Microsoft® SQL Server® 2008 Reporting Services Step by Step

Stacia Misner

PUBLISHED BY
Microsoft Press
A Division of Microsoft Corporation
One Microsoft Way
Redmond, Washington 98052-6399

Library of Congress Control Number: 2008940501

Printed and bound in the United States of America.

1 2 3 4 5 6 7 8 9 QWT 4 3 2 1 0 9

Distributed in Canada by H.B. Fenn and Company Ltd.

A CIP catalogue record for this book is available from the British Library.

Microsoft Press books are available through booksellers and distributors worldwide. For further information about international editions, contact your local Microsoft Corporation office or contact Microsoft Press International directly at fax (425) 936-7329. Visit our Web site at www.microsoft.com/mspress. Send comments to mspinput@microsoft.com.

Acquisitions Editor: Ken Jones
Developmental Editor: Sally Stickney
Project Editor: Carol Vu
Editorial Production: Custom Editorial Productions, Inc.
Technical Reviewer: Rozanne Murphy Whalen; Technical Review services provided by Content Master, a member of CM Group, Ltd.
Cover: Tom Draper Design

Body Part No. X15-28148

Contents at a Glance

Table of Contents

What do you think of this book? We want to hear from you!

Microsoft is interested in hearing your feedback so we can continually improve our books and learning resources for you. To participate in a brief online survey, please visit:

www.microsoft.com/learning/booksurvey

Part II Developing Reports

Part III **Managing the Report Server**

What do you think of this book? We want to hear from you!

Microsoft is interested in hearing your feedback so we can continually improve our books and learning resources for you. To participate in a brief online survey, please visit:

www.microsoft.com/learning/booksurvey

Acknowledgments

Each time I start a new book project, I am amazed to see the way it develops a life of its own after it leaves my custody. Many other people have left their mark on this book's pages as they made the changes necessary to improve upon my initial work and I'm so grateful for their commitment to quality and accuracy. As always, I enjoy working with Microsoft Press and appreciate the great team of people they have brought together for this project.

In particular, I would like to thank Ken Jones and Sally Stickney for their efforts in the initial stages of the book, and my project editor, Carol Vu, for nudging me along gently but persistently until the manuscript was complete. Rozanne Murphy Whalen provided a thorough technical review of the book by ensuring that each step performed exactly as described. Linda Allen of Custom Editorial Productions, Inc., Susan McClung, and Julie Hotchkiss were outstanding in their respective contributions to the book as they moved the manuscript through the editing process and continually rechecked the work to ensure that new errors weren't introduced as old errors were cleaned up. They have done the most thorough job I have ever seen and I believe that any author would be lucky to work with this group.

Of course, my family deserves many thanks as well. My husband, Gerry, has learned to indulge me in my writing projects and patiently sacrifices some of our time together so that I can focus on writing, but he's also my biggest cheerleader and encourages me every step of the way. For this, and all he has done for me in our many years together, I am eternally grateful.

I also appreciate my daughter's help on this project. Erika's glimmer of understanding of what I do for a living first developed when she provided feedback from a "newbie's" perspective on my last book, *Microsoft SQL Server 2005 Express Edition: Start Now!* (Microsoft Press, 2007). Little did either of us realize at the time that she would decide to learn more about what I do and eventually join me in my practice as a business intelligence consultant. Her experience using Reporting Services 2005 on a variety of projects since that time has given her an excellent perspective on the features that make Reporting Services 2008 compelling, and consequently, she was a great help to me in preparing many of the procedures in this book to highlight those features. I look forward to many more collaborative ventures together in the future.

Introduction

Microsoft Reporting Services is the component of Microsoft SQL Server 2008 that provides an enterprise-ready and extensible presentation layer for the Microsoft business intelligence platform. In its third release, Reporting Services continues its support for the three stages of the reporting life cycle, but it now includes several new features that improve the report development, management, and delivery processes. The new tablix and chart controls give you more options for presenting data in a report, and the new server architecture makes it easier for administrators to manage server resources and for users to access and page through large reports. As you complete the step-by-step procedures in this book, you are introduced to these and other new features, in addition to all the other features that have made Reporting Services a popular choice for implementing a reporting platform in organizations of all sizes since its initial release in 2004.

When you have finished the book, you will know how to build reports using each type of structure supported by Reporting Services and how to enhance reports with interactivity and data visualization techniques. You use these reports to learn how to move reports from the development workstation to the server environment and how to manage and secure the reports once they're on the report server. Then you use these reports again to learn how users can access reports online and subscribe to reports for delivery on a scheduled basis. You also learn how to build and use a report model for ad hoc reporting. If you have programming skills, you can continue learning about the extensibility of Reporting Services by enhancing the reports with custom code, by developing tools to manage the report server, and by exploring techniques for integrating access to reports managed by Reporting Services into portals and custom applications.

Who This Book Is For

Because Reporting Services is a platform of technologies rather than a single application, a variety of people serving in different roles and having different skill sets all need to learn how to work with some aspect of Reporting Services. Whether you're a report developer, IT administrator, or business user, you can use this book to learn how to perform the tasks for which you are responsible. If you're completely new to Reporting Services, this book teaches you the fundamental concepts required to build, manage, and access reports. You need no prior experience with Reporting Services to use this book successfully. On the other hand, if you're already familiar with an earlier version of Reporting Services, this book gives you a guided tour of the new features found in Reporting Services 2008.

Finding Your Best Starting Point in This Book

Even if your primary responsibility with Reporting Services requires you to focus on only one component, you benefit from an understanding of all the capabilities that Reporting Services supports. For this reason, if you have time, you should work through the book from beginning to end for the best experience.

Because this book can be used by readers with different needs, you can also choose to work through only the chapters that focus on your area of responsibility. Each part of the book contains related chapters in which the procedures are designed to build up your skills progressively and are necessarily interconnected. For the best experience, you should read all the related chapters and perform the steps in these chapters in sequence. Where applicable, instructions at the beginning of a chapter alert you to a requirement to complete procedures in a previous chapter before continuing. If you plan to read only about the features that apply to you, use the following table to find your best starting point.

If You Are	Follow These Steps
A business user who wants to access managed reports online	1. Install the sample files as described in the section entitled "Sample Files," later in this Introduction. 2. Work through the first two chapters to learn about Reporting Services and to install it on your computer. 3. Complete Part IV, "Viewing Reports," to learn how to access reports that have been published to the report server.
A business user or report developer who uses report models for ad hoc reporting	1. Install the sample files as described in the section entitled "Sample Files," later in this Introduction. 2. Work through the first two chapters to learn about Reporting Services and to install it on your computer. 3. Complete Chapter 9, "Developing Report Models," to learn how to construct a report model, and Chapter 14, "Creating Ad Hoc Reports," to learn how to develop ad hoc reports using a report model. Even if you're a business user who is not responsible for report model development, you should complete Chapter 9 to learn key concepts and terminology and to build the report model that you will need when developing ad hoc reports in Chapter 14. 4. Review the remaining chapters in Part IV to learn how to access ad hoc and managed reports that have been published to the report server.

If You Are	Follow These Steps
A business user with some experience developing database queries who develops managed reports	1. Install the sample files as described in the section entitled "Sample Files," later in this Introduction. 2. Work through the chapters in Part I, "Getting Started with Reporting Services," to learn about Reporting Services, to install it on your computer, and to learn how to use Report Builder 2.0. 3. Review the chapters that interest you in Part II, "Developing Reports," to learn how to build more advanced reports. In many cases, you can adapt the procedures in these chapters for use with Report Builder 2.0. 4. Review the chapters that interest you in Part IV to learn how users access reports from the report server.
A report developer	1. Install the sample files as described in the section entitled "Sample Files," later in this Introduction. 2. Work through the chapters in Part I to learn about Reporting Services, to install it on your computer, and to learn how to use Report Builder 2.0. 3. Complete Part II to learn how to use all the report development features available in Reporting Services. 4. Review the chapters that interest you in Parts III and IV to become familiar with overall functionality in Reporting Services. 5. If you have programming skills, complete Chapter 16, "Programming Reporting Services," to learn how you can customize Reporting Services.
A server administrator	1. Install the sample files as described in the section entitled "Sample Files," later in this Introduction. 2. Work through Chapter 1, "Introducing Reporting Services," and Chapter 2, "Installing Reporting Services," to learn about Reporting Services and to install it on your computer. 3. Complete Part III to learn how to configure and manage the report server. 4. Review the chapters that interest you in Part IV to understand how users interact with the report server. 5. Skim Chapter 16 to discover how customization of Reporting Services might require changes on the report server and how to perform administrative tasks programmatically.

Conventions and Features in This Book

This book presents information using conventions designed to make the information readable and easy to follow. Before you start, read the following list, which explains conventions you see throughout the book and points out helpful features that you might want to use.

Conventions

- Each exercise is a series of tasks. Each task is presented as a series of numbered steps (1, 2, and so on). A round bullet (•) indicates an exercise that has only one step.

- Notes labeled "Tip" provide additional information or alternative methods for completing a step successfully.

- Notes labeled "Important" alert you to information you need to check before continuing.

- Text that you type appears in **bold.**

- A plus sign (+) between two key names means that you must press those keys at the same time. For example, "Press Alt+Tab" means that you hold down the Alt key while you press the Tab key.

Other Features

- Sidebars throughout the book provide more in-depth information about the exercise. The sidebars might contain background information, design tips, or features related to the information being discussed.

- Each chapter ends with a section entitled "Quick Reference," which contains brief reminders of how to perform the tasks that you learned in the chapter.

Hardware and Software Requirements

You'll need the following hardware and software to complete the exercises in this book:

- Windows Vista Home Premium, Windows Vista Business, Windows Vista Ultimate, Windows Vista Enterprise, Windows Server 2003 Standard SP2, Windows Server 2003 Data Center SP2, Windows Server 2003 Enterprise SP2, Windows Server 2008 Standard, Windows Server 2008 Data Center, or Windows Server 2008 Enterprise. The exercises also run using Microsoft Windows XP Professional SP2.

- Microsoft SQL Server 2008 Standard, SQL Server 2008 Enterprise, SQL Server 2008 Developer, or SQL Server 2008 Evaluation.

- Optional: Microsoft Windows SharePoint Services 3.0 or Microsoft Office SharePoint Server 2007.

- Optional: Microsoft Visual Studio 2008 Standard or Professional with either the Microsoft Visual Basic .NET or Microsoft Visual C# .NET library, and Visual Studio 2008 Service Pack 1.

Note Visual Studio 2008 is required only to complete Chapter 16. If you install it before you complete the other chapters, you will notice that the steps that you must follow to start a new project or to open an existing project will vary slightly from the steps written in those chapters. These steps were written with the assumption that you do not install Visual Studio 2008 until you reach Chapter 16.

- 1 gigahertz (GHz) Pentium III+ processor, or faster, with 2 GHz recommended.

- 512 GB of available, physical RAM with 2 GB recommended.

- Video (1,028 x 768 or higher resolution) monitor with at least 256 colors.

- CD-ROM or DVD-ROM drive for installation from disc.

- Microsoft mouse or compatible pointing device.

You also need to have Administrator access to your computer to configure SQL Server 2008 Reporting Services.

Sample Files

The companion CD inside this book contains the sample files that you use as you perform the exercises. By using these sample files, you won't waste time creating files that aren't relevant to the exercise. The files and the step-by-step instructions in the lessons also let you learn by doing, which is an easy and effective way to acquire and remember new skills.

Digital Content for Digital Book Readers: If you bought a digital-only edition of this book, you can enjoy select content from the print edition's companion CD.
Visit **http://go.microsoft.com/fwlink/?LinkId=139877** to get your downloadable content. This content is always up-to-date and available to all readers.

Installing the Sample Files

Perform the following steps to install the sample files and required software on your computer so that you can use them with the exercises.

1. Remove the companion CD from the package inside this book and insert it into your CD-ROM drive.

Note A license agreement should open automatically. If this agreement does not appear, open My Computer on the desktop or Start menu, double-click the icon for your CD-ROM drive, and then double-click StartCD.exe.

2. Review the license agreement. If you accept the terms, select the Accept option and then click Next.

    A menu appears with options related to the book.

3. Click Install Practice Files.

4. Follow the instructions that appear.

    The code samples are installed to the Microsoft Press\Rs2008sbs folder in your Documents folder on your computer. If your computer's operating system is Windows Vista or Windows Server 2008, your Documents folder is located at C:\Users*<login>*\ Documents, where *<login>* is your login name. If the operating system is Windows XP or Windows Server 2003, your Documents folder is located at C:\Documents And Settings*<login>*\My Documents.

Using the Practice Files

Each chapter in this book explains when and how to use any practice files for that chapter. When it's time to use a practice file, the book lists the instructions for how to open the files.

Uninstalling the Code Samples

Perform the following steps to remove the code samples from your computer.

1. In Control Panel, open Add Or Remove Programs.

2. From the list of Currently Installed Programs, select Microsoft SQL Server 2008 Reporting Services Step by Step.

3. Click Remove.

4. Follow the instructions that appear to remove the code samples.

Find Additional Content Online

As new or updated material becomes available that complements your book, it will be posted online on the Microsoft Press Online Developer Tools Web site (*www.microsoft.com/learning /books/online/developer*). The type of material you might find includes updates to book content, articles, links to companion content, errata, sample chapters, and more. This Web site is updated periodically.

Support for This Book

Every effort has been made to ensure the accuracy of this book and the contents of the companion CD. As corrections or changes are collected, they will be added to a Microsoft Knowledge Base article.

Microsoft Press provides support for books and companion media at the following Web site:

http://www.microsoft.com/learning/support/books/

Questions and Comments

If you have comments, questions, or ideas regarding the book or the companion CD, or questions that are not answered by visiting the sites above, please send them to Microsoft Press via e-mail to

mspinput@microsoft.com

Or via postal mail to

Microsoft Press
Attn: *Microsoft SQL Server 2008 Reporting Services Step by Step* Editor
One Microsoft Way
Redmond, WA 98052-6399

Please note that Microsoft software product support is not offered through the preceding addresses.

Part I
Getting Started with Reporting Services

The chapters in Part I provide you with a foundation to Microsoft SQL Server 2008 Reporting Services in preparation for learning about its features in detail throughout the remainder of this book. In Chapter 1, "Introducing Reporting Services," you learn about the features and architecture of Reporting Services. In Chapter 2, "Installing Reporting Services," you learn how to plan for and complete an installation. Then, in Chapter 3, "Exploring Reporting Services," you get your first hands-on experience with report development and deployment.

Chapter 1
Introducing Reporting Services

After completing this chapter, you will be able to:

- Describe the key characteristics of a reporting platform.
- Explain the reporting life cycle.
- Identify the components of the Reporting Services architecture.

In this chapter, you learn how the capabilities of Microsoft SQL Server 2008 Reporting Services create a reporting platform. You also discover how this reporting platform supports each stage of the reporting life cycle and how each component of the platform fits together architecturally. This introduction gives you a better understanding of how you might use Reporting Services as a reporting platform in your organization.

A Reporting Platform

Put simply, a *report* is a structured arrangement of information. Typically, the information in a business report comes from data in a business application, although report information can be derived from a variety of sources. A *reporting platform* is an integrated set of applications that supports all required activities in a managed report environment, including report development, management, and viewing.

Historically, reports were available only as part of the business applications used in an organization and were not managed separately from these applications. However, preprogrammed reports like these rarely answered all the questions that business users needed answered. Increasing demand for access to the underlying data in these business applications prompted software vendors to include report-generation tools in their applications and eventually to allow direct access to the database with third-party client-side reporting tools. When only a limited number of people required access to reports, these reporting solutions were adequate. However, when the need to deliver reports to a larger audience arose, organizations found that reporting tools with a server component capable of scaling to a large number of users were expensive, complex to implement and manage, and difficult to integrate into custom applications and technical infrastructures.

The Reporting Services reporting platform was introduced in 2004 as an additional component of Microsoft SQL Server 2000 to address these problems. Since then, organizations small and large have migrated to Reporting Services to take advantage of the many benefits it has to offer. The current version of Reporting Services available in SQL Server 2008 makes it even easier for report developers, administrators, and business users to use this reporting platform to accomplish their respective objectives.

One of the primary reasons that organizations implement Reporting Services is to provide *managed reports* to a large number of internal users. This type of report is typically characterized by detailed operational data or summarized management information that is gathered from a variety of data sources and formally organized into a central repository. Often, managed reports must conform to specific formatting standards. Reports intended for print also require precise page layout and pagination. Consequently, a limited group of report developers is usually responsible for creating managed reports. Users can access these reports online by navigating through a report catalog when they need information, or they can receive reports as e-mail attachments on a scheduled basis. Some organizations also distribute information externally, making reports available to customers or partners by incorporating Reporting Services into an extranet environment.

With the proliferation of data in an organization, IT departments are challenged to keep up with the requests to develop new reports. To help solve this problem, Reporting Services includes a tool to develop *ad hoc reports* called Report Builder. With ad hoc reporting capabilities, users with limited technical skills can produce new, simple reports on their own, and they can choose whether to save them privately or to share them with others by publishing to the Reporting Services centralized store. Because ad hoc reports usually don't have the same layout requirements as managed reports and because Report Builder is easy to use, typically anyone with permission to see data used for reporting is allowed to create ad hoc reports.

To support business users creating ad hoc reports, a more technical user can develop a *report model* that describes the tables and columns in a database in a user-friendly format. The user then accesses the report model to construct an ad hoc report and thereby automatically generate the query language required to retrieve the requested data. Reports built using a report model can be a springboard for data exploration because the user can click information in the report to generate a series of drillthrough reports automatically to display related details.

In addition to managed and ad hoc reports, you can use Reporting Services to develop and manage *embedded reports* for an organization's portals or custom applications. This capability means that Reporting Services is more than a reporting application. As a fully extensible system, it's also a development platform that can be used by in-house developers or third-party independent software vendors to create either Microsoft Windows or Web reporting applications.

Another important feature of the Reporting Services platform is its ability to reproduce a report in a variety of formats. This process of converting the report layout and report data into a specific file format is called *rendering*. Many times, a user's question might be answered by simply locating and viewing a report rendered online in Hypertext Markup

Language (HTML) format. Other times, the user might want to analyze the data further by rendering the data as a Microsoft Office Excel workbook and adding calculations to the data, or the user might want to share information with someone else by rendering the report as a Portable Document Format (PDF) file.

Finally, system administrators need the right tools to manage a reporting platform. Reporting Services provides configuration and management tools with a graphical user interface (GUI) to manage server resources, organize content, and implement security. For repetitive tasks, a utility to execute scripts is available. Alternatively, developers can create custom applications to perform administrative tasks if an alternative tool is desired.

Reporting Life Cycle

The *reporting life cycle* is the sequence of activities associated with a report from creation to delivery. Reporting Services fully supports the three phases of the reporting life cycle, which include report development, management of the report server, and report access by users.

Report Development

Regardless of which tool you use to develop reports, the process is very similar. You develop reports on your own computer by selecting data for the report, organizing the report layout, and enhancing the report with formatting and, optionally, interactive features. At any time during report development, you can preview the report to test its appearance and any interactive features you added. If you're building a managed report, you can deploy the report from the authoring tool to the report server or to a Microsoft Office SharePoint Server 2007 Web site. If you're building an ad hoc report instead, you can choose to store it on your computer, but you also have the option to deploy it to the report server or a SharePoint site.

When you select data for your report, you can choose from a wide variety of data sources, typically relational or multidimensional databases or hierarchical data files. If Reporting Services doesn't provide a data source that you need for a report, you can develop or purchase custom data processing extensions, which are discussed further in the section "Server Extensions," later in this chapter. You can also use SQL Server 2008 Integration Services to extract and transform data before using it in Reporting Services if you have other types of data sources to include in your report or you need to perform complex operations on the data to prepare it for reporting.

After defining the data query or choosing a report model for your report, you organize the data fields into a table, cross-tab, or chart layout. Alternately, you can use free-form text boxes to present the data in a less-structured format. You can also use gauges for displaying key performance indicators. You might add grouping to the data layout to display subtotals.

You can also add calculations to display information such as averages or record counts or to concatenate strings into a single result, such as a first name and last name.

Today's business users have become increasingly sophisticated and expect reports to be designed with flexibility and interactivity in mind. With Reporting Services, you can build flexible reports by using parameters to filter content or change the appearance of the report. You can also add interactive features to allow the user to sort data or to hide or show details. Interactive features in Reporting Services also include the ability to add a document map for easy navigation within a large report and to add links to allow the user to jump to a related report or Web location.

Report Administration

Administrators manage the technical environment for the reporting platform. The administrative responsibilities might be performed by one individual or might be distributed among several people. Before reports can be deployed to the report server and accessed by users, an administrator must configure the report server and optionally integrate the report server with SharePoint. Occasionally, an administrator might reconfigure the report server to fine-tune its performance.

Administrators also manage the location, security, and execution properties of reports, although you might also delegate these responsibilities to some power users. Report developers can deploy reports directly to the report server if given permission to do so, or they can provide reports to an administrator to upload directly to the report server or to deploy in batch using a script utility. After a report is deployed to the report server, as an administrator, you can place the report in a folder with other related reports. You can then apply security to the report or the folder containing the report to control who can view the report and who can modify report properties.

In addition to security, a report has many properties that you can configure to control what happens when a user views the report. You can change the data source connection information, for example, to have the report's queries access a production database server instead of a test server.

By default, a report executes on demand, which means that the report queries run to retrieve data from the applicable data sources at the time the user opens the report for viewing. Configuring a report's execution properties allows you to balance when the report queries execute against the acceptable level of data latency. For example, you can cache the report for faster viewing of a frequently requested report if the underlying data isn't volatile, or you can create a snapshot report to execute a report at a time when most users are offline if the queries take a long time to complete. You can save multiple snapshots of a report in history to preserve the report data at specific points in time.

Report Access

The most common way for users to access reports is to use a browser and navigate to a central report repository. As another alternative, you can create your own portal application with links to guide users to reports in Reporting Services. A user can also optionally store a selection of reports in a personal folder for easy access or can create a subscription to a report to receive it on a scheduled basis in an e-mail inbox, a network file share, or a SharePoint document library.

By default, you view a report rendered in HTML format, but you can instead render it to a PDF or Tagged Image File Format (TIFF) format to share your report in printed form or to Comma Separated Values (CSV) or Extensible Markup Language (XML) format to import the report data into other applications. You can also request a specific format for subscription delivery of reports.

Another way that you might access Reporting Services reports is through corporate applications. Reports might be embedded into applications developed by your organization or by third-party vendors. Reports can also be used to provide supplemental information for scorecard and planning applications in Microsoft Office PerformancePoint Server 2007.

Reporting Services Architecture

To deliver the functionality required by a reporting platform, Reporting Services uses a variety of components, extensions, and application programming interfaces (APIs) in a multi-tier architecture with data, application, and server tiers. For most reporting scenarios, implementation of the standard architecture suffices, but the modular nature of the architecture allows you flexibility when you plan to use only some features or when you need to distribute components across multiple servers for scalability.

Reporting Services can run in native mode (the default configuration), in which it runs as a stand-alone application server, or in integrated mode, which requires the report server to run in a SharePoint farm. More information about integrated mode is found later in this chapter in the section "SharePoint Integrated Mode."

Figure 1-1 illustrates the relationship between components across the three tiers in native mode.

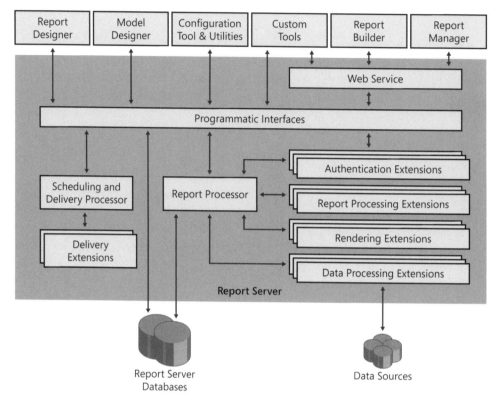

FIGURE 1-1 Component architecture

Data Tier

The data tier in the Reporting Services architecture consists of a pair of databases to support the reporting platform. The ReportServer database is the primary database for permanent storage of reports, report models, and other data related to the management of the report server. The ReportServerTempDB database stores session cache information and cached instances of reports for improved report delivery performance. In a scale-out deployment of Reporting Services across multiple report servers, these two databases in the data tier are the only requirements. These databases do not need to be on the same server as the report server.

The data presented in the reports comes from many possible sources. These data sources are typically located on separate servers from the report server. A connection string embedded in a data source defined for the report provides the information required by the report server to connect and authenticate to the data server.

Application Tier

The application tier in the Reporting Services architecture is the collection of tools that you use to develop reports and manage the reporting platform.

Report Development Tools

When a new report must be developed, you first must decide which of the available report development tools to use. Three report development tools are provided for Reporting Services 2008: Report Designer, Report Builder 1.0, and Report Builder 2.0. For report model development, you use Model Designer. If you are embedding report authoring capabilities into a custom application, you can create a custom authoring tool.

Report Designer   For the full range of report development features, you use Report Designer, a project template available in SQL Server Business Intelligence Development Studio (BI Dev Studio), one of the management tools you install with Reporting Services. Business Intelligence Development Studio might look familiar if you've ever used Microsoft Visual Studio. That's because BI Dev Studio is a Visual Studio 2008 shell that enables you to use the same integrated development environment that developers use to build applications. You are not required to install Visual Studio 2008 to use BI Dev Studio. You learn how to use Report Designer in Chapter 4, "Designing Reports."

Report Builder   For an ad hoc report, you can choose between Report Builder 1.0 and Report Builder 2.0. Report Builder was first available in Reporting Services 2005 and continues to be supported in Reporting Services 2008. Using Report Builder 1.0, you can build a simple report that displays data from a single data source as defined by a report model. This tool is most useful for business users who need access to information but lack the skills to write a Structured Query Language (SQL) query. You learn about Report Builder 1.0 in Chapter 14, "Creating Ad Hoc Reports." Report Builder 2.0 is new in Reporting Services 2008 and provides the same features you use in Report Designer using an interface much like the Office 2007 family of products. In Chapter 3, "Exploring Reporting Services," you learn how to use Report Builder 2.0.

Model Designer   You use Model Designer in BI Dev Studio to develop and publish a report model that can be used in Report Builder for ad hoc reporting. You create this model to hide the technical details about accessing data and generating queries from users while still supporting their exploration of data through ad hoc reporting. For relational sources in SQL Server, Oracle, and Teradata databases, you can generate and edit a report model directly in Model Designer. You use Model Designer in Chapter 9, "Developing Report Models."

Programmatic Interface for Report Development   Reporting Services includes APIs that allow you to build a custom report development tool. You can also build a program to produce a Report Definition Language (RDL) file, which is the same output generated by the Report Designer and Report Builder tools.

What's New in Reporting Services 2008 for Authoring?

If you are already familiar with a previous version of Reporting Services, you might be interested in a concise list of the changes in report development features in Reporting Services 2008:

- A new Teradata data processing extension for report and report model data sources

- A new Chart data region to provide more advanced chart types and more flexibility in chart design to support secondary axes, multiple chart areas, and calculated series, among other new features

- A new Gauge data region to display key performance indicator data in reports

- A new Tablix data region, which merges the capabilities of the Table and Matrix data regions used in previous versions for greater flexibility in data layout

- An enhanced Text Box report item to support rich text formatting or HTML

- Report variables and group variables for use in calculated expressions

- An enhanced Report Designer, which organizes all report information on a single page and enables greater precision over report layout

- A new version of Report Builder, which supports multiple data regions, multiple data sources, and queries to data sources without a report model

Report Viewers

Reporting Services provides three ways to view reports: Report Manager, SharePoint, or a programmatic interface. Within a single instance of Reporting Services, you can use either Report Manager or SharePoint as a standard user interface, but you cannot use both tools in the same instance. Whether Reporting Services runs in native mode or SharePoint mode, you can use a programmatic interface in addition to or instead of the standard user interface.

Report Manager   To view a report on a server running in native mode, you use a Web application called Report Manager to locate and render the desired report for online viewing. You can page through a large report, search for text within a report, zoom in or out to resize a report, render a report to a new format, print the report, and change report parameters using a special toolbar provided in the report viewer. Report Manager requires Microsoft Internet Explorer 6.0 or Windows Internet Explorer 7.0 and later. You learn how to use Report Manager for report viewing in Chapter 13, "Accessing Reports Online."

SharePoint   In SharePoint Integrated mode, you can navigate to a SharePoint document library to locate and render a report much as you can when using Report Manager. A Web Part is also available for embedding a report into a SharePoint Web page, such as a dashboard. Whether you open the report in a document library or in a Web Part, the same capabilities to page, search, zoom, render, print, and select parameters available in Report Manager are available in SharePoint. You learn how to work with reports in SharePoint in Chapter 13.

Programmatic Interface for Viewing or Delivering Reports   You can integrate report viewer functionality into a custom application by using the Reporting Services API or by accessing reports using URL endpoints. You can also extend standard functionality by customizing security, data processing, rendering, or delivery options. You can find examples for customizing user access to reports in Chapter 16, "Programming Reporting Services."

Management Tools

Following the installation of Reporting Services, you have several tools available to further configure application services and service properties or to disable server features. You also can use management tools to configure security. On an ongoing basis, you can use the provided management tools to manage report content and job schedules using a graphical user interface (GUI), or you can use scripting tools to perform these tasks in batch mode. As with other features of Reporting Services, you can develop custom tools to perform these administrative tasks.

Reporting Services Configuration Manager   You use the Reporting Services Configuration Manager to configure a local or remote Reporting Services installation. Using this tool, you can assign service accounts for running the service and for processing reports for schedule operations. You also use this tool to configure the URLs to be used by the Reporting Service application, create the report server databases to host the application data, or convert a report server to native mode or integrated mode. If you plan to use e-mail delivery of reports, you use this tool to identify the Simple Mail Transfer Protocol (SMTP) server in your network. Finally, you use this tool to connect a report server to a scale-out deployment if you require multiple servers to support your reporting environment. You learn how to use the Reporting Services Configuration Manager to complete an installation in Chapter 2, "Installing Reporting Services."

SQL Server Management Studio   This tool is the management interface for many of the server components in SQL Server. You can connect to a local or remote report server using this tool. In Chapter 12, "Performing Administrative Tasks," you learn how to manage the report server with this tool.

SQL Server Configuration Manager   You use SQL Server Configuration Manager when you need to start or stop the report server Windows service.

Report Manager   You use Report Manager in a native mode report server environment to organize and configure reports, which you learn about in Chapter 10, "Deploying Reports to a Server." You also use Report Manager to secure reports, which you learn how to do in

Chapter 11, "Securing Report Server Content." You also perform system administration, such as report model management (described in Chapter 14) and subscription management (described in Chapter 15, "Working with Subscriptions").

> **Note** For a report server in SharePoint integrated mode, you perform these same tasks, but you use a SharePoint interface. More information about how to perform a particular task in SharePoint is provided in each chapter describing management tasks using Report Manager.

Command-Line Utilities   For performing repetitive tasks in bulk, whether on a local or remote report server, you can use the Reporting Services command-line utilities. For example, you can publish reports to a server and configure report properties or security in bulk by creating a Microsoft Visual Basic .NET script that you can execute with a command-line utility called Rs.exe (described in Chapter 16). Other command-line utilities let you manage encryption keys used to provide access to report server databases after moving to a new server or restoring from a backup. You learn more about these utilities in Chapter 12.

Programmatic Interface for Management   All the management tasks that you can perform using Report Manager can be built into a custom application using the Reporting Services API. However, some capabilities supported in a native mode environment are not supported in SharePoint integrated mode.

What's New in Reporting Services 2008 for Management?

If you have had the opportunity to work with a previous version of Reporting Services, you will find that the configuration and management tools have been revised to eliminate overlap in functionality. The following list summarizes these revisions:

- Use SQL Server Management Studio (SSMS) to enable Reporting Services features, configure server properties, define shared schedules and role definitions, and manage scheduled jobs.

- Use Report Manager (for native mode) or a SharePoint site (for SharePoint integrated mode) to manage content, including permissions, report properties, subscriptions, and report models.

- Use Reporting Services Configuration Manager to define settings for the Web service, service accounts, URL endpoints, report server databases, SMTP servers, unattended execution, scale-out, and SharePoint integration.

Server Tier

The server tier is the central layer of the Reporting Services architecture. Within this tier lie the processor components that respond to and process requests to the report server. These components delegate certain functions to subcomponents called *server extensions*, which are simply processors that perform very specific functions. These components are implemented as a Windows service.

Processor Components

Activity on the report server is managed by two processor components: the Report Processor and the Scheduling and Delivery Processor. The Report Processor receives all requests that require execution and rendering of reports. The Scheduling and Delivery Processor receives all requests for scheduled events such as snapshots and subscriptions.

Report Processor   The tasks performed by the Report Processor depend on whether the user requests an on-demand report, a cached report, or a report snapshot. For a request for an on-demand report, the Report Processor calls a data processing extension to execute the report queries and then merges the query results into a temporary format that organizes the data according to the defined layout but is not yet the finished report. A cached report is stored in the ReportServerTempDB database in this temporary format while a report snapshot is stored in the ReportServer database in the temporary format. After generating the report in temporary format, or retrieving it from the applicable database, the Report Processor then calls a rendering extension to finalize the report for the user. You learn about all the report processing options in Chapter 10.

If a report uses a report model as a data source, the Report Processor also reads the report model and generates the query required to display the report as well as any drillthrough reports the user might request (described in Chapter 14).

Scheduling and Delivery Processor   When a user creates a snapshot or subscription schedule for a report, the Scheduling and Delivery Processor in turn creates a SQL Server Agent job. Later, when the job executes, SQL Server Agent sends a request to the Scheduling and Delivery Processor, which in turn forwards the request to the Report Processor to execute and render the report. The Report Processor returns the finished report to the Scheduling and Delivery Processor, which calls a delivery extension to e-mail the report or store it on a network share as applicable.

Server Extensions

The server extensions in Reporting Services are the processor components that perform very specific tasks. This modular approach within the server tier allows you to disable an out-of-the-box extension or add your own extension, whether developed in-house or by a third party. Reporting Services includes five types of server extensions: authentication, data processing, report processing, rendering, and delivery.

Authentication Extension   By default, Reporting Services uses Windows authentication to allow users to access the server and to authorize the content that users can see and the tasks that users can perform. Unlike other server extensions, there can be only one active authentication extension per report server instance. If you want to use a custom security extension, you must remove the default security extension provided by Reporting Services.

Data Processing Extension   The Report Processor sends query requests to the applicable data processing extension, which in turn connects to a data source, executes a query (with query parameters if applicable), and returns the query results to the Report Processor. Reporting Services includes data processing extensions for the following data sources: SQL Server, Analysis Services, Hyperion Essbase, Oracle, SAP Netweaver Business Intelligence, Teradata, Object Linking and Embedding Database (OLE DB), and Open Database Connectivity (ODBC).

Report Processing Extension   The report processing extension is an optional component used to process custom report items from third-party vendors. For example, you can obtain charting or mapping add-ins to enhance your reports. To merge the data into the format required by these add-ins, the Report Processor calls a report processing extension to produce the temporary format of the report. You can, of course, develop your own report items and the report processing extension required for the server to include these custom report items in a report.

Rendering Extension   The Report Processor calls a rendering extension to convert a report in temporary format into a finished format for the user. The rendering extensions included with Reporting Services are HTML, Excel, CSV, XML, Image, PDF, and Microsoft Office Word. If you need a different output format, you can develop your own rendering extension. You learn more about rendering in Chapter 13.

Delivery Extension   The Scheduling and Delivery Processor uses delivery extensions (described in Chapter 15) to handle scheduled report requests, as follows:

- The e-mail delivery extension sends an e-mail message to one or more recipients with the report embedded in the report body, attached as a file, or referenced as a URL link to the report on a report server.

- The file share delivery extension saves a report in a specified format to a network share that is independent of the reporting platform for archiving or providing a more scalable storage and access mechanism for large reports.

- The null delivery provider is a mechanism for caching a report in advance of user requests.

To meet other requirements for report delivery, you can develop a custom delivery extension for sending reports to other destinations, such as a fax device or printer, or to another application.

What's New in Reporting Services 2008 for Report Processing?

The following list outlines the enhancements made to Reporting Services 2008 for report processing:

- Improved rendering to Excel and to CSV formats

- New Word rendering extension that can produce a document compatible with Word 2000 or later

- Better memory management to support the processing of large reports and improve the scalability of the report server

- Consistent paging behavior among different rendering formats

Service Architecture

Reporting Services includes several applications running as a single process that supports the functioning of the server tier. Figure 1-2 illustrates the relationship between these features.

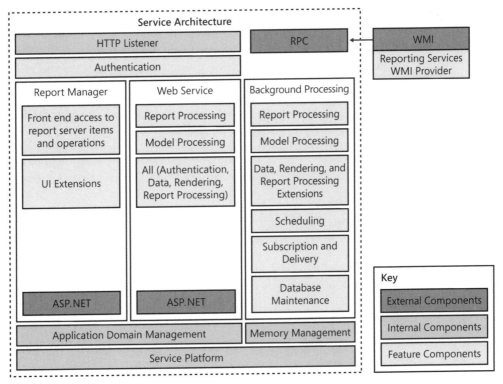

FIGURE 1-2 Reporting Services service architecture

HTTP Listener   In a significant departure from previous versions of Reporting Services, Reporting Services 2008 does not require an installation of Internet Information Services (IIS). Instead, Reporting Services now uses Http.sys directly from the server's operating system to accept requests directed to URLs and ports configured for Reporting Services. This architectural change allows Reporting Services to exist without IIS and still provides the same functionality. Even if IIS is installed on the same server with Reporting Services, the HTTP listener continues to manage Reporting Services requests. When a request is received, the HTTP listener forwards the request to the service's authentication layer.

Authentication   The authentication layer supports both Windows-based and custom authentication to confirm the identity of the user or application making the request. Reporting Services uses Windows integrated security by default using either NT LAN Manager (NTLM) or Kerberos authentication, but it also supports basic and anonymous access authentication. You can use anonymous authentication only if you implement custom ASP.NET Forms authentication. You can use only one authentication type on a report server and within a scale-out deployment. You learn about configuring authentication in Chapter 11. The authentication layer calls the Report Server Web service after the request is authenticated.

Application Domains   The application domain layer contains the following separate feature areas of Reporting Services, which you can enable or disable independently: Report Manager, Report Server Web service, and background processing. Combining the application domains as a single Windows service makes it easier to configure and maintain Reporting Services. The application domain layer also hosts the ASP.NET and Microsoft .NET Framework technologies that are part of SQL Server common language runtime (CLR) integration.

Report Manager   Report Manager is a front-end component provided so that users and server administrators can interact with the Report Server Web service when viewing reports, managing content, or managing server operations.

Report Server Web Service   The Report Server Web service is the report and model processing engine and programmatic interface for custom applications if you choose not to use Report Manager.

Background Processing   The background processing component manages scheduling, subscriptions, and delivery as well as data, rendering, report processing, and database maintenance.

Application Domain Management   The application domain management layer replaces the functionality of IIS.

Memory Management   The memory management layer extends SQL Server memory management features to Reporting Services and is responsible for monitoring thread processing.

Service Platform   The service platform allows Reporting Services to take advantage of SQL Server services for networking as well as CLR and .NET Framework support.

Remote Procedure Call (RPC)   RPC supports execution of procedures on a remote server and is used by the Reporting Services Windows Management Instrumentation (WMI) provider.

Internet Information Services Eliminated

Earlier versions of Reporting Services required the installation of IIS. In Reporting Services 2008, this requirement has been removed due to the redesign of the server architecture.

The benefits of eliminating IIS include the following:

- Easier configuration because IIS settings for other applications affected Reporting Services. IIS settings were a common cause of configuration problems in previous versions of Reporting Services, and much of the IIS functionality was not even used by Reporting Services.

- Better resource management because IIS was designed for displaying static or dynamic HTML pages, not for executing large reports for many concurrent users. Reporting Services now uses the memory management and thread monitoring capabilities of SQL Server to support better scalability.

- Consolidation of two services into one, which eliminates the overhead of the communication process between services and enables more efficient allocation of memory across the server processes. In earlier versions of Reporting Services, the two-service model created resource contention issues in large-scale environments.

- Elimination of deployment obstacles. SQL Server database administrators (DBAs) do not always have the skills necessary to deploy and maintain IIS, and some organizations have policies preventing the installation of IIS and SQL Server on the same server.

If you are upgrading a report server from Reporting Services 2000 or Reporting Services 2005, the settings in IIS for Internet Protocol (IP) addresses, host headers, ports, Secure Sockets Layer (SSL) server certificates, and security will be re-created seamlessly in Reporting Services 2008. For most modifications following the migration, you can use the Reporting Services Configuration Manager. If you need to change security settings, you must modify the RSReportServer configuration file (described in Chapter 12).

IIS settings for anonymous or digest authentication, client certificates, or Internet Server Application Programming Interface (ISAPI) are ignored during an upgrade.

SharePoint Integrated Mode

The architecture of a report server running in integrated mode requires a Windows SharePoint Services 3.0 or Microsoft Office SharePoint Server 2007 farm. By integrating Reporting Services with SharePoint, you can use a single security model for user access to enterprise content and take advantage of SharePoint features such as versioning, workflows, and dashboard integration that are not available in native-mode Reporting Services. The report server continues to process, render, and deliver reports, and a SharePoint site replaces Report Manager in providing front-end access to view reports and manage content. You learn how to configure an environment for SharePoint integration in Chapter 2.

> **Note** You can install and register SharePoint Web Parts for Reporting Services to enable users to locate and view reports stored on a report server in native mode from a SharePoint site. This approach is much simpler to deploy, but it prevents you from using the collaboration and document management features of SharePoint that are otherwise available if you configure the report server to run in integrated mode.

Figure 1-3 illustrates the architecture of a report server in integrated mode.

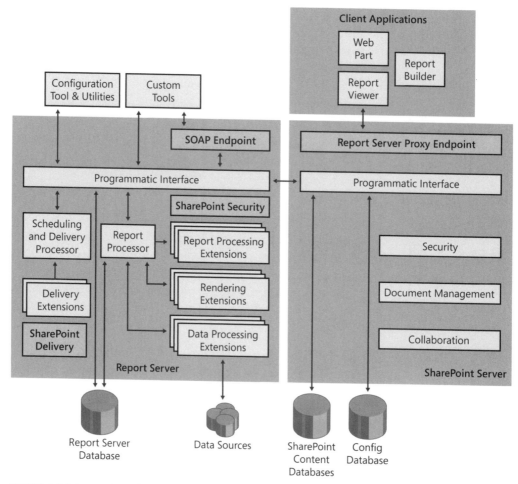

FIGURE 1-3 Integrated-mode report server architecture

SharePoint Server

To support Reporting Services integration, you must install the Microsoft SQL Server 2008 Reporting Services Add-in for Microsoft SharePoint Technologies on a SharePoint server. The add-in installs a proxy endpoint for the report server, adds a Report Viewer Web Part to the SharePoint gallery, and adds application pages to SharePoint for viewing and managing report server content on a SharePoint site.

SharePoint Content Database

Reports, models, data sources, and security permissions are stored in the SharePoint content database.

SharePoint Configuration Database

The configuration database stores information about the report server, including the URL, authentication information, and default server settings.

Report Server

When you configure a report server for SharePoint integration, the configuration process adds a Simple Object Access Protocol (SOAP) endpoint for the report server and SharePoint security and delivery extensions. In addition, the report server database is no longer the primary storage for reports and other content.

Report Server Databases

The report server databases continue to store snapshots, subscriptions, schedules, server settings, and cached reports. The ReportServer database also keeps a copy of the reports stored in the SharePoint content database to facilitate faster processing. When you add, replace, or open a report in SharePoint, the report server compares the time stamp of the copy in the ReportServer database with the time stamp of the report in the SharePoint content database. If the time stamps are different, the report server copies the newer version to the ReportServer database.

After reading this introduction to the features and architecture of Reporting Services and the activities performed during the reporting life cycle, you are probably ready to roll up your sleeves and put together your own reporting platform. In Chapter 2, you prepare the environment and perform an installation in preparation for building, managing, and viewing reports throughout the remainder of this book.

Chapter 1 Quick Reference

This Term	Means This
Report	A structured arrangement of information, such as business data
Reporting platform	An integrated set of applications that supports all activities related to a report, including report development, server management, and access to reports
Managed report	Information gathered from one or more data sources in report form and formally managed in a central report repository
Ad hoc report	A report that can be developed by a user with limited technical skills and saved privately or shared with others by publishing to the Reporting Services centralized store
Report model	A logical description of the tables and columns in a database in a user-friendly format
Embedded reports	A report integrated into an organization's portals or custom applications
Rendering	The conversion of the report layout and report data into a specific file format
Server extension	A processor subcomponent with a very specific function, such as authentication, data processing, rendering, or delivery

Chapter 2
Installing Reporting Services

After completing this chapter, you will be able to:

- Choose an appropriate edition, server mode, and deployment topology of Reporting Services for your reporting requirements.

- Install Reporting Services.

- Configure Reporting Services in native mode or SharePoint integrated mode.

In Chapter 1, "Introducing Reporting Services," you learned how Reporting Services components create a reporting platform. In this chapter, you learn how your reporting platform can be deployed on one or more servers, what requirements must be met before installing Reporting Services, and what steps to perform to install and configure Reporting Services correctly.

Planning for Installation

Before you can begin installing Reporting Services, you must make several decisions and perform a number of preparation tasks. First, you need to understand the features supported in each of the six editions so you can choose the one most appropriate for your reporting needs. Then, you must decide whether to implement Reporting Services in native mode or SharePoint integrated mode and whether you should deploy it in a single-server or multiserver topology. You also have to review the hardware and software requirements for Reporting Services to ensure that the installation completes successfully. Finally, you must consider whether you need to create Microsoft Windows accounts or whether you want to use built-in accounts for use as service accounts.

Choosing an Edition

Reporting Services is one of the features included in SQL Server 2008 and is included in all editions of the software except SQL Server 2008 Express and SQL Server Compact. Each edition supports a different set of features to meet specific scalability, performance, and pricing requirements. You can choose from the following editions:

- **SQL Server 2008 Express with Advanced Services** For use in desktop and small single-server applications with limited reporting functionality using only local relational data sources. You cannot add custom security roles, and Reporting Services is limited to 4 gigabytes (GB) of memory. There is no support for ad hoc reporting, caching, snapshots, subscriptions, history, scheduling, or SharePoint integration.

- **SQL Server 2008 Web**   For use with a Web site with limited reporting functionality using only local relational data sources. You cannot add custom security roles, and Reporting Services is limited to 4 GB of memory. There is no support for ad hoc reporting, caching, snapshots, subscriptions, history, scheduling, or SharePoint integration.

- **SQL Server 2008 Workgroup**   For use in branch locations with limited reporting functionality using only local relational data sources. This edition includes support for ad hoc reporting. Reporting Services is limited to 4 GB of memory. There is no support for caching, snapshots, subscriptions, history, scheduling, or SharePoint integration.

- **SQL Server 2008 Standard**   For department use or small-scale applications using local or remote data sources and nonrelational data sources. In this edition, all features are supported except scale-out deployment, infinite clickthrough (described in Chapter 14, "Creating Ad Hoc Reports"), and data-driven subscriptions (described in Chapter 15, "Working with Subscriptions"). There is no memory limit for Reporting Services.

- **SQL Server 2008 Enterprise**   For use in enterprise applications that support all reporting features. There is no memory limit for Reporting Services.

- **SQL Server 2008 Developer**   For use in the development and testing of reports in Reporting Services. This edition supports all features included in Enterprise Edition and is not licensed for use on a production server.

- **SQL Server 2008 Evaluation**   For use in evaluating the full range of Reporting Services features supported in SQL Server Enterprise for a 180-day trial period.

Choosing a Server Mode

Two server modes are available for Reporting Services: native mode and SharePoint integrated mode. The server mode you select is closely connected to the structure and usage of the report server databases. If you configure one of these server modes for Reporting Services and later switch to the other mode, you must create a new report server database using the Reporting Services Configuration Manager.

> **Important** You cannot migrate any reports that you have previously published to the report server, so you must keep a copy of the report definitions to publish again after switching the report server to a different mode.

The default server mode for Reporting Services is native mode, which runs the report server as a stand-alone application server. Even if you don't want to use Reporting Services in SharePoint integrated mode, you can still use a native-mode report server with SharePoint by using SharePoint Web Parts in a partial integration mode. These Web Parts work with Microsoft Windows SharePoint Services 2.0, Windows SharePoint Services 3.0, Microsoft SharePoint Portal Server 2003, and Microsoft Office SharePoint Server 2007. One Web Part lets you navigate through folders and lists of reports on a native-mode report server. A second Web Part lets you view a selected report.

In SharePoint integrated mode, the report server runs in a Windows SharePoint Services 3.0 or Office SharePoint Server 2007 server farm. In either edition of SharePoint, you can locate, view, manage, and secure reports in a SharePoint library. Office SharePoint Server provides several additional business intelligence features that enable you to integrate reports into dashboard pages using a Report Viewer Web Part with SharePoint filter Web Parts. SharePoint integrated mode does have two important limitations, however. It does not support linked reports (described in Chapter 10, "Deploying Reports to a Server"), nor does it support performing administrative tasks such as report deployment in batch mode using the Rs utility (also described in Chapter 10).

Choosing a Deployment Topology

After choosing an edition, your next decision is to select a deployment topology. Your topology options are limited by the server mode and edition that you plan to implement.

Native-Mode Topology

A standard deployment is a single native-mode report server instance that stores the application databases in a local or remote Microsoft SQL Server instance. Using a remote SQL Server instance requires you to have two SQL Server licenses: one for the remote instance and one for the local report server instance. You cannot distribute SQL Server features on multiple servers using a single license.

> **Note** You are not limited to SQL Server 2008 to host the application databases. You can instead use either SQL Server 2000 or SQL Server 2005 for a native-mode report server.

In a scale-out deployment, you create multiple report server instances that all use the same application database, which can also be located on the same server as one of the report server instances. You can implement only a scale-out deployment if you're using SQL Server 2008 Enterprise, SQL Server 2008 Developer, or SQL Server 2008 Evaluation. The benefit of a scale-out deployment is the increased availability of the servers and scalability. The processing of scheduled reports and subscriptions runs faster in a scale-out deployment, for example. In addition, you can load-balance the report servers in the scale-out deployment to maximize performance for on-demand reports. However, you need to implement a software or hardware solution to support Network Load Balancing (NLB) because no server cluster management tool is provided with Reporting Services. Likewise, you can install the Reporting Services application databases on a SQL Server 2005 failover cluster that is already configured. Reporting Services itself cannot run as part of a failover cluster, although it can run on the same server on which a failover cluster is installed.

The procedures in this chapter assume that you are installing a standard deployment using a local SQL Server instance to host the application database. In a production environment, however, your decision to host the application database on the same server as the report server should factor in the potential for resource contention between the database engine and the report server. Both applications require CPU time, memory, and disk space to process jobs, so you need to adjust your minimum hardware specifications to accommodate a high demand on these resources.

The disk space required to store the application database will increase over time, and it is difficult to predict in advance. Disk space is affected most by storing image files, collateral resources such as Portable Document Format (PDF) documents, and snapshots in the report server database, and by storing cached instances of reports in the report server temporary database. You need to monitor your database size over time to ensure that plenty of disk space is available.

SharePoint Integrated-Mode Topology

The simplest topology is a single-server deployment, in which you install SQL Server, Reporting Services, and SharePoint on the same server. You should use this approach only when you have a small number of users and relatively few reports to manage because the risk of resource contention is very high in this topology as a result of the dependency on SQL Server databases by both Reporting Services and SharePoint.

A more practical approach for managing resources is to implement a distributed topology. There are many possible variations, but understanding three common configurations should give you ideas about how to implement a distributed topology in your technical environment:

- **SharePoint stand-alone**   You install all SharePoint components, including the configuration and content databases, on a single server, and install Reporting Services on a separate server.

- **Remote SQL Server**   You install SharePoint components on one server, and install the SharePoint databases and Reporting Services on a second server.

- **SharePoint farm**   You create a SharePoint farm to support several Web front-end servers, and install Reporting Services on one of the Web front-end servers.

Reviewing Hardware and Software Requirements

Before you proceed with the installation of Reporting Services as a feature of SQL Server 2008, you should make sure your computer has the right operating system, ample memory, and plenty of hard disk space.

You can install SQL Server 2008 on most 32-bit or 64-bit operating systems: Windows XP Professional, Windows Vista (Business, Ultimate, or Enterprise edition), Windows Server 2003 SP2 (Standard, Data Center, or Enterprise edition), or Windows Server 2008 (Standard, Data Center, or Enterprise edition). You can install 32-bit SQL Server 2008 only on a 32-bit operating system, and likewise install 64-bit SQL Server 2008 only on a 64-bit operating system. The management tools run in 32-bit mode and are supported by Windows on Windows 64-bit (WOW64), which allows you to install these tools on a 64-bit system. Be sure to install all operating system service packs before beginning the installation of SQL Server 2008.

Note For a complete review of requirements and a full list of supported operating systems, refer to "Hardware and Software Requirements for Installing SQL Server 2008," at *http: //msdn.microsoft.com/en-us/library/ms143506(SQL.100).aspx*.

Although the minimum memory requirement is 512 megabytes (MB), the recommended memory is 2 GB. You should have as much available memory as possible to get the best performance from Reporting Services.

Before installation, your computer must have 2 GB of hard disk space available for temporary files. Reporting Services requires 120 MB for the report server components. Additional disk space (up to 1.6 GB) might be required if you install other SQL Server 2008 features on the same computer.

If you plan to deploy Reporting Services in SharePoint integrated mode, you must use one of the following SQL Server 2008 editions: Developer, Evaluation, Standard, or Enterprise. The report server must have an instance of Windows SharePoint Services 3.0 or Office SharePoint Server 2007 (Standard or Enterprise edition) installed, but you can install Reporting Services before or after installing SharePoint. If you are installing Reporting Services in a SharePoint farm, you need only install the SharePoint Web front-end on the report server.

Note You can find more information about hardware and software requirements for Windows SharePoint Services 3.0 at *http://technet.microsoft.com/en-us/library/cc288751.aspx*. Similar information for Office SharePoint Server 2007 is available at *http://technet.microsoft.com/en-us /library/cc262485.aspx*.

An additional software component, Microsoft Reporting Services Add-in for SharePoint Technologies, must be installed on the SharePoint server or on each Web front-end server in the SharePoint farm that hosts reporting. You learn how to obtain and install this component later in this chapter.

Important Although you can use a SQL Server 2000 or SQL Server 2005 database for Reporting Services in native mode, you must use a SQL Server 2008 database if you plan to run Reporting Services in SharePoint integrated mode.

Planning Accounts for Reporting Services

Before you install Reporting Services, you must decide whether to run the report server service under a built-in service account or a Windows account on your computer or in your network domain. If you use a Windows account, the account you use should be a least-privilege account with permission to connect to the network and the Allow Log On Locally permission on the report server and the computer hosting the report server database, if they are different. Ideally, you should dedicate this account to only the report server service.

> **Important** If you plan to use a Windows account, be sure to create the account before starting the installation of Reporting Services.

By default, the report server service account is also used for connecting to the report server database, although you can change this to a domain account or a SQL Server login by using the Reporting Services Configuration Tool (as explained later in this chapter). This connection account is used when the report server needs to store and retrieve reports, metadata, and server state information and is the only account requiring access to the report server database.

If you're deploying Reporting Services in SharePoint integrated mode, there are some constraints on service accounts that depend on your deployment topology to consider:

- **Single server**   You can use the built-in local system or network service accounts or use a local or domain Windows user account.

- **SharePoint stand-alone**   You can use the built-in network service account or a Windows user account but cannot use the local system account.

- **Remote SQL Server with report server on the same server as SharePoint databases**   You can use only a domain Windows user account. Built-in and local user accounts are blocked.

- **Remote SQL Server with report server on a separate server from SharePoint databases**   You can use the built-in network service account or a Windows user account but cannot use the local system account.

> **Important** When you create a SharePoint Web application, you must specify an account to run the application pool process. Generally, you should use a domain user account, although it is permissible to use Network Service. However, if the report server is running on a separate computer from SharePoint, and if Reporting Services Integration is configured in Trusted Account mode (explained later in this chapter), you must use a domain user account to run the application pool process.

Performing the Installation

You can install Reporting Services by using a setup wizard or by using a command-line executable. The installation process includes installation of prerequisites, installation of setup support files, and feature selection and configuration. You can install Reporting Services on the same server as other SQL Server components, as described in this chapter, or you can install it alone. If you install Reporting Services alone, the report server requires access to a SQL Server for hosting the report server database.

Important To run Setup on your computer, you must be logged into the computer with an account that is a member of the local administrator group.

Note The procedures in this section apply when you are performing a new installation of SQL Server 2008 and its components, including Reporting Services and Analysis Services, with all components on a single server. You must install Analysis Services if you intend to complete the procedures in Chapter 7, "Using Analysis Services as a Data Source." If you have already installed SQL Server 2008 but have not yet installed Reporting Services or Analysis Services, refer to *http://msdn.microsoft.com/en-us/library/cc281940.aspx* for instructions to how to add features to an existing SQL Server 2008 instance.

Installing Prerequisites

The installation of SQL Server 2008 components requires the Microsoft .NET Framework 3.5 SP1 and Microsoft Windows Installer 4.5 or later. When you start the SQL Server Installation Center by running Setup, a check for these prerequisites occurs. If the prerequisites are missing, the setup process begins with steps to install them.

In this procedure, you start the SQL Server Installation Center.

Start the SQL Server Installation Center

1. On the server where you want to install Reporting Services, run Setup from your SQL Server 2008 installation CD or from a network share containing the contents of the installation CD.

   A message box explains that SQL Server 2008 requires the .NET Framework and that an updated Windows Installer will also be installed before Setup continues.

2. In the message box, click OK.

3. In the Welcome To Setup page of the Microsoft .NET Framework 3.5 SP1 Setup wizard, review the license agreement, select I Have Read And ACCEPT The Terms Of The License Agreement, and click Install.

   The installation might take several minutes. When the Setup Complete page appears, click Exit. If a reboot of your computer is required, a message box displays to alert you. Click OK and then restart your computer manually.

Installing Setup Support Files

The installation process begins with a test of the configuration of your computer. If your computer passes this test, the process continues with the installation of the support files required for setup.

In this procedure, you continue with installation of SQL Server 2008 by installing the setup support files.

Install the setup support files

1. Run Setup from your SQL Server 2008 installation CD or from a network share containing the contents of the installation CD.

2. In the left pane of the SQL Server Installation Center, click Installation.

3. In the right pane, click New SQL Server Stand-alone Installation Or Add Features To An Existing Installation.

> **Note** The installation process checks your computer to make sure all setup requirements are met. For example, your computer must use a supported operating system, you must be an administrator, and the Windows Management Instrumentation (WMI) service must be running. You can review a list of all requirements after the check finishes.

4. On the Setup Support Rules page of the wizard, you can click Show Details to view the requirements and the status of each requirement. If your computer passes, click OK.

   You must correct any problems before continuing with the installation. You can leave the SQL Server 2008 Setup wizard open, fix a problem, return to the wizard, and click Re-Run to run the requirement tests again.

5. On the Product Key page of the wizard, select Specify A Free Edition, and then select Enterprise Evaluation from the drop-down list. If you have already purchased a SQL

Server 2008 license for installation on your computer, you should instead select Enter The Product Key and type the product key into the box. Click Next.

6. On the License Terms page of the wizard, review the agreement, select the I Accept The License Terms check box, and click Next.

7. On the Setup Support Files page of the wizard, click Install.

   The installation of the setup support files will take several minutes.

8. When the installation completes, the wizard displays a new Setup Support Rules page. This page automatically displays the status of additional setup requirements. Click the View Detailed Report link to review the status of the installation, and then click Next.

 Note If you see a warning in the Status column for Windows Firewall, refer to *http://msdn.microsoft.com/en-us/library/cc646023.aspx* for instructions on how to allow SQL Server access through a firewall.

Installing SQL Server 2008 Features

After the setup support files are installed, you must select which SQL Server 2008 features to install. If you have a remote server running SQL Server available to host the report server databases, you need only install Reporting Services and the Management Tools. You can install the Business Intelligence Development Studio (BI Dev Studio) and Client Tools Connectivity on the same computer if you plan to use it for report development, or install these features later on a separate computer.

 Important If you configure Reporting Services to use a remote server running SQL Server, your account needs permission to create and access databases on that server.

In this procedure, you continue the installation of SQL Server 2008 by selecting the SQL Server 2008 features to install.

Install SQL Server 2008 features

1. On the Feature Selection page of the SQL Server 2008 Setup wizard, in the Features list, select the Database Engine Services, Analysis Services, Reporting Services, Business Intelligence Development Studio, Client Tools Connectivity, SQL Server Books Online, and Management Tools – Complete check boxes.

The Feature Selection page of the wizard looks like this:

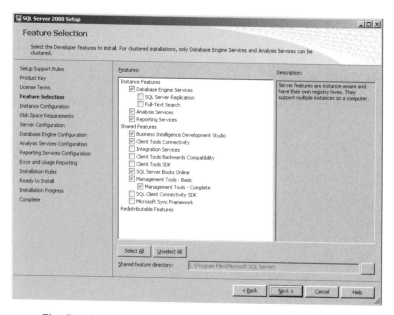

❑ The Database Engine Services feature is required to host the Reporting Services databases. If another instance of SQL Server 2008 is on your computer or is available on a remote server, you can ignore this selection.

❑ The Analysis Services feature is required to complete the procedures in Chapter 7 If you intend to skip that chapter, you can ignore this selection.

❑ The Reporting Services feature is the focus of this book, of course; therefore, it is a required selection on this page.

❑ You use the BI Dev Studio to build reports and report models in the chapters of Part II, "Developing Reports," so it is also a required selection.

❑ The Client Tools Connectivity feature includes the components and network libraries that Reporting Services uses for Open Database Connectivity (ODBC) and Object Linking and Embedding Database (OLE DB) connectivity when executing report queries.

❑ SQL Server Books Online is not required, but it is useful to install on your computer as a reference tool. Alternatively, you can refer to SQL Server Books Online at *http://msdn.microsoft.com/en-us/library/ms130214(sql.100).aspx*.

❑ The Management Tools – Complete feature includes SQL Server Management Studio with the necessary tools for managing the report server. This feature is required to complete the procedures in Chapter 11, "Securing Report Server Content," and Chapter 12, "Performing Administrative Tasks."

The default location for installation of the SQL Server 2008 features is C:\Program Files \Microsoft SQL Server, but you can choose a different location if you prefer.

2. On the Feature Select page, click Next to continue.

3. On the Instance Configuration page, shown here, keep the default selection of Default Instance.

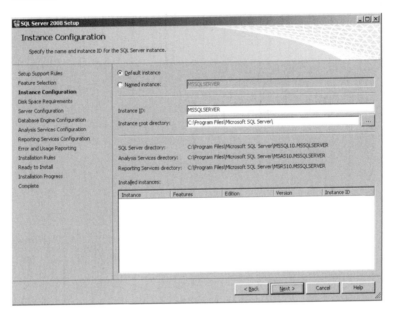

Alternatively, you can select Named Instance and specify a name for the instance. You can also change the root directory of the instance from the default of C:\Program Files \Microsoft SQL Server.

Notice the directory for Reporting Services is C:\Program Files\Microsoft SQL Server \MSRS10.MSSQLServer. This naming convention makes it much easier to identify where Reporting Services files are found in the SQL Server root directory as compared to previous versions of Reporting Services. You need to know this location if you want to change configuration files later or to review logs, which are covered in Chapter 12.

4. On the Instance Configuration page, click Next to continue.

5. On the Disk Space Requirements page, confirm that you have enough disk space on your computer to install the selected features, and click Next to continue.

6. On the Server Configuration page, in the Account Name drop-down list, select NT AUTHORITY\NETWORK SERVICE as the service account for SQL Server Agent, SQL Server Database Engine, SQL Server Analysis Services, and SQL Server Reporting Services.

The Server Configuration page looks like this:

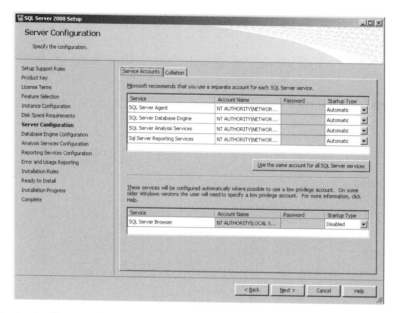

7. In the Startup Type drop-down list for SQL Server Agent, select Automatic.

   SQL Server Agent must be running to configure schedules for caching, snapshots, and subscriptions.

> **Note** Microsoft recommends that you establish separate service accounts for each service. In this book, your computer is assumed to be a development environment contained within a single computer, so you can safely use NT AUTHORITY\NETWORK SERVICE, which is a low-privilege account and satisfies the minimum security requirements.

If you plan to use a domain account for each service, you can click Use The Same Account For All SQL Server Services. A dialog box displays, in which you can provide the account name and password for all services in a single step. Otherwise, for each service, you need to select Browse in the Account Name drop-down list and locate an account.

8. On the Server Configuration page, click Next to continue.

9. On the Database Engine Configuration page, shown here, click Add Current User to add your user account as a SQL Server administrator:

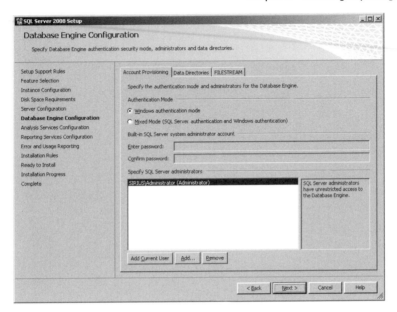

 Note If you prefer to use a different data directory for your SQL Server 2008 databases, you can click the Data Directories tab to specify an alternate location.

10. On the Database Engine Configuration page, click Next to continue.

11. On the Analysis Services Configuration page, click Add Current User, and then click Next. If you did not install Analysis Services, skip to step 12.

 Note If you prefer to use a different data directory for your Analysis Services 2008 databases, you can click the Data Directories tab to specify an alternate location.

12. On the Reporting Services Configuration page, shown here, select Install The Native Mode Default Configuration.

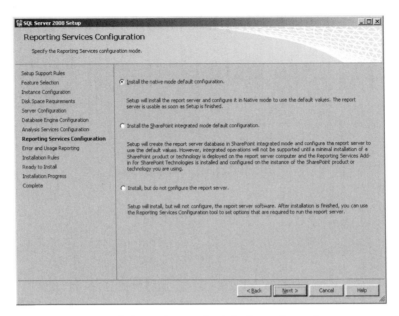

The option to install the native mode default configuration appears only when you install Reporting Services in the same instance that hosts the Database Engine and the account running Setup has permissions to access and create databases on that instance. Otherwise, you must use the Install, But Do Not Configure The Report Server option.

Important If you are installing Reporting Services 2008 on a computer that is already running Reporting Services 2005 and uses the default port 80 for the virtual directories ReportServer and Reports, you must choose the Install, But Do Not Configure The Report Server option to prevent Reporting Services 2008 from blocking access to Reporting Services 2005.

If you know now that you want to implement SharePoint integrated mode, you can instead select Install The SharePoint Integrated Mode Default Configuration. This option does not require you to have SharePoint installed on your computer, but the report server is not available until you install SharePoint and finish configuring the report server to work in SharePoint integrated mode, as explained later in this chapter.

Note It's very easy to change the configuration settings if you change your mind, so don't worry too much about your choices at this point. The main consideration to keep in mind when configuring a report server for native mode or SharePoint integrated mode is to plan to redeploy the content if you later want to switch to the other mode. Therefore, you should decide which mode to support before you start deploying reports to the report server. You might set up two evaluation computers to try out each mode before deciding which configuration to install in your production environment.

13. On the Reporting Services Configuration page, click Next.

14. On the Error And Usage Reporting page, click Next.

15. On the Installation Rules page, click Next.

16. On the Ready To Install page, click Install.

    Installation might take up to an hour, especially if you followed the steps in this procedure to install all the features required to complete the procedures throughout this book.

17. On the Installation Progress page, click Next.

18. On the Complete page, click Close.

19. Close the SQL Server Installation Center window.

Configuring Reporting Services

When you choose the option to install the native mode default configuration, Reporting Services is ready to use, although there are more configuration steps that you might need to complete if you intend to use e-mail subscriptions or use remote data sources. In addition, to protect the report server database, you should also back up the encryption key using the Reporting Services Configuration Manager. Finally, if you have implemented a scale-out deployment, you use the Reporting Services Configuration Manager to add servers to the scale-out.

In this procedure, you use the Reporting Services Configuration Manager to complete the configuration of your report server.

Use the Reporting Services Configuration Manager

1. Click Start, select All Programs, Microsoft SQL Server 2008, Configuration Tools, and finally Reporting Services Configuration Manager.

2. If you installed Reporting Services as the default instance on your local computer, in the Reporting Services Configuration Connection dialog box, click Connect. Otherwise, change the Server Name and the Report Server Instance to the applicable server and instance, and then click Connect.

The Report Server Status page of the Reporting Services Configuration Manager displays, as shown here.

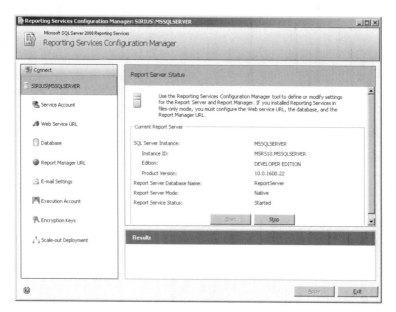

3. In the left pane, click Service Account, and you see the account used to run the report server Windows service. If you followed the steps described in the previous procedure, the built-in account Network Service displays here. You can change the service account to a different built-in account or to a domain account at any time. After you specify a new service account, click Apply to implement the change.

> **Important**   Because it's a Windows service, you see Reporting Services listed in the Services management console. You might be tempted to change the service account in that interface. However, it's recommended that you always use the Reporting Services Configuration Manager to make service account changes.

4. In the left pane, click Web Service URL to view the current settings, as shown here.

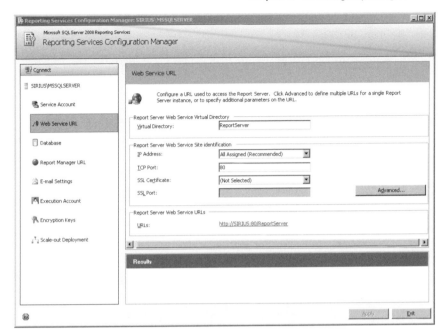

 Note If you installed Reporting Services in Files-Only mode, you need to configure the Web Service URL before you can deploy reports to the report server.

On this page of the Reporting Services Configuration Manager, you configure the virtual directory for the Web service as well as the *URL reservation*, which describes one or more URLs that can be used to access the report server Web service. You use the Web service URL when you want to bypass the Report Manager and access a report directly (as described in Chapter 16, "Programming Reporting Services").

When you define the URLs for Report Manager and the report server using the Reporting Services Configuration Manager, you create a URL reservation that defines a URL endpoint. That endpoint is registered on the server when the Report Server service starts, if the service is enabled in SQL Server Surface Area Configuration. A request queue is created at that time and HTTP.SYS can route requests to the report server's request queue when registration completes.

The URL reservation consists of four elements:

- **Scheme** Identifies the protocol used to send a request to Reporting Services, such as Hypertext Transfer Protocol (HTTP) or Hypertext Transfer Protocol Secure (HTTPS).

- **Host name** Defines the server hosting Reporting Services, such as adventureworks.com.

- **Port**   Specifies the port configured to listen for HTTP requests, which is port 80 by default.

- **Virtual directory**   Refers to the name that identifies the URL reservation, similar to an Internet Information Services (IIS) virtual directory, such as ReportServer for the report server Web service.

You can have multiple URLs configured for the report server Web service (or the Report Manager, which you'll configure later in this chapter), but you must keep the same virtual directory for all those URLs. For example, you might require multiple URLs when supporting both intranet and extranet deployment scenarios by the same report server.

HTTP.SYS uses the following hierarchical system of URL reservation types to determine how to route requests:

- **All Assigned**   All requests on the specified port for the specified virtual directory are routed to Reporting Services. This type of URL reservation (for example, *http://+:80/ReportServer*) uses the plus (+) sign as a strong wildcard and is the default for Reporting Services.

- **Specific**   Only requests matching the host, port, and virtual directory are sent to Reporting Services, such as *http://adventureworks.com:80/ReportServer.*

- **All Unassigned**   Any request not already handled by another reservation is sent to Reporting Services, such as *http://*:80/ReportServer.* In this case, the asterisk (*) symbol is used as a weak wildcard.

To configure the URL reservation, you select a value for the IP Address, which by default is All Assigned (Recommended). You can choose an alternative value in the drop-down list to create a specific or All Unassigned reservation type. In addition, you specify a port number in the TCP Port box.

If you have a Secure Sockets Layer (SSL) certificate installed on the report server, it appears in the SSL Certificate drop-down list. After you select the certificate, you can specify a port to use for SSL communications.

Important If you install Reporting Services 2008 on a computer that already has Reporting Services 2005 installed, you must change the URL reservation. Reporting Services 2005 uses *http://<servername>:80/ReportServer* (or *http://<servername>:8080 /ReportServer* on a Windows XP 32-bit system). For Reporting Services 2008, use a different port number or a different virtual directory name in the URL reservation to avoid a conflict between the two versions.

5. You use the Advanced Multiple Web Site Configuration dialog box to configure multiple identities for the same report server Web service. Click Advanced to add, edit, or delete a URL reservation, as shown here:

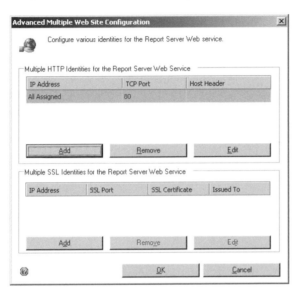

6. Under Multiple HTTP Identities For The Report Server Web Service, click Add. The Add A Report Server HTTP URL dialog box displays, as shown here:

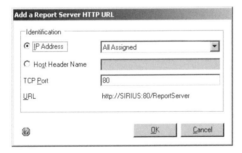

Here you can specify the reservation type All Assigned, All Unassigned, or a specific Internet Protocol (IP) address as well as the port number for a URL reservation. The full URL displays in the dialog box to allow you to confirm the configuration.

7. Click Cancel to close the Add A Report Server HTTP URL dialog box, and then click Cancel to close the Advanced Multiple Web Site Configuration dialog box.

8. Click the Report Server Web service URL. A browser window opens and displays the version information for Reporting Services. You might be prompted for credentials before you can view the Web service page shown here:

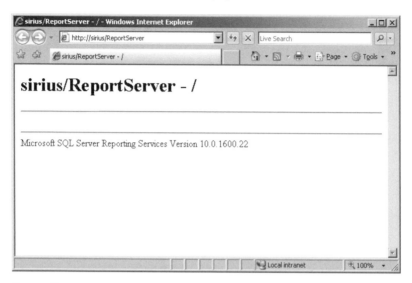

Depending on your operating system and Windows Internet Explorer settings, you might also be prompted to enable intranet settings. If so, click the yellow bar at the top of the page, click Enable Intranet Settings, and click Yes in the message box to confirm.

You can easily check each URL reservation that you configure in the Reporting Services Configuration Manager by clicking the applicable link here to verify the report server Web service is responding correctly.

9. Close the Internet Explorer window to continue.

10. In the left pane, click Database.

If you installed Reporting Services in Files-Only mode, you need to configure the report server database in the Reporting Services Configuration Manager, as shown here.

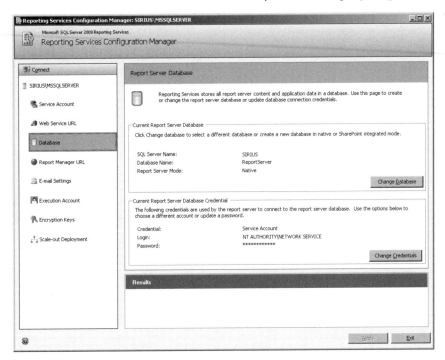

On this page, you can see the server hosting the report server database and the database name, which defaults to ReportServer. You can also see the current server mode for the report server. Finally, you can see the account used to connect to the report server database.

If you want to switch to SharePoint integrated mode or if you want to set up a new report server database in the current server mode, click Change Database. An example of creating a SharePoint integrated-mode report server database is described later in this chapter.

To change the report service connection account, click Change Credentials.

Note If you installed Reporting Services in Files-Only mode, you need to configure the Report Manager URL.

11.   In the left pane, click Report Manager URL, as shown here.

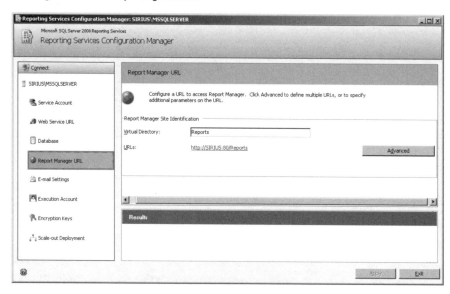

On this page of Reporting Services Configuration Manager, you configure the virtual directory used to access Report Manager. As you learned in Chapter 1, Report Manager is the Web application that is the standard user interface for accessing reports and performing certain administrative tasks.

As with the Report Server Web Service URL, you can click Advanced to configure multiple URL reservations. Each URL reservation listed in the URLs section is a link that you can use to confirm that Report Manager opens on request.

12. Click the URL to display Report Manager, as shown here:

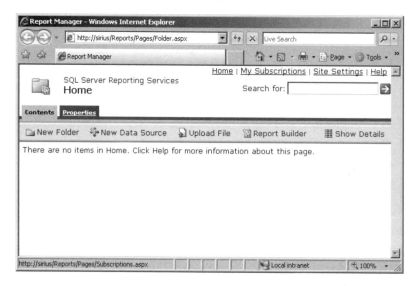

By opening Report Manager, you confirm that Reporting Services is correctly installed and configured. You learn more about Report Manager in Chapter 13, "Accessing Reports Online."

13. Close the Report Manager window.

14. In the left pane, click E-mail Settings to view the page shown here:

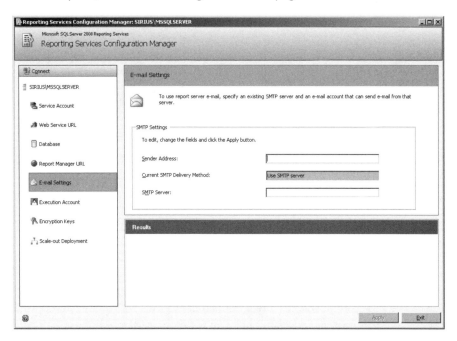

15. In the Sender Address box, type a valid e-mail account in your computer's domain in the format *sendername@domain*. Reporting Services uses this account to specify the sender in an e-mail subscription delivered to recipients.

16. In the SMTP Server box, type the name of a Simple Mail Transfer Protocol (SMTP) server in your domain. If you are using a stand-alone server as a development environment, you can type **localhost**. Click Apply.

Note To test e-mail delivery, you must have SMTP installed on your computer or accessible on the network by your computer.

17. In the left pane, click Execution Account to view the page shown here:

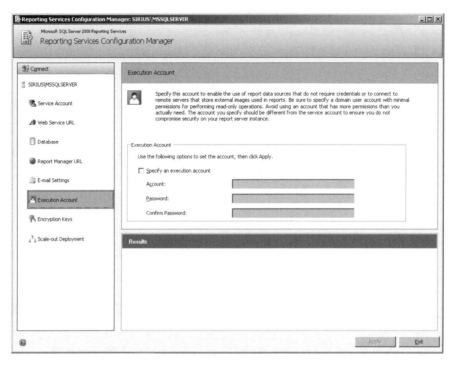

If the reports that you manage on the report server require access to data on remote servers, you must configure a domain user account to enable access to the server. Reporting Services uses this account for reports using database authentication or to connect to servers hosting data for which access to the data itself does not require authentication. Reporting Services also uses the execution account for authenticating image files that are used in a report but that are stored in a separate location that does not allow Anonymous access.

18. In the left pane, click Encryption Keys to view the page shown here:

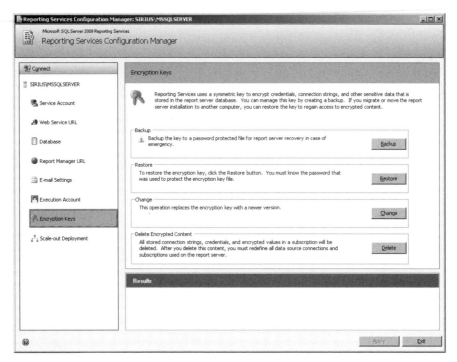

19. Click Backup.

If you later need to restore the ReportServer database, you need a backup of the en-cryption key used to store data in that database. You learn more about the encryption key in Chapter 12.

20. In the Backup Encryption Key dialog box, type a file location and filename, such as **C:\Backup\RS.snk**.

 Note You must create the folder for the file location before you attempt to save the file.

21. In the Password box, type a strong password, retype the password in the Confirm Password box, and then click OK.

 Tip To learn more about creating strong passwords, refer to *http://www.microsoft.com /protect/yourself/password/create.mspx*.

22. In the left pane, click Scale-out Deployment to view this page:

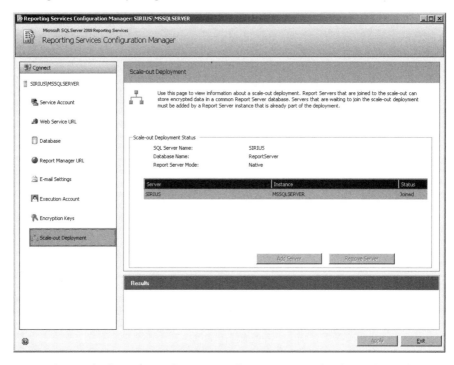

In a scale-out deployment, only one set of report server databases is used. Using Reporting Services Configuration Manager, you connect to a report server that is already part of a scale-out deployment (or the first server in the scale-out deployment), and then use the Scale-out Deployment page to add one or more report servers to the scale-out.

23. Click Exit to close Reporting Services Configuration Manager.

Configuring Windows Firewall for Windows XP

If your computer's operating system is Windows XP SP2, Windows Firewall blocks HTTP requests for port 80 by default. To correct this problem, you must configure Windows Firewall to open port 80 to use Reporting Services on your computer. To configure Windows Firewall, follow these steps:

1. Click Start, select Control Panel, and click Windows Firewall.

2. In the Windows Firewall dialog box, click the Exceptions tab, and then click Add Port.

3. In the Name box, type **Reporting Services (TCP 80)**.

4. In the Port Number box, type **80**.

5. Select the Transmission Control Protocol (TCP) protocol, and click OK. Click OK to close the Windows Firewall dialog box.

Installing Report Builder 2.0

The Report Builder 2.0 component is a free download that provides an alternative interface for building managed or ad hoc reports. Power users will appreciate the familiar Office 2007 appearance. You learn how to use Report Builder 2.0 in Chapter 3, "Exploring Reporting Services."

In this procedure, you download and install Report Builder 2.0.

Download and install Report Builder 2.0

1. Open Internet Explorer, navigate to *http://www.microsoft.com/downloads /details.aspx?FamilyID=9f783224-9871-4eea-b1d5-f3140a253db6*, and click the Download button next to ReportBuilder.msi.

2. In the File Download – Security Warning message box, click Save.

3. In the Save As dialog box, navigate to a location on your computer or network to store the downloaded file, and click Save.

4. When the download completes, open Windows Explorer, navigate to the location in which you saved the downloaded file, and double-click the downloaded file.

5. In the Open File – Security Warning message box, click Run.

6. On the Welcome page of the Microsoft SQL Server Report Builder wizard, click Next.

7. On the License Agreement page of the wizard, select I Accept The Terms In The License Agreement, and click Next.

8. On the Registration Information page of the wizard, type your name and company name in the text boxes provided, and click Next.

9. On the Feature Selection page of the wizard, click Next to accept the default installation.

10. On the Default Target Server page of the wizard, type **http://<*servername*> /reportserver** for a native-mode report server or type **http://<*servername*>/sites /ssrs** for a SharePoint integrated-mode report server, replacing <*servername*> with the name of your server. You create the SSRS site for SharePoint in the "Creating a Report Center Site" section later in this chapter.

11. On the Ready To Install The Program page of the wizard, click Install.

12. When installation completes, click Finish.

Installing Sample Databases

Beginning with the release of SQL Server 2008, Microsoft no longer packages sample databases with the installation media. Instead, the sample databases are available for download from the CodePlex community Web site. To complete procedures in this book, you use the AdventureWorksDW2008 sample database for SQL Server 2008, which uses a star schema database design typical in data warehouses that are often used as reporting sources. Of course, you can use other data sources in reports, but a star schema design is easier to query and is useful for learning how to build reports in the report development chapters of this book.

> **Note** A star schema design denormalizes multiple tables in a transactional database into a set of fact tables and dimension tables. A fact table contains numeric columns for data, such as sales, quantities, and foreign key columns, to dimension tables. The foreign key columns function as a compound primary key for the fact table. A dimension table contains a primary key and one or more columns to store attributes relating to a dimension record.

In this procedure, you download and install the AdventureWorksDW2008 sample database.

Download and install the sample database

1. Open Internet Explorer and navigate to *http://www.codeplex.com /MSFTDBProdSamples/Release/ProjectReleases.aspx?ReleaseId=16040.*

2. Click the SQL2008.AdventureWorks_DW_BI_v2008.x86.msi link if your computer has a 32-bit operating system, or click the SQL2008.AdventureWorks_DW_BI_v2008.x64.msi link if your computer has a 64-bit operating system.

3. In the Microsoft Public License message box, click I Agree.

4. In the File Download – Security Warning message box, click Save.

5. In the Save As dialog box, navigate to a location on your computer or network to store the downloaded file, and click Save.

6. When the download completes, open Windows Explorer, navigate to the location in which you saved the downloaded file, and double-click the downloaded file. If necessary, click Run to continue the process.

7. On the Welcome page of the Setup Wizard, click Next.

8. On the End-User License Agreement page of the wizard, select the I Accept The Terms In The License Agreement check box, and click Next.

9. On the Custom Setup page of the wizard, click the icon for Restore AdventureWorks DBs, select Entire Feature Will Be Installed On Local Hard Drive, and click Next.

10. On the Database Setup page of the wizard, in the Select Local Database Instance For AdventureWorks drop-down list, select MSSQLSERVER (or a named instance if you created one during installation of SQL Server 2008), and click Next.

11. On the Ready To Install page of the wizard, click Install. When the installation completes, click Finish.

Configuring SharePoint Integrated Mode

As you learned in Chapter 1, you can integrate Reporting Services with Windows SharePoint Services 3.0 or Office SharePoint Server 2007. Regardless of the deployment topology that you choose to implement to integrate these technologies, you must configure the report server for SharePoint integrated mode, install an add-in component for SharePoint, and configure SharePoint for integration with Reporting Services. The order of installation of Reporting Services and SharePoint doesn't matter, but you must follow the configuration steps in sequence as described in this section.

> **More Info** SharePoint installation is beyond the scope of this book. To follow the procedures in this book, you can download an evaluation edition of Office SharePoint Server 2007 at *http://technet.microsoft.com/en-us/evalcenter/bb727242.aspx.* Follow the instructions to install and configure SharePoint on a single computer at *http://msdn.microsoft.com/en-us/library /bb677368(SQL.100).aspx.* If you want to use a server farm, follow the instructions at *http: //msdn.microsoft.com/en-us/library/bb677365(SQL.100).aspx.*

If you're using a single-server topology, your computer should have everything installed before you continue. If you're using one of the distributed topologies, you need to install a SharePoint Web front-end on your report server. You can find instructions at *http: //msdn.microsoft.com/en-us/library/aa905869(SQL.100).aspx.*

Configuring the Report Server

When you choose the installation option for SharePoint integrated mode, Setup configures the report server service account and the Web service URL, but you must configure the report server database. The Report Manager URL is no longer required because SharePoint is now the point of access for reports. All other configuration steps are optional and follow the same steps as described previously in this chapter. Until you complete the configuration of the report server and the SharePoint server, Reporting Services will not function.

Configure the report server

1. Click Start, select All Programs, Microsoft SQL Server 2008, and Configuration Tools, and then click Reporting Services Configuration Manager.

2. If you installed Reporting Services in the default instance on your local computer, in the Reporting Services Configuration Connection dialog box, click Connect. Otherwise, change the Server Name and the Report Server Instance to the applicable server and instance, and then click Connect.

3. In the left pane, click Web Service URL, and then click Apply to accept the default configuration.

   Of course, you can change the URL setting to apply a different IP address or TCP port. You can also add more URLs if necessary.

4. In the left pane, click Database, and then click Change Database.

5. In the Report Server Database Configuration Wizard, click Next to create a new report server database, as shown here.

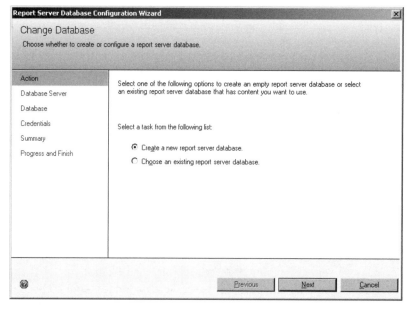

6. On the next page of the wizard, shown here, click Next to accept the default user if your database server uses integrated security.

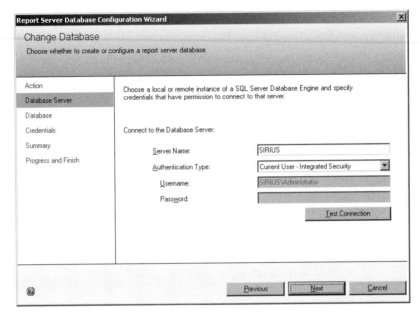

The credentials you specify here are used to create the report server database on the database server. You can change the Authentication Type to SQL Server Account if you must authenticate with a SQL Server login.

7. On the next page of the wizard, shown here, select SharePoint Integrated Mode and click Next.

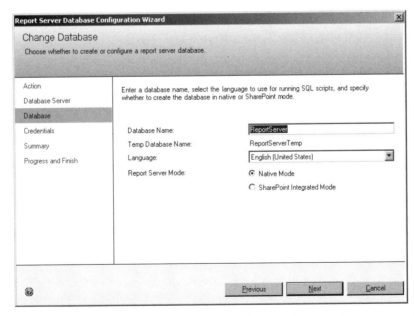

You can change the Database Name from the default ReportServer to an alternative name if you prefer.

8. On the Credentials page of the wizard, click Next.

   The default Authentication Type is Service Credentials. The service account is used to connect to the report server database. Alternatively, you can change the Authentication Type to Windows Credentials or SQL Server Credentials if you prefer the service to use a different account for this connection.

9. On the Summary page of the wizard, click Next.

10. When the database creation and configuration process completes, click Finish.

> **Note** At this time, you can perform additional configuration steps as described previously in this chapter. Be sure to change the service account to a domain user account if the SharePoint databases are on the same computer as the report server in a Remote SQL Server deployment topology.

11. Click Exit to close the Reporting Services Configuration Manager.

Installing the Reporting Services Add-in for SharePoint Technologies

To use Reporting Services features in SharePoint, you must download and install the Microsoft SQL Server 2008 Reporting Services Add-in for SharePoint technologies. This component adds Web application pages to SharePoint for managing content and adds a Report Viewer Web Part for viewing reports online and exporting reports to an alternate format. Furthermore, the component adds support for synchronization between the SharePoint content database and the report server database and for custom security to control access to reports and reporting tasks using the SharePoint security model.

> **Important** If you are implementing a distributed deployment, you need to download and install the .NET Framework 3.0 redistributable package on the SharePoint server. You can download it from *http://go.microsoft.com/fwlink/?LinkID=86634* and run Setup to install.

In this procedure, you download and install the Reporting Services Add-in for SharePoint Technologies.

Download and install the Reporting Services Add-in for SharePoint Technologies

1. Open Internet Explorer, and navigate to *http://go.microsoft.com/fwlink/?LinkID=112120.*

2. Click the Download button for RsSharePoint.msi if your computer has a 32-bit operating system, or click the Download button for RsSharePoint_x64.msi if your computer has a 64-bit operating system.

3. In the File Download – Security Warning message box, click Save.

4. In the Save As dialog box, navigate to a location on your computer or network to store the downloaded file, and click Save.

5. When the download completes, open Windows Explorer, navigate to the location in which you saved the downloaded file, and double-click the downloaded file.

> **Important** You must be both a SharePoint Web farm administrator and a site collection administrator to install the Reporting Services Add-in.

6. In the Open File – Security Warning message box, click Run.

7. On the Welcome page of the SQL Server 2008 Reporting Services Add-in For SharePoint wizard, click Next.

8. On the License Agreement page of the wizard, select I Accept The Terms In The License Agreement, and click Next.

9. On the Registration Information page of the wizard, type your name and company name if default values are not provided, and click Next.

10. On the Ready To Install The Program page of the wizard, click Install.

11. When installation completes, click Finish.

> **Note** If you have a SharePoint farm, you must install the Reporting Services Add-in on all Web front-end servers in the farm except the computer hosting the report server.

Configuring SharePoint for Reporting Services Integration

The Reporting Services Add-in modifies the Application Management page in the SharePoint Central Administration site with links to pages you use to configure Reporting Services. Using these pages, you identify the URL for the report server and the type of authentication to use with the report server. You also run a procedure to grant the report server service account permission to access the SharePoint content database. Finally, you can configure server defaults for Reporting Services for logging, ad hoc reporting, and other server-based limits.

In this procedure, you use the SharePoint Central Administration application to configure SharePoint for Reporting Services Integration.

Configure SharePoint for Reporting Services Integration

1. On the SharePoint server, click Start, select Administrative Tools, and select SharePoint 3.0 Central Administration.

> **Important** You must be both a SharePoint Web farm administrator and a site collection administrator to configure SharePoint for Reporting Services integration.

2. Click the Application Management tab.

3. In the Reporting Services section, click the Grant Database Access link to view this page:

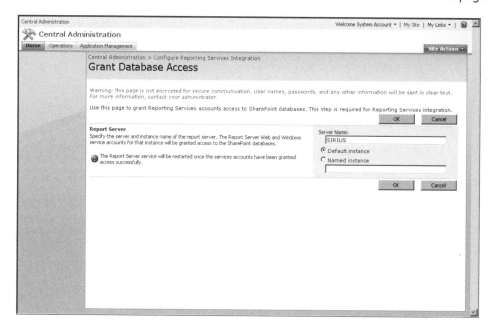

> **Note** If you do not see the Reporting Services section on the Application Management page of Central Administration, you must activate the report server integration feature. To do this, on the Site Actions, choose Site Settings, click the Site Collection Features link, and finally click the Activate button to the right of Report Server Integration Feature.

4. On the Grant Database Access page, in the Server Name box, type the name of your report server, and select Default Instance. If you installed Reporting Services as a named instance, select Named Instance and type the name of the instance. Click OK.

5. In the Enter Credentials – Webpage Dialog box, type the user name and password of an account that is a member of the local administrator group on the report server and then click OK.

6. In the Reporting Services section, click Manage Integration Settings.

7. On the Reporting Services Integration page, in the Report Server Web Service URL section, type the Web service URL for Reporting Services that you configured in step 4 of the "Use the Reporting Services Configuration Manager" procedure earlier in this chapter. You can omit the port number if the Web service is using port 80.

8. In the Authentication Mode drop-down list, select Windows Authentication.

The Reporting Services Integration page, shown here, appears.

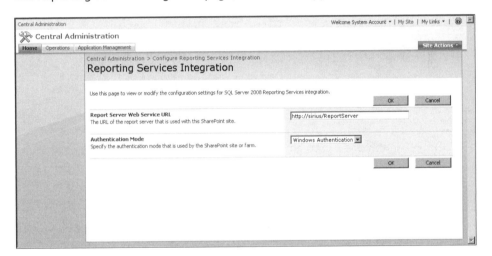

Anonymous access is not supported, so you must use a different authentication provider for the SharePoint Web application used for reporting. When you use Trusted Account, queries in your reports that access a report server run only in the context of the trusted account that is defined for the query's data source. If you configure your environment to use Kerberos authentication or if your report data is hosted on the SharePoint server, you can then use Windows authentication, which passes the current user's credentials to the data source for authentication. You learn more about configuring security in Chapter 11.

9. Click OK to apply the settings.

The report server service is now given Write and Execute permissions on the SharePoint configuration and content database as part of the integration process.

10. In the Reporting Services section, click the Set Server Defaults link.

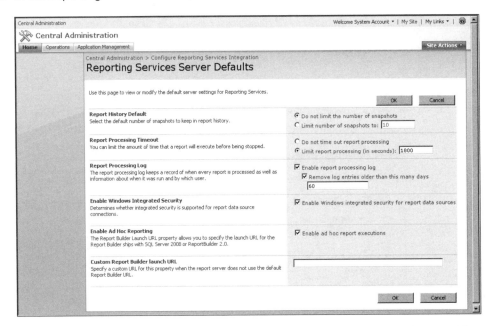

On this page, you can specify default values for report history, timeout values, and log-ging. You can also enable Windows Integrated Security for report data sources and en-able ad hoc reporting. You learn more about configuring these report server properties in Chapter 12.

11. Click Cancel to return to the Application Management page without changing settings, but keep the Central Administration window open for the next procedure.

Creating a SharePoint Web Application

At this point, after the report server and SharePoint are configured, you're ready to create a SharePoint Web application to host the document libraries in which you store reports and data sources. Essentially, the Web application defines the URL and port used to connect to those document libraries and stores its content in a database associated with an applica-tion you create. If you already have a SharePoint Web application available, you can skip this procedure.

In this procedure, you use the SharePoint Central Administration application to create a SharePoint Web application.

Create a SharePoint Web application

1. On the Application Management page of Central Administration, in the SharePoint Web Application Management section, click the Create Or Extend Web Application link.

2. On the Create Or Extend Web Application page, click the Create A New Web Application link.

3. On the Create New Web Application page, shown here, for the Create A New IIS Web Site option, you must specify a port number for the application.

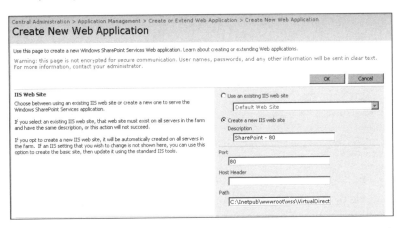

If this is the first Web application created for SharePoint, you can use the default port 80. SharePoint suggests an alternative port number if port 80 is not available. You can provide a different available port number if you prefer.

4. In the Security Configuration section, shown here, keep the default authentication provider NTLM to complete the procedures throughout this book.

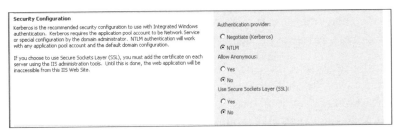

You can select Negotiate (Kerberos) if you have configured Kerberos for Reporting Services and for SharePoint in your network.

5. In the Application Pool section, shown here, under Create New Application Pool, select Predefined and keep the default Network Service.

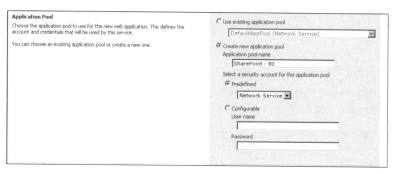

Alternatively, you can provide a domain account for the application pool if you prefer.

 Important If the report server is running on a separate computer from SharePoint, and if Reporting Services Integration is configured in Trusted Account mode, you must use a domain user account to run the application pool process.

6. In the Database Name And Authentication section, in the Database Server box, type the name of a database server to host the content database for the Web application.

7. Click OK to create the Web application.

Creating a Report Center Site

Now you're ready to create a SharePoint site collection and a site for the Web application that you just created. A site collection is a container for one or more sites. In turn, each site is a set of one or more Web pages that organizes content for a particular purpose, such as team collaboration or document management. To access and view reports, you can use any site that includes a SharePoint document library.

The Enterprise Edition of Office SharePoint Server 2007 has a Report Center site, which contains document libraries and other business intelligence features that use Reporting Services reports. However, you're not required to use Enterprise Edition to implement Reporting Services in SharePoint integrated mode. Using the Report Center site enables you to integrate Reporting Services reports with other SharePoint content on dashboard pages, which you learn how to do in Chapter 13, more easily.

In this procedure, you use the SharePoint Central Administration application to create a Report Center site.

Create a Report Center site

1. In Central Administration, click the Application Management tab.

2. In the SharePoint Site Management section, click the Create Site Collection link.

3. If the Web application that you created in the previous procedure does not display in the Web Application box, click the link in the box, and click Change Web Application. In the Select Web Application – Webpage dialog box, click the correct Web application to select it.

4. On the Create Site Collection page, in the Title box, type a name for your site, such as Reporting Services Step by Step.

5. In the URL drop-down list, select /sites/, and in the box to the right, type **ssrs**.

6. In the Template Selection section, click the Enterprise tab, and select Report Center, like this:

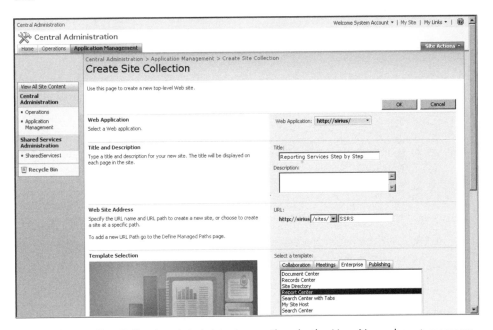

7. In the Primary Site Collection Administrator section, in the User Name box, type your user name, and click the Check Names icon on the right.

   You are not required to supply a secondary site collection administrator.

8. Click OK to create the site collection.

9. On the Top-Level Site Successfully Created page, click OK.

Adding Reporting Services Content Types to a SharePoint Document Library

The final step is to configure the SharePoint site to use Reporting Services. First, you activate the Report Server Integration Feature. Then you add SharePoint content types to the document libraries in the site in which you want to use reports, data sources, and report models. Two document libraries are included in the site template in the Report Center site, to which you should add the Reporting Services content types, Reports and Data Connections. You learn more about these document libraries in Chapter 10. You can also add Reporting Services content types to any document library in a site collection in which the Report Server Integration Features has been activated.

In this procedure, you add Reporting Services content types to the Reports and Data Connections document libraries.

Add Reporting Services content types to a SharePoint document library

1. In Internet Explorer, open *http://<servername>/sites/ssrs*.

> **Note** If you receive the Server Application Unavailable error when you attempt to open the SharePoint site, follow the steps detailed in the sidebar entitled "Configuring Permissions for the ASPNET User" later in this chapter.

2. In the upper-right corner, on the Site Actions menu, choose Site Settings, and click the Modify All Site Settings link.

3. In the Site Collection Administration section, click the Site Collection Features link.

4. To the right of Report Server Integration Feature, click Activate.

5. Click the Reporting Services Step by Step tab at the top of the page to return to the site collection home page.

6. In the list of navigation links on the left, click Reports.

7. Click Settings and then click Document Library Settings.

8. In the Content Types section, click Add From Existing Site Content Types.

9. In the Available Site Content Types list, select Report Builder Model, and then, while pressing the CTRL key, select Report Builder Report. Click Add.

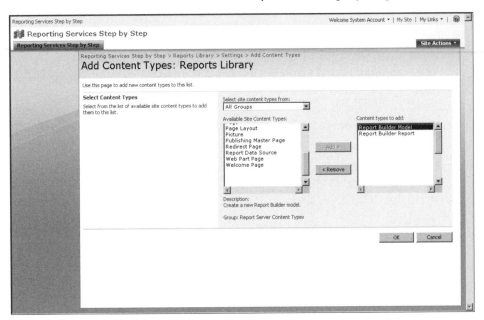

10. Click OK.

11. Click the Reporting Services Step by Step tab at the top of the page to return to the site collection home page.

12. In the list of navigation links on the left, click Data Connections.

13. Click Settings and then click Document Library Settings.

14. In the Content Types section, click Add From Existing Site Content Types.

15. In the Available Site Content Types list, select Report Data Source, click Add, and click OK.

16. Close Internet Explorer.

Configuring Permissions for the ASPNET User

If you are unable to open your SharePoint site due to the following error, "Server Application Unavailable," your error is likely a permissions issue for the ASPNET user. To resolve this problem when using a computer running Windows XP or Windows Server 2003, follow these steps:

1. Open Windows Explorer, and navigate to C:\Windows.

2. Right-click the folder Microsoft.NET and select Sharing And Security.

3. In the Select Users Or Groups dialog box, click Find Now.

4. In the Search Results list, select ASPNET, and click OK.

5. In the Select Users Or Groups dialog box, click OK.

6. Confirm that the ASPNET account has Read & Execute permissions, and click OK.

7. In the Security message box, click OK.

8. Open a command prompt window, type **iisreset**, and press Enter.

The SharePoint site should open correctly now. If not, open the Event Viewer and check the Application log on your computer for the error that you can use to search for troubleshooting information.

Tip For partial integration of a native-mode report server with a SharePoint product, you can install SharePoint 2.0 Web Parts on your SharePoint server. For more information, refer to Viewing Reports with SharePoint 2.0 Web Parts available online at *http://msdn.microsoft.com/en-us/library/ms159772(SQL.100).aspx*. Despite the reference to SharePoint 2.0 in the title, you can use these Web Parts with Windows SharePoint 3.0 or Office SharePoint Server 2007, but you must first add the Web Part assemblies to the global assembly cache (GAC).

By following the procedures outlined in this chapter, you have successfully installed and configured Reporting Services in either native mode or SharePoint integrated mode. Furthermore, by performing the steps to open Web pages for the report service Web service URL, the Report Manager URL, or for the SharePoint content types, you have verified Reporting Services is working properly. Now you're ready to start building reports to add content to the report server. In Chapter 3, you learn how to use Report Builder 2.0 to build your first report quickly and easily.

Chapter 2 Quick Reference

To	Do This
Test or learn the features of Reporting Services before implementing it in a production environment	Use SQL Server 2008 Evaluation Edition in a single-server deployment.
Implement Reporting Services in native mode	Use any edition of Reporting Services.
Implement Reporting Services in SharePoint integrated mode	Use Standard, Enterprise, Developer, or Evaluation edition of Reporting Services.
Install Reporting Services	Double-click Setup.exe on the installation CD or run the setup command-line executable with command-line arguments or a template file.

To	Do This
Change the report server service account	Open Reporting Services Configuration Manager, click Service Account, specify a built-in or Windows user account and its password, and click Apply.
Configure the Web service URL	Open Reporting Services Configuration Manager, click Web Service URL, type a virtual directory name, select an IP address or wildcard, type a port number, and click Apply. You also can select an SSL certificate and specify an SSL port.
Create a report server database or switch to a different report server mode	Open Reporting Services Configuration Manager, click Database, click Change Database, and complete the wizard.
Configure the Report Manager URL for a native-mode report server	Open Reporting Services Configuration Manager, click Report Manager URL, and type a virtual directory name. You can click Advanced to specify an IP address or wildcard, TCP port, SSL certificate, and SSL port, if necessary.
Configure e-mail settings	Open Reporting Services Configuration Manager, click E-mail Settings, provide a sender address, type the SMTP server name, and click Apply.
Configure an unattended execution account	Open Reporting Services Configuration Manager, click Execution Account, select the Specify An Execution Account check box, type a Windows user account and its password, and click Apply.
Back up an encryption key	Open Reporting Services Configuration Manager, click Encryption Keys, click Backup, type a file location and filename, type a strong password twice, and click OK.
Configure SharePoint integrated mode	Open Reporting Services Configuration Manager, click Database, click Change Database, and complete the wizard after selecting SharePoint Integrated Mode as the report server mode. Install the Reporting Services Add-in on the SharePoint server. Use the Application Management page of Central Administration to configure SharePoint using the links Grant Database Access and Reporting Services Integration.

Chapter 3
Exploring Reporting Services

After completing this chapter, you will be able to:

- Use Report Builder 2.0 to develop and preview a simple report.

- Publish a report to a native-mode or SharePoint integrated-mode report server.

- Use Report Manager to set report properties.

- Use the HTML Viewer to interact with a report.

In Chapter 1, "Introducing Reporting Services," you learned about the variety of features that Reporting Services provides in a complete reporting platform. Then, in Chapter 2, "Installing Reporting Services," you learned how to install and configure all these features. Now it's time to explore some of these features firsthand in each stage of the reporting life cycle. You start by developing a basic report using Report Builder 2.0 and then publishing your report. You continue your exploration by performing some administrative tasks to manage content on the server, and then complete the life cycle by accessing your report online and using Reporting Service's interactive viewing features.

Developing a Simple Report

Recall from Chapter 1 that Reporting Services has three tools for developing reports: Report Designer, Report Builder 1.0, and Report Builder 2.0. Most report developers use Report Designer because it has the most complete feature set and it has been part of the Reporting Services platform since the release of the initial version. You learn all about Report Designer in Part II, "Developing Reports." Business users can use Report Builder 1.0, which was first released as part of Reporting Services 2005, to develop simple ad hoc reports based on a report model. You learn how to work with Report Builder 1.0 in Chapter 14, "Creating Ad Hoc Reports." Report Builder 2.0, a new tool first available in Reporting Services 2008, is simple enough for a business user and yet includes enough features to satisfy a more technically skilled report developer.

Whereas Report Builder 1.0 requires a report model on the report server before you can develop a report, Report Builder 2.0 allows you to define your own data source and a query to return results from that data source. You then design the layout of the query results. After you have the information positioned in the report layout, you can fine-tune the appearance of your report by grouping query results to display subtotals and by applying formatting. At any point during report development, you can preview your report to incrementally test the changes you make to the report design.

Introducing Report Builder 2.0

You can use Report Builder 2.0 to develop both ad hoc and managed reports. It has a Ribbon interface similar to Microsoft Office 2007 to organize commonly used commands for adding items to a report, formatting report items, and setting display options. Report Builder 2.0 is very similar in functionality to Report Designer, although the interface is different and you are limited to working on one report at a time.

In this procedure, you explore the user interface of Report Builder 2.0.

Explore the Report Builder 2.0 interface

1. Click Start, select All Programs and Microsoft SQL Server 2008 Report Builder, and then select Report Builder 2.0. The application window, shown here, opens.

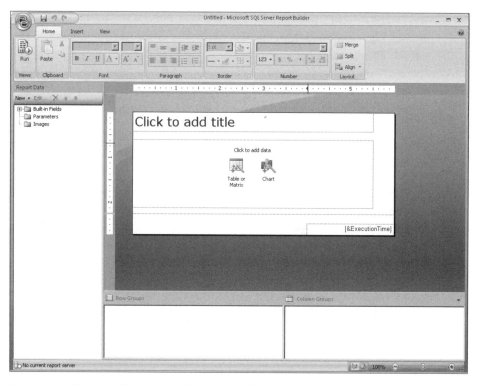

At the top of the application window is the Ribbon, which organizes commands into logical groups. On the left side of the application window is the Report Data pane, which organizes information used in the report, such as built-in fields, report parameters, images, data sources, and data sets. At the bottom of the application window is the Grouping pane, which displays groups that you create in the report layout. In the center of the application window is the report design surface, which you use to arrange and configure report items.

2. On the Ribbon, click the Insert tab to view the commands to add objects to your report, as shown here.

On the Insert tab, there are four groups:

- **Data Regions**   A *data region* is a special type of report item that you add to the report layout that is bound to a data set, such as a table, matrix, chart, gauge, or list. When using Report Builder 2.0, you can add one or more data regions to your report.

- **Report Items**   You use report items to add graphical elements, such as an image or line to a report. Using a text box, you can display static text, such as a report title, or text from a data set.

- **Subreports**   A *subreport* is a report item used to display another report inside the current report.

- **Header & Footer**   The header and footer are optional sections of a report page that you can remove if you prefer not to use them.

You learn more about each of these features in Chapter 4, "Designing Reports," and Chapter 8, "Visualizing Data." These same features are also available in Report Designer, although the method to add them to your report layout differs. In Report Builder 2.0, you simply click an item to add it to your report.

3. Click the View tab on the Ribbon to view the commands that it contains, as shown here.

On the View tab, there is one group:

- **Show/Hide**   You use the check boxes in this group to toggle the display of the Report Data pane, the Grouping pane, the Properties pane, and the Ruler. The Properties pane displays a list of properties associated with a report item selected on the design surface. Sometimes you might find it easier to work on your report when you hide all the panes, thereby maximizing the design surface in the application window. The ruler is useful for sizing and positioning report items on the design surface.

4. Click the Home tab on the Ribbon, to view its commands, as shown here.

On the Home tab, there are seven groups:

- **Views**   When you are in the Design view, this group contains the Run command to preview the report. When you are in the Report preview, this group contains the Design command to return to the Design view.

- **Clipboard**   You can use the Clipboard to cut, copy, and paste report items.

- **Font**   To format text, you can select a font style, size, color, and other properties.

- **Paragraph**   You can choose a command to align text horizontally or vertically within a text box, to increase or decrease the indent level of a paragraph, or to start a bulleted or numbered list.

- **Border**   You can select a command to define properties for a text box border, including border width, line color, style, and fill color.

- **Number**   You can use these commands to format numerical values.

- **Layout**   You can merge or split cells in a data region or align the edges of selected items.

5. Click Run.

Of course, there is no report to view yet, so you see an empty report, but you can see how easy it is to switch from the Design view to the preview of the report.

Another way to open the report preview is to click the Run button (to the right of the Design button) on the status bar, shown here:

The status bar at the bottom of the application window not only allows you to toggle between Design view and preview, but it also lets you use the slider to zoom in and out in either view.

6. On the Home tab, click Design to return to the Design view of the report. Alternatively, you can click the Design button on the toolbar at the bottom of the window.

Adding a Data Source

Before you can build a report, you must add a data source to the report definition to identify the source of the data that you'll display in the report. A data source provides the information necessary for executing queries to the report processor, such as a data source type, a connection string, and authentication information.

With Report Builder 2.0, you can access nine different types of data sources: Microsoft SQL Server, Object Linking and Embedding Database (OLE DB), Microsoft SQL Server Analysis Services, Oracle, Open Database Connectivity (ODBC), Extensible Markup Language (XML), SAP NetWeaver BI, Hyperion Essbase, and TERADATA. The type of data source that you select determines the structure of the connection string you must provide.

In this procedure, you add the AdventureWorksDW2008 database as a data source.

Add a data source

1. In the Report Data pane, click New, and then select Data Source.

2. In the Data Source Properties dialog box, in the Name text box, type **AdventureWorksDW2008**.

    It's considered good practice to provide a more meaningful name than DataSource1, such as the name of a database, to make it easier for yourself and others to recognize the source of the data if it becomes necessary to modify the report later.

3. Select Use A Connection Embedded In My Report, and then click Build.

    Rather than type the connection string, you can use the Build button to open the Connection Properties dialog box, which builds the connection string for you.

4. In the Connection Properties dialog box, in the Server Name text box, type **localhost** (or the name of your server running SQL Server if you're accessing data on a remote server).

5. In the Select Or Enter A Database Name drop-down list, select AdventureWorksDW2008, and click OK.

    The correct connection string now displays in the Data Source Properties dialog box, as shown here.

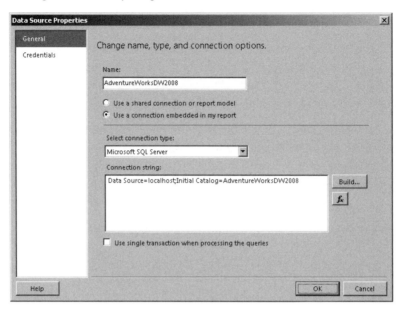

In this procedure, you're creating an *embedded data source*, which means the data source is associated only with this report. If you later want to change the data source definition to point to the same database on a different server, you must open the report to change the data source's connection string. In Chapter 4, you learn about using a shared data source reference.

6. Click Credentials, as shown here.

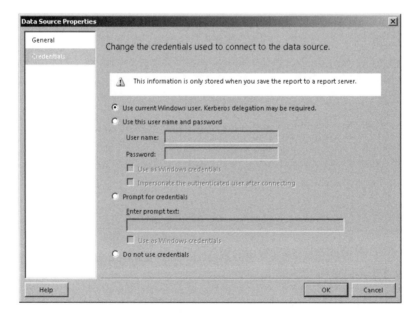

The Use Current Windows User option is the default method for authenticating a data source. When a user runs the report, the user's Windows account must have permissions to read the data source. If you prefer, you can give a specific user account Read permissions on the database, and then select the Use This User Name And Password option and provide the user name and password for that account. A less commonly used approach is the Prompt For Credentials option, which forces the user to type a user name and password before viewing the report. For reports requiring no security at all, you can use the Do Not Use Credentials option.

7. Click OK to close the Data Source Properties dialog box.

   Notice that the data source appears in the Report Data pane, as shown here:

Adding a Dataset

Now that you have a data source available, you can define a *dataset* to retrieve data for your report. A dataset is a container for the information used by the Report Processor to execute a query and return results, such as a pointer to the data source, the query string to execute, and a field list describing the data types of the query results.

In this procedure, you create a dataset to return Internet sales amounts grouped by product for the calendar year 2004.

Add a dataset

1. In the Report Data pane, click New, and then select Dataset.

2. In the Dataset Properties dialog box, in the Name text box, type **InternetSales2004**.

3. Below Query, click Import.

4. In the Import Query dialog box, navigate to the C:\Users\<*Username*>\Documents \Microsoft Press\Rs2008sbs\Chap03 folder. In the Items Of Type drop-down list, select All Items (*.*), and then double-click InternetSales2004.sql. Click Import to confirm that you want to import the selected query.

 Note If you're using Windows XP, navigate to C:\Documents and Settings\<*Username*> \My Documents\Microsoft Press\Rs2008sbs\Chap03.

The query displays in the Query text box, as shown here.

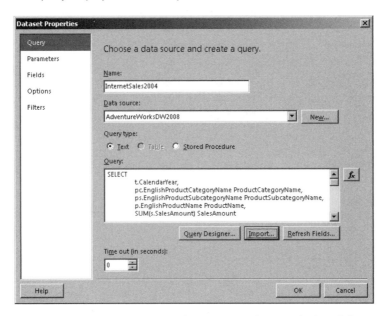

You can scroll in the Query text box to view the remainder of the query. The purpose of this query is to return Internet sales amounts grouped by product category, product subcategory, and product for the 2004 calendar year.

You learn more about the other properties in the Dataset Properties dialog box in Chapter 4.

5. Click Query Designer.

6. In the Query Designer window, click the Run button (which displays as an exclamation point) to run the query, as shown here.

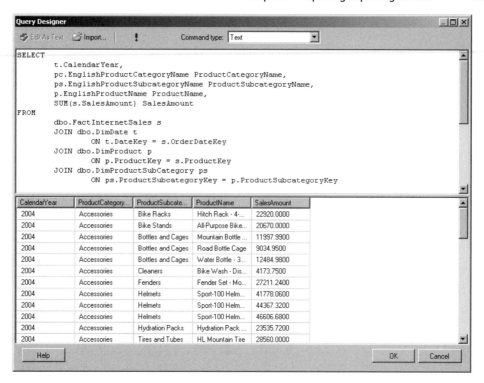

It's useful to view the query results before you begin the report design to ensure that you have the data you expect for your report.

7. Click OK to close the Query Designer window, and then click OK again to close the Dataset Properties dialog box.

The dataset appears below the data source in the Report Data pane, as shown here.

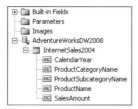

Each column returned by the query also displays as a field below the dataset. You learn more about dataset fields in Chapter 4.

Adding a Report Title

You can use a text box report item to hold static text for your report title. If you place the text box in the page header of your report, it will repeat on each page of the report by default. You can change the print options for the page header to display the page header on the first page only.

In this procedure, you add a report title to the page header of your report.

Add a report title to the page header

1. On the report design surface, click in the text box containing the text Click To Add Title and type **Internet Sales 2004**.

2. Click anywhere in the report layout, and then click the edge of the text box to select it.

3. On the Home tab, in the Font group, in the Font Size drop-down list, select 14.

4. On the Ribbon, click Bold.

5. Drag the right edge of the text box to the left until the text box is about 2.5 inches wide, according to the horizontal ruler, as shown here.

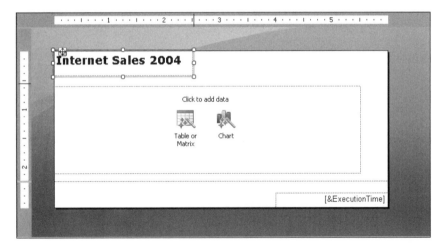

As you move the cursor across the design surface, the current position of the cursor is marked on both the horizontal and vertical rulers, which makes it very easy to resize a report item or move it to a specific location.

6. Right-click anywhere in the page footer section, and select Footer Properties, as shown here.

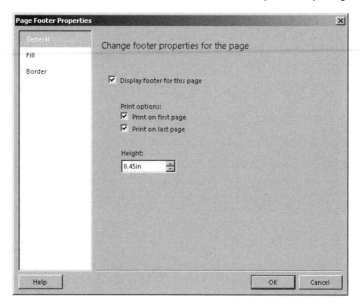

Notice the options Print On First Page and Print On Last Page, which control whether the page footer should be included on the first page only or on the last page only, respectively. You can also set the height of the page footer section using the *Height* property in this dialog box. To remove the page footer entirely from your report, simply clear the Display Footer For This Page check box.

On the Fill and Border tabs of the Page Footer Properties dialog box, you can set the background color and border style of the page footer section separately from the body of the report.

7. In the Page Footer Properties dialog box, click Cancel to keep the default selections.

Adding a Table

A table is a data region that contains a fixed number of columns and a dynamic number of rows. That is, the number of rows in the table depends on the number of rows returned by the dataset query. At each intersection of a column and row is a text box, into which you can type static text or insert a field from a dataset. If you want, you can add a total row to your table as well.

Note You can use fields from only one dataset in a data region at a time. To display information from multiple datasets in the same report, you must use separate data regions for each dataset.

You can add a table to a new report by launching the Table wizard either by clicking the Table Or Matrix icon on the report design surface or by using the Table Wizard command on the Insert tab of the Ribbon. You can also add a table by selecting the Insert Table command on the Insert tab of the Ribbon.

In this procedure, you add a table to the design surface by using the Insert Table command.

Add a table

1. Click the edge of the box in the center of the report body labeled Click To Add Data, and then press the Delete key to remove this item from the report.

2. On the Insert tab of the Ribbon, in the Data Regions group, click Table, select Insert Table, and then click on the report just below the report title and at the left edge of the report to insert the table, as shown here.

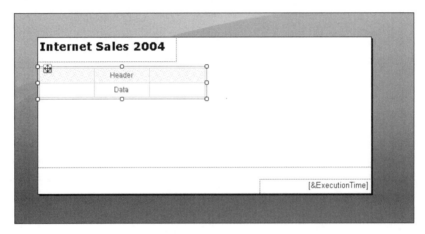

3. From the Report Data pane, drag ProductName into the cell in the first column of the data row, as shown here.

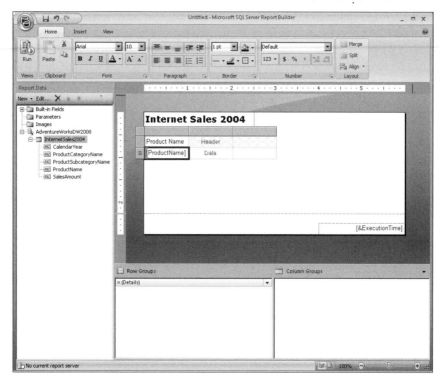

Notice that, although you added a field to the data row, a column title also displays in the header row. The column title is derived from the field name. Report Builder 2.0 uses the capitalized letters in the field name to identify separate words and inserts a space between each word. Similarly, if your field name uses an underscore symbol (_) between words, Report Builder 2.0 replaces the underscore with a space to create a column title.

Notice also that a Details row group displays in the Row Groups section of the Grouping pane. You can access properties associated with the Details row group when you right-click the group in the Grouping pane, and then choose Group Properties. You learn more about these properties in Chapter 4.

Finally, notice that the field in the data row displays with brackets around the field name. This syntax is an expression placeholder for the expression *=Fields!ProductName. Value,* which is stored in the report definition and evaluated by the Report Processor when executing the report. If you are familiar with earlier versions of Reporting Services, you know that it's sometimes difficult to see the name of a field in a narrow column because only the beginning of the expression is visible. The new expression placeholder display on the design surface allows you to see more easily which field is defined for the text box.

4. Point to the second column of the data row, click the Field List icon that displays when you point to the text box, as shown below, and select SalesAmount.

You can also type the field expression *=Fields!SalesAmount.Value* directly into the text box, but it's best to use drag-and-drop or use the field list to make sure the spelling and capitalization are correct. Expressions in Reporting Services are case-sensitive, and failure to use the correct case is a common problem for report developers new to Reporting Services.

5. Right-click [SalesAmount] in the data row, and select Add Total.

Important You must right-click [SalesAmount] without selecting text to display the shortcut menu that includes Add Total.

Notice the expression placeholder for the Sales Amount total, *[Sum(SalesAmount)]*. The full syntax for this expression is *=Sum(Fields!SalesAmount.Value)*. You learn more about expressions, such as this aggregate function, in Chapter 5, "Developing Expressions."

6. In the first text box of the table footer, type **Total Sales**. The design surface now looks like this:

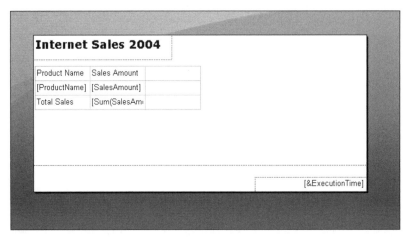

When you add a total row to the table, the *Sum* aggregate function is used automatically with the field you selected. You learn more about aggregate functions in Chapter 5.

Grouping Data

When you have a lot of detail rows to display in your report, you can organize rows with a common field value into a *group*. For example, you can create a group by ProductSubcategoryName to display all products with a ProductSubcategoryName value of *Bike Racks* as one group instance and all products with a ProductSubcategoryName value of *Bottles And Cages* as another group instance. You can also display a total for each group instance.

In this procedure, you add groups to display data by product subcategory and product category.

Group data in a table

1. In the table, right-click [ProductName], select Add Group, and select Parent Group in the Row Group section.

   The Tablix Group dialog box opens.

2. From the Group By drop-down list, select [ProductSubcategoryName].

   You can control whether the group has a header, a footer, or both in step 3.

3. Select the Add Group Header and Add Group Footer check boxes, as shown here.

   You might be wondering why this dialog box refers to a Tablix group when you are working with a table in your report. In the report definition, your table is actually represented as a special type of data region called a *tablix*, which is described in more detail in Chapter 4.

4. Click OK.

   As you add each row group to your table, a new column appears in the table with the field name and a column title, as shown here.

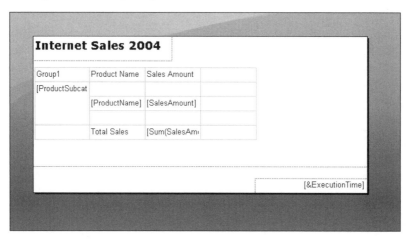

You can, however, design a more compact structure for your table by eliminating this new column and placing the *[ProductSubcategoryName]* field in the same column as *[ProductName]*.

5. If necessary, click the table to display the *row* and *column handles*, which are the gray borders along the left and top edge of the table, respectively.

6. Right-click the column handle of the first column (containing the column title Group1), and select Delete Columns.

7. In the group header row above *[ProductName]*, click the Field List icon and select ProductSubcategoryName.

8. Click the Field List icon in the group footer row between *[SalesAmount]* and *[Sum(SalesAmount)]*, and click SalesAmount to update the table, as shown here.

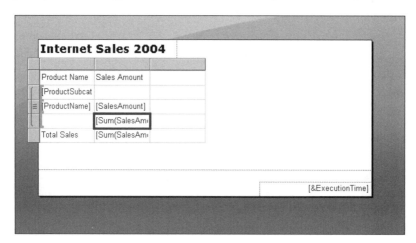

When you add a numeric field to a group header or footer, the *Sum* aggregate function is added automatically.

Notice the icons in the row handles, which help you identify the details and group. The icon with three horizontal lines indicates the Details group, which currently contains only a single row. The icon spanning three row handles to the left of the Details icon identifies a group containing a group header row, the details row, and a group footer row.

Currently, because the [Sum(SalesAmount)] text box is selected, an orange bracket displays to the right of the row handles, just inside the table, to indicate the set of rows that belong to the group containing the selected text box. When you have many groups within the data region, this orange group indicator helps you identify the relationship between a text box and each report group easily.

9. Right-click the first text box of the group footer below *[ProductName]*, and then select Expression.

10. In the Expression dialog box, in the Category list, click Fields (Internet Sales2004), and then, in the Values list, double-click ProductSubcategoryName.

11. In the Set Expression For: Value text box, at the end of the expression, type **& " total"** to construct the following expression:

```
=Fields!ProductSubcategoryName.Value & " total"
```

12. Click OK. Notice that the expression placeholder displays *<<Expr>>* in the text box. This placeholder displays for any expression that does not evaluate as a single field or an aggregate function.

Now you're ready to add another group for ProductCategoryName, but this time you use the Grouping pane to create the group.

13. In the Row Group section of the Grouping pane, right-click Group1, select Add Group, and select Parent Group.

14. In the Group By drop-down list, select [ProductCategoryName].

15. Select the Add Group Header and Add Group Footer check boxes, and click OK.

16. Right-click the column handle of the first column (containing the column title Group2), and select Delete Columns.

17. In the group header row above *[ProductSubcategoryName]*, click the Field List icon, and select ProductCategoryName.

18. In the group footer row between *[Sum(SalesAmount)]* and *[Sum(SalesAmount)]*, click the Field List icon, and click SalesAmount.

19. Right-click the first text box of the new group footer, then select Expression.

20. In the Expression dialog box, construct the following expression:

```
=Fields!ProductCategoryName.Value & " total"
```

21. Click OK. Your report design surface now looks like this:

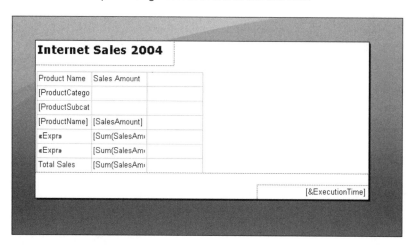

Inserting Page Breaks

By default, the Report Processor fits as many rows as possible on a single page as determined by the vertical size defined for your report. As each page fills up, the Report Processor inserts a page break to begin a new page. You can override this behavior by configuring a page break for a row group. For example, you can force a page break in your report when the product category group instance value changes from *Accessories* to *Bikes*.

In this procedure, you insert a page break between the instances of the category group.

Insert a page break between each instance of a group

1. In the Row Groups section of the Grouping pane, right-click Group2, and select Group Properties. The Group Properties dialog box opens.

2. In the left pane, click Page Breaks.

3. Select the Between Each Instance Of A Group check box, as shown here.

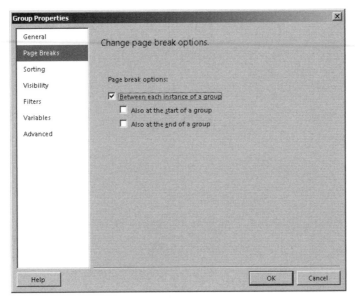

4. Click OK. When a data region spans multiple pages, you can choose to repeat the header on each page to improve the readability of your report.

5. If necessary, click anywhere in the data region to display the row and column handles.

6. Right-click any handle, and select Tablix Properties. The Tablix Properties dialog box opens.

7. Select the Repeat Header Rows On Each Page check box, as shown here.

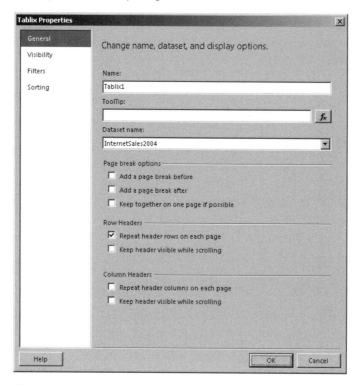

8. Click OK.

Formatting a Report

You can use a number of properties to control the appearance of individual text boxes in a data region. You can also set properties for an entire row or column in a data region. Several commands on the Home tab are available to set format properties, such as font color and style. You can access many more format properties by opening the Properties pane.

In this procedure, you improve the appearance of your report by setting formatting properties.

Set format properties

1. If necessary, click anywhere in the data region to display the row and column handles.

2. Click the row handle of the header row (containing the column titles) to select it.

   When you select an entire row or column, the property you configure applies to the selected row or column.

3. On the Home tab, in the Font group, click Bold.

4. On the View tab, in the Show/Hide group, select the Properties check box.

5. In the Properties pane, below Fill, from the BackgroundColor drop-down list, select More Colors, select DarkGray, and click OK.

6. Click the column handle of the SalesAmount column.

7. In the Properties pane, below Number, in the Format box, type **c0,** as shown here.

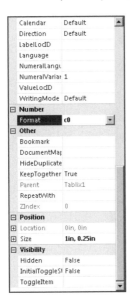

You can use any Microsoft Visual Basic .NET format string in the *Format* property. For a complete list of permissible format strings, refer to *http://msdn.microsoft.com/en-us /library/dwhawy9k.aspx*.

8. Click the column handle of the Product Name column.

9. In the Properties pane, below Position, expand the *Size* property, and then, in the *Width* property, replace the current value with **2in** to widen the column.

   You can also adjust the column width manually by positioning your cursor on the line between column handles and dragging the column to the right to increase the column width, or to the left to decrease the column width. Use the *Width* property when you need to set a precise value.

10. Right-click the column handle of the third column in the table, and select Delete Columns to remove the empty column.

   You can apply more formatting to this report to improve the readability later, but for now, you should have a good understanding of the principles and can continue with your exploration of Report Builder 2.0.

Previewing a Report

At any time during the report development process, you can preview your report to check your progress. You can then switch back to Design view to make changes to the report if necessary. The preview of your report shows you exactly what the report will look like when accessed from the report server. You can also preview the print layout and the export formats before you publish the report.

In this procedure, you preview and save your report.

Preview a report

1. On the Home tab, click Run to view the report, as shown here.

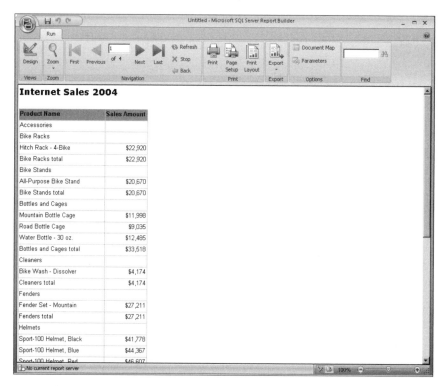

   On the first page of the report is the Accessories group.

2. On the toolbar above the report, click the Next button, represented by the blue arrow pointing right.

   The second page of the report begins the next group, Bikes.

3. Click the Report Builder button in the upper-left corner of the window, and click Save.

4. In the Save As Report dialog box, navigate to the Microsoft Press\Rs2008sbs \Workspace folder in your Documents folder. In the File Name box, type **Internet Sales 2004**, and click Save.

You can save a report that you created by using Report Builder 2.0 to a local folder for personal use without publishing it to the report server.

Managing a Report

The second phase of the report life cycle includes all activities related to managing reports. After a report is published, you can then configure properties that control the report's appearance on the server, its query execution, and processing of the report, to name only a few of the tasks you can perform. In Part III, "Managing the Report Server," you learn everything you need to know about report management, but in this section, you explore only a few of the features as a quick introduction to Reporting Services.

Publishing a Report

Whether you're using a native mode or SharePoint integrated-mode server doesn't matter during the report development process. However, when you move into the management phase of the report life cycle, the procedures you follow differ, although you'll find they are very similar. You can publish a report to a report server directly from the report development tool, although there are other publishing methods that you learn about in Chapter 10, "Deploying Reports to a Server."

In this procedure, you publish your report to a native-mode report server.

Publish a report to a native-mode report server

1. In Report Builder 2.0, click Report Builder, and then select Save As.

2. In the Save As Report dialog box, in the Name text box, type **http://<servername> /reportserver**, where *<servername>* is the name of your server, and press Enter.

To publish the report, you use the name of the virtual directory that you configured for the Web service in Chapter 2. If you configure a port number other than 80, or a different virtual directory name, you must change the Report Server URL in the Deployment Settings dialog box to match the Web service URL.

Note If you specified a default target server during installation of Report Builder 2.0 as described in Chapter 2, you can quickly navigate to that server instead of typing the URL by clicking Recent Sites And Servers in the Save As dialog box, and then clicking the URL in the list of sites that displays.

3. In the Name box, type **Internet Sales 2004**, and click Save.

The URL *http://*<servername>*/reportserver* places the report in the main folder of the report server. As you add folders to the server to organize content, you can target a specific folder when publishing your report by navigating to the target folder after typing the URL.

In this procedure, you publish your report to a SharePoint integrated-mode report server.

Publish a report to a SharePoint integrated-mode report server

1. In Report Builder 2.0, click Report Builder, and then click Save As.

2. In the Save As Report dialog box, in the Name box, type **http://<*servername*>/sites /ssrs/ReportsLibrary**, where <*servername*> is the name of your server, and press Enter.

> **Note** If you specified a default target server during installation of Report Builder 2.0 as described in Chapter 2, you can quickly navigate to that server instead of typing the URL by clicking Recent Sites And Servers in the Save As dialog box, and then clicking the URL in the list of sites that displays. You can then navigate to the ReportsLibrary folder in the site collection.

The report server URL must match the URL that you configured for the site collection you created for Reporting Services in Chapter 2.

The report folder must match the name of a shared document library in the Report Center site included in the URL. If you created a site collection using the Report Center template as described in Chapter 2, the shared document library is named ReportsLibrary.

3. In the Name box, type **Internet Sales 2004**, and click Save.

Adding a Description

You can add a report description to provide more details about a report which help a user decide if the report contains the information needed. When a user wants to locate a report using the Search feature in Report Manager, if a match is found in either the report name or its description, the report is included in the search results.

In this procedure, you add a description to your report in Report Manager.

Add a report description in Report Manager

1. Open Windows Internet Explorer.

2. Type the URL **http://localhost/Reports** to open the Report Manager.

   The Home page of Report Manager displays in list view, as shown here.

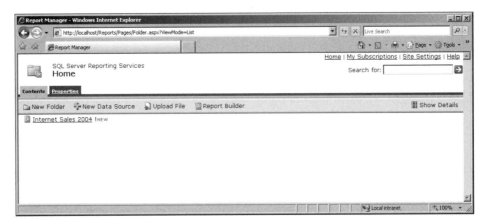

3. Click Show Details on the right side to display the report server content in details view, as shown here.

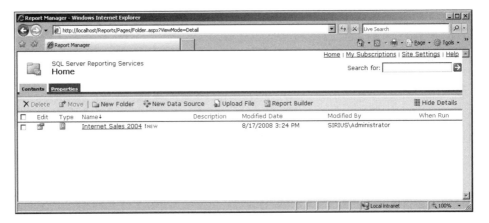

   When you view the report server content in details view, you can access report properties directly without first viewing the report.

4. In the Edit column, click the Properties icon.

5. In the Description text box, type **Actual Internet sales for 2004 by product category and by product subcategory,** as shown here.

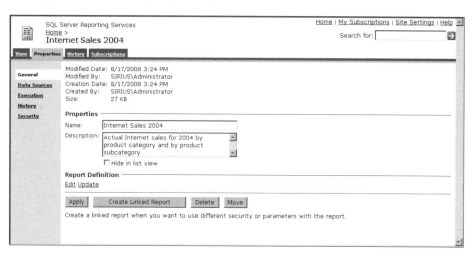

This report description displays on the Contents page in the Report Manager and is visible only to users who have been granted permission to view the report.

6. Click Apply.

7. Click the Home link at the upper-left corner of the browser window to view the report in list view with its description below the report name, as shown here.

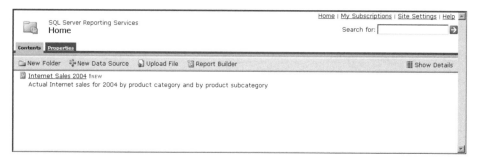

In this procedure, you add a description to your report in the SharePoint document library.

Add a report description in a SharePoint document library

1. Open Internet Explorer.

2. Type the URL **http://<*servername*>/sites/ssrs/ReportsLibrary** (where <*servername*> is the name of your server) to open the shared document library in the SSRS SharePoint site, as shown here.

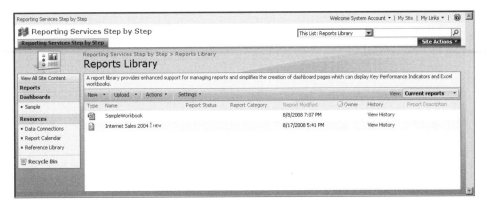

3. Point to Internet Sales 2004, click the Edit button (to the right of the report title) to display the report menu, and select Edit Properties.

4. In the Report Description text box, type **Actual Internet sales for 2004 by product category and by product subcategory**, as shown here.

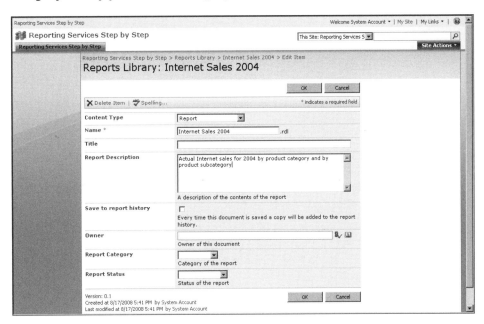

This report description displays in the Current Reports view of the Shared Documents library and is visible only to users who have been granted permission to view the report.

5. Click OK.

6. Click the Home link at the upper-left corner of the browser window to view the report in list view with its description below the report name, as shown here.

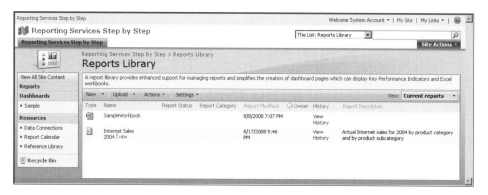

Reviewing Execution Properties

You can use a report's execution properties to improve the user experience with Reporting Services when the report returns a large volume of data and requires a lot of processing time. By default, a report runs on demand, which means that the query is not executed until the user opens the report. To eliminate waiting time for the user, you can use execution properties to implement caching or a report snapshot to execute a report in advance of the user's request for the report. You learn more about the impact of changing execution properties in Chapter 10.

In this procedure, you review the execution properties of your report in Report Manager.

Open the Execution Properties page of a report in Report Manager

1. Click Show Details on the right side to display report server content in details mode.

2. In the Edit column, click the Properties icon.

3. Click the Execution link in the left frame of the page to view the Execution Properties page, as shown here.

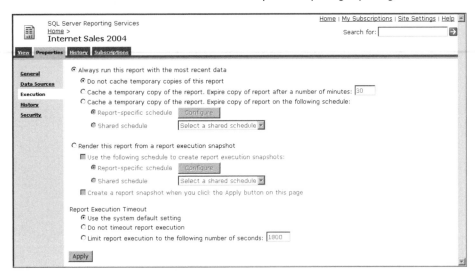

As you can see, the default selection is Always Run This Report With The Most Recent Data. In addition, the option Do Not Cache Temporary Copies Of This Report is selected. As a result, each time a user opens this report, the report query executes and the Report Processor must render the report with the query results. When you select one of the caching options, the first user who opens the report must wait for the query execution and rendering of the report, but subsequent users opening the same report only wait for the report to render using the query results generated by the first report execution. Rendering a report usually processes much faster than executing a query. When you configure a report snapshot, the query execution occurs in advance of any user's request for the report, so all users will wait only for report rendering, which shortens their waiting time.

You can also use the Execution Properties page to configure the report execution timeout. The system default setting limits report execution to 1800 seconds, but you can override this setting to prevent a timeout completely or to use a different timeout value for the selected report.

In this procedure, you review the execution properties of your report in SharePoint.

Open the Execution Properties page of a report in SharePoint

1. Point to Internet Sales 2004, click the Edit button (to the right of the report title) to display the report menu, and select Manage Processing Options. The Manage Processing Options window opens, as shown here.

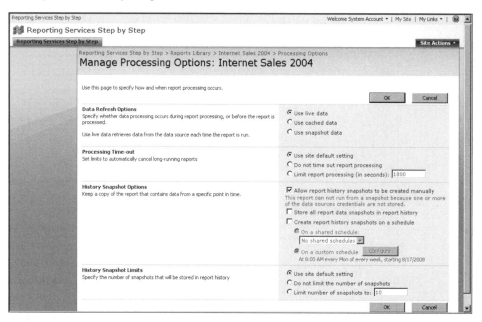

Although the names of the processing options differ from the execution properties accessible in Report Manager, their functions are the same. The Use Live Data option executes the report query and renders the report on demand. The Use Cached Data option executes the query on the first request of the report and renders the cached results each time a user requests the report. The Use Snapshot Data option produces a report snapshot that permanently stores the query results and renders the snapshot on demand.

You can set processing timeout values on this page as well as set limits on the number of history snapshots that accumulate on the report server.

2. In the Data Refresh Options section, select Use Cached Data.

Notice a new section, Cache Options, displays between Data Refresh Options and Processing Time-out. The selection of a data refresh option changes the options you can configure.

At this time, you cannot configure cache options because the data source credentials are configured to use the current user's Windows account, rather than a stored account. You learn more about stored data source credentials in Chapter 10.

3. Click Cancel.

Viewing a Report

The third phase of the report life cycle concerns user accessing of reports. For a native-mode report server, you use Report Manager to find and view reports. You use a SharePoint Web application to find and view reports managed by a SharePoint integrated-mode report server. While the user interface depends on the report server mode, the same functionality is available in either mode, as you learn in this section.

Opening a Report

You use Report Manager not only to manage report server content, but also to view reports. You navigate through a list of reports and click the report link to view the report.

In this procedure, you open a report listed in Report Manager.

Open a report on a native-mode report server

1. In Report Manager, click the Home link at the upper-left corner of the window, and then click the Internet Sales 2004 link. You can also click the View tab when you're viewing one of the report's properties pages.

   The Report Processor executes the query, renders the report in Hypertext Markup Language (HTML) format, and displays the report, as shown here.

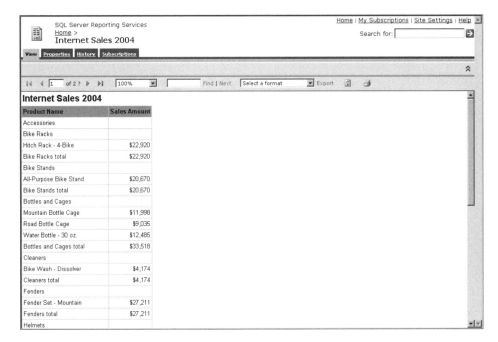

Notice that the display of the report using Report Manager matches the way the preview of the report looked in Report Builder 2.0.

2. On the toolbar above the report, click Next Page (the blue arrow) to view the second page of the report.

In this procedure, you open a report listed in a SharePoint shared document library.

Open a report in a SharePoint shared document library

1. In the Current Reports view of the Reports Library, click the Internet Sales 2004 link to open the report, as shown here.

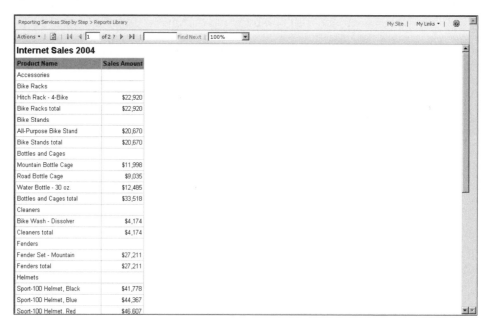

2. On the toolbar above the report, click Next Page (the blue arrow) to view the second page of the report.

Using the HTML Viewer

The HTML Viewer is a special toolbar that displays when you view a report. You can use the HTML Viewer to navigate through the pages of your report, change the zoom factor of the page, search text in the report, export the report to another format, refresh the report, or print the report. You explore the HTML Viewer in more detail in Chapter 13, "Accessing Reports Online."

In this procedure, you search for a specific string in your report.

Search for a string in a report

1. In the Find text box, located to the right of the Zoom drop-down list, type **racing**, and then click Find.

> **Note** The steps to search for a string in a report are exactly the same whether you are viewing a report on a native-mode report server or a SharePoint integrated-mode report server.

The first instance of the string displays as shown here. Notice that the search is not case-sensitive.

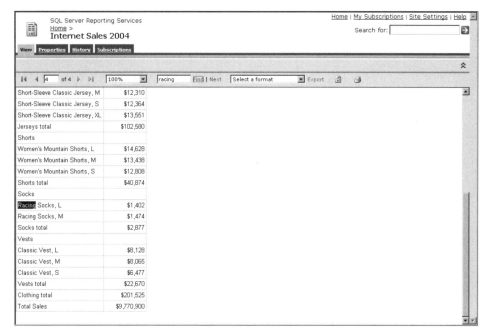

2. Click Next twice to continue the search, and click OK in the message box.

Each time you click Next, the search continues to the next instance until you reach the end of the report.

By completing the procedures in this chapter, you have toured all three phases of the report life cycle: development, administration, and access. This tour introduced you to several key features, but there's much more to learn. Each of the remaining chapters of this book covers these features in greater detail to help you master Reporting Services.

Chapter 3 Quick Reference

To	Do This
Open Report Builder 2.0	Click Start, select All Programs and Microsoft SQL Server 2008 Report Builder 2.0, and select Report Builder 2.0.
Add a data source	In the Report Data pane, click New, select Data Source, type a name for the data source, select a connection type, and type a connection string, or use the Build button to access the Connection Properties dialog box to build a connection string by using a GUI.
Add a dataset	In the Report Data pane, click New, select Dataset, type a name for the dataset, and type a query string or click Import to import a query stored in an SQL script file.
Add a report title to the page header section	Click inside the text box containing the text Click To Add Title, and type a text string.
Add a table to a report by using the Insert Table command	On the Insert tab of the Ribbon, in the Data Regions group, click Table, select Insert Table, click a location on the report design surface to position the upper-left corner of the table, and drag fields from the Report Data pane to cells in the table.
Add a parent row group	In the data region, right-click a field, select Add Group, select Parent Group in the Row Group section, select a field for grouping in the Group By expression drop-down list, and optionally select the Add Group Header and Add Group Footer check boxes; *or* In the Row Group section of the Grouping pane, right-click an existing group, select Add Group, select Parent Group, select a field for grouping in the Group By expression drop-down list, and optionally select the Add Group Header and Add Group Footer check boxes.
Add a page break between each instance of a group	In the Grouping pane, right-click a group, select Group Properties, click Page Breaks, and select the Between Each Instance Of A Group check box.
Open the Properties pane	On the View tab, in the Show/Hide group, and select the Properties check box.
Set format properties	Select a text box, row, or column, and click a style button on the Home tab of the Ribbon or set a property value in the Properties pane.
Preview a report	On the Home tab, click Run, or click the Run button at the bottom of the Report Builder 2.0 window.

To	Do This
Publish a report	Click Report Builder, click Save As, type the report server URL, navigate to the target folder, and type a name for the report. For a native-mode report server, use the following default URL: *http://*<servername>*/reportserver* For a SharePoint integrated-mode server, use the following default URL: *http://*<servername>*/sites/*<sitename>; and the following default folder: *http://*<servername>*/sites/*<sitename>*/ReportsLibrary*.
Manage report properties	For a native-mode report server, open Report Manager at *http://*<servername>*/Reports*, click Show Details, click the Properties icon, click the applicable link in the left frame to access properties, set the property value, and click Apply. For a SharePoint integrated-mode server, open the shared document library at *http://*<servername>*/sites/*<sitename>*/ReportsLibrary*, point to the report, click the drop-down arrow, and click the applicable command, such as Manage Processing Options.
View a report	For a native-mode report server, open Report Manager at *http://*<servername>*/Reports*, and click the report link. For a SharePoint integrated-mode server, open the shared document library at *http://*<servername>*/sites/*<sitename>*/ReportsLibrary*, and click the report link.

Part II
Developing Reports

The chapters in Part II teach you a variety of report development techniques that take advantage of the rich set of features available in Reporting Services. In Chapter 4, "Designing Reports," you learn how to use Report Designer in Business Intelligence Development Studio to build basic reports. In Chapter 5, "Developing Expressions," you learn how to enhance reports by adding calculations and using expressions to change properties dynamically. Then, in Chapter 6, "Adding Interactivity," you build more advanced reports to support user interaction with online reports. In Chapter 7, "Using Analysis Services as a Data Source," you learn how to use the MDX query designer to retrieve Analysis Services data for the reporting environment. Later, in Chapter 8, "Visualizing Data," you explore the many ways to communicate information visually by using charts and gauges. Finally, in Chapter 9, "Developing Report Models," you learn how to construct a report model to support ad hoc reporting for non-technical users. After completing the procedures in these chapters, you will be well prepared to develop your own reports to meet a variety of reporting requirements.

Chapter 4
Designing Reports

After completing this chapter, you will be able to:

- Create a report server project in Business Intelligence Development Studio.

- Add a new or existing report to a report server project.

- Add a shared data source to a report server project.

- Define a dataset.

- Design a report using data regions and report items.

- Group and total data in a data region.

- Embed a report in another report as a subreport.

- Use properties to define placement and appearance of report items.

- Define page breaks and set properties related to paging.

- Add report items to the page header and page footer.

In this chapter, you learn how to use Report Designer in Business Intelligence Development Studio (BI Dev Studio) to develop reports. Many of the principles that you have already learned about using Report Builder 2.0 are also applicable to using Report Designer, so you can use either tool comfortably when you finish this chapter. You start by preparing a report server project to contain your reports and creating a data source and dataset to provide data for your report. Then you learn a variety of techniques for structuring data in a report and enhancing the appearance of your report.

Getting Started with Report Designer

Before you start report development using Report Designer, you must first perform some tasks to prepare the environment. Whereas Report Builder 2.0 supports development of one report at a time, as explained in Chapter 3, "Exploring Reporting Services," the integrated development environment in BI Dev Studio allows you to work with multiple reports in the same environment. You use a *report server project* as a container to store these reports in a common location. Another difference from Report Builder 2.0 that you encounter when using BI Dev Studio is the ability to create a *shared data source* to store data source connection information independently of the reports. After creating a shared data source, you define the query used to extract data from the source for display in the report. After finishing these tasks, you're ready to start developing reports.

Creating a Report Server Project

BI Dev Studio is a Microsoft Visual Studio shell program that provides many of the features of Visual Studio without requiring you to purchase and install Visual Studio. If you're new to the Visual Studio integrated environment, don't worry. You don't need to be a programmer to use this tool effectively. Before you start report development, you must create a report server project, which is a folder created to store a set of reports and shared data sources. When you create a new report server project, you define the location for this folder and a name for the solution to contain the report server project. A solution is simply a container for one or more projects, which can be any combination of project types supported by Visual Studio, including a report server project.

In this procedure, you create a report server project in BI Dev Studio.

Create a report server project

1. Click Start, select All Programs and Microsoft SQL Server 2008, and click SQL Server Business Intelligence Development Studio.

2. On the File menu, point to New, and click Project.

3. In the New Project dialog box, in the Templates pane, select Report Server Project.

   When you create a new project, you have three templates from which to choose: Report Server Project Wizard, Report Server Project, and Report Model Project. You can use the Report Server Project Wizard to accelerate basic report design using a wizard interface. (To learn more about the Report Project Wizard, refer to the sidebar, "Using the Report Project Wizard," later in this chapter.) To meet specific report design requirements, however, you will likely find it better to use the Report Server Project as you learn how to do in this procedure. You learn how to use the Report Model Project in Chapter 9, "Developing Report Models."

4. In the Name box, type **Sales**.

5. In the Location box, type **C:\Users\<*Username*>\Documents\Microsoft Press \Rs2008sbs\Workspace,** as shown here.

> **Note** If you're using Microsoft Windows XP or Windows Server 2003, navigate to C:\Documents and Settings\<*Username*>\My Documents\Microsoft Press\Rs2008sbs \Workspace.

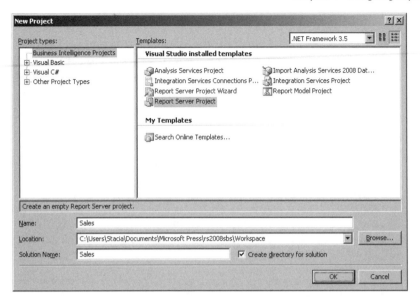

6. Click OK.

Using the Report Project Wizard

The Report Project Wizard walks you step by step through the report development process. You define an embedded or shared data source, provide a query string, select a report layout, define groupings, and apply a style to set colors and fonts for the report. The wizard limits you to using a tabular or matrix layout. However, after the report is created, you can continue to fine-tune the report to meet your specifications.

Adding a Report to a Project

Now that you have a report server project ready, you can add a report to your report server project by using the Report Project Wizard, adding a new report manually, or importing a report from Microsoft Office Access.

In this procedure, you add a report to your report server project.

Add a report to a report server project

1. In Solution Explorer, right-click the Reports folder, select Add, and click New Item.

   You might be tempted to click the Add New Report command on the context menu for Reports, but this command starts the Report Project Wizard. The Report Project Wizard is useful for quickly producing a basic report, but most report developers prefer to build a report manually.

2. In the Templates pane, select Report.

In addition to the Report template, the list of available templates includes the Report Project Wizard and Data Source templates. The Report Project Wizard template produces the same result as using the Add New Report command from the Reports context menu. Similarly, the Data Source template displays the same dialog box as the Add New Data Source command in the Shared Data Sources context menu.

3. In the Name box, type **Reseller Sales Summary.rdl,** and click Add.

 Note You must provide the file extension .rdl for the file you are adding to the report server project.

After you click Add, the report appears in the solution and Report Designer displays in the document window.

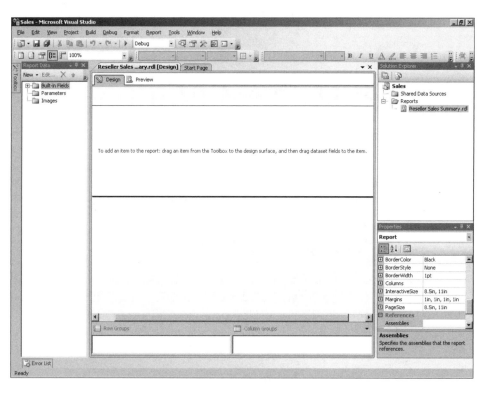

Before continuing to develop your report, take a few moments to become familiar with the layout of the design environment:

- **Toolbox**   The Toolbox window is hidden by default when you first open a report and appears only as a tab on the left side of the window. The Toolbox window is similar to the Ribbon in Report Builder 2.0 introduced in Chapter 3. You use this window to add controls that define your report layout.

- **Report Data**   The Report Data window displays to the left of the report layout. It contains three folders: Built-in Fields, Parameters, and Images. You use Built-in Fields to add commonly used expressions, such as *ReportName* or *PageNumber,* to your report. You learn how to work with the Parameters folder in Chapter 6, "Adding Interactivity." The Images folder stores images you use in the report, as you do later in this chapter. After you add a data source and a dataset to your report, these objects display in the Report Data window as well. Thus, the Report Data window organizes many of the key items you use within your report.

- **Report Designer**   The Report Designer occupies the central window in the development environment and consists of two tabs. On the Design tab, you arrange the layout of data and graphical elements on your report. On the Preview tab, you can test the rendering of the report to different formats without first deploying your report to the report server. The Grouping pane appears at the bottom of the Report Designer window and displays a hierarchical view of groups defined for a selected data region.

- **Solution Explorer**   This window appears to the right of Report Designer and displays the files associated with each project within your solution.

- **Properties**   Each item you add to the report, as well as each area of the report (such as the body, page header, page footer, and even the report itself), has a set of properties to define its appearance and behavior. When you select an item or report area in Report Designer, you see its related properties in the Properties window, which displays to the right of Report Designer.

You can rearrange these windows while developing your report to give more space to Report Designer or to access items better in a window. For example, you can use the Auto Hide feature to minimize the Toolbox, Report Data, Solution Explorer, or Properties window. You can also undock a window from its default location and drag it to a new location.

4. Point to the Toolbox tab on the left side of the window, and then click the Auto Hide button (which looks like a pushpin and is displayed next to the Close button for the window) to open and lock the Toolbox window, shown here.

Notice that the Toolbox overlays the Report Data window to conserve the amount of space used on your screen. You use the tabs at the bottom of the current window to switch to the other window.

5. Click the Report Data tab to switch the visible window.

Instead of using the Auto Hide feature, you can close a window to maximize screen space for the Report Designer.

6. In the upper-right corner of the Report Data window, click the Close button (which appears as an X).

At any time, you can open a closed window by using the View menu.

7. On the View menu, click Report Data.

Creating a Data Source

A report requires a data source to identify where the data for the report is found and how the user is authenticated to determine whether permissions exist to retrieve the report data. You can choose to embed a data source within the report or to use a shared data source that is available to multiple reports. By using a shared data source, you can maintain connection and authentication information in a single location, which is generally the recommended approach. However, if you need to use a dynamic data source, such as when you need to use different servers for different users, then you must use an embedded data source.

In this procedure, you create a shared data source for the AdventureWorksDW2008 database.

Create a shared data source

1. In the Report Data window, click New, and then click Data Source.

2. In the Data Source Properties dialog box, in the Name text box, type **AdventureWorksDW2008.**

> **Note** When you define a name for a data source, you cannot include spaces in the name and you must use a letter as the first character.

You can choose either to create an embedded connection or to use a shared data source reference. When you use an embedded connection, you can define an explicit connection string, as you did in Chapter 3, or you can click the Expression button (to the left of the Edit button) to build a dynamic connection string, which you learn how to do in Chapter 5, "Developing Expressions."

3. Select Use Shared Data Source Reference, and click New.

> **Note** Because no shared data sources exist in the report server project, you must create a new data source before you can select a reference.

4. In the Shared Data Source Properties dialog box, in the Name text box, type **AdventureWorksDW2008.**

5. Open the Type drop-down list, review the available data providers, and select Microsoft SQL Server.

You can choose from the following data providers: Microsoft SQL Server, Object Linking and Embedding Database (OLE DB), Microsoft SQL Server Analysis Services, Oracle, Open Database Connectivity (ODBC), Extensible Markup Language (XML), Report Server Model, SAP NetWeaver BI, Hyperion Essbase, and Teradata. You must supply a connection string applicable to the selected data provider. If the Edit button is available after you select a data provider, you can use it to open the Connection Properties dialog box, which provides a graphical interface that prompts you for the properties required to construct the appropriate connection string.

6. Click Edit.

7. In the Connection Properties dialog box, in the Server Name text box, type **localhost**.

8. In the Select Or Enter A Database Name drop-down list, select AdventureWorksDW2008, and click OK.

9. In the Shared Data Source Properties dialog box, click Credentials.

As you learned in Chapter 3, you must specify whether the report uses Windows authentication to pass through the current user's credentials, a hard-coded value for user name and password, a prompt at report execution to request the user to enter credentials, or no credentials at all. Unless the data source has no security defined, which is highly unusual, the credentials are used by the data source to authenticate the user before the query executes. Accordingly, the user account must have at least Read permissions on the data source.

10. Click OK to close the Shared Data Source Properties dialog box.

Notice that the AdventureWorksDW2008.rds file has been added to the Sales solution in the Shared Data Sources folder in the Solution Explorer window. AdventureWorksDW2008.rds is an XML file containing all the information required to connect to the data source. The shared data source deploys to the report server when you deploy the report, as you learn in Chapter 10, "Deploying Reports to a Server."

11. In the Data Source Properties dialog box, in the Use Shared Data Source Reference drop-down list, select AdventureWorksDW2008, as shown here.

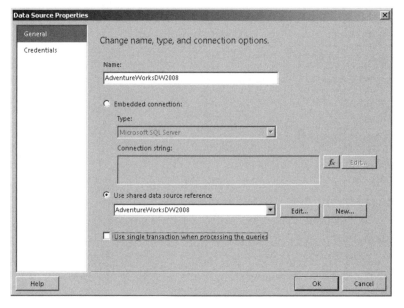

Notice the Use Single Transaction When Processing The Queries check box at the bottom of the dialog box. You should select this check box when your report contains multiple datasets that reference the same shared data source and your data source cannot handle several parallel connections, or if you want the queries to execute as a single transaction. In other words, when this option is selected, if one query to the data source fails, then all queries to the same data source should also fail. If you leave this check box cleared, then the dataset queries execute in parallel.

12. Click OK to close the Data Source Properties dialog box.

Notice that the data source now appears in the Report Data window. This data source is actually a pointer to the data source file that you see in Solution Explorer. If you later change connection information in the shared data source file, you won't need to update the connection in your report because your report automatically uses the new connection information.

Creating a Dataset

As you learned in Chapter 3, a dataset defines a query for your report and contains the field list of data columns returned by the query. The Dataset Properties dialog box allows you to use a query designer for supported data sources, such as SQL Server or Analysis Services, to build the query text or to import the query text from a file saved on your computer or network. You can also test the query to be sure you're retrieving the right data before developing your report.

In this procedure, you add a dataset to return reseller sales amounts grouped by sales territory and by business type for the calendar year 2004.

Add a dataset

1. In the Report Data window, click New, and then click Dataset.

2. In the Dataset Properties dialog box, in the Name text box, type **ResellerSales.**

   As with a data source, your dataset name cannot include spaces and must have a letter as the first character.

   Notice that the data source is already selected. If you have multiple data sources defined in your report, then you must be sure to select the correct data source. You also have the option to create a new data source at this time if you skipped that step before attempting to create a dataset.

   If you plan to write your own query, select Text as the query type, which is the default. Many database administrators prefer that reports use stored procedures to retrieve data from a database. When you select Stored Procedure as the query type, a list of available stored procedures displays in a drop-down list from which you make a selection. If you are using an OLE DB or ODBC data provider to connect to a SQL Server database, you can select Table as the query type to use the TableDirect feature of SQL Server to return all fields within a table.

   Instead of providing static query text for a dataset, you can construct a query dynamically by specifying an expression. You learn how to do this in Chapter 5.

3. Click Query Designer.

4. On the toolbar, click Import.

5. In the Import Query dialog box, navigate to the Microsoft Press\Rs2008sbs\Chap04 folder in your Documents folder, and double-click ResellerSalesSummary2004.sql. This query retrieves sales for each sales territory group, sales territory country, and reseller business type for the calendar year 2004.

6. On the toolbar, click the Run button (which displays as an exclamation point) to run the query, as shown here.

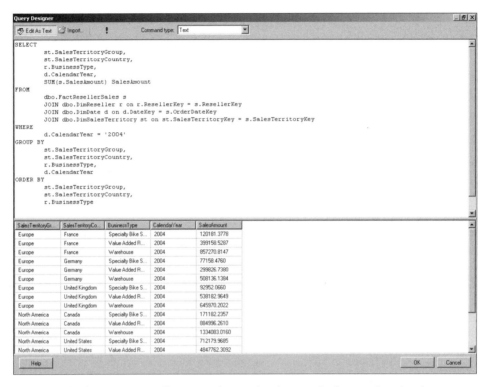

You can edit the query text if you need to make changes before saving the dataset query.

7. On the toolbar, click Edit As Text to disable the text editor and view the Query Designer.

 Tip If you prefer a GUI, you can click Edit As Text to toggle to the Query Designer if it's supported by the selected data provider.

8. Click OK to close the Query Designer window and return to the Dataset Properties, as shown here.

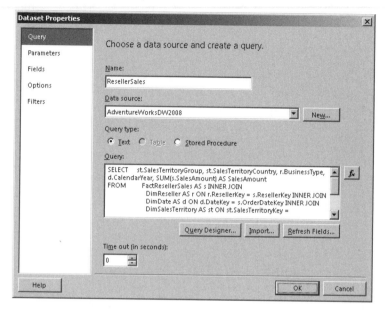

You can specify a time-out value in seconds to end execution if the query cannot execute within a fixed period of time. If you clear the value from the Time Out (In Seconds) box so that it's empty, the query never times out.

Notice also that the Dataset Properties dialog box has several other tabs, as follows:

- **Parameters**   You can provide default values for query parameters if they are supported by the data source. These default values can alternatively be linked to report parameters, which you learn about in Chapter 6.

- **Fields**   In addition to fields retrieved for the dataset by executing the query, you can define calculated fields, which you learn about in Chapter 5.

- **Options**   You can specify options for your data, such as collation, case sensitivity, accent sensitivity, kanatype sensitivity, and width sensitivity. This page also includes an option for specifying whether subtotal rows in your dataset should be treated as detail rows in your report, which is explained in more detail in Chapter 7, "Using Analysis Services as a Data Source."

- **Filters**   If you are unable to filter data at the data source by using a WHERE clause in your query, you can filter the data in the dataset by defining filter rules. You learn how to use filters in Chapter 6.

9. Click OK to close the Dataset Properties dialog box.

The dataset appears in the Report Data window as a node of the AdventureWorksDW2008 data source. Notice the fields below the data set, as shown here. Each field is a column returned by the query for this dataset.

Designing the Report Structure

Now that you have completed the preparation for report development, you're ready to start designing the layout of data on the report. You use one or more data regions to present data in a structured or unstructured format in the report layout. As you work, you can switch to Preview mode to confirm you're achieving the desired results. Your report specifications might require you to define groupings and totals, add supporting elements such as a text box, line, or image, or even embed another report within the report you're currently developing.

Adding a Data Region

A data region is the primary report item that you use to display data in your report. Reporting Services provides four different data regions: tables, matrixes, lists, and charts. You link a data region to a single dataset and specify how fields in that dataset are positioned within the data region.

To start your first report, you use a table. A table has a fixed number of columns, and the number of detail rows depends on the number of rows returned by the dataset query. Much as a spreadsheet is a collection of cells, a Reporting Services table is a collection of text boxes organized as rows and columns. You can define a header row in a table for column labels or a footer row for aggregated values. To organize detail rows better, you can add groups and define subtotals for these groups.

In this procedure, you add a table to the report design.

Add a table

1. In the Toolbox window, double-click Table to add it to the design surface, or you can drag the table from the Toolbox to the design surface.

> **Tip** If you can't see the Toolbox window, click the Toolbox tab on the left if the window is currently configured to Auto Hide, or click the Toolbox tab at the bottom of the Report Data window if the window is currently configured as a tabbed document. If you still can't see the Toolbox window, use the View menu to open the Toolbox window.

When you double-click a control in the Toolbox window, the control is placed as near the upper-left corner of the design surface as possible. You can be more specific with the placement of the control if you drag it from the toolbox to the desired location.

The default table includes three columns. You can add or remove columns to meet your requirements.

2. Right-click the top row of the third column, and click Delete Columns.

Now your table has two columns that you can use to display Business Type and Sales Amount from the ResellerSales dataset.

Binding Data to a Data Region

A data region must be bound to a dataset so that you can position fields from that dataset within the data region. To associate a dataset with a data region, you can set the *DatasetName* property for the data region or you can drag a dataset field from the Report Data window to a text box in the data region. After you have bound a data region to a dataset, you cannot add fields from a different dataset to that data region.

In this procedure, you add fields to your table.

Add fields to a table

1. Open the Report Data window, and then drag the BusinessType field to the second row of the first column, as shown here.

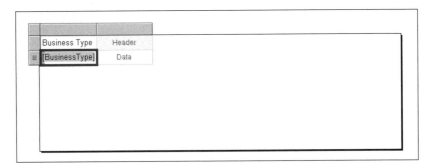

When you add a field to a detail row in a table, Report Designer displays the field name in the column header automatically. You can change the text if you prefer a different label. If the field's data type is numeric, the text box automatically is right-justified.

Tip If you place data in a wrong field, or do anything you didn't intend, for that matter, click the Undo button on the toolbar to revert to the previous state of your report. This action undoes the last action that you performed, so you need to do it immediately after you recognize your error. You can undo up to your last five actions.

2. Point to the second row of the second column, click the Field List icon, and click SalesAmount.

   You can either drag fields from the Report Data window or use the Field List to select a field from the dataset bound to the data region. By adding BusinessType to the table, you bound the ResellerSales dataset to the table.

3. In the Properties window, open the drop-down list at the top of the window, select Tablix1, and scroll to locate the *DataSetName* property in the General section to confirm the binding to the ResellerSales dataset.

Note You might be wondering why the data region is called a tablix here rather than a table, but first it's important to develop an understanding of data regions in general. You learn more about the tablix later in this chapter.

4. Click the Preview tab to view the report, as shown here.

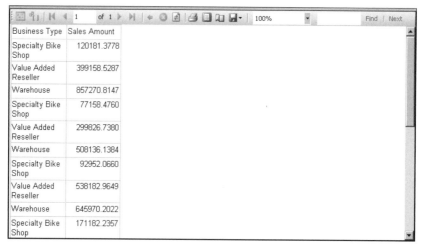

Business Type	Sales Amount
Specialty Bike Shop	120181.3778
Value Added Reseller	399158.5287
Warehouse	857270.8147
Specialty Bike Shop	77158.4760
Value Added Reseller	299826.7380
Warehouse	508136.1384
Specialty Bike Shop	92952.0660
Value Added Reseller	538182.9649
Warehouse	645970.2022
Specialty Bike Shop	171182.2357

   Notice the repetition of the business types: Specialty Bike Shop, Value Added Reseller, and Warehouse. Each row in the table is a detail row and reproduces the same sequence of rows that you saw when you executed the dataset query in a previous procedure in this chapter. In the dataset, these detail rows are grouped by sales territory group and country. You'll also add these groups to your table in the next procedure.

5. Close the Output window.

Each time you preview your report, the Output window appears. Any errors or warnings display in this window to alert you to problems to be corrected in your report. This window stays open even when you switch back to the Design tab, but you can close it at any time.

Previewing a Report in Report Designer

You can preview a report without first deploying it to a server to make sure it looks the way you intend for online viewing. You also can use the Print Layout button to see how the printed version of the report will look, which is an important step to remember. Commonly, new report developers focus on a report design that looks great online, but they forget to check the print version. A data region might render across multiple pages unintentionally or blank pages might appear—problems that become evident only when you print or export the report while in Preview mode.

The Preview toolbar includes several buttons to test your report. Use the Page Setup button to define page size, orientation, and margins, and then use the Print button to send your report to a printer. Be sure to test rendering to other formats by using the Export button to view the report in XML, Comma-Separated Value (CSV), Tagged Image File Format (TIFF), Portable Document Format (PDF), MIME Encapsulation of Aggregate HTML Documents (MHTML), Microsoft Office Excel, or Microsoft Office Word formats.

Grouping Data

You can use groups to combine detail rows into related sets, and you can include subtotal values as an aggregation of numeric fields in the detail rows. For a table, you define row groups only. You can right-click a text box in a data region to create a new group, and then select a dataset field to use for grouping, or alternatively define an expression.

You can see groups in the Grouping pane at the bottom of Report Designer. This Grouping pane makes it easier to see which groups are defined for the data region and, if multiple groups are defined, how the groups relate to one another hierarchically. Furthermore, in the Grouping pane, you can access properties for each group or add additional groups easily.

In this procedure, you add groups to your table.

Group data in a table

1. Click the Design tab.
2. Right-click the second row of the first column, select Add Group, and then, in the Row Group section, click Parent Group.

There are also options to add a column group or an adjacent group. You learn more about working with these other group types later in this chapter.

3. In the Tablix Group dialog box, in the Group By drop-down list, select [SalesTerritoryGroup], as shown here.

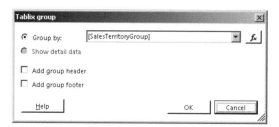

You have the option to add a header or footer for the group. When you choose these options, rows are added to the table above and below the details row. For this report, you are creating a more compact table and will not use header and footer rows for each group.

4. Click OK to close the Tablix Group dialog box.

Notice that the group appears in a new column to the left of the existing columns, as shown here. A default column label, Group1, also displays, which you can change, of course.

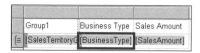

5. Right-click the second row of the first column (containing *[SalesTerritoryGroup]*), select Add Group, and then, in the Row Group section, click Child Group.

When you add a group to a data region that already contains at least one group, you must decide how the groups will relate to each other. If the new group will contain the existing group or detail rows, you create a parent group. If the new group will be contained by the existing group, you create a child group, as you did here.

6. In the Tablix Group dialog box, in the Group By drop-down list, select [SalesTerritoryCountry], and click OK.

The labels for the groups default to Group1 and Group2, as shown here, which you can change by replacing the text in the table header row.

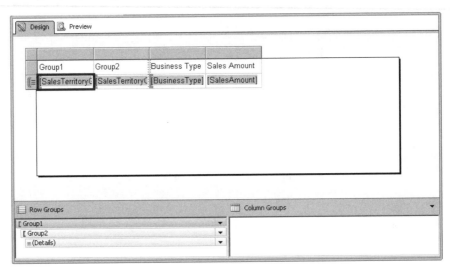

7. Click in the first row of the first column, highlight Group1, and type **Group**.

8. Click in the first row of the second column, highlight Group2, and type **Country**.

 Note Changing the labels does not change the name of the groups in the Grouping pane. Instead, you must access the Group properties to change the group names to identify them more easily in the Grouping pane.

 Tip Although you are not required to provide names for the groups yourself, you will find it helpful to use a more meaningful name than the default generic name when multiple groups display in the Grouping pane.

9. In the Grouping pane, right-click Group1, and click Group Properties.

10. In the Group Properties dialog box, in the Name text box, type **SalesTerritoryGroup,** as shown here.

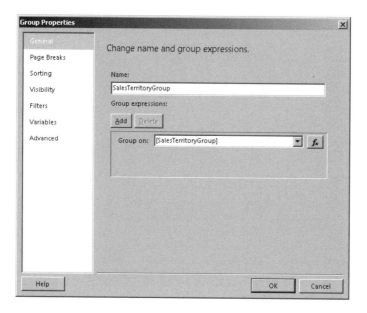

Note Group names, like data source and dataset names, cannot contain spaces and must start with a letter.

Notice that you can define multiple group expressions for a single group by clicking Add and selecting a new field. Instead of using a dataset field as a group expression, you can construct a formula expression for grouping. You learn more about expressions in Chapter 5.

You can define many other types of properties for each group: Page Breaks, Sorting, Filters, Variables, and Advanced. You learn more about Page Breaks and Sorting later in this chapter. Defining a filter for a data region is similar to defining a filter for a dataset, except that the data region filter applies only to the data region. You learn more about group variables in Chapter 5 and about the options on the Advanced tab in Chapters 5 and 6.

11. Click OK to close the Group Properties dialog box.

12. In the Grouping pane, right-click Group2, and click Group Properties.

13. In the Group Properties dialog box, in the Name box, type **SalesTerritoryCountry**, and click OK.

Tip From time to time, it's a good idea to save your work. Notice the asterisk on the Report Designer tab. The asterisk lets you know that you have made changes to the report that you have not yet saved to disk, and it disappears when you save your report.

14. On the File menu, click Save, or click the Save Selected Items button on the toolbar.

15. Click the Preview tab to view the current state of your report, as shown here.

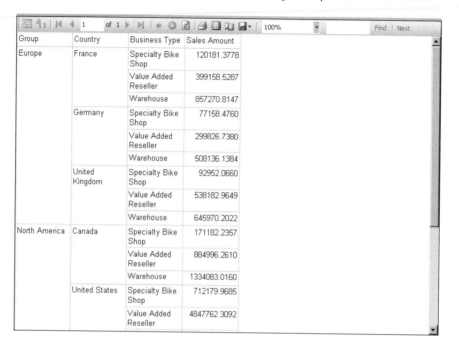

Adding a Total

When you use a table in your report, you can use the Add Total command to add a row to sum detail rows for a group, or for the entire table. By default, the Add Total command inserts an expression using the *Sum()* function, but you can change the expression to use an alternative aggregate function such as *Average()* or *Min()*. You learn more about aggregate functions in Chapter 5.

In this procedure, you add totals for each group in your table.

Add totals to row groups

1. Click the Design tab.

2. Right-click the text box containing *[SalesAmount]*, and click Add Total.

A new row appears as a group footer row for the *SalesTerritoryCountry* group.

3. Click the new text box containing *[Sum(SalesAmount)]*, as shown here.

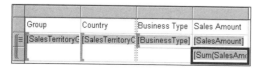

When you click a text box containing an aggregate function, an orange bar appears to the left of the row group to which the aggregate function applies. In this case, the sum of the Sales Amount column entries represents the sum of all sales amounts for the *SalesTerritoryCountry* group.

4. Right-click the text box containing *[Sum(SalesAmount)]*, and click Add Total.

When you apply the Add Total command to a group total, Report Designer adds another group footer row for the total of the parent group, which in this case is the *SalesTerritoryGroup*. Because *SalesTerritoryGroup* has no parent group, a label for Total displays in the new group footer row.

Notice also the icons in the row handles on the left side of the table. The set of three horizontal lines identifies the detail row. The line spanning the second and third rows of the table shows the scope of the innermost group, *SalesTerritoryCountry*, and the line spanning the second, third, and fourth rows of the table shows the scope of the *SalesTerritoryGroup* group. These visual cues are helpful when you add many groups and multiple rows per group to a table.

5. In the text box to the left of *[Sum(SalesAmount)]* in the group footer row of the *SalesTerritoryCountry* group (in the third row of the third column), type **Country Total**.

6. In the *SalesTerritoryGroup* group footer row, replace Total by typing **Group Total** in the text box.

7. Click Save Selected Items, and then click the Preview tab to view the report, as shown here.

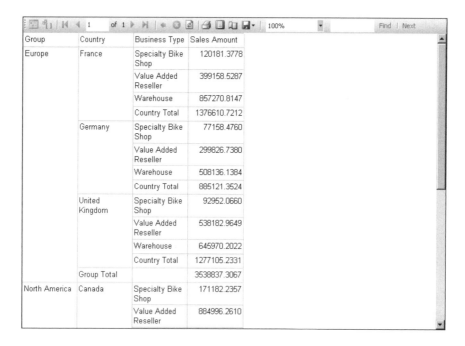

Reviewing the RDL File

The purpose of Report Designer is to provide a graphical interface for the construction of a Report Definition Language (RDL) file, which is an XML representation of your report using Report Definition Language, an open schema developed by Microsoft. Instead of reports stored in a proprietary format that can be used only within specific applications, Reporting Services allows you to create a report definition to describe the report's data query, fields, layout, properties, and so on. The report definition describes how to get the data required for the report and what the final report should look like, but not how to produce it.

You can view the RDL of your report at any time. In Solution Explorer, right-click the report, and click View Code. You can make edits to the RDL in Code view, but be careful. If you inadvertently remove a required tag, you can no longer work with the report in Report Designer. Be sure to make a copy of your report before modifying the RDL as a safeguard.

Using a Matrix

Another type of data region that you will find useful is a matrix. Whereas a table has a fixed number of columns and a dynamic number of rows, both the rows and columns of a matrix are dynamic. A matrix displays data in a structure much like a crosstab or pivot table, and can use groups on either rows or columns with optional subtotals.

In this procedure, you add a matrix to your report.

Add a matrix

1. Click the Design tab.

   You can reuse the same dataset in multiple data regions on your report, or you can use separate datasets for each data region. In the current report, you add a new dataset to summarize reseller sales by sales territory group and by year.

2. Open the Report Data window, click New, and click Dataset.

3. In the Dataset Properties dialog box, in the Name box, type **ResellerSalesByTerritoryByYear**.

4. In the Dataset Properties dialog box, click Import.

5. In the Import Query dialog box, navigate to the Microsoft Press\Rs2008sbs\Chap04 folder in your Documents folder, double-click ResellerSalesByTerritoryByYear.sql, and click OK.

6. Open the Toolbox window, and drag the Matrix control onto the design surface to the right of the table at the top of the report body, as shown here.

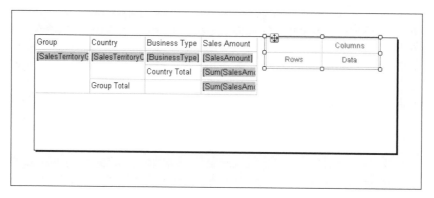

7. Point to the text box on the second row of the first column, click the Field List icon, point to AdventureWorksDW2008, point to ResellerSalesByTerritoryByYear, and click SalesTerritoryCountry.

When a dataset is not bound to a data region and multiple datasets exist, the first time you make a selection using the Field List, you must select the data source and data set before you can select a field. Of course, you can drag a field from the Report Data window and drop it into the text box instead of using the Field List.

Notice that the Grouping pane now shows only the group associated with the matrix. The rows and columns you add to a matrix are classified automatically as groups. There are no detail rows in a matrix, which is another characteristic differentiating a matrix from a table.

8. Point to the text box on the first row of the second column, click the Field List icon, and click CalendarYear.

Notice that CalendarYear appears now as a column group in the Grouping pane. The Grouping pane displays only groups associated with the currently selected data region.

9. In the matrix, point to the text box on the second row of the second column, click the Field List icon, and click SalesAmount.

Because there are no detail rows in a matrix, all data field text boxes, appearing at the intersections of rows and columns, automatically use the *Sum* aggregate function, although you can replace it with a different aggregate function.

Notice also that when you click in the data field text box, an orange bar appears to the left of the row group and above the column group to show the group scope affecting the current text box.

10. Save and then preview the report, as shown here.

Group	Country	Business Type	Sales Amount	Sales Territory Country	2002	2003	2004	2001
Europe	France	Specialty Bike Shop	120181.3778	France		857123.1784	2373804.0354	1376610.7212	
		Value Added Reseller	399158.5287	Germany			1098866.6849	885121.3524	
		Warehouse	857270.8147	United Kingdom		841757.7607	2160145.8328	1277105.2331	
		Country Total	1376610.7212	Canada	4822999.2021	5651305.4254	2390261.5127	1513359.4563
	Germany	Specialty Bike Shop	77158.4760	United States	17622549.5128	20071116.4827	9362059.3657	6552075.8490
		Value Added Reseller	299826.7380	Australia			847430.9640	746904.4127	

The matrix renders to the right of the table. Notice that the years display out of sequence, however. The dataset query for the table includes an ORDER BY clause to display the table rows in the desired order without any further change required. If the dataset query does not include an ORDER BY clause, or if you want to override the ORDER BY clause, you can change the sorting property of the group.

 Tip For better performance, you should let the database engine perform sort operations. Use report properties only when the database engine can't perform a required operation, such as certain types of calculations that you learn about in Chapter 5.

11. Click the Design tab, click the matrix, right-click the *CalendarYear* group in the Grouping pane, and click Group Properties.

12. In the Group Properties dialog box, in the left pane, click Sorting.

13. Click Add, and then, in the Sort By drop-down list, select [CalendarYear], as shown here.

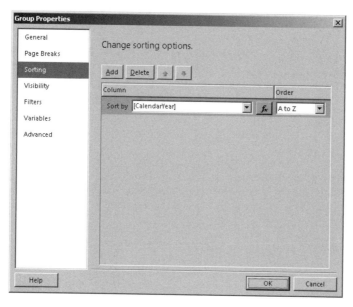

The default sort order is ascending, which is designated by A to Z in the Order drop-down list. You can define a sort based on multiple fields, each with its own sort order. You use the up and down arrow buttons to control the sequence in which the sorts apply. Instead of using dataset fields to define a sort, you can click the Expression button to the right of the Sort By drop-down list to use a formula as a sort expression. You learn about expressions in Chapter 5.

14. Click OK to close the Group Properties dialog box.

15. Click the Preview tab to verify that the sort order is now correct.

Using a List

When you use a table or matrix, you present data in text boxes that are arranged in rows or columns, but a list can create a more flexible layout than the other two data regions. You can, for example, use nothing but text boxes for a completely free-form layout, or you can use a combination of text boxes and other data regions to present some data in free form and other data in a structured layout. Unlike the table and matrix data regions, the list supports only one level of grouping, but you can implement multiple levels of grouping by nesting lists within lists.

In this procedure, you create a copy of your report and then use a list to display a text box and a matrix in your report.

Display a text box and a matrix in a list

1. Click the Design tab, and then click the Save Selected Items button on the toolbar.

2. In Solution Explorer, right-click Reseller Sales Summary.rdl, and click Copy.

3. In Solution Explorer, click the Reports folder, and press CTRL+V.

4. Right-click the new report, Copy Of Reseller Sales Summary.rdl, click Rename, type **Reseller Sales Summary List.rdl**, and press Enter.

5. In Solution Explorer, double-click Reseller Sales Summary List.rdl to open the new report.

> **Tip** After you make a copy of a report, it's very easy to start making design changes to the original report without realizing it. To ensure you're working on the new report copy, you can make sure only the current copy of the report is open by right-clicking the current report tab in the document workspace, and clicking Close All But This.

6. From the Toolbox window, drag the List control onto the design surface below the matrix, as shown here.

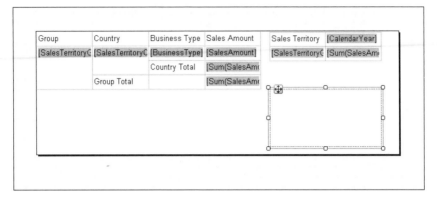

When you drag a new control onto the design surface near existing controls, you see
blue snap lines appear to help you align the controls. In this report, you move the list
later to a new position, so don't worry right now about getting the alignment perfect.

7. Right-click anywhere inside the matrix, point to Select, click Tablix2 to select the matrix
(as indicated by the crosshair), and then, using the crosshair, drag the matrix into the
list, as shown here.

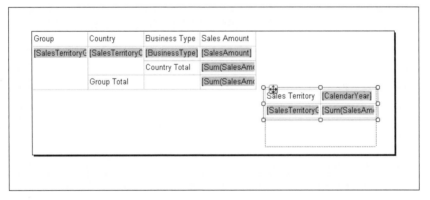

8. Right-click anywhere inside the list, point to Select, and click Tablix3 to select the list.

9. In the Properties window, in the DatasetName drop-down list, select
ResellerSalesByTerritoryByYear.

> **Important** The list and any data regions that you nest inside the list, such as the matrix in
> this example, must be bound to the same dataset.

10. In the Grouping pane, right-click the Details1 group, and click Group Properties.

The list differs from the table and matrix data regions because you define a group for
the details row.

11. In the Group Properties dialog box, click Add.

12. In the Group On drop-down list, select [SalesTerritoryGroup], and click OK.

13. Right-click the matrix inside the list, point to Select, click Tablix2, and then drag the matrix down inside the list to make room for a text box above the matrix.

14. From the Toolbox window, drag a text box control into the list above the matrix, and position the text box at the left edge of the list just above the matrix, as shown here.

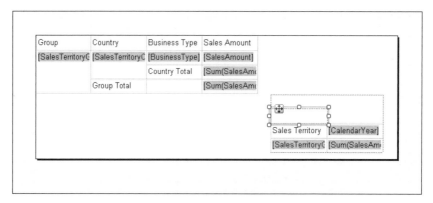

15. Point to the new text box, click the Field List icon, and click SalesTerritoryGroup.

You can bind data to a freestanding text box, but you must use an aggregate function, such as *Sum* for a numeric field or *First* for a string field.

16. Right-click anywhere inside the list, point to Select, click Tablix3 to select the list, and then drag the list to the top edge of the report body just to the right of the table.

17. Save and then preview the report, as shown here.

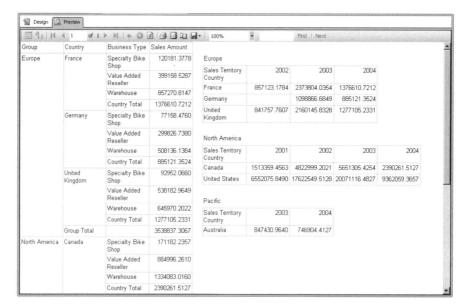

Introducing the Tablix

By completing the procedures up to this point in the chapter, you have developed experience with the table, matrix, and list data regions. To the report processing engine, these data regions are all treated as a *tablix*, which is a hybrid data region with a flexible grid layout that can be defined with fixed columns and dynamic rows like a table, or dynamic columns and dynamic rows like a matrix. Although you select a table control from the Toolbox window, the structure on the report design surface is really just a starting point. After starting to design a traditional table layout, if you decide you really need to add a column group or define dynamic columns, you can make the change easily without the need to discard your work and start development of a matrix instead. Similarly, you can add row or column groups to a list to convert it to a table or matrix structure. In addition, you can group data more flexibly. For example, you can nest groups in parent and child relationships, but you can also place groups adjacent to one another.

Defining Adjacent Groups

A traditional grouping structure in a table or matrix combines multiple groups into a hierarchical structure that refers to a containing group as a parent group and a contained group as a child group. A new feature in Reporting Services 2008 is the ability to create an adjacent group. One way you might use adjacent groups is to display data in a matrix that uses adjacent groups on columns. The data in each adjacent group represents all data from the dataset query. Each adjacent group provides different views of the same data.

In this procedure, you update an existing report by adding adjacent groups to a matrix.

Define adjacent groups

1. In Solution Explorer, right-click the Reports folder, point to Add, and click Existing Item.

    You can import a report definition file into your project instead of creating a report from scratch. When you do this, the report definition file is kept in its original location, and a copy of the file is added to the project folder. Any edits you make to the report affect only the file stored in the report server project.

2. In the Add Existing Item – Sales dialog box, navigate to the Microsoft Press\Rs2008sbs \Chap04 folder in your Documents folder, and double-click Reseller Sales By Year By Product.rdl.

3. In Solution Explorer, double-click Reseller Sales By Year By Product.rdl to open the report in the document workspace.

This report currently contains a matrix similar to the one you created in the "Add a Matrix" procedure earlier in this chapter. You are now going to add a second column group to the matrix as an adjacent group.

4. Right-click the text box containing *[CalendarYear]*, point to Add Group, and select Adjacent Right.

5. In the Tablix Group dialog box, in the Group By drop-down list, select Category, and click OK.

6. Point to the text box below *[Category]*, click the Field List icon, and click SalesAmount.

   In this example, you are creating an adjacent group displaying the same value as the first group, *SalesAmount*. However, you could select any field value or use an expression to display an entirely different value in the adjacent group.

7. Save and then preview the report.

8. To view the entire width of the matrix, as shown here, in the Zoom drop-down list in the center of the Preview toolbar, select 75%.

Sales Territory Group	2001	2002	2003	2004	Accessories	Bikes	Clothing	Components
Europe		12012879.2292	366 15372.2568	24690862.0687	308405.6472	7321530.0915	25700907.6880	39988270.1260
North America	53536179.1767	1669 15819.5194	1873 15606.3041	850 18037.8454	1704958.6356	71799716.3784	48295388.7888	370085579.0438
Pacific			5042726.9736	5004484.8156	33731.5680	358806.6596	96 15625.2816	41048.2800

Adding a Text Box

A text box is a report item that can exist independently of a data region. It can either contain static text or an expression that computes a value for the text box at the time of the report execution. You use freestanding text boxes for report titles and page numbers, for example.

In this procedure, you add a static title to your report.

Add a static report title

1. Click the Design tab.

2. On the Report menu, select Ruler.

   A vertical ruler appears along the left side of the document workspace and a horizontal ruler appears across the top of the workspace. You can use these rulers to help align an object as you drag it across the design surface.

3. Right-click anywhere inside the matrix, point to Select, click Tablix1 to select the matrix, and then drag the matrix down on the design surface so that the top edge is approximately at the ½-inch mark on the vertical ruler.

4. From the Toolbox window, drag a text box onto the design surface and position it in the upper-left corner of the report body.

5. Click in the new text box, and type **Reseller Sales by Year and by Product**.

6. Click anywhere in the report outside the text box, click inside the text box to select it, and then drag the right edge of the text box to the 3-inch mark on the horizontal ruler.

7. Save and then preview the report, as shown here.

Reseller Sales by Year and by Product								
Sales Territory Group	2001	2002	2003	2004	Accessories	Bikes	Clothing	Components
Europe		12012879.2292	366 15372.2568	24690862.0667	308405.6472	7321530.0915	25700907.6880	39988270.1260
North America	53536179.1767	1669 15819.5194	1873 15606.3041	85018037.8464	1704958.6356	71799716.3784	48295388.7888	370985579.0438
Pacific			5042726.9736	5004484.8156	33731.5680	356806.6596	96 15625.2816	41048.2800

Adding a Line

You can use a line to add visual effects to a report. A line has properties that you can set to define its length, width, and color, among other properties. Although you can configure many property values to change at report execution, as you learn in Chapter 5, a line always has a fixed length that cannot be changed dynamically.

In this procedure, you add a line below the text box containing the report title.

Add a line

1. Click the Design tab.

2. In the Toolbox window, double-click the Line control.

3. Click the left end of the line and drag it below the report title text box.

4. Click the right end of the line and drag the end of the line to stretch the line to the same length as the title text box at the same vertical position as the left end of the line.

   When the line length matches the text box width, you see a blue snap line connecting the two report items to indicate alignment. The snap line disappears when you release your mouse button. Your report layout now looks like this:

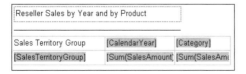

A line does nothing more than add decoration to a report. Later in this chapter, you learn how to use properties to add more visual interest to the line.

Adding an Image

You can use an image as a freestanding logo or picture in your report, or you can have pictures associated with rows of data, such as details for a product catalog. You can also use an image as a background for a text box, a data region, or the body of a report.

You can add images to a report in a number of ways. The most straightforward way is to import an image into the report and store it as an embedded image. If you need to refer to the same image in many reports, such as a corporate logo, you can store the image on a network share or on a Web server and embed a reference to the image in your report. Then, if the image later changes, you can update the image in one location, and all reports then use the new image. Finally, for the display of separate images in detail, you can retrieve images from a database.

In this procedure, you add a logo to your report as an embedded image.

Add an embedded image

1. From the Toolbox window, drag the image to the top edge of the design surface at approximately the 4-inch mark of the horizontal ruler.

2. In the Image Properties dialog box, in the Name text box, type **logo**.

3. Open the Select The Image Source drop-down list to review the available options: External, Embedded, and Database.

   When you select an option, the dialog box changes to prompt you for the information required to support the selected option.

4. In the Select The Image Source drop-down list, select Embedded.

   If you already have an embedded image in the report, you can select the image in the Use This Image drop-down list to use the same image in a new location. Because you have no images yet, you must import an image into the report.

5. Click Import.

6. In the Open dialog box, navigate to the Microsoft Press\Rs2008sbs\Chap04 folder in your Documents folder, select BMP Files in the Files Of Type drop-down list, and double-click Logo.bmp. The Image Properties box now looks like this:

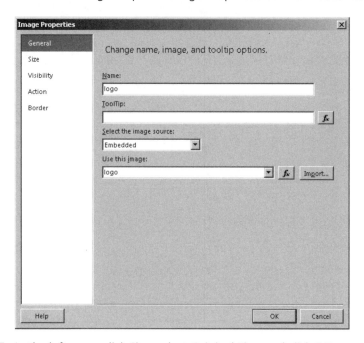

7. In the left pane, click Size, select Original Size, and click OK.

The image height interferes with the expansion of the matrix, but you can resize it to fit the page better.

8. Drag the bottom edge of the image approximately to the ½-inch mark on the vertical ruler to position it above the top edge of the matrix, as shown here.

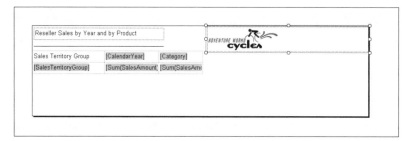

The image resizes proportionally as you manually adjust the height or width.

9. Save and then preview the report.

Linking Information with a Subreport

A subreport is a special report item that serves as a placeholder for another report that you want to embed in the report you are currently developing. You can build a report once and reuse it many times as a subreport. A popular way to use subreports is to combine many online reports into a single report for the purpose of producing a PDF document. You can pass parameter values from the report to the subreport to change the subreport's content dynamically, which you learn about in Chapter 6.

> **Note** The page header and page footer sections of the subreport do not render in the parent report.

In this procedure, you add a subreport to your report.

Add a subreport

1. Click the Design tab.

   First, to preview your report and subreport by using Report Designer, you should add the other report to your report server project if it's not already there. The subreport is not required to be stored in the same location as the parent report once deployed, but you need to provide the path to the report when you configure the subreport.

2. In Solution Explorer, right-click the Reports folder, point to Add, and click Existing Item.

3. In the Add Existing Item – Sales dialog box, navigate to the Microsoft Press\Rs2008sbs \Chap04 folder in your Documents folder, and double-click Reseller Sales By Business Type.rdl.

4. In the Reseller Sales By Year By Product report, from the Toolbox window, drag Subreport to the design surface below the matrix.

   A placeholder appears for the subreport. By default, this placeholder is three inches high and three inches wide, but you see when you preview the report that the subreport is not confined to these dimensions. You can resize the placeholder if you prefer.

5. Right-click the subreport, and select Subreport Properties.

6. In the Subreport Properties dialog box, in the Use This Report As A Subreport drop-down list, select Reseller Sales By Business Type, and click OK.

   The name of the report displays inside the subreport placeholder to help you identify the report that will display in that location.

7. Save, and then preview the report, as shown here.

Reseller Sales by Year and by Product

Sales Territory Group	2001	2002	2003	2004	Accessories	Bikes	Clothing	Components
Europe		12012879.2292	36615372.2568	24690862.0667	308405.6472	7321530.0915	25700907.6880	39988270.1260
North America	53536179.1767	166915819.5194	187315606.3041	85018037.8464	1704958.6356	71799716.3784	48295388.7888	370985579.0438
Pacific			5042726.9736	5004484.8156	33731.5680	356806.6596	9615625.2816	41048.2800

Group	Country	Specialty Bike Shop	Value Added Reseller	Warehouse
Europe	France	$120,181		
			$399,159	
				$857,271
	Germany	$77,158		
			$299,827	
				$508,136
	United Kingdom	$92,952		
			$538,183	
				$645,970
	Group Total	*$290,292*	*$1,237,168*	*$2,011,377*
North America	Canada	$171,182		
			$884,996	
				$1,334,083
	United States	$712,180		
			$4,847,762	
				$3,802,117
	Group Total	*$883,362*	*$5,732,759*	*$5,136,200*
Pacific	Australia	$165,542		
			$400,571	
				$180,791
	Group Total	*$165,542*	*$400,571*	*$180,791*

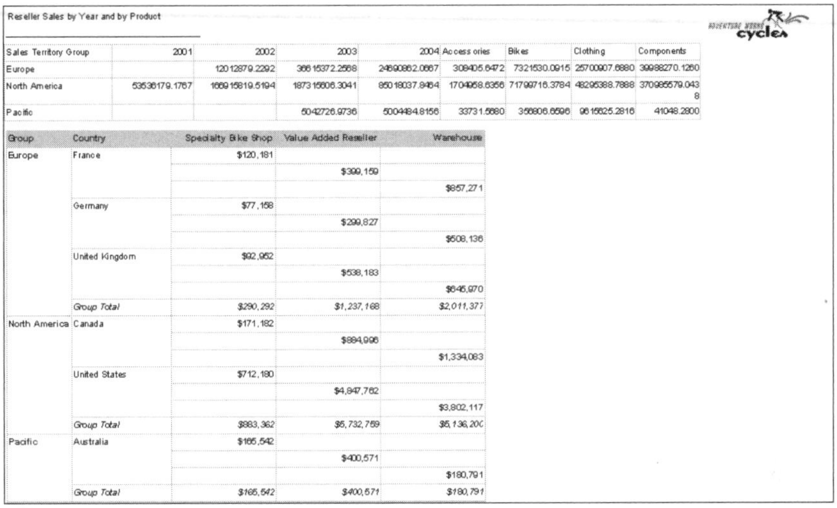

Enhancing the Report Appearance

After you finalize the data layout, you can then improve your report by configuring properties to manage the location and size of report items, change the formatting of report items, or control the paging of the report. For large reports, you might add page breaks to separate the report into logical groupings. If your report contains multiple pages, you might add page headers and page footers to repeat information on each page such as the report title and page number.

Configuring the Placement and Size of a Report Item

You can use drag-and-drop to move a report item or a data region to a new location, and you can drag the edges of a report item to make it larger or smaller. However, using drag-and-drop to perform these tasks might not provide the precision you need for a pixel-perfect report. Instead, you can use the *Location* and *Size* properties to configure the placement and size of a report item to meet exact specifications.

In this procedure, you reposition and resize the logo image.

Change the value of the *Location* and *Size* properties

1. Click the Design tab, and then, on the design surface, click the image. Alternatively, in the Properties window, select Logo.

2. In the Properties window, scroll down to locate the Location and Size boxes in the Position category.

   By default, properties are arranged by category. If you prefer, you can switch to an alphabetical arrangement by clicking the Alphabetical button on the Properties toolbar.

3. To the left of the Location box, click the plus sign (+) to expand the property.

   There are actually two values you must provide for the *Location* property: Left and Top. These values provide the coordinate for the upper-left corner of the selected report item.

4. In the Left box, type **3in**, and in the Top box, type **0in** if it contains a different value.

5. To the left of the Size box, click the plus sign (+) to expand the property.

6. In the Width box, type **1.5in**, and in the Height box, type **0.5in**.

7. Review the report design surface to see the new placement and size of the image.

Changing the Appearance of a Report Item

Many properties are available for configuring the appearance of a report item. Most commonly, you define format strings, font sizes, styles, and colors of text, but you can also use properties related to borders, padding, and background colors, among others. A new feature in Reporting Services 2008 allows you to set different formatting properties for selected text within a text box.

In this procedure, you use the Properties window to set report item properties.

Set report item properties

1. Click inside the text box containing the report title and highlight the text.

   Notice that the current report item in the Properties window is Selected Text. Rather than applying format properties to all the text in a text box (which was the only option in previous versions of Reporting Services), you can apply properties to selected text within a text box.

2. On the toolbar above the document workspace, click the Bold button.

> **Note** The Bold button, along with other buttons that define format properties, appears on the Report Formatting toolbar that displays by default in BI Dev Studio. If you don't see this toolbar, right-click any visible toolbar and select Report Formatting.

You can set a variety of properties for selected text, including *Indent*, *SpaceAfter*, *SpaceBefore*, *TextAlign*, *Color*, *Font*, or *LineHeight*. You can also define bulleted and numbered lists and list indention.

3. In the text box, select Reseller Sales, and then, in the Font Size drop-down list on the Report Formatting toolbar, select 12pt.

4. With Reseller Sales selected, in the Properties window, in the Color box, select Blue.

5. Click the tablix, and then click the row handle of the first row to select the entire row.

    You can apply formatting to all text boxes in a row or column by selecting the applicable handle in the data region.

6. On the Report Formatting toolbar, click the Bold button.

7. In the Properties window, in the BackgroundColor drop-down list, select Light Gray.

8. In the tablix, click the text box containing *[Category]*, and then, on the Report Formatting toolbar, click the Align Right button.

9. In the tablix, click the text box in the second column containing *[Sum(SalesAmount)]*, and then, while holding the Shift key, click the text box to its right.

10. In the Properties window, in the Format box, type **C0**.

> **Tip** Recall from Chapter 3 that you can use any Microsoft Visual Basic .NET format string for this property.

11. Click the line below the report title, and then, in the Properties window, in the LineColor drop-down list, select Blue.

12. In the LineWidth box, type **5pt**.

13. In the Location/Left box, type **0in**, and in the Location/Top box, type **0.4in**.

14. In the Properties window, in the report item drop-down list, select Textbox3, and then, in the Location/Left box, type **0in**, and in the Location/Top box, type **0in**.

15. Click Save Selected Items, click the Preview tab, and in the Zoom drop-down list, select 100% to better view the report, as shown here.

Reseller Sales by Year and by Product						
Sales Territory Group	**2001**	**2002**	**2003**	**2004**	**Accessories**	**Bikes**
Europe		$12,012,879	$36,615,372	$24,690,862	$308,406	$7,321,530
North America	$53,536,179	$166,915,820	$187,315,606	$85,018,038	$1,704,959	$71,799,716
Pacific			$5,042,727	$5,004,485	$33,732	$356,807

Group	**Country**	**Specialty Bike Shop**	**Value Added Reseller**	**Warehouse**
Europe	France	$120,181		
			$399,159	
				$857,271
	Germany	$77,158		
			$299,827	
				$508,136
	United Kingdom	$92,952		
			$538,183	
				$645,970
	Group Total	*$290,292*	*$1,237,168*	*$2,011,377*
North America	Canada	$171,182		
			$884,996	
				$1,334,083
	United States	$712,180		
			$4 847 763	

Setting Page Breaks

By default, the report processing engine will fit as much of a data region onto a page as it can before creating a page break. You can override this behavior by inserting page breaks relative to a data region, or when a group instance changes within a data region.

In this procedure, you add page breaks to your report.

Add page breaks

1. Click the Design tab.

2. In the Properties window, in the report item drop-down list, select Tablix1.

3. In the PageBreak drop-down list, select End.

When the report renders the tablix, a page break forces the subreport to start on the next page. The *PageBreak* property allows you to set a page break before the data region renders, after the data region renders, or both before and after rendering.

4. In Solution Explorer, double-click Reseller Sales By Business Type.rdl to open the report for editing.

5. In the Grouping pane, right-click the SalesTerritoryGroup, and click Group Properties.

6. In the Group Properties dialog box, click Page Breaks, select the Between Each Instance Of A Group check box, and click OK.

7. Save and then preview the report.

The first page of the report now contains only the tablix displaying sales by sales territory on rows and by business type on columns. The first group instance, Europe, displays.

> **Note** The question mark that appears to the right of the page number indicates that the report is not yet fully rendered and the total number of pages in the report is not yet available. When a report renders one page at a time, you experience better performance, especially when a report contains a lot of data.

8. On the Preview toolbar, click the Next Page button.

   On the second page of the report, you see the North America group instance. Each group instance appears on a separate page. Notice, however, that the column labels are missing. You can configure the data region to repeat column labels on each page.

9. Click the Design tab.

10. In the Grouping pane, click the arrow that appears to the right of the Column Groups label, and click Advanced Mode to display all groups, as shown here.

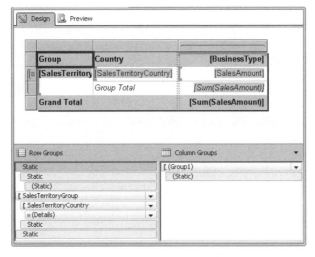

11. In the Row Groups section, click the first Static group, and then, in the Properties window, in the RepeatOnNewPage drop-down list, select True.

12. Save the report.

Adjusting the Report Size for Print-Ready Formats

Your report has properties, too. You might need to set page size and margin properties for reports that will be printed or exported to PDF format. You can also define background color or image properties, or add borders to your report. There is also a property to eliminate white space so that blank pages are not added to your report.

In this procedure, you change the *PageSize* property to change the report to a landscape format.

> ### Use the *PageSize* property to define a landscape format
>
> 1. In Solution Explorer, double-click Reseller Sales By Year By Product.rdl.
>
> 2. In the Properties window, in the report item drop-down list, select Report.
>
> 3. Expand the PageSize box, type **11in** in the Width box, and type **8.5in** in the Height box.
>
>   The *PageSize* property applies only to a report rendered to a print-ready format such as PDF or TIFF. To adjust sizing of a report for online viewing, you use the *InteractiveSize* property.
>
>   Because the first tablix in the report is very wide, you must make some additional adjustments to fit the data region onto a single page even though you have defined a landscape format by setting a page size of 11 inches by 8.5 inches. Changing margin size is one type of adjustment you can make.
>
> 4. Expand the Margins text box, type **0.25in** in the Left box, and type **0.25in** in the Right box.
>
>   Even after making adjustments to margins and page size, a data region still might not fit on a page. In this case, you can adjust the font size and column spacing to reduce the overall space required by the data region.
>
> 5. Click anywhere in the first tablix, click the first column handle, and then, while pressing the CTRL key, click the second and third column handles.
>
> 6. On the Report Formatting toolbar, in the Font Size drop-down list, select 8pt.
>
> 7. Click the second column handle, and then, in the Properties window, expand the Size text box and type **1in** in the Width box.
>
> 8. Preview the report, click the Print Layout button on the Preview toolbar, and click the Next Page button on the Preview toolbar.
>
>   Although you have adjusted the report to fit the first tablix on a single page, the second page of the report is blank, which indicates that the body and margins of the report are too wide for the report page size.
>
> 9. Click the Design tab, and notice the amount of white space to the right of Tablix1.
>
>   The white space in the body of your report is preserved by default, which can extend the body size beyond the width of the report and cause blank pages to appear. You can disable this behavior by setting the *ConsumeWhiteSpace* property of the report.
>
> 10. In the Properties window, in the report item drop-down list, select Report, and then, in the ConsumeContainerWhitespace drop-down list, select True.

11. Preview the report, click the Print Layout button on the Preview toolbar, and click the Next Page button on the Preview toolbar.

    The second page of the report now displays the first page of the subreport.

12. Continue paging through the report to observe the page break between group instances and the repeating column labels for each group instance.

Adding a Page Header and Page Footer

The page header and page footer sections of a report are optional and disabled by default. If you want to repeat information or images on all report pages, you can enable these report sections and then place a text box or image inside the desired section. You cannot add a dataset field to a text box in a page header or page footer, nor can you add a data region or subreport in these sections.

In this procedure, you add a report title to the page header that displays on all but the first page, and add page numbers to the page footer that display on all pages of the report.

Add a page header and a page footer

1. Click the Design tab.

2. On the Report menu, select Add Page Header.

3. In the Report Data window, expand the Built-in Fields folder, and drag Report Name to the page header, aligning the left edge of the text box with the left side of the report.

4. Drag the right edge of the text box to the same width as the report title text box in the body of the report.

    You can prevent the display of the text box in the page header on the first page only by changing the *PrintOnFirstPage* property. By default, the report items in the page header display on each page of the report.

 Important If you later decide to remove the page header, all report items contained in the page header will be deleted from the report.

5. Click anywhere in the page header to set it as the current report item in the Properties window, and then, in the PrintOnFirstPage drop-down list, select False.

6. Right-click in the area below the report body in the document workspace and click Add Page Footer.

7. From the Report Data window, drag Page Number to the left side of the page footer.

Because the page number is a numeric value, the page number aligns right when the report renders. If you position the page number on the left side of the page footer, you can change the text box to align left.

8. With the text box containing *[PageNumber]* selected, click the Align Left button on the Report Formatting toolbar.

9. Save and then preview the report. Page through the report to test the appearance of the page header and page footer.

10. On the File menu, select Close Project, and, if the Microsoft Visual Studio message box appears, click Yes to save the solution.

You've learned a lot about developing reports in this chapter, but there is still much more to learn. In the next chapter, you learn how to work with expressions to use calculations in your report and to change the content and appearance of your report dynamically.

Chapter 4 Quick Reference

To	Do This
Create a new report server project	Open Business Intelligence Development Studio; on the File menu, select New, Project, select Report Server Project in the Template list, and provide a name and location for the project.
Add a new report to your report server project	In Solution Explorer, right-click the Reports folder, select Add, click New Item, select Report in the Templates list, and provide a name for the report.
Create a shared data source	In the Report Data window, click New, click Data Source, provide a report data source name, click New, provide a shared data source name, select a provider type, specify a connection string, click Credentials, and select a report authentication method.
Create a dataset	In the Report Data window, click New, click Dataset, provide a dataset name, select a data source, and provide a query string.
Add a data region to the report lay out	In the Toolbox, double-click a table, matrix, or list control; *or* Drag a control from the Toolbox onto the Report Designer design surface.
Bind data to a data region	From the Report Data window, drag a field from a dataset into a text box in a data region; *or* Point to a text box in a data region, click the Field List icon, and click a dataset field.

To	Do This
Preview a report	Click the Preview tab.
Group data	Right-click a text box in a data region, select Add Group, and then, in the Row Group or Column Group section, select one of the following options: Parent Group, Child Group, Adjacent Above, Adjacent Below, Adjacent Left, or Adjacent Right. In the Tablix Group dialog box, select a field in the Group By drop-down list, and add a group header or group footer if you want.
Add a total	Right-click a text box containing a value to total, and click Add Total.
Sort group instances	In the Grouping pane, right-click a group, select Group Properties, Sorting, Add, and then, in the Sort By drop-down list, select a field. In the Sort By drop-down list, select a sort direction.
Add a static report title	From the Toolbox window, add a text box to the design surface. Click in the new text box, and type a string for the report title.
Add a line	From the Toolbox window, add a line to the design surface, drag the line endpoints to the desired position, and set applicable properties, such as *LineColor* or *LineWidth*, in the Properties window.
Add an embedded image	From the Toolbox window, add an image to the design surface. In the Image Properties dialog box, provide a name for the image, select Embedded in the Select The Image Source drop-down list, click Import, navigate to the image location, and double-click the image file.
Add a subreport	From the Toolbox window, add a subreport to the design surface. Right-click the subreport, select Subreport Properties, and select a report in the Use This Report As A Subreport drop-down list.
Change the placement and size of a report item	On the design surface, select the report item, and then, in the Properties window, change the values of the Location/Top and Location/Left boxes for placement and the Size Height and Size Width boxes for size of the report item.
Change the appearance of text in a text box	Click inside the text box, highlight all or part of the text within the text box, and use the buttons on the Report Formatting toolbar, such as Bold, or change values of properties, such as Color, in the Properties window.
Resize a report	In the Properties window, in the report item drop-down list, select Report, expand the PageSize box, and change the values of Width and Height.

To	Do This
Set page breaks	In the Properties window, in the report item drop-down list, select a tablix item, and select a value in the PageBreak drop-down list to control a page break relative to a report item;
	or
	In the Grouping pane, right-click a group, select Group Properties, Page Breaks, Between Each Instance Of A Group, and (if you want) Also At The Start Of A Group or Also At The End Of A Group.
Eliminate blank pages	In the Properties window, in the report item drop-down list, select Report, and select True in the ConsumeContainer-Whitespace drop-down list.
Add a page header or page footer	On the Report menu, click Add Page Header or Add Page Footer.

Chapter 5
Developing Expressions

After completing this chapter, you will be able to:

- Use expressions to calculate values for display in a text box.

- Create aggregation functions in expressions to summarize data.

- Develop expressions to change the appearance or behavior of report items.

- Use variables to extend the flexibility of expressions.

- Build dynamic connection strings and query strings.

- Use expressions for data in a recursive hierarchy group.

You can build many reports that rely exclusively on data that comes straight from the data source using the techniques you learned in Chapter 4, "Designing Reports," but often the real value of information in reports comes from enhancing the data. You can include derived information in your report by creating calculations based on dataset fields. You can also enhance a report by including the name of a report, its location, and the date of execution in the report using a special set of expressions. In addition, expressions are useful for changing format properties, sorting data, and even hiding data based on predefined conditions. Expressions, in general, support a lot of flexibility in your report design, but you have even more options with group and report variables, data source and dataset expressions, and expressions that help you display and summarize hierarchical data. In this chapter, you learn everything you need to know about developing expressions in your reports.

Adding Calculations to a Report

To add a calculation to a report, you must build an expression. Technically speaking, each time you add a field from a dataset to the report design surface, you are adding an expression to the report. However, the process is streamlined to make it easy for you to work with field expressions by using a *simple expression* on the report design surface to display the field name enclosed in brackets. A simple expression is a reference to a single item, such as a dataset field, a built-in field, or a parameter. When you drag a field into a text box, the simple expression is created for you, like *[SalesAmount]*, but you can also type this expression directly into the text box.

Many of the expressions that you add to reports are operations that perform mathematical or string manipulation operations on fields in a dataset and require you to build a longer *complex expression*, which was the only option for expressions in earlier versions of Reporting

Services. A complex expression can reference multiple fields, parameters, or built-in fields, include operators to combine several expressions into a compound expression, and specify calls to functions. Usually, you open the Expression dialog box to create or edit an expression, but you can type it directly into a text box or property box as well. The Report Designer converts a complex expression to *<<Expr>>* on the design surface, so you must open the Expression dialog box to view the expression.

Whether you use simple or complex expressions, you interact with one or more of the built-in collections available in Reporting Services: dataset fields, report items, parameters, and variables. To reference a collection item in an expression, you use standard Microsoft Visual Basic collection syntax: `Collection!ObjectName.Property`. For example, to refer to the *SalesAmount* field, you use `Fields!SalesAmount.Value` in your expression.

Adding a Calculated Field

A calculated field in your dataset is equivalent to adding an expression to the SELECT clause in a Transact-SQL (T-SQL) statement. In fact, ideally you create a derived column in your dataset query to get the desired value into the dataset from the data source, but in the case when you have no control over the source, such as when you're accessing a view or a stored procedure, you can create the calculation you need.

In this procedure, you add a calculated field to a dataset, and then use the calculated field in a data region.

Add a calculated field

1. Click Start, select All Programs, Microsoft SQL Server 2008, and click SQL Server Business Intelligence Development Studio.

2. On the File menu, select Open, and click Project/Solution.

3. In the Open Project dialog box, navigate to the Microsoft Press\Rs2008sbs\Chap05 folder in your Documents folder, and double-click Sales.sln.

4. In Solution Explorer, double-click Reseller Sales Margin Analysis.rdl.

   This report contains a dataset that includes SalesAmount and TotalProductCost, which you use to create a calculated field for profit margin.

5. In the Report Data pane, right-click the ResellerSales dataset, and select Add Calculated Field.

6. In the Dataset Properties dialog box, in the empty row at the bottom of the field list, in the Field Name text box, type **ProfitMargin**.

Note You cannot include spaces in the name of the calculated field, and you must use a letter as the first character.

7. To the right of the Field Source text box, click the Expression button.

8. In the Expression dialog box, in the Category list, select Fields (ResellerSales), and then, in the Values list, double-click SalesAmount.

    You can use the expression lists at the bottom of the Expression dialog box to build an expression by choosing a category, selecting a category item, and then selecting a value. When you choose the Fields category for a particular dataset, you can choose a value that corresponds to a field available in the selected dataset. Notice that your selection creates an expression, =Fields!SalesAmount.Value.

Important The equal sign (=) is required in your expression. Be careful not to remove it.

9. In the Category list, expand Operators, select Arithmetic, and then double-click the minus sign (–).

    Notice the red wavy line below the division symbol in the Set Expression For: Value box. This line is a visual cue that the expression currently contains an error, and in this case, it displays because the expression is incomplete. When you correct the problem, the wavy line disappears. This feature alerts you to a problem before you try to preview the report.

10. In the Set Expression For: Value text box, click at the end of the expression, type **Fields!**, and then, in the drop-down list that appears, double-click TotalProductCost.

    Instead of using the expression lists to build an expression, you can type the expression directly into the expression box. As an aid to typing the expression, the Expression dialog box uses IntelliSense to display a list of valid fields when you begin an expression using the *Fields* collection syntax. This feature ensures that you get the correct name and case for the field name. However, the expression is not yet complete. You must still specify which property of the *Fields* collection item to use in the expression.

11. At the end of the expression, type a period (.), and then, in the drop-down list that appears, scroll down and double-click Value.

    All properties available to the *Fields* collection item display in the IntelliSense list. Most of the time, you use the *Value* property in your expressions. Many of the properties you see listed are used only when you use an Analysis Services data source, which you learn about in Chapter 7, "Using Analysis Services as a Data Source."

    The Expression dialog box now looks like this:

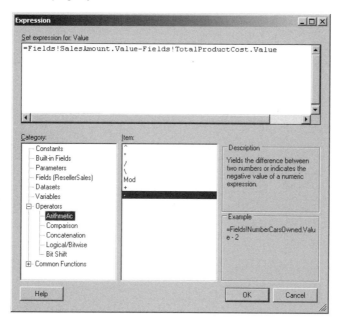

Notice that the red wavy line no longer appears because your expression now validates correctly.

12. Click OK to close the Expression dialog box.

In the Field Source box for the calculated field, *ProfitMargin*, a placeholder for your expression appears, as shown here.

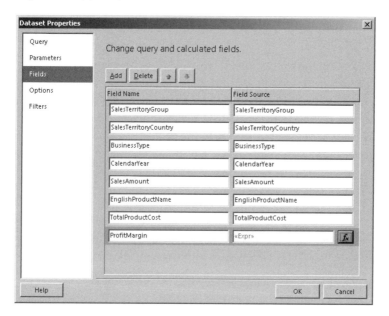

13. Click OK to close the Dataset Properties dialog box.

    You can now use the *ProfitMargin* calculated field just as you would use any other field that comes directly from the dataset. In fact, you cannot distinguish the calculated field from other fields by looking at the list of fields in the Report Data pane. The only way to know if a field is calculated is to open the Dataset Properties dialog box and review the contents of the Field Source text box.

14. Click the tablix, right-click the Sales Amount column handle, point to Insert Column, and select Right to add a new column.

15. In the new column, in the detail row (to the right of *[SalesAmount]*), click the Field List icon, and select ProfitMargin.

16. Click the ProfitMargin column handle, and then, in the Properties window, in the Format text box, type **C2**.

17. Save and then preview the report, as shown here.

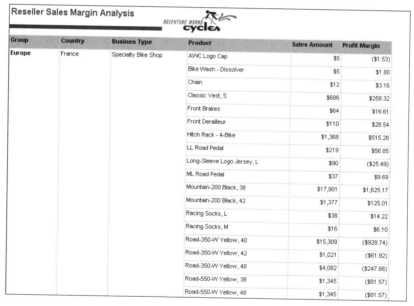

Group	Country	Busines Type	Product	Sales Amount	Profit Margin
Europe	France	Specialty Bike Shop	AWC Logo Cap	$5	($1.53)
			Bike Wash - Dissolver	$5	$1.80
			Chain	$12	$3.16
			Classic Vest, S	$686	$258.32
			Front Brakes	$64	$16.61
			Front Derailleur	$110	$28.54
			Hitch Rack - 4-Bike	$1,368	$515.28
			LL Road Pedal	$219	$56.85
			Long-Sleeve Logo Jersey, L	$90	($25.49)
			ML Road Pedal	$37	$9.69
			Mountain-200 Black, 38	$17,901	$1,625.17
			Mountain-200 Black, 42	$1,377	$125.01
			Racing Socks, L	$38	$14.22
			Racing Socks, M	$16	$6.10
			Road-350-W Yellow, 40	$15,309	($928.74)
			Road-350-W Yellow, 42	$1,021	($61.92)
			Road-350-W Yellow, 48	$4,082	($247.66)
			Road-550-W Yellow, 38	$1,345	($81.57)
			Road-550-W Yellow, 48	$1,345	($81.57)

Reseller Sales Margin Analysis

You could, of course, create a text box expression to calculate the profit margin. However, whenever you have complex calculations that you use multiple times in the report, it is easier to define the calculation once and refer to it as needed.

Creating a Text Box Expression

A tablix is comprised of text boxes, each of which displays either static text or an expression. Thus far, you have used expressions to display a field value or an aggregate of a field value. In the last procedure, you developed a calculated field that you can use in your report just like any other dataset field, as many times as needed. When you intend to use an expression only once in the report, you can instead create an expression for the text box.

In this procedure, you create a text box expression to display a calculation in a tablix.

Create a text box expression

1. Click the Design tab.

2. Click the tablix, right-click the Profit Margin column handle, point to Insert Column, and select Right to add a new column.

3. In the new column, in the detail row (to the right of *[ProfitMargin]*), right-click the text box, and click Expression.

4. In the Expression dialog box, type the following expression into the Set Expression For: Value box (or use the expression lists to build the expression):

   ```
   =Fields!ProfitMargin.Value/Fields!SalesAmount.Value
   ```

   Whether you create an expression for a calculated field, a text box, or any property that accepts an expression as a value, you use the same Expression dialog box.

5. Click OK to close the Expression dialog box.

   The tablix displays a placeholder for the expression. The only way to view the expression is to open the Expression dialog box.

6. In the header text box above the new expression, click twice to insert the cursor inside the text box, and type **Profit Margin Pct**.

7. Click the Profit Margin Pct column handle, and then, in the Properties window, in the Format text box, type **P2**.

   You use the formatting string P2 to apply a percentage format using two decimal places.

8. Save and then preview the report.

Using a Report Item Expression

Sometimes you need to use the result of a text box expression in the expression for another text box. For example, you might use the aggregated value of detail rows in a group in a different text box. As you know, the total that appears in a group header or footer uses the *Sum* function to calculate the text box value. As an alternative to using the same expression over and over, which can often be quite long, the *ReportItems* collection provides you with a pointer to the expression.

In this procedure, you add a text box using a report item expression to the tablix to display the percent contribution of a product to the business type group's sales.

Use a report item expression in a new text box

1. Click the Design tab.

2. In the tablix, click the text box in the row below the details row (just below the text box containing *[SalesAmount]*), and then, in the Properties window, in the Name text box, type **BusinessTypeTotal**.

   By replacing the generic text box name, you can identify the text box more easily when building a report item expression.

3. Click the tablix, right-click the Profit Margin Pct column handle, select Insert Column, and select Right to add a new column.

4. In the new column, in the detail row (to the right of *<<Expr>>*, right-click the text box, and select Expression.

5. In the Expression dialog box, type the following expression into the Set Expression For: Value box:

   ```
   =Fields!SalesAmount.Value/ReportItems!BusinessTypeTotal.Value
   ```

   You cannot use the expressions list in the Expression dialog box to construct an expression that uses the *ReportItems* collection, but the IntelliSense feature prompts you with a list of available items.

> **Note** In this example, you could also use an expression with the *Sum* function aggregating *SalesAmount* and using a *Scope* argument to limit the aggregation to a specific group within the data region. You can also use the *Scope* argument to apply the aggregation to an entire dataset or a data region.

6. Click OK to close the Expression dialog box.

7. In the header text box above the new expression, click twice to insert the cursor inside the text box, and type **Pct Contribution**.

8. Click the Pct Contribution column handle, and then, in the Properties window, in the Format text box, type **P2**.

9. Save and then preview the report, as shown here.

Reseller Sales Margin Analysis							
Group	**Country**	**Busines Type**	**Product**	**Sales Amount**	**Profit Margin**	**Profit Margin Pct**	**Pct Contribution**
Europe	France	Specialty Bike Shop	AWC Logo Cap	$5	($1.53)	-28.33 %	0.00 %
			Bike Wash - Dissolver	$5	$1.80	37.67 %	0.00 %
			Chain	$12	$3.16	26.00 %	0.01 %
			Classic Vest, S	$686	$258.32	37.67 %	0.57 %
			Front Brakes	$64	$16.61	26.00 %	0.05 %
			Front Derailleur	$110	$28.54	26.00 %	0.09 %
			Hitch Rack - 4-Bike	$1,368	$515.28	37.67 %	1.14 %
			LL Road Pedal	$219	$56.85	26.00 %	0.18 %
			Long-Sleeve Logo Jersey, L	$90	($25.49)	-28.33 %	0.07 %
			ML Road Pedal	$37	$9.69	26.00 %	0.03 %
			Mountain-200 Black, 38	$17,901	$1,625.17	9.08 %	14.89 %
			Mountain-200 Black, 42	$1,377	$125.01	9.08 %	1.15 %
			Racing Socks, L	$38	$14.22	37.67 %	0.03 %
			Racing Socks, M	$16	$6.10	37.67 %	0.01 %
			Road-350-W Yellow, 40	$15,309	($928.74)	-6.07 %	12.74 %
			Road-350-W Yellow, 42	$1,021	($61.92)	-6.07 %	0.85 %
			Road-350-W Yellow, 48	$4,082	($247.66)	-6.07 %	3.40 %
			Road-550-W Yellow, 38	$1,345	($81.57)	-6.07 %	1.12 %
			Road-550-W Yellow, 48	$1,345	($81.57)	-6.07 %	1.12 %

Although using the *ReportItems* collection can be a simple way to refer to a text box value within a data region, it is the only way to refer to a text box value in an expression that is external to the data region. You learn how to use a report item expression in an external expression later in this chapter.

Using Built-in Fields

In the Report Data window, the Built-in Fields folder contains eight fields that you can use to add an expression quickly to a text box when you want to display information that is specific to your report, such as the *Execution Time* or the *Report Server URL*. You can use a built-in field in any text box in your report, but you can use the built-in fields *Page Number* and *Total Pages* only in the report's page header or page footer. A simple expression for a built-in field includes an ampersand symbol (&) in front of the field name. To reference a built-in field in a more complex expression, you use the *Globals* collection.

Note Built-in fields were called global collections in previous versions of Reporting Services.

In this procedure, you add built-in fields to your report.

Use built-in fields

1. Click the Design tab.

2. In the Report Data window, expand the Built-in Fields folder, as shown here.

3. From the Report Data window, drag *Report Name* to the text box containing the report title, Reseller Sales Margin Analysis.

> **Tip** By using the *Report Name* built-in field instead of static text for a report title, you make your report design more flexible. For example, you can modify the report title visible in Report Manager (or a Microsoft SharePoint document library) after deploying the report to the report server, but a report title using static text would not reflect the modification. If you use the built-in field instead, the report title displaying in the report always matches the title displayed in Report Manager.

4. On the Report menu, select Add Page Footer.

5. From the Toolbox window, drag a text box into the page footer.

6. With the text box selected, in the Properties window, in the Location/Left text box, type **0in**, and then, in the Location/Top text box, type **0in**.

7. In the Properties window, in the Size/Width text box, type **2.5in**.

8. From the Report Data window, drag *Page Number* into the page footer text box.

9. Click in the text box twice at the end of the simple expression, *[&PageNumber]*, press the spacebar, and type **of [&TotalPages]**.

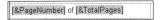

In addition to dragging a built-in field from the Report Data window, you can type the simple expression for a built-in field directly into the text box.

10. From the Report Data window, drag *Execution Time* into the page footer to the right of the page number text box.

You can drag a built-in field directly to the report design surface without first adding a text box.

11. With the text box selected, in the Properties window, in the Location/Left text box, type **4in**, in the Location/Top text box, type **0in**, and in the Size/Width text box, type **2in**.

12. Click anywhere inside the page footer, but outside the text boxes, and then, in the Properties window, in the Height text box, type **0.25in**.

13. Save and then preview the report. Scroll the bottom of the page, if necessary, to view the page footer.

Using Aggregate Functions

You use aggregate functions primarily to summarize many records of numerical data, such as giving a total or average value. You can also use aggregate functions to get the first or last string value in a group of records.

To work successfully with aggregate functions, you must first understand how the location of an expression in the report affects when it is evaluated. An expression in the report body has access to the dataset and therefore can reference an object directly in the *Fields* collection. However, an expression in the page header or page footer is evaluated after the report body is processed when the dataset is no longer available. Although you can no longer use the *Fields* collection, you can access the results of the report processing by referencing an object in the *ReportItems* collection.

Standard aggregate functions available in Reporting Services are shown in Table 5-1.

TABLE 5-1 Standard Aggregate Functions

Use This Aggregate Function	To Calculate
Aggregate	A custom aggregation of non-null values as defined by the data provider
Avg	The average of non-null numerical values in scope
Count	The count of values in scope
CountDistinct	The count of distinct values in scope
CountRows	The count of rows in scope
First	The first value in scope
Last	The last value in scope
Max	The highest value in scope
Min	The lowest value in scope
RunningValue	The current cumulative value of rows in scope
StDev	The standard deviation of non-null values in scope
StDevP	The population standard deviation of non-null values in scope
Sum	The sum of numerical values in scope
Var	The variance of non-null values in scope
VarP	The population variance of non-null values in scope

Using the *Scope* Argument

An aggregate function uses scope to determine which detail rows to include in the aggregation. If you omit the *Scope* argument when using an aggregate function, the scope is inferred by the location of the expression. If the expression appears in a text box in a group (or a property of that text box), then the scope is limited to the dataset rows associated with that group. If you want to use a scope other than the inferred scope, you must specify the scope explicitly in the aggregate function. To specify the scope, you provide the name of a dataset, data region, or group. Any reference to one of these objects must match the actual case used in the name, or the expression fails. You only know if the expression succeeds or fails due to a case mismatch if you attempt to preview the report because no warning displays in the Expression dialog box to alert you to the mistake.

In this procedure, you use the *Scope* argument to display the aggregated value of a dataset.

Use the *Scope* argument

1. In Solution Explorer, double-click Reseller Sales Cumulative Sales.

2. From the Toolbox window, drag a textbox control to the right of the image at the top of the report.

3. With the text box selected, in the Properties window, in the Location/Left text box, type **4.75in**, in the Location/Top box, type **0in**, and in the Size/Width text box, type **2in**.

4. In the Font/FontWeight drop-down list, select Bold.

5. Right-click the text box, and select Expression.

6. In the Expression dialog box, in the Category list, expand Common Functions, select Aggregate, and then select Sum, as shown here.

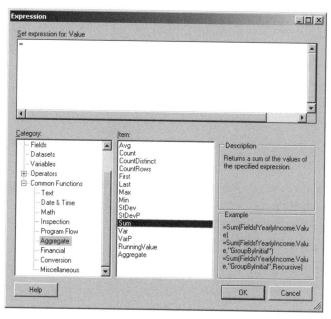

When you select a function in the Expression dialog box, a description and an example of the function both display to help you understand how to use the function.

7. Double-click the *Sum* function.

Whether you type a function or use the expressions list to add the function to the Set
Expression For: Value box, the IntelliSense feature displays syntax information in the
Set Expression For: Value box to help you properly construct the expression. When the
function has more than one possible syntax, you see a visual cue, such as "1 of 3." You
can click the arrow icons to review each syntax example.

8. Click the down arrow icon once to view the syntax for the *Sum* function that includes
the *Scope* argument, as shown here.

```
=Sum(
  ◄ 2 of 3 ►  Sum (Expression as Object, Scope as String) as Single
  Expression:
    The expression to aggregate.
```

The first argument of the *Sum* function requires an expression, such as a field item.
The second argument requires a string value that represents a scope, which can be the
name of a dataset, a data region, or a group.

 Important The scope name is case-sensitive. Be sure to use the exact name for the item
you use to define the scope.

9. Clear the text in the Set Expression For: Value box, and then type **=**.

10. In the Category list, select Datasets, and then, in the Values list, double-click
Sum(SalesAmount) to create the following expression:

```
=Sum(Fields!SalesAmount.Value, "ResellerSales")
```

Because this text box is not bound to a dataset, you cannot use the Fields category in
the Category list to select a specific field, nor can you use IntelliSense to prompt you
for the field item.

11. Click between the equal sign (=) and the *Sum* function, and type **"Total Sales: " &
CStr(FormatCurrency(**.

You can combine static text with an expression result by enclosing the static text in
double quotes and using an ampersand (&) as a concatenation operator. You must convert a numeric value to a string using the *CStr* function to concatenate it with a string.
In addition, you should use the *FormatCurrency* function to format the numeric value.

12. Click to position the cursor at the end of the expression, and type **,0))** to define
the number of decimal places for the *FormatCurrency* function and to add closing
parentheses to the *FormatCurrency* and *CStr* functions. The completed expression looks
like this:

```
="Total Sales: " & CStr(FormatCurrency(Sum(Fields!SalesAmount.Value,
"ResellerSales"),0))
```

> **Note** Because you are working with a freestanding text box that is not bound to a da-
> taset, IntelliSense detects an error related to *Fields!SalesAmount.Value*, but you can safely
> ignore the warning.

13. Click OK to close the Expression dialog box.

14. Save and then preview the report, as shown here.

Using an Aggregate Function in a Data Region

The main difference between using an aggregate function in a freestanding text box and using one in a data region is the *Scope* argument. Whereas this argument is required in a freestanding text box, you can omit the *Scope* argument in a data region if Reporting Services
can infer the scope correctly. An exception to this rule is the *RunningValue* function, which
not only requires you to specify scope but also requires you to specify an aggregate function
to use to accumulate values.

To better understand how you might use the *RunningValue* function, consider a request from
a business user to facilitate comparisons of product mixes across reseller business types.
More specifically, the business user wants to see which products contribute most to sales
for each reseller business type. To support this analysis, your report must show the products
grouped by reseller business type. You must calculate the cumulative sales for each product within the group and the cumulative percentage of total sales for the group. When the
products are sorted in descending order, the user can see easily which products collectively
contribute to a target percentage of sales, such as the top 20 percent of sales or the top 50
percent of sales.

In this procedure, you use the *RunningValue* function to compute the cumulative sales and
percentage of cumulative sales by product for each business type.

Use the *RunningValue* function in a tablix

1. Click the Design tab, click the tablix, right-click the Sales Amount column handle, select
Insert Column, and select Right to add a new column.

2. In the new column, in the detail row (to the right of *[SalesAmount]*), right-click the text
box, and select Expression.

3. In the Set Expression For: Value box, create the following expression:

```
=RunningValue(Fields!SalesAmount.Value, Sum, "BusinessType")
```

> **Important** Be careful to match the case exactly when specifying the *Scope* argument in an aggregate function. Note that you must enclose the scope name in double quotes. When using the *RunningValue* function, be sure to include the aggregate function without quotes.

4. Click OK to close the Expression dialog box.

5. In the Properties window, in the Name text box, type **CumulativeSales**.

6. In the header text box above the new expression, click twice to insert the cursor inside the text box, and then type **Cumulative Sales**.

7. Click the column handle of the new column, and then, in the Properties window, in the Format text box, type **C0**.

8. Right-click the Cumulative Sales column handle, select Insert Column, and select Right to add a new column.

9. In the new column, in the detail row (to the right of <<*Expr*>>), right-click the text box, and select Expression.

10. In the Expression dialog box, create the following expression:

    ```
    =ReportItems!CumulativeSales.Value/ReportItems!BusinessTypeTotal.Value
    ```

    This expression computes the percentage of sales for the cumulative sales value of the current record.

11. Click OK to close the Expression dialog box.

12. In the header text box above the new expression, click twice to insert the cursor inside the text box, and type **Cumulative Sales Pct**.

13. Click the Cumulative Sales Pct column handle, and then, in the Properties window, in the Format text box, type **P0**.

14. Save and then preview the report.

15. Click the Next Page button on the Preview toolbar to view the second page and confirm the cumulative sales value resets to 0 when the next business type instance begins, as shown here.

Group	Country	Busines Type	Product	Sales Amount	Cumulative Sales	Cumulative Sales Pct
Europe	France	Specialty Bike Shop	Touring-3000 Yellow, 44	$3,118	$111,727	93 %
			Touring-3000 Yellow, 50	$445	$112,172	93 %
			Touring-3000 Yellow, 62	$5,345	$117,517	98 %
			Water Bottle - 30 oz.	$45	$117,562	98 %
			Women's Mountain Shorts, L	$1,008	$118,570	99 %
			Women's Mountain Shorts, M	$420	$118,990	99 %
			Women's Mountain Shorts, S	$1,191	$120,181	100 %
			Business Type Total	*$120,181*		
		Value Added Reseller	AWC Logo Cap	$22	$22	0 %
			Bike Wash - Dissolver	$33	$55	0 %
			Chain	$121	$176	0 %
			Classic Vest, M	$229	$405	0 %
			Classic Vest, S	$267	$672	0 %
			Front Brakes	$831	$1,502	0 %
			Front Derailleur	$714	$2,216	1 %
			Half-Finger Gloves, M	$88	$2,304	1 %
			Half-Finger Gloves, S	$15	$2,319	1 %
			Hitch Rack - 4-Bike	$648	$2,967	1 %
			HL Bottom Bracket	$437	$3,404	1 %
			HL Crankset	$3,402	$6,806	2 %
			HL Mountain Frame - Black, 42	$2,429	$9,235	2 %

Currently, because the product data is not sorted, products are listed in the order that the records are returned from the database. When working with cumulative sales data, you can sort the data in descending order by sales amount to easily see which set of products represent a particular percentage of sales.

16. Click the Design tab, and then, in the Row Groups pane, right-click (Details), and click Group Properties.

17. In the Group Properties dialog box, click Sorting.

18. Click Add, and then, in the Sort By drop-down list, select [SalesAmount].

   Notice the Expression button to the right of the Sort By drop-down list. Instead of sorting by a field in the dataset, you can define an expression to sort data, which you learn to do in the next section of this chapter.

19. In the Order drop-down list, select Z To A to sort in descending order, and click OK.

20. Save and then preview the report, as shown here.

Group	Country	Busines Type	Product	Sales Amount	Cumulative Sales	Cumulative Sales Pct
Europe	France	Specialty Bike Shop	Mountain-200 Black, 38	$17,901	$17,901	15 %
			Touring-1000 Yellow, 46	$15,735	$33,636	28 %
			Road-350-W Yellow, 40	$15,309	$48,945	41 %
			Touring-1000 Yellow, 60	$14,304	$63,249	53 %
			Touring-1000 Blue, 46	$11,444	$74,693	62 %
			Touring-2000 Blue, 54	$5,831	$80,524	67 %
			Touring-1000 Blue, 60	$5,722	$86,246	72 %
			Touring-3000 Yellow, 62	$5,345	$91,591	76 %
			Road-350-W Yellow, 48	$4,082	$95,673	80 %
			Touring-3000 Yellow, 44	$3,118	$98,791	82 %
			Touring-2000 Blue, 60	$2,916	$101,707	85 %
			Touring-3000 Blue, 50	$2,672	$104,379	87 %
			Road-750 Black, 48	$2,268	$106,647	89 %
			Touring-3000 Blue, 54	$1,782	$108,429	90 %
			Mountain-200 Black, 42	$1,377	$109,806	91 %
			Hitch Rack - 4-Bike	$1,368	$111,174	93 %
			Road-550-W Yellow, 38	$1,345	$112,518	94 %
			Road-550-W Yellow, 48	$1,345	$113,863	95 %

Reseller Sales Cumulative Sales — ADVENTURE WORKS cycles — Total Sales: $16,038,063

In the report, you can now see that in specialty bike shops in France, four products represent more than 50 percent of all sales.

Changing Report Item Properties by Using Expressions

The power of Reporting Services lies in the ability to use expressions to control virtually every property of each report item. You can use expressions to set a fixed value for a property or to change a property's value dynamically according to conditions at report execution. These conditions can be determined by a value returned in the data, by a user selection, or by the result of a calculation.

Using an Expression to Sort Data

By default, rows in a data region display in the same order that records are returned in the dataset. For large data volumes, you get the best performance when you let the database engine sort records by adding an ORDER BY clause to the query string. You can override the default sort order in the report by configuring the sorting of rows in a group or data region.

In this procedure, you add an expression to sort detail rows using the percent contribution expression.

Use an expression to sort data

1. In Solution Explorer, double-click Reseller Sales Margin Analysis.rdl.

2. Click the Preview tab, if necessary.

Currently, the details in this report appear to sort in order by product name. To better locate products with a high contribution percentage, you can sort the details by the expression used to calculate the percentage.

3. Click the Design tab, and then, in the Row Groups pane, right-click Details, and select Group Properties.

4. In the Group Properties dialog box, click Sorting.

5. Click Add, and then, to the right of the Sort By drop-down list, click the Expression button.

6. In the Expression dialog box, create the following expression:

```
=Fields!SalesAmount.Value/Sum(Fields!SalesAmount.Value, "BusinessType")
```

Because the text box displaying the contribution percentage contains an expression that refers to a report item, you cannot use the same expression as a sort expression. Instead, you must use the *Sum* function with a *Scope* argument to calculate the correct denominator for the contribution percentage expression. In this case, the *Scope* argument refers to the *BusinessType* group.

7. In the Expression dialog box, click OK.

8. In the Order drop-down list, select Z To A to sort in descending order, and click OK.

9. Save and then preview the report, as shown here.

Reseller Sales Margin Analysis

Group	Country	Busines Type	Product	Sales Amount	Profit Margin	Profit Margin Pct	Pct Contribution
Europe	France	Specialty Bike Shop	Mountain-200 Black, 38	$17,901	$1,625.17	9.08 %	14.89 %
			Touring-1000 Yellow, 46	$15,735	($566.45)	-3.60 %	13.09 %
			Road-350-W Yellow, 40	$15,309	($928.74)	-6.07 %	12.74 %
			Touring-1000 Yellow, 60	$14,304	($514.96)	-3.60 %	11.90 %
			Touring-1000 Blue, 46	$11,444	($411.97)	-3.60 %	9.52 %
			Touring-2000 Blue, 54	$5,831	($209.93)	-3.60 %	4.85 %
			Touring-1000 Blue, 60	$5,722	($205.98)	-3.60 %	4.76 %
			Touring-3000 Yellow, 62	$5,345	($192.42)	-3.60 %	4.45 %
			Road-350-W Yellow, 48	$4,082	($247.66)	-6.07 %	3.40 %
			Touring-3000 Yellow, 44	$3,118	($112.24)	-3.60 %	2.59 %
			Touring-2000 Blue, 60	$2,916	($104.96)	-3.60 %	2.43 %
			Touring-3000 Blue, 50	$2,672	($96.21)	-3.60 %	2.22 %
			Road-750 Black, 48	$2,268	($137.59)	-6.07 %	1.89 %
			Touring-3000 Blue, 54	$1,782	($64.14)	-3.60 %	1.48 %
			Mountain-200 Black, 42	$1,377	$125.01	9.08 %	1.15 %
			Hitch Rack - 4-Bike	$1,368	$515.28	37.67 %	1.14 %
			Road-550-W Yellow, 38	$1,345	($81.57)	-6.07 %	1.12 %
			Road-550-W Yellow, 48	$1,345	($81.57)	-6.07 %	1.12 %
			Women's Mountain Shorts, S	$1,191	$432.17	36.28 %	0.99 %

You can now see the top contributors to sales in specialty bike shops in France in descending order and the percentage contribution to sales for each product. Notice that the top contributors to sales are the same products that you saw in the Reseller Sales Cumulative Sales report, but the individual product percentage contributions are listed in this report. If you add the contribution percentages for the first two products and round up, the result is 28 percent, which corresponds to the cumulative percentage for these products in the Reseller Sales Cumulative Sales report. Thus, you have two reports that present similar information in different ways to support different types of analysis.

Applying Conditional Formatting

By using *conditional formatting*, you can change most, but not all, format properties of a report item dynamically at run time based on specified conditions. For example, you can use an expression to set format properties affecting appearance, such as *BorderStyle*, *Color*, *FontFamily*, or *Padding*. Similarly, you can set format properties affecting behavior, such as *Hidden* (which you learn about in Chapter 6, "Adding Interactivity"), using an expression. However, you cannot use expressions to set properties that specify size or location.

> **Tip** You can determine whether a property supports conditional formatting by checking the property's drop-down list in the Properties window. If <Expression...> is available in the drop-down list, you can use the property to apply conditional formatting.

In this procedure, you use conditional formatting to change the font color in a text box based on its value.

Use conditional formatting to highlight values

1. Click the Design tab.

2. In the Pct Contribution column, click the text box containing *<<Expr>>*.

3. In the Properties window, in the Name text box, type **PctContribution**.

   Although you can't refer to a report item in a sort expression, you can use a report item expression for conditional formatting. Providing a name for the text box makes it easier to build a conditional formatting expression.

4. In the Properties window, in the Color drop-down list, select Expression....

5. In the Expression dialog box, delete the constant expression B1ack.

6. In the Category list, expand Common Functions, and select Program Flow.

   To create an expression for conditional formatting, you use one of the program flow functions: *Choose*, *Iif*, or *Switch*. These functions evaluate an expression to determine the value to return. The *Iif* function, the mostly commonly used function, uses the following syntax:

   ```
   =Iif(Expression as Boolean, TruePart as Object, FalsePart as Object)
   ```

   For the first argument, you provide an expression that returns either a *True* or *False* value. The second argument contains the value to return if the first argument is true, while the third argument contains the value to return if the first argument is false. The second and third arguments can be static text or an expression that evaluates to a string, numeric, or Boolean value.

7. In the Set Expression For: Value box, type an equal sign (=), and then, in the Item list, double-click Iif.

8. In the Set Expression For: Value box, complete the expression to look like this:

```
=Iif(ReportItems!PctContribution.Value > .1, "Green", "Black")
```

This expression changes the *Color* property to Green only when the contribution percentage value is greater than 10 percent.

9. Click OK, and then preview the report.

The first four rows in the report have a contribution percentage greater than 10 percent, helping you identify the rows exceeding the defined threshold.

Color might not always be the best way to highlight information in a report when some readers could be colorblind. In addition to using conditional formatting to change font color, you can use it to display a specific image. This technique is popular for reports displaying key performance indicators (KPIs).

10. Click the Design tab.

11. In the Report Data pane, right-click the Images folder, and click Add Image.

12. In the Open dialog box, navigate to the Microsoft Press\Rs2008sbs\Chap05 folder in your Documents folder.

13. In the Files Of Type drop-down list, select BMP Files, and double-click Green kpi.bmp.

Notice the names assigned to the images in the Images folder. You will refer to these image names later in this procedure.

14. Repeat the previous three steps to add the image file Red kpi.bmp to the report.

15. In the tablix, right-click the Pct Contribution column, select Insert Column, and select Right.

16. In the new column, click the text box to the right of the *<<Expr>>* placeholder in the Pct Contribution column.

17. In the Properties window, expand *BackgroundImage*, and then, in the Source drop-down list, select Embedded.

18. In the Value drop-down list, select <Expression...>.

19. In the Expression dialog box, construct the following expression:

```
=Switch(ReportItems!PctContribution.Value > .1, "greenkpi",
ReportItems!PctContribution.Value < .02, "redkpi")
```

To apply one formatting rule to a specific condition, and a second formatting rule to a different condition, you use the *Switch* function. In fact, you can add as many formatting rules as you like to the *Switch* function, which makes it very flexible. You add a pair of arguments to the function, with the first argument representing a Boolean expression and the second argument representing the value to return.

20. In the BackgroundRepeat drop-down list, select Clip.

> **Note** The Clip option prevents the image from repeating.

21. In the Pct Contribution column, click the text box containing *<<Expr>>*, and then, in the Properties window, in the Color drop-down list, select Expression....

22. Modify the expression so that it looks like this:

```
=Switch(ReportItems!PctContribution.Value > .1, "green",
ReportItems!PctContribution.Value < .02, "red")
```

Now the report uses font color and an image to identify values that are above and below the specified thresholds.

23. Save and then preview the report, as shown here.

Reseller Sales Margin Analysis							
Group	**Country**	**Busines Type**	**Product**	**Sales Amount**	**Profit Margin**	**Profit Margin Pct**	**Pct Contribution**
Europe	France	Specialty Bike Shop	Mountain-200 Black, 38	$17,901	$1,625.17	9.08 %	14.89 % ●
			Touring-1000 Yellow, 46	$15,735	($566.45)	-3.60 %	13.09 % ●
			Road-350-W Yellow, 40	$15,309	($928.74)	-6.07 %	12.74 % ●
			Touring-1000 Yellow, 60	$14,304	($514.96)	-3.60 %	11.90 % ●
			Touring-1000 Blue, 46	$11,444	($411.97)	-3.60 %	9.52 %
			Touring-2000 Blue, 54	$5,831	($209.93)	-3.60 %	4.85 %
			Touring-1000 Blue, 60	$5,722	($205.98)	-3.60 %	4.76 %
			Touring-3000 Yellow, 62	$5,345	($192.42)	-3.60 %	4.45 %
			Road-350-W Yellow, 48	$4,082	($247.66)	-6.07 %	3.40 %
			Touring-3000 Yellow, 44	$3,118	($112.24)	-3.60 %	2.59 %
			Touring-2000 Blue, 60	$2,916	($104.96)	-3.60 %	2.43 %
			Touring-3000 Blue, 50	$2,672	($96.21)	-3.60 %	2.22 %
			Road-750 Black, 48	$2,268	($137.59)	-6.07 %	1.89 % ◆
			Touring-3000 Blue, 54	$1,782	($64.14)	-3.60 %	1.48 % ◆
			Mountain-200 Black, 42	$1,377	$125.01	9.08 %	1.15 % ◆
			Hitch Rack - 4-Bike	$1,368	$515.28	37.67 %	1.14 % ◆
			Road-550-W Yellow, 38	$1,345	($81.57)	-6.07 %	1.12 % ◆
			Road-550-W Yellow, 48	$1,345	($81.57)	-6.07 %	1.12 % ◆
			Women's Mountain Shorts, S	$1,191	$432.17	36.28 %	0.99 % ◆

Working with Variables

As you learned earlier in this chapter, the location of an expression within a report affects when it is evaluated. In addition, the expression's location determines how many times it is evaluated. As you switch from page to page in a report, expressions on the requested page are evaluated when you open the page. You can manage the evaluation of expression-based values by using variables.

Variables are a new feature in Reporting Services 2008. You can store an explicit value in a variable, or use an expression that calculates a value at run time. You can scope a variable to a group or to the report. A group variable evaluates when the group instance changes, so it can potentially change even on the same page of a report. By contrast, a report variable evaluates only once and persists for the lifetime of the report.

Changing Expression Evaluation by Using a Group Variable

A group variable evaluates once for each distinct value defining a group. After you add a group variable to a group, you can reference it in an expression for any group or text box contained by the group for which the variable is defined.

In this procedure, you create a group variable to assign a different conditional formatting threshold to each sales territory group.

Create and use a group variable

1. Click the Design tab.

2. In the Row Groups pane, right-click SalesTerritoryGroup, and click Group Properties.

3. In the Group Properties dialog box, click Variables.

4. Click Add, and then in the Name text box, type **GroupThreshold**.

   Notice that you can create multiple group variables for the same group.

5. To the right of the Value text box, click the Expression button.

6. In the Expression dialog text box, create the following expression:

   ```
   =Switch(Fields!SalesTerritoryGroup.Value="Europe", .13,
   Fields!SalesTerritoryGroup.Value="North America", .15,
   Fields!SalesTerritoryGroup.Value="Pacific", .09)
   ```

   This expression assigns a value to the variable based on the current group instance. You use this variable value to assign a percentage to the *BackgroundImage/Value* property and thereby change the threshold that displays the green KPI image according to sales territory group.

7. In the Expression dialog box, click OK to return to the Group Properties dialog box, as shown here.

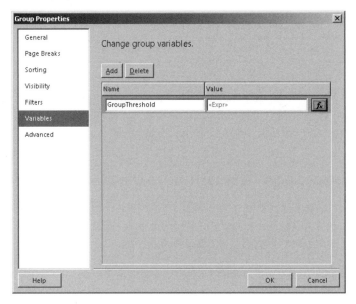

8. In the Group Properties dialog box, click OK.

9. In the last column in the tablix, click the text box to the right of the *<<Expr>>* place-holder in the Pct Contribution column, and then, in the Properties window, expand the *BackgroundImage* property.

10. In the Value drop-down list, click <Expression...>.

11. In the Expression dialog box, modify the expression to look like this:

```
=Switch(ReportItems!PctContribution.Value > Variables!GroupThreshold.Value,
"greenkpi",
ReportItems!PctContribution.Value < .02, "redkpi")
```

 Note IntelliSense displays an error for the *Variables!GroupThreshold.Value* property, but you can safely ignore it.

12. In the Expression dialog box, click OK.

13. Save and then preview the report, as shown here.

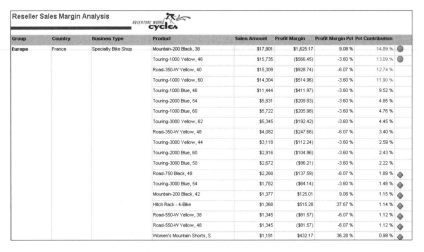

Group	Country	Busines Type	Product	Sales Amount	Profit Margin	Profit Margin Pct	Pct Contribution	
Europe	France	Specialty Bike Shop	Mountain-200 Black, 38	$17,901	$1,625.17	9.08 %	14.89 %	●
			Touring-1000 Yellow, 46	$15,735	($566.45)	-3.60 %	13.09 %	●
			Road-350-W Yellow, 40	$15,309	($928.74)	-6.07 %	12.74 %	
			Touring-1000 Yellow, 60	$14,304	($514.96)	-3.60 %	11.90 %	
			Touring-1000 Blue, 46	$11,444	($411.97)	-3.60 %	9.52 %	
			Touring-2000 Blue, 54	$5,831	($209.93)	-3.60 %	4.85 %	
			Touring-1000 Blue, 60	$5,722	($205.98)	-3.60 %	4.76 %	
			Touring-3000 Yellow, 62	$5,345	($192.42)	-3.60 %	4.45 %	
			Road-350-W Yellow, 48	$4,082	($247.66)	-6.07 %	3.40 %	
			Touring-3000 Yellow, 44	$3,118	($112.24)	-3.60 %	2.59 %	
			Touring-2000 Blue, 60	$2,916	($104.96)	-3.60 %	2.43 %	
			Touring-3000 Blue, 50	$2,672	($96.21)	-3.60 %	2.22 %	
			Road-750 Black, 48	$2,268	($137.59)	-6.07 %	1.89 %	◆
			Touring-3000 Blue, 54	$1,782	($64.14)	-3.60 %	1.48 %	◆
			Mountain-200 Black, 42	$1,377	$125.01	9.08 %	1.15 %	◆
			Hitch Rack - 4-Bike	$1,368	$515.28	37.67 %	1.14 %	◆
			Road-550-W Yellow, 38	$1,345	($81.57)	-6.07 %	1.12 %	◆
			Road-550-W Yellow, 48	$1,345	($81.57)	-6.07 %	1.12 %	◆
			Women's Mountain Shorts, S	$1,191	$432.17	36.28 %	0.99 %	◆

Notice that the circle KPI image (which displays in green on your computer display) now appears only for the two rows above 13 percent that apply to the Europe sales territory group.

14. In the Find box on the Preview toolbar, type **pacific**, and click Find.

Now the green KPI image appears for all values above 9 percent, reflecting the lower threshold assigned by the group variable. To finish this report, you could adjust the expression in the PctContribution *Color* property to use the same threshold value.

Maintaining Consistency by Using a Report Variable

Because a report variable evaluates only once during report processing, it is especially useful in expressions closely linked to time, such as currency rates or time stamps. As you page through a report, you get consistent results in these types of calculations only if the expression calculating time is stored in a report variable.

In this procedure, you compare the use of the *Now* function as a text box expression and as a report variable expression.

Use the *Now()* function in a report variable

1. Click the Design tab.

2. Click inside the text box containing *[&ExecutionTime]*, delete the expression, and type **=Now()**.

3. From the Toolbox window, drag a text box to the page footer to the right of the text box containing *<<Expr>>*.

4. On the Report menu, click Report Properties.

5. In the Report Properties dialog box, click Variables, and click Add.

6. In the Name text box, type **TestNowFunction**.

7. In the Value text box, type **=Now(),** as shown here.

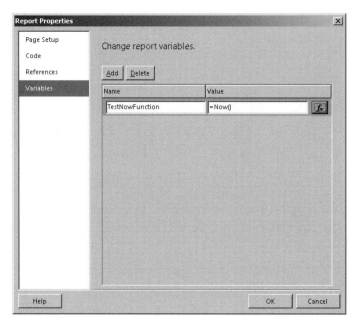

Click OK to close the Report Properties dialog box.

8. Right-click the empty text box in the page footer, and select Expression.

9. In the Expression dialog box, in the Category list, select Variables, and then, in the Values list, double-click TestNowFunction to construct the following expression:

```
=Variables!TestNowFunction.Value
```

10. In the Expression dialog box, click OK.

11. Save and then preview the report.

12. Scroll to the bottom of the page to view the date and time values in the text boxes in the page footer.

    The first date and time value you see is calculated when the page renders. The second date and time value is calculated when the report begins execution.

13. On the Preview toolbar, click the Next Page button, and scroll to the bottom of the page to compare the date and time values.

    Not only is the first date and time value different from the second date and time value on this page, but it is also different from the value calculated for *Now* on the first page due to the time elapsed between the time you executed the report and the time you paged forward. If you were to return to the first page, you would find the first date and time value has changed yet again, while the text box containing the report variable remains consistent as you page forward or backward.

Using Expressions for Dynamic Connections and Datasets

The data that displays in your reports will change, of course, as data is inserted into or deleted from your source database. But what if you need to change the actual source of the data at run time, or even the query string that executes to retrieve the data? All the reports in your project currently use a static data source and static datasets. The data source and the datasets remain the same no matter how many times you run each report and no matter who runs the report. You can use expressions to evaluate the connection string or the query string before processing the data for the report.

Creating a Dynamic Connection String

To use a dynamic connection string, you must use an embedded data source rather than a shared data source. Typically, you use a reference to the *Parameters* collection to get a value retrieved from a dataset, specified by a user, or evaluated from an expression and incorporate this reference into a concatenation of static text and parameter references that resolves as a valid connection string.

> **Note** If your goal is simply to switch the server name from a development server to a production server, you would typically leave the data source connection string configured using a hardcoded value, and then override this value by editing the data source object on the production server. You learn more about working with data sources on the report server in Chapter 10, "Deploying Reports to a Server."

In this procedure, you use a report parameter to store a server name, and then use the report parameter value to generate a dynamic connection string for the AdventureWorksDW2008 data source.

Create a dynamic connection string

1. Click the Design tab.

2. In the Report Data window, right-click the Parameters folder, and select Add Parameter.

3. In the Report Parameter Properties dialog box, in the Name text box, type **ServerName**.

> **Note** When you refer to an item in the *Parameters* collection, you use this name. A parameter name cannot contain spaces, and must start with a letter.

4. In the Prompt text box, type **Server Name**.

   The value in this text box displays to the user when viewing the report online, unless you choose to hide the parameter by selecting the *Hidden* value for parameter visibility.

For example, you could build a table that maps user accounts from Active Directory directory service to specific servers (or from Active Directory Domain Services if you're using Windows Server 2008). You could store the result of retrieving the server name from the table in a report parameter, but hide the parameter value so that the server name could not be changed on demand by the user.

5. Click Default Values, select Specify Values, and then click Add.

6. In the Value text box, type **localhost**, and click OK.

> **Note** In this scenario, you are using a report parameter to store a static server name to keep the procedure simple because it is assumed you're working only with one server as you step through these procedures. However, you could develop an expression that uses a conditional expression to assign a server name dynamically or use a table lookup to assign the server name to the report parameter. Regardless of how you provide a value for the report parameter, you use it to build a dynamic connection string for the data source. You learn about report parameters in more detail in Chapter 6.

7. In the Report Data window, right-click AdventureWorksDW2008, and select Data Source Properties.

8. In the Data Source Properties dialog box, select Embedded Connection.

9. In the Type drop-down list, select Microsoft SQL Server.

10. Click the Expression button to the right of the Connection String text box.

11. In the Expression dialog box, construct the following expression:

```
="Data Source=" + Parameters!ServerName.Value + ";Initial
Catalog=AdventureWorksDW2008"
```

You can replace any argument value in a connection string with a parameter item to create an expression that generates the applicable connection string when the report executes.

> **Important** Before you define an expression for the data source connection string, you should run your report with the static connection string to ensure that you have a valid connection string at the start and you have connectivity to the source server and database.

12. In the Expression dialog box, click OK.

13. In the Data Source Properties dialog box, click Credentials, select Use Windows Authentication (Integrated Security), and then click OK.

14. Save and then preview the report.

If the report displays, then you know that the connection string for the data source was generated correctly. Notice the report parameter at the top of the page above the Preview toolbar. You can type a new value in this box to generate a different connection string.

15. In the Server Name text box, type **localhost**, as shown here, and click View Report.

Again, if the report displays, the expression to build the connection string is correct. If you have access to the AdventureWorksDW2008 database on another server, you could type the server name in the Server Name box as another test of the connection string.

Creating a Dynamic Dataset

The use of query parameters, as you learn in Chapter 6, allows you to filter query results dynamically, but what if you need to modify the query itself dynamically? The ability to create a query dynamically provides enormous flexibility. However, with flexibility comes responsibility. You must take care that the structure of the result set is the same regardless of which version of the dynamic query executes. That is, the number of columns, the column names, and the column data types must match each and every time the query executes.

In previous editions of Reporting Services, the only way to accomplish this objective was to create a stored procedure to which the report would pass parameter values that would affect construction of the query string. However, there are situations in which you as a report developer require access to a data source, but you have no ability to add a stored procedure to the source database. Creation of a dynamic dataset in the report itself allows you to define the right query without requiring a change in the database.

In this procedure, you create a report parameter that you use to generate a dataset dynamically.

Create a dynamic dataset

1. Click the Design tab.
2. In the Report Data window, right-click the Parameters folder, and click Add Parameter.
3. In the Report Parameter Properties dialog box, in the Name text box, type **CostBasis**.
4. In the Prompt text box, type **Cost Basis**.
5. Click Default Values, select Specify Values, and then click Add.
6. In the Value text box, type **Total**, and click OK.
7. In the Report Data window, right-click ResellerSales, and select Dataset Properties.

8. In the Dataset Properties dialog box, click the Expression button to the right of the Query text box.

9. In the Expression dialog box, delete the current expression.

10. Click Start, and click Explore to open Windows Explorer.

11. Navigate to the Microsoft Press\Rs2008sbs\Chap05 folder in your Documents folder, and double-click DynamicDataset.txt.

The query to copy looks like this:

```
="SELECT st.SalesTerritoryGroup, st.SalesTerritoryCountry, r.BusinessType,
d.CalendarYear, p.EnglishProductName, SUM(s.SalesAmount) AS SalesAmount, " +
Switch(Parameters!CostBasis.Value="Total", "SUM(s.TotalProductCost)",
Parameters!CostBasis.Value="Standard", "SUM(s.ProductStandardCost)") + " AS
TotalProductCost FROM FactResellerSales AS s INNER JOIN DimReseller AS r ON
r.ResellerKey
= s.ResellerKey INNER JOIN  DimDate AS d ON d.DateKey = s.OrderDateKey INNER JOIN
DimSalesTerritory AS st ON st.SalesTerritoryKey = s.SalesTerritoryKey INNER JOIN
DimProduct AS p ON p.ProductKey = s.ProductKey WHERE  (d.CalendarYear = '2004') GROUP BY
st.SalesTerritoryGroup, st.SalesTerritoryCountry, r.BusinessType, d.CalendarYear,
p.EnglishProductName ORDER BY st.SalesTerritoryGroup, st.SalesTerritoryCountry,
r.BusinessType"
```

This query is the same as the query that you deleted from the Set Expression For: Value box, except that it has been converted to a string expression by placing an equal sign at the beginning of the expression and enclosing the string with double quotes.

In addition, to replace the single column Sum(s.TotalProductCost), the *Switch* function (highlighted in bold) returns the string to sum a numeric column based on the current value of the *CostBasis* report parameter:

```
Switch(Parameters!CostBasis.Value="Total", "SUM(s.TotalProductCost)",
Parameters!CostBasis.Value="Standard", "SUM(s.ProductStandardCost)")
```

12. Click in Notepad, press CTRL+A to select the entire expression, press CTRL+C to copy the expression to the Clipboard, press ALT+TAB until you switch back to the Expression dialog box, press CTRL+V to paste the clipboard contents into the Set Expression For: Value box, and then click OK.

13. In the Dataset Properties dialog box, click OK.

14. In the message box explaining you can no longer update the field list, shown here, click OK.

 Important You should wait until you have finished your report design before you replace the static query string with an expression because the field list will not update and you cannot access the Query Designer for the dataset. If the field list is not current, you cannot add fields to a data region.

15. Save and then preview the report.

If the report displays, then the dynamic query string is correct. Take note of the current values in the Profit Margin for comparison in the next step.

16. In the Cost Basis text box, type **Standard**, and click View Report.

The profit margin now uses the ProductStandardCost column in its calculation and changes considerably for many products in this report.

 Note Another way to achieve the same result is to adjust the dataset query string to return both *TotalProductCost* and *ProductStandardCost,* and then use a conditional expression in the *ProfitMargin* calculated field to use the applicable column.

Developing Expressions for Hierarchical Data

Hierarchical data comes from a table with a self-referencing join, which is sometimes referred to as a parent-child table. You can recognize a table of hierarchical data by the presence of a foreign key column with a relationship to a primary key column in the same table. This type of data structure is useful when multiple levels of data exist, such as you might find in an organizational chart of employees, but a different number of levels exist in each branch from the top of the hierarchy.

Reporting Services allows you to create a group to organize rows into hierarchical levels as defined by the foreign key relationships. A special function is available to show the level of a row within the hierarchy, which can be useful for applying formatting.

Creating a Recursive Hierarchy Group

Unlike the groups you created in the previous chapter for which group properties are maintained separately from the details row, a recursive hierarchy group is defined by changing the detail row's group properties. You define the initial grouping of the hierarchy based on the primary key column, and then you define the foreign key column as the recursive parent. No separate grouping for the recursive hierarchy group appears in the Row Groups pane.

In this procedure, you create a recursive hierarchy group in a tablix.

Create a recursive hierarchy group

1. In Solution Explorer, double-click Employee Organization.rdl.

2. Click the tablix to select it, and then, in the Row Groups pane, right-click (Details), and click Group Properties.

3. In the Group Properties dialog box, click Add.

4. In the Group On drop-down list, select [EmployeeKey].

    For a recursive hierarchy group, you create a group using the field containing a unique value for each row in the group, such as a primary key column like EmployeeKey.

5. Click Advanced, and then, in the Recursive Parent drop-down list, select [ParentEmployeeKey], as shown here.

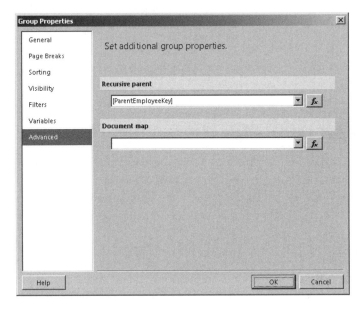

By specifying a recursive parent, the detail records are arranged by ParentEmployeeKey in your report.

6. In the Group Properties dialog box, click OK.

7. Save and then preview the report, as shown here.

Employee Name	Title	
Sánchez, Ken	Chief Executive Officer	
Bradley, David	Marketing Manager	
Brown, Kevin	Marketing Assistant	
Harnpadoungsataya, Sariya	Marketing Specialist	
Gibson, Mary	Marketing Specialist	
Williams, Jill	Marketing Specialist	
Eminhizer, Terry	Marketing Specialist	
Benshoof, Wanida	Marketing Assistant	
Wood, John	Marketing Specialist	
Dempsey, Mary	Marketing Assistant	
Bradley, David	Marketing Manager	
Duffy, Terri	Vice President of Engineering	
Tamburello, Roberto	Engineering Manager	
Walters, Rob	Senior Tool Designer	
Walters, Rob	Senior Tool Designer	
Erickson, Gail	Design Engineer	
Goldberg, Jossef	Design Engineer	
Miller, Dylan	Research and Development Manager	
Margheim, Diane	Research and Development Engineer	

Although the data is grouped by manager, you cannot see the difference between the detail rows for subordinate employees and the group header row for the manager. You can use conditional formatting to distinguish detail rows from group header rows.

Identifying a Level in a Recursive Hierarchy

The *Level* function returns a numerical value to specify the number of levels between the top of the hierarchy and the row for which the expression is being evaluated. You can include a *Scope* argument to limit the function to evaluating within a group, data region, or dataset. If you omit the argument, then the function assigns a value of *0* to the top of the hierarchy, and then increments this value by 1 for each level within the hierarchy to the reach the evaluating row. Typically, you use this function to apply different formatting styles to different levels of a hierarchy.

In this procedure, you apply conditional formatting based on the level of a record in a recursive hierarchy.

Use the *Level* function

1. Click the Design tab, and then, in the tablix, click the text box containing *[EmployeeName]*.

2. In the Properties window, expand the *Padding* property, and in the Left drop-down list, select <Expression...>.

3. In the Expression dialog box, construct the following expression:

   ```
   =CStr(2 + Level()*10) + "pt"
   ```

4. In the Expression dialog box, click OK.

5. In the Properties window, expand the *Font* property, and in the FontWeight drop-down list, select <Expression...>.

6. In the Expression dialog box, construct the following expression:

   ```
   =Iif(Level() < 2, "Bold","Normal")
   ```

   This expression displays all employees with a level below 2 using a bold font. As a result, the names of the chief executive officer and all employees reporting directly to the chief executive officer are bold.

7. In the Expression dialog box, click OK.

8. In the Row Groups pane, right-click (Details), click Group Properties, click Sorting, and click Add.

9. In the Sort By drop-down list, select [EmployeeName], and click OK.

   The sort of employee names applies only within a group. That is, the employees are grouped first by manager, and then alphabetically within their respective groups.

10. Save and then preview the report, as shown here.

Employee Name	Title	
Sánchez, Ken	Chief Executive Officer	
Bradley, David	Marketing Manager	
Benshoof, Wanida	Marketing Assistant	
Brown, Kevin	Marketing Assistant	
Dempsey, Mary	Marketing Assistant	
Eminhizer, Terry	Marketing Specialist	
Gibson, Mary	Marketing Specialist	
Harnpadoungsataya, Sariya	Marketing Specialist	
Williams, Jill	Marketing Specialist	
Wood, John	Marketing Specialist	
Bradley, David	Marketing Manager	
Duffy, Terri	Vice President of Engineering	
Tamburello, Roberto	Engineering Manager	
Cracium, Ovidiu	Senior Tool Designer	
D'Hers, Thierry	Tool Designer	
Galvin, Janice	Tool Designer	
Erickson, Gail	Design Engineer	
Goldberg, Jossef	Design Engineer	
Miller, Dylan	Research and Development Manager	

Employee Organization — ADVENTURE WORKS cycles

Using a Recursive Aggregate Function

Because hierarchical data is structured into a recursive grouping, the process of aggregating values within the grouping works differs from standard aggregation calculations. You can use the same aggregate functions, but to account for the difference in data structure, you include the *Recursive* keyword as a third argument in the aggregate function.

In this procedure, you create an expression to count records in a recursive hierarchy.

Count records in a recursive hierarchy

1. Click the Design tab, and then, in the third column, right-click the text box in the detail row to the right of *[Title]*, and select Expression.

2. In the Expression dialog box, construct the following expression:

   ```
   =Count(Fields!EmployeeKey.Value, "Details", Recursive) - 1
   ```

   When you use the *Recursive* keyword with an aggregate function, such as the *Count* function shown here, the aggregation applies to the scope of the specified group. In this example, the scope is the Details row group, which includes each instance of a manager record plus the number of employee records associated with that manager. To get the right count of employees for a manager, you must subtract 1 from the result returned by the *Count* function.

3. In the Expression dialog box, click OK.

4. In the header row above *<<Expr>>*, type **Employee Count**, and widen the column by dragging the edge of the column handle to the right until the static text displays on one line.

5. Save and then preview the report, as shown here.

Employee Name	Title	Employee Count
Sánchez, Ken	Chief Executive Officer	295
Bradley, David	Marketing Manager	8
Benshoof, Wanida	Marketing Assistant	0
Brown, Kevin	Marketing Assistant	0
Dempsey, Mary	Marketing Assistant	0
Eminhizer, Terry	Marketing Specialist	0
Gibson, Mary	Marketing Specialist	0
Harnpadoungsataya, Sariya	Marketing Specialist	0
Williams, Jill	Marketing Specialist	0
Wood, John	Marketing Specialist	0
Bradley, David	Marketing Manager	0
Duffy, Terri	Vice President of Engineering	14
Tamburello, Roberto	Engineering Manager	13
Cracium, Ovidiu	Senior Tool Designer	2
D'Hers, Thierry	Tool Designer	0
Galvin, Janice	Tool Designer	0
Erickson, Gail	Design Engineer	0
Goldberg, Jossef	Design Engineer	0
Miller, Dylan	Research and Development Manager	3

Employee Organization — ADVENTURE WORKS cycles

Expressions are the key to informative, flexible, and dynamic reports. By using expressions, you can enhance the data retrieved from the data source and modify the appearance and behavior of data in your report. In Chapter 6, you continue to work with expressions and report items properties to add interactive features to your report.

Chapter 5 Quick Reference

To	Do This
Add a calculated field to a dataset	In the Report Data pane, right-click the dataset, click Add Calculated Field, type a name in the Field Name text box in the bottom row, click the Expression button, and construct an expression for the calculated field by typing the expression or using the expression lists.
Create a text box expression	Right-click a text box, click Expression, and construct an expression.
Refer to the value in another text box	Assign a name to the text box (if you want), and then create an expression using the *ReportItems* collection. For example, to return the value of the BusinessTypeTotal text box, use this expression: `=ReportItems!BusinessTypeTotal.Value`
Add global report information to the report, such as a report title or page number	From the Toolbox window, expand the Built-in Fields folder, and drag an item, such as *Report Name* or *Page Number* to the design surface.
Use a simple expression	For a dataset field, enclose the field name in brackets like this: `[SalesAmount]`, *or* For a built-in field, enclose the field name in brackets and precede the field name with an ampersand, like this: `[&PageNumber]`
Use an aggregate function	Construct an expression for the function by defining the function, expression to aggregate, and optional scope, like this: `Sum(Fields!SalesAmount.Value, "ResellerSales")`
Sort data using an expression	In the Row Groups pane, right-click the group to sort, select Group Properties, Sorting, Add, click the Expression button, and construct an expression on which to base the sort. In the Group Properties dialog box, in the Order drop-down list, select A To Z for an ascending sort and Z To A for a descending sort.
Apply conditional formatting	Select a report item on the design surface, and then, in the Properties window, in the drop-down list for a formatting property (such as *Color* or *BackgroundImage/Value*), select <Expression...>, and create an expression using a program flow function: *Choose, Iif,* or *Switch*.
Create a group variable	In the Row Groups pane, right-click a group, select Group Properties, Variables, Add, type a name for the group variable, click the Expression button, and create an expression to provide a value for the group variable.

To	Do This
Create a report variable	On the Report menu, select Report Properties, Variables, Add, type a name for the report variable, click the Expression button, and create an expression to provide a value for the report variable.
Use a group variable or report variable in an expression	Use the following syntax: *Variables!VariableName.Value* where *VariableName* is the name of the group variable or report variable.
Create a simple report parameter and assign a default value	In the Report Data window, right-click the Parameters folder, select Add Parameter, type a name for the report parameter, and type a prompt string; select Default Values, Specify Values, Add, and type a value.

Create a dynamic connection string	In the Report Data window, right-click a data source, select Data Source Properties, Embedded Connections, select a connection type in the Type drop-down list, click the Expression button, and construct an expression to concatenate static text and a report parameter, similar to this:
	
	`="Data Source=" +`
	`Parameters!ServerName.Value + ";Initial`
	`Catalog=AdventureWorksDW2008"`

Create a dynamic dataset	In the Report Data window, right-click a dataset, select Dataset Properties, click the Expression button, and construct an expression to concatenate static text and a report parameter, similar to this:
	
	`="select col1, col2," +`
	`Parameters!ColumnName.Value + "from`
	`table1"`

Create a recursive hierarchy group	In the Row Groups pane, right-click (Details), select Group Properties, Add, select the primary key field in the Group On drop-down list, click Advanced, and select the parent key in the Recursive Parent drop-down list.
Identify a level in a recursive hierarchy	Use the *Level* function in an expression, like this: =Level()

Aggregate values in a recursive hierarchy group	Specify the name of the recursive group and add the *Recursive* keyword to an aggregate function, like this:
	
	`=Count(Fields!EmployeeKey.Value,`
	`"Details", Recursive)`

Chapter 6
Adding Interactivity

After completing this chapter, you will be able to:

- Implement interactive report layout features such as interactive sorting and floating headers.

- Toggle the visibility of one or more text boxes.

- Use a report parameter as a filter for report content or as a query parameter.

- Add navigation features to a report to move to a different page within the same report or to access information in a different location.

In Chapter 4, "Designing Reports," and Chapter 5, "Developing Expressions," you learned how to structure report content by using data regions, how to change the appearance and behavior of report content by using properties, and how to add calculations and change properties dynamically by using expressions. If users access and view reports online most of the time, you should consider adding interactive features to make it easier for them to use your reports. For example, you can allow the user to change the sort order of data, hide or show selected data, or filter data to show only a selected subset of data in the report. You can also use navigation aids to help the user easily move to information located in the same report or to access information contained in a related report or Web page. In this chapter, you explore a variety of techniques for enhancing the interactive report experience.

Changing the Report Layout Interactively

When you design a report that contains many detail rows of data, spend some time thinking about how users might want to interact with the report. Although you define a specific sort order for report data based on an established specification, you will invariably find that some users want to view the data using a different sort order. Also, when the dataset contains several columns and a large number of rows, the column headers could move out of view as the user scrolls down the page. Finally, some users will want to see all the detail data, while other users might prefer to see only a summary of the detail data. In this section, you learn how to use the interactive features included in Reporting Services to address these particular issues.

Implementing Interactive Sorting

You can give the user direct control over the sort order of report data by implementing the interactive sort feature on any text box that you want the user to click to change sort order.

Usually, the text box for which you enable this feature is a column header or row header in a data region. As an example, when you have many numeric columns, you can configure each column header to use interactive sort, and the user can sort one column at a time or create a more complex sort by selecting multiple columns to sort.

In this procedure, you configure interactive sort on column header text boxes.

Enable interactive sort options

1. Click Start, select All Programs, Microsoft SQL Server 2008, and then click SQL Server Business Intelligence Development Studio.

2. On the File menu, point to Open, and click Project/Solution.

3. In the Open Project dialog box, navigate to the Microsoft Press\Rs2008sbs\Chap06 folder in your Documents folder, and double-click Sales.sln.

4. In Solution Explorer, double-click Reseller Sales Margin Analysis Interactive.rdl.

5. Right-click the text box in the second column of the table header row containing the constant value *Sales Amount,* and select Text Box Properties.

6. Click Interactive Sort.

7. Select the Enable Interactive Sort On This Text Box check box.

8. Keep the default selection of Details Rows, and then, in the Sort By drop-down list, select [SalesAmount], as shown here.

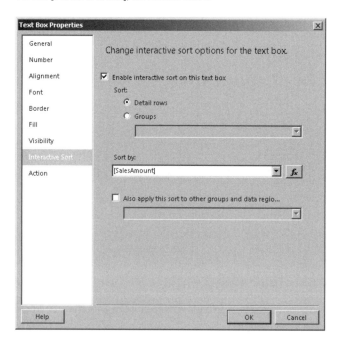

Instead of sorting by a dataset file, such as Sales Amount in this example, you can also sort by an expression. Notice also, you can select a check box to apply the sort to other groups within the same data region or to a completely different data region. In this way, you can keep sorting consistent across the report, rather than limiting the sort to the current data region.

When you sort by detail rows, as you do in this procedure, the detail rows within each group are sorted in ascending or descending order independently of other groups. Instead, you can choose to sort by group. For example, if you sort by the *[BusinessType]* group, the group total is used to determine which business type group instance appears first in the report, which instance appears second, and so on. The detail rows would continue to sort in the order in which the rows are returned in the query.

9. Click OK.

10. Repeat the previous five steps to enable interactive sort on the remaining numeric columns: Profit Margin, Profit Margin Pct, and Pct Contribution. Instead of selecting a value in the Sort By drop-down list, click the Expression button and provide the applicable expression. Use Table 6-1 to determine the value for the sort expression.

TABLE 6-1 **Configure the Sort Expression**

For This Column	Use This Expression
Profit Margin	[ProfitMargin]
Profit Margin Pct	=Fields!ProfitMargin.Value/Fields!SalesAmount.Value
Pct Contribution	=Fields!SalesAmount.Value/sum(Fields!SalesAmount.Value, "BusinessType")

Note These expressions represent the same values that display in the respective columns. You cannot use report item references, such as ReportItems!BusinessTypeTotal.Value, in a sort expression.

11. Click the column handle above the Pct Contribution text box to select the entire column, and in the Properties window, in the Size/Width box, type **1.1in**.

Tip Enabling interactive sort adds an icon to the selected text box and can force the text in the text box to wrap to a new line. Consequently, you might need to adjust the width of a text box after enabling interactive sort.

12. Save and preview the report.

Notice the double arrow icon that appears next to the numeric column labels in the header row. This icon indicates that the user can use interactive sort on each of these four columns.

13. In the Sales Amount text box, click the icon once. The arrow points upward, indicating that the detail rows now display in ascending numeric order.

14. Click the icon again. The arrow points downward, and the detail rows now display in descending numeric order.

15. In the Profit Margin Pct text box, click the icon. Notice that the first four rows all have the same profit margin percentage (-28.33%), and that this column displays in ascending numeric order.

16. While pressing the Shift key, in the Sales Amount text box, click the icon twice. Pressing the Shift key preserves any existing sorts, and clicking the icon twice changes the sort to a descending sort order. Your report now displays detail rows in ascending order of profit margin percentage, and then in descending order of sales amount, as shown here.

Reseller Sales Margin Analysis Interactive						ADVENTURE WORKS cyclea
Product	**Sales Amount**	**Profit Margin**	**Profit Margin Pct**	**Pct Contribution**		
Europe					◆	
France					◆	
Specialty Bike Shop					◆	
Short-Sleeve Classic Jersey, XL	$680	($192.74)	-28.33 %	0.57 %	◆	
Short-Sleeve Classic Jersey, L	$227	($64.25)	-28.33 %	0.19 %	◆	
Long-Sleeve Logo Jersey, L	$90	($25.49)	-28.33 %	0.07 %	◆	
AWC Logo Cap	$5	($1.53)	-28.33 %	0.00 %	◆	
Road-350-W Yellow, 40	$15,309	($928.74)	-6.07 %	12.74 %		
Road-350-W Yellow, 48	$4,082	($247.66)	-6.07 %	3.40 %		
Road-350-W Yellow, 42	$1,021	($61.92)	-6.07 %	0.85 %	◆	
Road-550-W Yellow, 38	$1,345	($81.57)	-6.07 %	1.12 %	◆	
Road-550-W Yellow, 48	$1,345	($81.57)	-6.07 %	1.12 %	◆	
Road-750 Black, 48	$2,268	($137.59)	-6.07 %	1.89 %	◆	
Touring-3000 Yellow, 62	$5,345	($192.42)	-3.60 %	4.45 %		
Touring-3000 Yellow, 44	$3,118	($112.24)	-3.60 %	2.59 %		
Touring-3000 Blue, 50	$2,672	($96.21)	-3.60 %	2.22 %		

Adding Fixed Headers

When a full page of data in your report is larger than the vertical size of your screen, you must scroll to view the data near the bottom of the page. As a result, the column headers might scroll off the screen. You can pin the column headers into position at the top of the screen so that they remain visible as the user scrolls the page.

In this procedure, you set the *FixedData* property to prevent the tablix header columns from scrolling out of view.

Adding a fixed column header

1. Click the Design tab.

2. In the Grouping pane, display the Column Groups shortcut menu by clicking the arrow that appears to the right of the Column Groups label, and click Advanced Mode.

3. In the Row Groups section, click the first *Static* group (displayed above SalesTerritoryGroup), and then, in the Properties window, in the FixedData drop-down list, select True.

4. Save and preview the report.

5. Scroll to the bottom of the page and notice that the column headers remain visible, as shown here.

Product	Sales Amount	Profit Margin	Profit Margin Pct	Pct Contribution	
Touring-2000 Blue, 60	$2,916	($104.96)	-3.60 %	2.43 %	
Touring-3000 Blue, 50	$2,672	($96.21)	-3.60 %	2.22 %	
Road-750 Black, 48	$2,268	($137.59)	-6.07 %	1.89 %	◆
Touring-3000 Blue, 54	$1,782	($64.14)	-3.60 %	1.48 %	◆
Mountain-200 Black, 42	$1,377	$125.01	9.08 %	1.15 %	◆
Hitch Rack - 4-Bike	$1,368	$515.28	37.67 %	1.14 %	◆
Road-550-W Yellow, 38	$1,345	($81.57)	-6.07 %	1.12 %	◆
Road-550-W Yellow, 48	$1,345	($81.57)	-6.07 %	1.12 %	◆
Women's Mountain Shorts, S	$1,191	$432.17	36.28 %	0.99 %	◆
Road-350-W Yellow, 42	$1,021	($61.92)	-6.07 %	0.85 %	◆
Women's Mountain Shorts, L	$1,008	$379.62	37.67 %	0.84 %	◆
Classic Vest, S	$686	$258.32	37.67 %	0.57 %	◆
Short-Sleeve Classic Jersey, XL	$680	($192.74)	-28.33 %	0.57 %	◆
Touring-3000 Yellow, 50	$445	($16.03)	-3.60 %	0.37 %	◆
Women's Mountain Shorts, M	$420	$158.18	37.67 %	0.35 %	◆
Short-Sleeve Classic Jersey, L	$227	($64.25)	-28.33 %	0.19 %	◆
LL Road Pedal	$219	$56.85	26.00 %	0.18 %	◆

1 of 48

Tip When using the *FixedData* property to pin a row or column into a fixed position, you should also set the *BackgroundColor* property of the row or column. If no color is defined, the background is transparent, and you see the data scrolling behind the text in the fixed headers.

Controlling Visibility

When a report requires both summary and detail data, you might consider creating a *drill-down report,* in which only the summary data displays when the user opens the report and the detail data displays when the user clicks a text box that has been configured to toggle the visibility of details. To achieve this behavior, you configure an entire row, an entire column, or a specific text box using visibility properties to hide the selection when the document opens. You also configure the *ToggleItem* property of the selection to reference a text box in the report. When the report renders, a plus sign displays in that referenced text box to indicate to the user that the item can be expanded to show additional information.

In this procedure, you configure row visibility and report item visibility to present summary information when the report opens and to toggle the display of details on demand.

Configure visibility

1. Click the Design tab.

2. Click anywhere in the tablix region to display the table handles, right-click the row handle for the Details row (the row that displays *[EnglishProductName]* in the Product column), and select Row Visibility.

3. In the Row Visibility dialog box, select Hide.

4. Select the Display Can Be Toggled By This Report Item check box, and then, in the drop-down list, select BusinessType, as shown here.

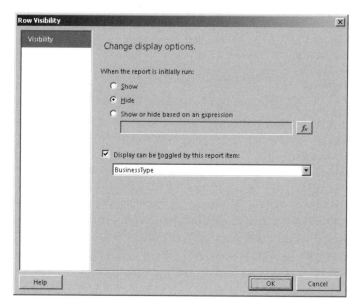

Tip If you plan to use a text box as a toggle item for report item visibility, be sure to give it a name to help you find the right text box in this drop-down list. In this example, the text box name was assigned automatically when you added the field to the text box.

If you use the Hide option, as you do in this procedure, the row is always hidden when the user first opens the report. You can also use a conditional expression to control which rows display and which rows hide when the report renders. For example, you could create an expression that checks the business type name and returns *False* if the business type is Specialty Bike Shop and returns *True* for all other business types. As a result, the report displays only the Specialty Bike Shop details and hides all other business types.

5. Click OK.

6. Repeat the previous three steps to hide the Business Type Total row, using the same toggle item, BusinessType.

7. Save and preview the report, as shown here.

Reseller Sales Margin Analysis Interactive					
Product	**Sales Amount**	**Profit Margin**	**Profit Margin Pct**	**Pct Contribution**	
Europe					●
France					●
⊞ Specialty Bike Shop					◆
⊞ Value Added Reseller					◆
⊞ Warehouse					◆
Country Total	$1,376,611				
Germany					◆
⊞ Specialty Bike Shop					◆
⊞ Value Added Reseller					◆
⊞ Warehouse					◆
Country Total	$885,121				
United Kingdom					◆
⊞ Specialty Bike Shop					◆
⊞ Value Added Reseller					◆
⊞ Warehouse					◆
Country Total	$1,277,105				

8. Click the plus sign to the left of Specialty Bike Shop. The detail rows are now visible, as well as the Business Type Total, which you can see if you scroll the page.

9. Click the minus sign to the left of Specialty Bike Shop to hide the detail rows.

As an improvement to this report, you can display the subtotals for the business type on the visible rows when the details are hidden, and hide these subtotals when the details are visible. Remember that the business type subtotals are visible below the details when you expand a specific business type.

10. Click the Design tab.

11. Click the text box containing *[Sum(SalesAmount)]* in the Business Type Total row, and press CTRL+C to copy the contents into the Clipboard.

> **Tip** You can tell that the text box is selected because the border of the text box displays with dark lines. If the cursor is blinking inside the text box, the text box is not selected. You must click outside the text box and then click the text box again to select it.

12. Click the text box in the Sales Amount column in the [BusinessType] row, which appears above the Details row, and press CTRL+V to paste the copied text box content into the destination text box.

13. In the Properties window, expand the Visibility category if necessary. In the ToggleItem drop-down list, select BusinessType.

14. Save and preview the report, as shown here.

Product	Sales Amount	Profit Margin	Profit Margin Pct	Pct Contribution	
Europe					◆
France					◆
⊞ *Specialty Bike Shop*	$120,181				◆
⊞ *Value Added Reseller*	$399,159				◆
⊞ *Warehouse*	$857,271				◆
Country Total	$1,376,611				
Germany					◆
⊞ *Specialty Bike Shop*	$77,158				◆
⊞ *Value Added Reseller*	$299,827				◆
⊞ *Warehouse*	$508,136				◆
Country Total	$885,121				
United Kingdom					◆
⊞ *Specialty Bike Shop*	$92,952				◆
⊞ *Value Added Reseller*	$538,183				◆
⊞ *Warehouse*	$645,970				◆
Country Total	$1,277,105				

Reseller Sales Margin Analysis Interactive — ADVENTURE WORKS cycles

Now the business type totals display in the group header rows when the report renders. When you click the toggle icon, the totals in the group header are hidden, while the totals in the group footer row display.

Working with Parameters

By using parameters, you can add flexibility to your reports. A common way to use a parameter is to prompt the user for input. For instance, you can use the input value to change the behavior of the report by using it in an expression, as you learned in Chapter 5. Another way to use a parameter is to filter the contents of a report. In this case, you can use the input value either as a filter on a data region or as a query parameter to limit the data retrieved by a dataset.

Prompting the User for Input

You can prompt the user for input using a report parameter in two ways. It's considered best practice to provide the user with a list of valid values, but you can also let the user simply type a value. When you provide a list of valid values, you must specify whether the user can choose only one value or can select multiple values. You can type a static list of valid values for the report parameter or generate a list of values from a dataset. In all cases, you can provide a default value to allow the report to execute before the user selects a parameter value.

In this procedure, you create a report parameter with a static list of available values.

Create a report parameter with static available values

1. In Solution Explorer, double-click Reseller Sales Cumulative Sales.rdl.

2. In the Report Data window, right-click the Parameters folder, and select Add Parameter.

3. In the Report Parameters dialog box, in the Name text box, type **SalesTerritoryGroup**.

    The parameter name cannot contain spaces or special characters.

4. In the Prompt box, type **Sales Territory Group**.

    The prompt is the string that displays as a label for the drop-down list or the text box for the report parameter. This string can contain spaces and special characters.

5. Select the Allow Multiple Values check box, as shown here.

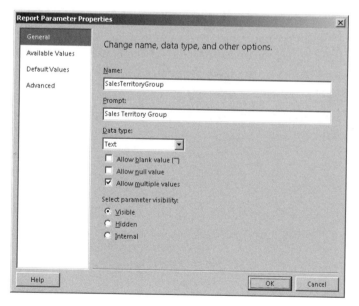

In this case, the data type of the parameter value is text. If you are passing the report parameter value to a query parameter, the query fails if the report parameter's data type is not correct.

Notice that you can also elect to allow blank or null values. A blank value is interpreted as an empty string.

By default, the user can select only one value for the report parameter. You must explicitly enable support for multiple values, which will display in a drop-down list. If you enable this option, you cannot allow null values.

Notice also the choices you have for parameter visibility. Of course, if you want the user to provide a value, the parameter must be visible. You use the Hidden option if you don't want to display the prompt when viewing the report, but still need the ability to set the parameter value using URL access (described in Chapter 16, "Programming Reporting Services") or when creating a subscription (described in Chapter 15, "Working with Subscriptions"). You use the Internal option when you need to use a parameter value in a report, but set the parameter value without user interaction. For example, you can get a parameter value by evaluating an expression or retrieving a value from a dataset, and thereby bypass the need to prompt the user.

6. In the left pane, click Available Values.

7. Select Specify Values.

8. Click Add.

9. In the Label text box, type **Europe**, and then, in the Value text box, type **Europe**.

In this procedure, the values in the Label and the Value boxes are identical, but sometimes you might require the two values to be different. Value is the default passed to a parameter expression and to a query parameter, whereas Label is the text that displays in the report parameter's drop-down list.

10. Repeat the previous two steps to add **North America** and **Pacific** to the available values list, as shown here.

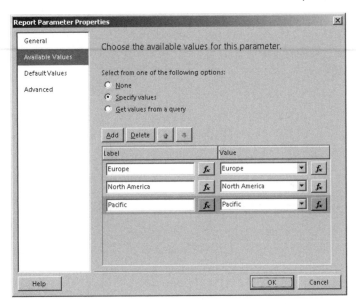

Notice that you can specify an expression rather than a static value for both Label and Value.

11. In the left pane, click Default Values.

    This report parameter is now configured correctly even if you omit default values. However, the report does not render until the user selects a value.

12. Select Specify Values.

13. Click Add.

14. Type **Europe** in the Value text box, or select it from the drop-down list.

15. Repeat the previous two steps to add **North America** and **Pacific**, as shown here.

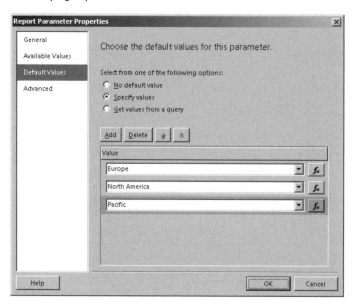

When you configure a parameter to allow multiple values, you can specify one or more default values. Just as with the available values, you can use expressions to specify default values instead of using static text.

16. Click OK, and then save and preview the report. Notice the parameter drop-down list, which allows you to select values different from the default values of Europe, North America, and Pacific, as shown here.

17. In the drop-down list for the *Sales Territory Group* parameter, clear the (Select All) check box, then select the Pacific check box and click View Report.

Notice the report data hasn't changed. You must alter the dataset to use the new parameter.

Using a Date/Time Report Parameter

When you set the data type of a report parameter to Date/Time, the user can type a date into the report parameter text box, or click a calendar icon to display a calendar control, as shown here.

It is common practice to set a default value for a date parameter. You can set the current date as the default value by using =**Today()** as the expression. Alternatively, you can set a specific date relative to the current date, such as the last day of the previous month, which you define by using =**DateSerial(Year(Now()),Month(Now()),0)** as the expression.

Using a Report Parameter as a Filter

You can apply a filter to a dataset, a data region, or a group to limit the detail rows within the applicable scope to those rows satisfying the condition you define for the filter. To create a dynamic filter based on user input, you can use a report parameter to store the user's selection and then reference that parameter in the filter condition.

Because a filter is applied to the dataset rows after the query executes, even if you apply the filter to the dataset, the time to render the report after selecting a new report parameter value is quite low. When you want to both minimize the number of query executions against the source database and maximize report performance when changing report parameter values, use a report filter on the dataset. When you need access to all data in some data regions and filtered data in other data regions on the same report, use a report filter on the applicable data regions instead.

In this procedure, you use a report parameter value to filter the report dataset.

Define a filter on a dataset

1. Click the Design tab.

2. In the Report Data window, right-click Reseller Sales, and select Dataset Properties.

3. In the Dataset Properties dialog box, in the left pane, click Filters.

4. Click Add, and then, in the Expression drop-down list, select [SalesTerritoryGroup].

5. In the Operator drop-down list, select In.

   In this procedure, you use the In operator to compare the current *SalesTerritoryGroup* value to multiple values specified in the report parameter. Use Table 6-2 to learn about other operators.

TABLE 6-2 Available Filter Operators

This Operator	Performs This Action
=, <>, >, >=, <, <=, Like	Compares the expression to the value
Top N, Bottom N	Compares the expression to a single integer value
Top %, Bottom %	Compares the expression to a single integer or float value
Between	Determines whether the expression is between two values, inclusive
In	Determines whether the expression is found in a list of values

6. In the Value text box, type **[@SalesTerritoryGroup]**, as shown here.

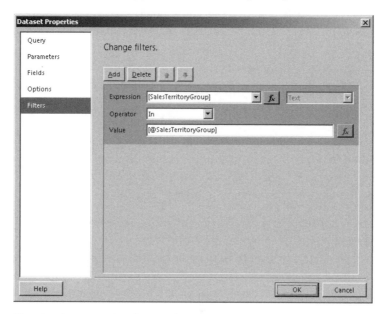

The simple expression format for a report parameter adds an @ symbol in front of the report parameter name and encloses the resulting string in brackets.

7. Click OK, and then save and preview the report.

8. In the Sales Territory Group drop-down list, clear the (Select All) check box, select the Pacific check box, and then click View Report.

Notice that when you select Pacific this time, only the data for Pacific displays in the report.

9. In the Sales Territory Group drop-down list, select North America.

10. Page through the report to confirm that only the data for North America and Pacific display in the report.

Mapping Report Parameters in a Subreport

When you configure a report for use as a subreport, you have the option to configure its parameter properties as well. On the Parameters page of the Subreport Properties dialog box, you can select a parameter name in the subreport and assign that parameter a value. Valid values that you can assign to the parameter name include a reference to a field in the dataset in the source report, a parameter value in the source report, or a custom expression.

Using a Dataset for Report Parameter Values

Whenever possible, you should use a dataset to provide a list of available values for a report parameter. Ideally, your dataset should reference a view in your data source. Then, if you need to add or remove items in the list, you can manage the change in the data source and can thereby avoid the need to edit the report parameter list in each report using the same list. When you use a dataset to supply report parameter values, you typically have two columns in the dataset, one for the parameter value and one for the parameter label. You can, however, use a single column as both a value and a label.

In this procedure, you replace a static list of available values with values from a query.

Get a list of available values from a query for a report parameter

1. Click the Design tab.
2. In the Report Data window, click New, and then click Dataset.
3. In the Name text box, type **SalesTerritoryGroup**.
4. Click Query Designer.
5. Click Edit As Text.
6. In the Query Designer, in the SQL pane, type the following statement:

   ```
   SELECT DISTINCT SalesTerritoryGroup FROM DimSalesTerritory
   ```
7. Click Run to view the query results.
8. Click OK twice.
9. In the Report Data window, expand the Parameters folder if necessary, right-click SalesTerritoryGroup, and select Parameter Properties.
10. In the Parameter Properties dialog box, in the left pane, click Select Available Values.
11. Select Get Values From A Query.

12. In the Dataset drop-down list, select SalesTerritoryGroupLookup.

13. In the Value Field drop-down list, select SalesTerritoryGroup, and then, in the Label Field drop-down list, select SalesTerritoryGroup, as shown here.

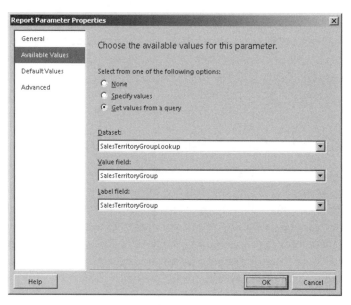

14. In the left pane, click Default Values.

15. Select Get Values From A Query.

16. In the Dataset drop-down list, select SalesTerritoryGroupLookup, and then, in the Value Field drop-down list, select SalesTerritoryGroup, as shown here.

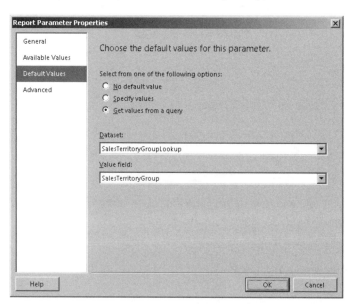

17. Click OK, and then save and preview the report.

Notice that the *Sales Territory Group* parameter list appears the same as previously, but now it also includes an NA value in the list. Otherwise, nothing has changed. As new sales territories are added to the source table for the dataset query, they automatically appear in the default values list. You can add a WHERE clause to your dataset query if you prefer to limit the sales territories to a specific set.

Adding a Query Parameter to a Dataset

When it's important to reduce the amount of network traffic caused by returning a dataset's query results to a report, you should use a query parameter to filter the data at the source. You start by adding a query parameter to the WHERE clause of your dataset query, and then you associate the query parameter with an expression. This expression is typically a reference to a report parameter value, but it can also be an expression that evaluates current conditions in the report at execution, such as the date or the current user.

In this procedure, you create a report parameter that passes a value to a dataset's query parameter.

Link a report parameter to a query parameter

1. Click the Design tab.

2. In the Report Data window, click New, and click Dataset.

3. In the Dataset Properties dialog box, in the Name text box, type **YearLookup**.

4. In the Query text box, type the following query:

```
SELECT DISTINCT CalendarYear FROM DimDate ORDER BY CalendarYear
```

This dataset creates a list of years that you can then use as the list of available values for a new report parameter that prompts the user to select a year.

 Note You can also use query parameters with a stored procedure. The stored procedure must return a single result set. To configure a dataset to use a stored procedure instead of a query, change the Query Type to Stored Procedure in the Dataset Properties dialog box.

5. Click OK.

6. In the Report Data window, right-click the Parameters folder, and select Add Parameter.

7. In the Report Parameter Properties dialog box, in the Name text box, type **Year**, and then, in the Prompt box, type **Year**.

8. Select the Allow Multiple Values check box.

9. In the left pane, select Available Values, and then select Get Values From A Query.

10. In the Dataset drop-down list, select YearLookup.

11. In the Value Field drop-down list, select CalendarYear, and then, in the Label Field drop-down list, select CalendarYear.

12. In the left pane, click Default Values.

13. Select Get Values From A Query.

14. In the Dataset drop-down list, select YearLookup, and then, in the Value Field drop-down list, select CalendarYear.

    When you use a query to set the default values of a report parameter, you must ensure that the query returns only one record if the report parameter accepts only one value. If you enable Allow Multiple Values, as you have done in this procedure, the query must return at least one record. If these conditions are not met, the report fails to execute.

> **Tip** You can instead create a dynamically changing default value by using an expression like =Year() to set the current year as the default value. Because the AdventureWorksDW2008 reseller sales data includes only data between 2001 and 2004, using the =Year() expression as a default for the report parameter works the same as if you had not specified a default value because the current year does not match any value in the available values list.

15. Click OK.

    Now that the report parameter is configured, your next step is to modify the ResellerSales dataset to use a query parameter and then you can link it to the *Year* report parameter.

16. In the Report Data window, right-click ResellerSales, and then select Dataset Properties.

17. Click Query Designer, and then click Edit As Text.

18. Modify the WHERE clause of the query to look like this:

    ```
    WHERE (d.CalendarYear IN (@Year))
    ```

> **Note** Remember that the report parameter is configured to allow multiple values. Consequently, you must use the In operator to use multiple values for comparison in the WHERE clause. If you allowed the user to select only one value, then the WHERE clause could be WHERE (d.CalendarYear = @Year).

19. Click OK.

20. In the Dataset Properties dialog box, click Parameters.

21. In the Parameter Value drop-down list, select [@Year], as shown here.

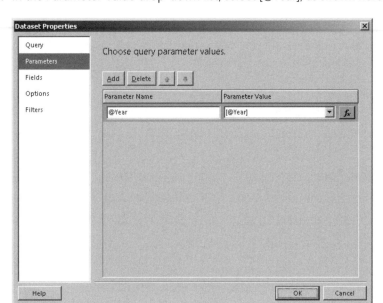

Notice that you can also use an expression for the parameter value. For example, you can concatenate the value selected by the user with static text, or you could use an expression that is completely independent of report parameters. In Chapter 11, "Securing Report Server Content," you learn how to implement security at the data level by using a query parameter value that represents the current user.

22. Click OK, and then save and preview the report.

23. In the Year drop-down list, clear the (Select All) check box, select the 2001 check box, and then click View Report to confirm that the selection of a specific year changes the values that display in the report.

Displaying a Message When a Dataset Is Empty

When a dataset returns no data, any data regions associated with that dataset do not render when the report executes. When this condition occurs, you can display a message in place of each missing data region by configuring the *NoRowsMessage* property for the data region. To configure this property, follow these steps:

1. In the Report Designer Design view, click anywhere in the data region.

2. Click the box in the upper-left corner of the data region to select the data region and display its properties in the Properties window.

3. In the NoRowsMessage text box, type the message text to display when the dataset is empty, such as **No data available**.

Creating Cascading Parameters

Sometimes you might need to create the available values list for a report parameter based on the user's selection of a value for a different report parameter. This dependency between parameters is called *cascading parameters*.

In this procedure, you create a report parameter that passes a value to a dataset's query parameter.

Create cascading parameters

1. Click the Design tab.

2. In the Report Data window, click New, and click Dataset.

3. In the Dataset Properties dialog box, in the Name box, type **QuarterLookup**.

4. Click Import.

5. In the Import Query dialog box, navigate to the Microsoft Press\Rs2008sbs\Chap06 folder in your Documents folder, and double-click CalendarQuarter.sql.

> **Note** This query includes two columns, CalendarQuarterValue and CalendarQuarterLabel, which you use to populate the list of available values and default values for a report pa-rameter that you add later in this procedure. *CalendarQuarterValue* is the value that the report parameter passes to a query parameter, and the CalendarQuarterLabel is the label that displays in the report parameter drop-down list. The query also includes a query pa-rameter, *@Year,* that requires the user to select a year before the valid quarters for that year display.

6. In the left pane, click Parameters.

   Notice that the *@Year* query parameter is linked automatically to the *[@Year]* report parameter.

7. Click OK.

8. In the Report Data window, right-click the Parameters folder, and select Add Parameter.

9. In the Report Parameter Properties dialog box, in the Name text box, type **Quarter**, and then, in the Prompt text box, type **Quarter**.

10. Select the Allow Multiple Values check box.

11. In the left pane, select Available Values, and then select Get Values From A Query.

12. In the Dataset drop-down list, select QuarterLookup.

13. In the Value Field drop-down list, select CalendarQuarterValue, and then, in the Label Field drop-down list, select CalendarQuarterLabel.

14. In the left pane, click Default Values.

15. Select Get Values From A Query.

16. In the Dataset drop-down list, select QuarterLookup, and then, in the Value Field drop-down list, select CalendarQuarterValue.

17. In the left pane, click Advanced, and select Always Refresh, as shown here.

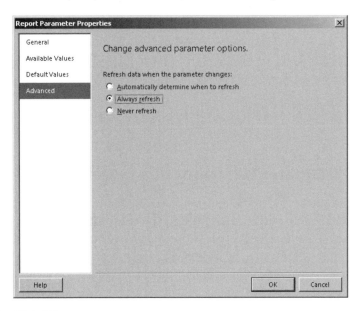

18. Click OK.

19. In the Report Data window, right-click Reseller Sales, and select Query.

20. Modify the WHERE clause of the query to look like this:

```
WHERE (d.CalendarYear IN (@Year) AND d.CalendarQuarter IN (@Quarter))
```

Now the query filters the results by both year and quarter, based on the user selection of the *Year* and *Quarter* report parameter values.

21. Click OK, and then save and preview the report.

22. In the Year drop-down list, clear the (Select All) check box, select the 2001 check box, and then click anywhere in the toolbar to close the drop-down list.

Notice that the *Quarter* values automatically change to *Q3* and *Q4* to reflect the two quarters of data available in 2001.

23. Click View Report to confirm that the report executes correctly, as shown here.

Group	Country	Business Type	Product	Sales Amount	Cumulative Sales	Cumulative Sales Pct
North America	Canada	Specialty Bike Shop	Mountain-100 Black, 42	$28,350	$28,350	14 %
			Mountain-100 Black, 44	$24,300	$52,650	26 %
			Mountain-100 Black, 38	$24,300	$76,950	38 %
			Mountain-100 Black, 48	$20,250	$97,200	48 %
			Mountain-100 Silver, 42	$18,360	$115,560	57 %
			Mountain-100 Silver, 38	$16,320	$131,880	65 %
			Mountain-100 Silver, 44	$16,320	$148,200	73 %
			Road-450 Red, 52	$13,997	$162,196	80 %
			Mountain-100 Silver, 48	$8,160	$170,356	84 %
			Road-450 Red, 58	$7,873	$178,229	87 %
			Road-650 Black, 52	$5,872	$184,102	90 %
			Road-650 Red, 44	$5,034	$189,135	93 %
			Road-650 Black, 58	$4,614	$193,749	95 %
			Road-650 Red, 60	$4,614	$198,363	97 %
			Road-650 Red, 62	$2,936	$201,300	99 %
			Road-650 Red, 48	$1,678	$202,977	100 %
			Long-Sleeve Logo Jersey, L	$490	$203,468	100 %
			LL Road Frame - Red, 44	$184	$203,652	100 %

Reseller Sales Cumulative Sales — Total Sales: $8,065,435

Displaying Parameter Selections in a Report

Because a report is often printed out or exported to another format, it is important to preserve the context of the report as specified by the report parameter selections. You can create a freestanding text box to display the parameter selections as a subtitle in the report or as a footnote in the page footer. By default, a parameter expression evaluates the value field of a report parameter. When the label field differs from the value field, you can modify the parameter expression to evaluate the label field instead.

In this procedure, you create a report parameter that passes a value to a dataset's query parameter.

Add parameter labels to a report

1. Click the Design tab.

2. From the Toolbox window, drag a textbox control to the page footer and position it to the right of the text box containing *[&ExecutionTime]*.

3. Right-click the text box, and select Expression.

4. In the Expression dialog box, construct the following expression:

```
="Filters: " + Join(Parameters!SalesTerritoryGroup.Value, ",") + " - " +
Join(Parameters!Year.Value, ",") + " - " + Join(Parameters!Quarter.Label, ",")
```

If you use the builder functions to build the portion of the expression containing a *Parameters* collection (e.g., *Parameters!SalesTerritoryGroup*), you discover that the default expression references the first item in an array, such as *Parameters!SalesTerritoryGroup(0)*. This behavior occurs only when you allow multiple values for the parameter. To display values in a multiselect parameter, you must use the *Join* function to concatenate the selected parameter values as a single delimited string that you can display in a text box.

Notice that the delimiter string is the second argument of the *Join* function. In this case, the delimiter is a comma followed by a space.

Notice also that the second *Parameters!Quarter* collection reference uses the *Label* property. In this case, the label differs from the integer-based value. The other two report parameters have the same value and label fields, so no modification of the expression is necessary.

5. Click OK.

6. Select the text box containing the filter labels, and then in the Size/Width text box in the Properties window, type **5in**.

7. In the Font/FontSize box, type **8pt**.

8. Save and then preview the report.

9. Scroll to the bottom of the page to view the contents of the newly added text box, as shown here.

Touring-2000 Blue, 54	$8,018	$225,946	54 %
Mountain-200 Silver, 38	$7,457	$233,403	56 %
Touring-1000 Blue, 60	$7,152	$240,556	57 %
Road-650 Red, 62	$7,047	$247,603	59 %
Mountain-200 Silver, 46	$6,214	$253,817	61 %
Road-350-W Yellow, 48	$6,124	$259,940	62 %
Road-650 Black, 52	$6,107	$266,048	64 %
Touring-2000 Blue, 54	$5,831	$271,879	65 %
Touring-1000 Blue, 60	$5,722	$277,601	66 %
Road-650 Red, 44	$5,356	$282,956	68 %
Touring-3000 Yellow, 62	$5,345	$288,301	69 %
Touring-1000 Yellow, 46	$4,387	$292,688	70 %
Road-650 Red, 48	$4,228	$296,916	71 %
Road-650 Red, 62	$4,228	$301,144	72 %
Road-350-W Yellow, 48	$4,082	$305,227	73 %
Road-350-W Yellow, 40	$4,082	$309,309	74 %
Road-650 Red, 44	$3,758	$313,067	75 %
Road-650 Black, 58	$3,758	$316,826	76 %

9/26/2008 10:35:38 AM   Filters: Europe,NA,North America,Pacific - 2001,2002,2003,2004,2006 - Q1,Q2,Q3,Q4

Adding Navigation Features

Reporting Services includes several navigation features that you can implement. You can configure a document map to help users go to a new location in the same report. You can also use an action to go to a bookmark in the report, go to a URL, or go to another

Reporting Services report. Finally, you can use Hypertext Markup Language (HTML) markup to create a link that opens a Web page or a mail application.

Configuring a Document Map

The Document Map feature allows you to configure bookmarks for each instance in a group and display this list of bookmarks next to the report. In effect, this list of bookmarks is a table of contents for the report that enables the user not only to see the group instances at a glance, but also to jump to the location of a specific instance. When the report includes nested groups, the document map displays the list of bookmarks in a tree form. The user must expand a specific group instance to view the instances of groups contained by the selected group.

In this procedure, you add a document map to a report to support navigation to different instances of a group.

Add a document map

1. Click the Design tab.

2. In the Row Groups pane, right-click SalesTerritoryGroup, and select Group Properties.

3. In the Group Properties dialog box, in the left pane, click Advanced.

4. In the Document Map drop-down list, select [SalesTerritoryGroup], as shown here.

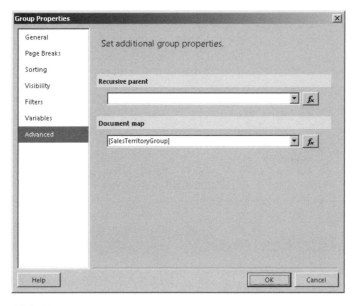

5. Click OK.

6. In the Row Groups pane, right-click SalesTerritoryCountry, and select Group Properties.

7. In the Group Properties dialog box, in the left pane, click Advanced.

8. In the Document Map drop-down list, select [SalesTerritoryCountry], and click OK.

9. In the Row Groups pane, right-click BusinessType, and select Group Properties.

10. In the Group Properties dialog box, in the left pane, click Advanced.

11. In the Document Map drop-down list, select [BusinessType], and click OK.

12. Save and preview the report.

   The document map displays on the left side of the report, as shown here.

13. In the Document Map pane, expand Europe, as shown here, and click United Kingdom.

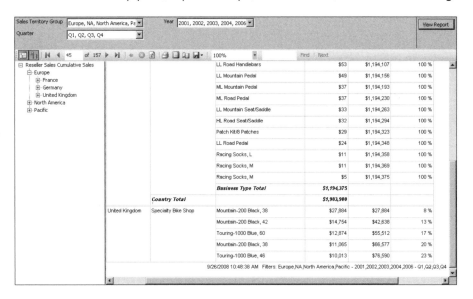

Jumping to a Report

Each text box and image has an *Action* property that you can use to define a target location for display when the user clicks the text box or image. To configure a Go To Report action, you define a target report, and if you want, you can also map expressions in the source report to parameters in the target report. Consequently, the target report can display information using the same context as the source report if the target report is designed to filter based on report parameter values.

You use the Go To Bookmark action to help the user quickly navigate to another location in the same report. You must first define a text box as a bookmark. In the *Bookmark* property, you type a string or select an expression to use as a label for the bookmark.

A third option for navigation is the Go To URL action. You simply type a URL or select an expression that evaluates to a URL. When the user clicks the link, the target destination opens in the browser window.

In this procedure, you add an action to a text box to open another report when the user executes the action.

Add a Go To Report action to a text box

1. Click the Design tab.

2. Right-click the cell containing *[SalesTerritoryGroup]* and select Text Box Properties.

3. In the Text Box Properties dialog box, in the left pane, click Action.

4. Select Go To Report.

5. In the Select A Report From The List drop-down list, select Reseller Sales Margin Analysis by Sales Territory.

> **Important** When the target report is contained in the same project as the report for which you are implementing the Go To Report action, you can select the report in the drop-down list. Otherwise, you can type the name of the report in the box. So long as the two reports are stored in the same folder on the report server, you can simply use the report name. If the two reports are stored in separate folders, you must provide the folder path in addition to the report name. For example, if the target report Sales Analysis is stored in the Sales folder, you type **/Sales/Sales Analysis** to identify both the location and the name of the report. If you change the location of the target report, you must correct the path in the source report's *Action* property.

6. Click Add.

7. In the Name drop-down list, select SalesTerritoryGroup, and then, in the Value drop-down list, select [SalesTerritoryGroup].

   When the user clicks a specific *Sales Territory Group* value in the report, that value is assigned to the *SalesTerritoryGroup* report parameter in the target report.

> **Note** When you define a target report for the Go To Report action that is not in the current project, the target report's parameter name is not available in the Name drop-down list. You must type the report parameter name manually. Remember that this property is case-sensitive, so take care to match the case in the report parameter's name exactly.

8. Click Add.

9. In the Name drop-down list, select Year, and then, in the Value box, type **[@Year]**.

In this case, the current report parameter value selection for Year in the source report passes to the target report's *Year* report parameter. When configuring the Go To Report action, you can map any expression to a report parameter in the target report, such as a current field value or a report parameter selection, as you have done in this procedure, or you can develop a custom expression to map to a target report parameter.

10. Click Add.

11. In the Name drop-down list, select Quarter, and then, in the Value box, type **[@ Quarter],** as shown here.

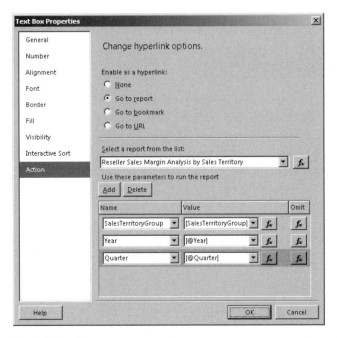

As with the *Year* parameter, the current report parameter value selection for Quarter passes to the target report's *Quarter* report parameter.

12. Click OK.

13. Right-click the cell containing *[SalesTerritoryGroup]* and select Text Box Properties.

14. In the Text Box Properties dialog box, in the left pane, click Font.

15. Click the Color drop-down list, and select Blue (in the sixth column on the second row).

Although the text box now has an active link that opens the target report when clicked, the user has no visual cue that indicates that a link exists in the text box. You can use *Font* properties to display the text in a blue font and with an underline effect to simulate the appearance of a hyperlink.

16. In the Effects drop-down list, select Underline, and then click OK.

17. Save and preview the report.

18. In the first row on the report, click Europe.

The Reseller Sales Margin Analysis by Sales Territory report displays data for Europe only for all years and quarters.

19. Click the Back To Parent Report button on the HTML Viewer toolbar, as shown here.

Using Embedded HTML Tags

You can use selected HTML markup tags in a report to control formatting in text to achieve a specific layout, but the <A href> tag in particular is useful for navigation. You can create a text expression that combines static text or an expression with HTML markup tags and evaluates as a URL or as a mail recipient. You assign this text expression to a placeholder that you must also configure to interpret HTML tags as style commands.

In this procedure, you configure placeholder text as HTML markup for e-mail addresses.

Configure placeholder properties to interpret HTML tags as styles

1. In Solution Explorer, double-click CustomerList.rdl.

2. Click the Preview tab.

The top of the report looks like this:

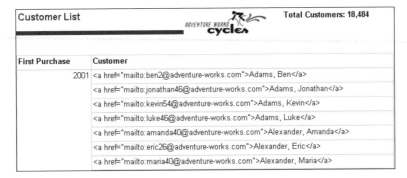

The dataset returns an HTML tag for a mail link to each customer. However, the report currently renders the HTML tag as text. You need to modify the properties for the text box containing the HTML tag to change this behavior.

3. Click the Design tab.

4. In the text box containing *[CustomerTag]*, click the *[CustomerTag]* placeholder three times to select the placeholder, as shown here.

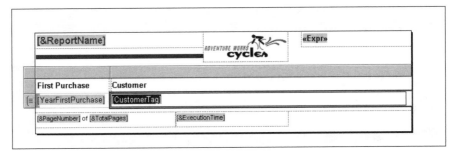

The first click selects the text box, the second click positions the cursor inside the text box to add more text, and the third click finally selects the placeholder.

5. Right-click the placeholder, and then select Placeholder Properties.

6. In the Placeholder Properties dialog box, under Markup Type, select HTML – Interpret HTML Tags As Styles.

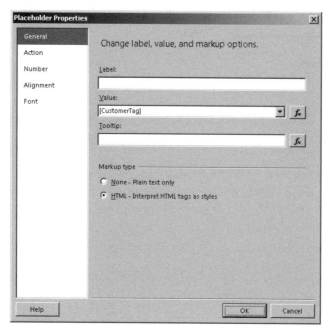

The placeholder text value can be a field from a dataset, a parameter value, or a custom expression. You can use the HTML tags shown in Table 6-3 in placeholder text.

TABLE 6-3 Use HTML Markup Tags

For This Tag Type	Select From These Markup Tags
Font	<FONT>
Header, style, and block elements	<DIV>, <H{n}>, <HN>, <LI>, <P>, <SPAN>
Hyperlink	<A href>
List	<LI>, <OL>, <UL>
Text format	<B>, <I>, <S>, <U>

Note Any HTML markup tag not shown in Table 6-3 is ignored when the report renders.

7. Click OK, and then save and preview the report.

The top of the report looks like this:

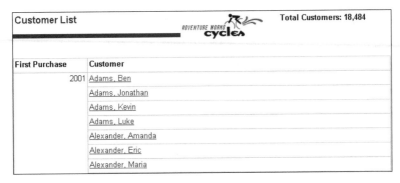

First Purchase	Customer
2001	Adams, Ben
	Adams, Jonathan
	Adams, Kevin
	Adams, Luke
	Alexander, Amanda
	Alexander, Eric
	Alexander, Maria

If you have a mail application installed on your computer, then when you click the link, a new message window opens and displays the selected customer's e-mail address in the To line, as shown here.

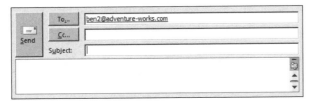

Reporting Services includes many features that provide a rich interactive experience for users. Both the interactive sort and report parameters make it possible to design a single report for many purposes and help eliminate the proliferation of reports that are only slightly different due to sort order or applied filters. In addition, the use of navigation features enables users to move within and across reports to information that is linked by context.

By completing this chapter and all the preceding chapters in Part II, "Developing Reports," you have been introduced to all the key features of Reporting Services report development. In Chapter 7, "Using Analysis Services as a Data Source," you primarily focus on the development of the dataset and report parameters when an Analysis Services cube is the source for your reports.

Chapter 6 Quick Reference

To	Do This
Enable interactive sort	Right-click a text box in a column or row header, select Text Box Properties, Interactive Sort, select the Enable Interactive Sort On This Text Box check box, select a Sort scope (detail rows or a group), and select a Sort By expression. If you want, select a group or data region to which the same sort definition should apply.
Add a fixed header	In the Grouping pane, select Advanced Mode. In either the Row Groups or Column Groups section, click the first Static group, and then, in the Properties window, in the FixedData drop-down list, select True.
Configure row or column visibility to toggle when the user clicks a text box	Right-click a row or column handle, select Row Visibility or Column Visibility, respectively, select Hide, select the Display Can Be Toggled By This Report Item check box, and then, in the drop-down list, select a text box name.
Configure text box visibility to toggle when the user clicks a different text box	In the Report Designer, select a text box, and then, in the Properties window, in the Visibility category, in the ToggleItem drop-down list, select a text box name. If the text box should be hidden when the report opens, in the Hidden drop-down list, select True.
Create a report parameter with static available values from which the user can select one or more values	In the Report Data window, right-click the Parameters folder, select Add Parameter, type a name in the Name box, type a prompt in the Prompt box, and select the Allow Multiple Values check box. On the Available Values page of the Report Parameter Properties dialog box, select Specify Values, and then, for each value, click Add, and type a label and a value in the Label and Value boxes, respectively.
Create a report parameter with a list of available values from a query, from which the user can select one or more values	In the Report Data window, right-click the Parameters folder, select Add Parameter, type a name in the Name box, type a prompt in the Prompt box, and select the Allow Multiple Values check box. On the Available Values page of the Report Parameter Properties dialog box, select Get Values From A Query, select a dataset, select a value field, and select a label field.
Configure a list of static default values for a report parameter	In the Report Parameter Properties dialog box, select the Default Values page, select Specify Values, and then, for each value, click Add, and type a value in the Value box.
Configure a list of default values for a report parameter from a query	In the Report Parameter Properties dialog box, select the Default Values page, select Get Values From A Query, select a dataset, and select a value field.

To	Do This
Define a filter on a dataset	In the Report Data window, right-click the dataset, select Dataset Properties, and, in the left pane, click Filters. Click Add, select an expression in the Expression drop-down list, select an operator in the Operator drop-down list, and then type an expression in the Value box.
Link a report parameter to a query parameter	In the Report Data window, right-click a dataset, select Dataset Properties, modify the WHERE clause of the query to include a query parameter like this: **WHERE (d.CalendarYear IN (@ Year))**. On the Parameters page of the Dataset Properties dialog box, select a report parameter in the Parameter Value drop-down list next to the corresponding query parameter in the Parameter Name box.
Create cascading parameters	Create a dataset with a query parameter that links to a report parameter, create a second report parameter with a list of available values from the new dataset, and then, on the Advanced page of the Report Parameter Properties dialog box, select Always Refresh.
Add parameter labels to a report	Add a textbox control to the report layout, right-click the text box, select Expression, and construct an expression that uses a reference to the report parameter, such as **Parameters!Quarter.Label** for a single value or **Join(Parameters!Quarter.Label, ", ")** for multiple values.
Add a document map	In the Row Groups pane, right-click a group, select Group Properties, Advanced, and then select a field placeholder or expression to display as a label in the document map.
Create a Go To Report action for a text box	Right-click a text box, select Text Box Properties, Action, Go To Report, and then select a report in the Select A Report From The List drop-down list. For each report parameter in the target report, click Add, select a report parameter in the Name drop-down list, select the name of the report parameter, and then, in the Value drop-down list, select an expression to map to the report parameter.
Render placeholder text as HTML	Select a placeholder in a text box, right-click, select Placeholder Properties, and select HTML – Interpret HTML Tags As Styles.

Chapter 7

Using Analysis Services as a Data Source

After completing this chapter, you will be able to:

- Create an Analysis Services data source.

- Use the MDX query designer to develop an MDX query.

- Use extended field properties for an Analysis Services dataset.

- Display server aggregates in a data region.

- Define parameters in the MDX query designer.

When you have a large database to query or your reports contain complex calculations that are difficult to perform by using relational queries, you can move your data into an *online analytical processing* (OLAP) database managed by Analysis Services. An OLAP database is characterized by a multidimensional data structure known as a cube, which provides fast responses to queries and includes spreadsheet-style formulas to centralize and simplify the business logic used to perform calculations. To query a cube, you must use the Multidimensional Expression (MDX) query language, which many people find difficult to learn. The good news is that Reporting Services includes a query designer that you can use to create the MDX query using a drag-and-drop operation if you're new to Analysis Services. If you're already experienced with MDX, you also have the flexibility to create your own MDX query or to modify the MDX query generated by the query designer.

In this chapter, you install a sample Analysis Services database to use as a data source for the reports that you use throughout this chapter. Then you learn how to use the MDX query designer to create a dataset for a report. You also learn how working with Analysis Services dataset fields and parameters differs from working with fields and parameters when using other data source types.

Note You don't need any prior experience with Analysis Services before you begin this chapter. All the information you need to build reports successfully using Analysis Services as a data source is provided in this chapter, but you can learn more about Analysis Services by referring to *Microsoft SQL Server 2008 Analysis Services Step by Step* (Microsoft Press, 2009).

Installing the Sample Database

As you learned in Chapter 2, "Installing Reporting Services," Microsoft provides sample databases for download from the CodePlex community Web site rather than packaging them with the SQL Server 2008 installation media. To complete the procedures in this chapter, you use the Adventure Works DW 2008 SE sample database for Analysis Services. This database includes a cube that contains the same data from the AdventureWorksDW2008 database that you've been using to create reports in previous chapters.

The difference between the cube and the SQL Server database for reporting purposes is the query language you use to retrieve data from each data source. In a production system in which data volumes are high, you would likely experience faster performance from the cube queries. However, the sample databases that you use throughout this book are too small to discern a difference in query performance between the OLAP and relational databases.

In this procedure, you download and install the Adventure Works DW 2008 SE sample database.

Download and install the sample database

1. Open Windows Internet Explorer and navigate to *http://www.codeplex.com /MSFTASProdSamples/Release/ProjectReleases.aspx?ReleaseId=16038*.

2. Click the SQL2008.Analysis_Services.Samples.x86.msi link if your computer has a 32-bit operating system, or click the SQL2008.Analysis_Services.Samples.x64.msi link if your computer has a 64-bit operating system.

3. In the Microsoft Public License message box, click I Agree.

4. In the File Download – Security Warning message box, click Save.

5. In the Save As dialog box, navigate to a location on your computer or network to store the downloaded file, and click Save.

6. When the download completes, open Windows Explorer, navigate to the location in which you saved the downloaded file, and double-click the downloaded file. In the Open File – Security Warning message box, click Run.

7. On the Welcome page of the Microsoft SQL Server 2008 Analysis Services RTM Samples Setup Wizard, click Next.

8. On the End-User License Agreement page of the wizard, select the I Accept The Terms In The License Agreement check box, and click Next.

9. On the Custom Setup page of the wizard, click Next.

10. On the Ready To Install page of the wizard, click Install.

11. When the installation completes, click Finish.

The wizard installs the solution and project files for the Analysis Services database, but it does not actually install the database on your Analysis Server. Before you can build reports using Analysis Services as a data source, you must give the Analysis Services service account read permissions on the AdventureWorksDW2008 database, which is the source database used to load data into the sample Analysis Services database. Then you must deploy the Analysis Services solution to the server to build and process the sample database.

12. Click Start, select All Programs, Microsoft SQL Server 2008, and click SQL Server Management Studio.

13. In the Connect dialog box, in the Server Type drop-down list, select Database Engine, and click Connect.

14. In Object Explorer, expand Security, and then expand Logins.

15. Right-click NT AUTHORITY\NETWORK SERVICE, and click Properties.

> **Note** Use the service account that you configured for Analysis Services during installation if you opted to use a different account.

16. In the Select A Page pane, click User Mapping.

17. Select the AdventureWorksDW2008 check box, and then, in the list of database roles, select the db_datareader check box. Click OK.

18. Click Start, select All Programs, Microsoft SQL Server 2008, and click SQL Server Business Intelligence Development Studio.

19. On the File menu, point to Open, and click Project/Solution.

20. In the Open Project dialog box, navigate to C:\Program Files\Microsoft SQL Server \100\Tools\Samples\AdventureWorks 2008 Analysis Services Project\Standard, and double-click Adventure Works.sln.

21. In Solution Explorer, right-click Adventure Works DW 2008 SE, and click Deploy.

> **Note** If you are using a named instance, or if you want to deploy the sample database to a server other than your local computer, you must change the deployment path of the project. To make this change, in Solution Explorer, right-click Adventure Works DW 2000 SE, and select Project Properties. In the left pane, click Deployment. In the Server text box, type the name of the server or the name of the server and instance, such as **localhost \AS2008** if the named instance is AS2008 on your local computer. Click OK, and then deploy the project as instructed previously.

The Deployment Progress window opens and displays the progress of processing the Analysis Services database objects. When you see the Deployment Completed Successfully message, the database is ready for you to use as a source for your reports.

Creating an Analysis Services Dataset

Before you can create an Analysis Services dataset, you must define a data source that stores the connection information for the Analysis Services server and database. Then, when you create the dataset, you provide an MDX query either by using a graphical interface to construct the query or by typing the MDX query directly into the query designer.

Creating an Analysis Services Data Source

The process to create an Analysis Services data source is very similar to building any other data source. Most often, you will select the Microsoft SQL Server Analysis Services data source type. This provider allows you to use the MDX query designer, which simplifies the process of constructing an MDX query, particularly if you're still learning the MDX query language.

If you're skilled in MDX and if your report specifications require you to build a dynamic expression for the MDX query, you can use the Object Linking and Embedding Database (OLE DB) data source type instead. With this data source type, you use the Microsoft OLE DB Provider for Analysis Services 10.0. However, this type of data source does not include a graphical designer, so you must be able to prepare the MDX query without assistance.

> **Note** Regardless of which data source type you select, you must use Windows Authentication as the credentials to connect to the data source because this is the only type of authentication supported by Analysis Services.

In this procedure, you add an Analysis Services shared data source to an existing report project.

Create an Analysis Services shared data source

1. In SQL Server Business Intelligence Development Studio, on the File menu, point to Open, and click Project/Solution.

2. In the Open Project dialog box, navigate to the Microsoft Press\Rs2008sbs \Chap07folder in your Documents folder, and double-click Sales.sln.

3. In Solution Explorer, right-click the Shared Data Sources folder, and click Add New Data Source.

4. In the Name text box, type **OLAP**, and then, in the Type drop-down list, select Microsoft SQL Server Analysis Services.

5. Click Edit.

6. In the Connection Properties dialog box, in the Server Name text box, type **localhost** (or the Analysis Server name) and then, in the Select Or Enter A Database Name drop-down list, select Adventure Works DW 2008 SE.

7. Click OK twice.

8. In Solution Explorer, right-click the Reports folder, point to Add, then select New Item.

9. In the Name text box, type **Reseller Sales OLAP.rdl**, and click Add.

10. In the Report Data window, click New, then select Data Source.

11. In the Data Source Properties dialog box, in the Name text box, type **OLAP**.

12. Select the Use Shared Data Source Reference option, and then, in the drop-down list, select OLAP. Click OK.

Building a Query

You use the MDX query designer to develop an MDX query to retrieve data from an Analysis Services cube. In the default Design Mode, you can drag items from a list of OLAP database objects into a data pane to view the results incrementally.

Note You can also use the DMX query designer to develop a Data Mining Expression (DMX) query. A DMX query retrieves data from an Analysis Services mining model. To learn more about building a DMX query, refer to the topic "Using the Analysis Services DMX Query Designer (Reporting Services)," in SQL Server Books Online.

In this procedure, you create a dataset and query by using the MDX query designer.

Use the MDX query designer to build a query

1. In the Report Data window, click New, and then click Dataset.

2. In the Dataset Properties dialog box, click Query Designer.

   The MDX query designer displays, as shown here.

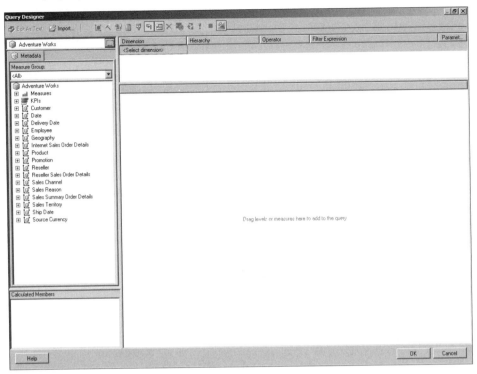

The query designer uses several panes to help you construct an MDX query:

- **Current Cube**   The current cube displays in the upper-left corner of the query designer. In this example, the current cube is Adventure Works. When an Analysis Services database contains many cubes, click the button in the Current Cube pane to select a different cube.

- **Metadata**   The Metadata pane displays below the Current Cube pane on the left side of the query designer. A list of database objects displays in this pane, beginning with Measures and key performance indicators (KPIs) at the top of the list and continuing with dimensions associated with the current cube. You build a query by dragging objects from the list into the Data pane.

- **Calculated Members**   In the lower-left corner of the query designer, you find the Calculated Members pane. You can create calculations to extend the measures and dimensions available in the current cube. These calculations display in this pane. You can then drag a calculation from this pane into the Data pane to add the calculation to the query.

- **Filter**   The Filter pane displays across the top of the query designer, just below the query designer toolbar. You use the Filter pane to limit the data retrieved from the cube by the query.

- **Data**   The Data pane displays the results of the current query in the area below the Filter pane. You drag items from the Metadata pane and the Calculated Members pane into the Data pane to view the results of the query.

The query designer also includes a toolbar, shown here, that contains buttons to help you as you build your MDX query.

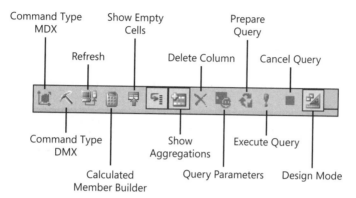

The following list describes the query designer toolbar buttons:

- **Command Type MDX**   Switch to the MDX query designer if the DMX query designer is currently active.

- **Command Type DMX**   Switch to the DMX query designer if the MDX query designer is currently active.

- **Refresh**   Update the list of objects in the Metadata pane if changes have occurred in the data source since you opened the query designer.

- **Add Calculated Member**   Display the Calculated Member Builder dialog box.

- **Show Empty Cells**   Add or remove the NON EMPTY keyword in the query by using this toggle button. By default, the empty cells are hidden, which means that the NON EMPTY keyword is included and any row for which no measure value exists is excluded from the query results.

- **Auto Execute**   Switch between viewing results on demand or deferring query execution until explicitly requested. By default, Auto Execute is enabled when you open the query designer.

- **Show Aggregations**   Add or remove server aggregations in the Data pane.

- **Delete**   Delete the currently selected column in the Data pane.

- **Query Parameters**   Display the Query Parameters dialog box when the query designer is in Query Mode.

- **Prepare Query** Prepare the query when the query designer is in Query Mode.

- **Execute Query** Run the query and display the query results in the Data pane.

- **Cancel Query** End a query that is currently executing.

- **Design Mode** Switch between Query Mode and Design Mode. In Design Mode, you drag objects to build the query, but in Query Mode, you edit the MDX query directly.

3. In the Metadata pane, expand Product, and then drag Category in the area labeled Drag Levels Or Measures Here To Add To The Query.

4. Expand Measures, expand Reseller Sales, and then drag Reseller Sales Amount to the right of Category.

5. Drag Reseller Gross Profit Margin to the right of Reseller Sales Amount.

The query automatically executes and the MDX Query Designer displays the results, as shown here.

Category	Reseller Sales ...	Reseller Gross Profit Margin
Accessories	571297.9278	0.342715392744332
Bikes	66302381.557	-0.014942146404625
Clothing	1777840.8391	0.130733537495775
Components	11799076.6584	0.0875463826285602

6. In the Filter pane above the query columns, in the Dimension drop-down list, select Date.

7. In the Hierarchy drop-down list, select Date.CalendarYear.

8. In the Filter Expression drop-down list, expand All Periods, select the CY 2004 check box, and then click OK.

The Filter pane looks like this:

Dimension	Hierarchy	Operator	Filter Expression	Parameters
Date	Date.Calendar Year	Equal	{ CY 2004 }	☐
<Select dimension>				

After you create the filter, the query executes once more and returns results for the calendar year 2004 only.

The default Operator is Equal, but you can choose other options. Use Table 7-1 to learn about other operators:

TABLE 7-1 Available MDX Filter Operators

This Operator	Performs This Action
Equal, Not Equal	Filters the results to include or exclude the selected dimension members
In, Not In	Filters the results to include or exclude members that are part of a named set defined in the cube
Contains, Begins With	Filters the results to include members whose names contain or start with the string defined as the filter expression (which you enter in the Filter Expression box without quotes)
Range (Inclusive)	Filters the results to include members in a range between a beginning member and an ending member defined as the filter expression, and includes the beginning and ending members
Range (Exclusive)	Filters the results to include members in a range between a beginning member and an ending member defined as the filter expression, but excludes the beginning and ending members
MDX	Filters the results to include members defined by an MDX expression

Adding a Calculation to the MDX Query

Because the MDX query designer automatically generates the MDX for you as you drag items from the Metadata pane into the Data pane, you are not required to know MDX before you can build a report using Analysis Services as a data source. However, if you learn MDX, then you can fine-tune the query by using the Query Mode of the query designer. Furthermore, you can add calculations to the dataset if the calculation you need is not already defined in the cube. Although you can add calculations to the query in Query Mode, you might find it easier to use the graphical interface in the Calculated Member Builder when the query designer is in Design Mode.

In this procedure, you review the MDX generated by the query designer and add a calculation for the variance between the gross margin percent goal and actual value.

Add a calculation to the MDX query

1. In the MDX query designer toolbar, click the Design Mode button (the last button on the right side of the toolbar) to switch to Query Mode to see the MDX generated by the query designer, as shown here.

```
SELECT NON EMPTY { [Measures].[Reseller Gross Profit Margin], [Measures].[Reseller
Sales Amount] } ON COLUMNS, NON EMPTY {
([Product].[Category].[Category].ALLMEMBERS ) } DIMENSION PROPERTIES
MEMBER_CAPTION, MEMBER_UNIQUE_NAME ON ROWS FROM { SELECT ( {
[Date].[Calendar Year].&[2004] } ) ON COLUMNS FROM [Adventure Works]) WHERE (
[Date].[Calendar Year].&[2004] ) CELL PROPERTIES VALUE, BACK_COLOR,
FORE_COLOR, FORMATTED_VALUE, FORMAT_STRING, FONT_NAME, FONT_SIZE,
FONT_FLAGS
```

Notice towards the end of the query that the MDX query designer automatically includes a request for cell properties that you can use to format values in the report. For example, in the sample database, both the Reseller Sales Amount and Reseller Gross Profit Margin measures have a property that defines the format string to be used by the client application when displaying the respective values. In addition, the Reseller Gross Profit Margin has a property controlling the font color based on the current value of the measure. Reporting Services does not automatically use these properties, but it includes them as extended field properties of the dataset. You can access these properties when designing the report layout, as you learn how to do in the section entitled "Using Extended Field Properties," later in this chapter.

If you're comfortable with developing MDX queries, you can modify the query directly while in Query Mode. However, after you make changes, you cannot switch back to Design Mode without losing any changes that you make in Query Mode. The rule to follow when designing your own MDX queries for Reporting Services is to use only measures on the column's axis.

> **Tip** To work around the "measures only" limitation on the columns axis of an MDX query, you can create a calculated member using the WITH clause. Create the new member as a member of the Measures dimension, and then include the new member in the set of measures defined for the columns axis in the SELECT statement.

As an alternative to modifying the MDX query in Query Mode when you want to add a calculated member, you can use the Calculated Members pane in Design Mode.

2. On the MDX Query Designer toolbar, click the Design Mode button to switch back to Design Mode.

3. On the MDX Query Designer toolbar, click the Add Calculated Member button.

4. In the Calculated Member Builder dialog box, in the Name text box, type **Goal Variance**.

5. In the Metadata pane, expand KPIs, expand Product Gross Profit Margin, and drag Value to the Expression text box.

    In the Calculated Member Builder dialog box, you can type an MDX expression directly into the Expression text box, or use the Metadata and Functions panes to drag and drop items into the Expression text box.

6. At the end of the expression, type a minus sign (–).

7. From the Metadata pane, drag Goal to the end of the expression in the Expression text box.

8. At the end of the expression, type the following text:

```
, FORMAT_STRING = "Percent"
```

You can define the formatting in your calculated member definition so that you can be consistent in using extended field properties for all values in the dataset, as shown here.

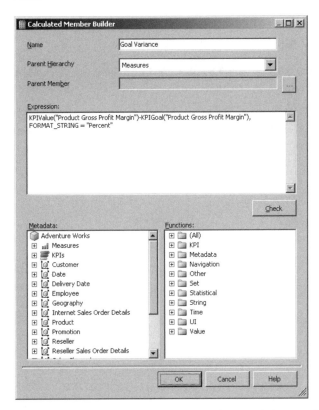

The cube contains several KPIs. A KPI is a special type of calculation stored in the Analysis Services cube to compare actual values to target values. The Goal Variance calculated member that you are creating computes the difference between the goal and the value. The resulting value is available as a field in the dataset when you add the calculated member to the query.

9. Click OK.

> **Note** A message box displays with a message regarding a syntax error in the calculated member. However, you can safely ignore this message. Just click OK to continue.

The new member displays in the Calculated Members pane, as shown here.

10. From the Calculated Members pane, drag Goal Variance to the right of Reseller Gross Profit Margin in the Data pane.

The formatted value for Goal Variance does not display in the Data pane. You must use extended field properties in the report layout, which you do in the section entitled "Using Extended Field Properties," later in this chapter.

11. On the MDX Query Designer toolbar, click the Design Mode button to switch back to Query Mode.

12. Click OK to close the Query Designer dialog box, and then click OK to close the Dataset Properties window.

Building a Report

After you have a dataset available, you are ready to build your report by arranging the dataset fields in data regions. For the most part, using fields from an Analysis Services dataset is no different from using fields from any other type of dataset. However, you'll find there are a few notable differences when you need to format or aggregate field values, which you learn about in this section.

Using an Analysis Services Dataset in a Report

After creating an Analysis Services dataset, you're ready to develop the report layout. The columns returned by the MDX query are added as fields to the dataset, and you can use these fields in a data region in the same way you learned to work with dataset fields in previous chapters.

In this procedure, you create a simple table that groups details from the Analysis Services dataset by business type and by sales territory.

Create a table with an Analysis Services dataset

1. In the Toolbox pane, double-click Table to add it to the design surface.

2. From the Report Data window, drag Category to the first text box of the details row of the table.

3. Drag Reseller_Sales_Amount to the text box next to [Product].

4. Drag Reseller_Gross_Profit_Margin to the text box next to [Reseller_Sales_Amount].

5. Right-click the column handle above Reseller Gross Profit Margin, select Insert Column, and click Right.

6. Drag Goal_Variance to the text box next to [Reseller_Gross_Profit_Margin].

7. Right-click the text box containing [Reseller_Sales_Amount], then click Add Total.

8. Repeat the previous step to add a total for the Reseller Gross Profit Margin and Goal Variance columns.

9. Select the row handle of the header row, and click the Bold button on the toolbar.

10. Select the row handle of the footer row, and click the Bold button on the toolbar.

11. Save and then preview the report, as shown here.

	Reseller Sales Amount	Reseller Gross Profit Margin	Goal Variance
Accessories	161794.3332	0.367493657064 622	0.15247280818 2663
Bikes	13399243.1836	- 0.018202659094 8453	0.03380549485 88823
Clothing	386013.1626	0.085850518352 2465	- 0.00592539782 90518
Components	2091011.9184	0.066004170796 6957	- 0.03399582920 33033
	16038062.5978	0.501145687118 719	0.14635707600 919

Notice that the numeric values are currently not formatted. Rather than use the format techniques you learned in Chapter 4, "Designing Reports," you can use the extended field properties to apply the format properties defined in the Analysis Services cube, which you learn how to do in the next procedure.

Using Extended Field Properties

The developer of an Analysis Services cube has the option to define a format string for each measure. You can access this format string by using the extended field properties that are available when you use an Analysis Services data source. The MDX query returns two results for the measure value in the dataset. The unformatted value is stored as a string in the *Value* property of the field, while the formatted value is stored as a string in the *FormattedValue* property. You can then display the formatted value in a text box by using the syntax `=Fields!MeasureName.FormattedValue,` where `MeasureName` is the name of your measure.

In this procedure, you format the numeric values in your report by using the extended field properties.

Use extended field properties to format values

1. Click the Design tab.

2. Right-click the text box containing [Reseller_Sales_Amount], and click Expression.

3. In the Set Expression For Value text box, change the expression to =Fields!Reseller_Sales_Amount.FormattedValue, and click OK.

4. Repeat the previous step to use the *FormattedValue* property in place of the *Value* property in the text boxes containing [Reseller_Gross_Profit_Margin] and [Goal Variance].

5. Click the text box containing [Sum(Reseller_Sales_Amount)], and then, in the Properties window, in the Format box, type **C2** to format the value as currency with two decimal places.

   When you use an aggregate function like *Sum*, you cannot use the *FormattedValue* property. Instead, you must use the *Format* property for the text box to apply the desired formatting.

6. Click the text box containing [Sum(Reseller_Gross_Profit_Margin)], and then, in the Properties window, in the Format box, type **P2** to format the value as a percentage with two decimal places.

7. Repeat the previous step to format the text box containing [Sum(Goal_Variance)].

8. Click the column header for the Reseller Sales Amount column, and then, while pressing the CTRL key, click the column headers for the Reseller Gross Profit Margin and Goal Variance columns.

9. On the toolbar, click the Align Right button.

10. Save and then preview the report, as shown here.

	Reseller Sales Amount	Reseller Gross Profit Margin	Goal Variance
Accessories	$161,794.33	36.75%	15.25%
Bikes	$13,399,243.18	-1.82%	3.38%
Clothing	$386,013.16	8.59%	-0.59%
Components	$2,091,011.92	6.60%	-3.40%
	$16,038,062.60	50.11 %	14.64 %

Note The text boxes containing fields with the *FormattedValue* property might appear empty when you preview the report the first time. Click the Refresh button on the toolbar to execute the report one more time to display the formatted values correctly.

Now the values are properly formatted using the currency or percentage format as applicable.

If you look carefully, however, you will notice that the totals for Reseller Gross Profit Margin and for Goal Variance are summing the individual rows. The report definition currently uses the *Sum* function to calculate each total by adding each detail row. However, these values are *nonadditive*. A nonadditive value cannot be summed because it is derived from a multiplication or division of other values that must be summed before the multiplication or division is performed, such as a ratio or percentage value. The cube can provide the correct percentage values for all product categories if you use the *Aggregate* function instead, which you do in the next procedure.

Using Extended Field Properties for Conditional Formatting

The developer of an Analysis Services cube can also define conditional formatting for calculations to set the font color, background color, font name, font size, and font flags to specify text decorations such as bold or underline. You can then use extended field properties to access these settings and configure text box properties, such as *Color* or *BackgroundColor*. For example, imagine that the Reseller Gross Profit Margin were defined in the cube to display the value using a red font whenever the value falls below a specified threshold and using a green font whenever the value falls above a different specified threshold. If that were the case, you could then use the definition stored in the cube to set the proper color of the value in your report by following these steps:

1. Click the Design tab.

2. Click the text box containing the calculation, and then, in the Properties window, in the Color drop-down list, select Expression.

3. In the Set Expression For Color box, construct the following expression:

   ```
   =Fields!Reseller_Gross_Profit_Margin.Color
   ```

   The condition determining which color to display is defined in the cube and returned by the query to the dataset as a cell property.

4. Click OK.

Using the *Aggregate* Function

As you learned in the previous procedure, some measures in a cube are nonadditive, such as Reseller Gross Profit Margin. When you use a client application to retrieve nonadditive measures from a cube, the Analysis Services engine returns the correct aggregation because it knows to sum the constituent components of the measure before performing the calculation defined for the measure. In the case of Reseller Gross Profit Margin, the constituent components are Reseller Sales Amount and Reseller Total Product Cost. When you use Reporting

Services, the MDX query returns the correctly aggregated value for each row in the results, but you might then design your report layout to include a total of these rows. To ensure that you get the proper results in the total row, you must replace the *Sum* function with the *Aggregate* function to instruct Reporting Services to retrieve the server aggregate instead of performing the calculation.

In this procedure, you modify the expressions used on the total row for nonadditive measures to use the *Aggregate* function.

Use the *Aggregate* function for nonadditive measures

1. Click the Design tab.

2. Right-click the text box in the footer row in the Reseller Gross Profit Margin column, and click Expression.

3. In the Set Expression For Value box, change the expression to =Aggregate(Fields! Reseller_Sales_Gross_Profit_Margin.Value), and click OK.

4. Repeat the previous step to use the *Aggregate* function in place of the *Sum* function in the text box for the Goal Variance total.

5. Save and then preview the report, as shown here.

	Reseller Sales Amount	Reseller Gross Profit Margin	Goal Variance
Accessories	$161,794.33	36.75%	15.25%
Bikes	$13,399,243.18	-1.82%	3.38%
Clothing	$386,013.16	8.59%	-0.59%
Components	$2,091,011.92	6.60%	-3.40%
	$16,038,062.60	-0.08 %	3.64 %

Now the values on the footer row use the aggregated values from the Analysis Services cube rather than the sum of the detail rows in the report.

Displaying Aggregate Values in Detail Rows

There might be times when a data region must include a combination of detail and aggregate rows. By default, the dataset ignores the aggregate rows, but you can override this behavior by changing an option in the Dataset Properties dialog box. On the Options page, you can change the Interpret Subtotals As Detail Rows value to *True*. When you change this value, the data region will correctly display the aggregate rows.

In this procedure, you change the dataset properties to display aggregate values in detail rows.

Interpret subtotals as detail rows

1. In Solution Explorer, double-click Reseller Sales by Category.rdl.

2. Preview the report.

Category	Subcategory	Reseller Sales Amount	Reseller Gross Profit Margin
Bikes	Mountain Bikes	$3,902,246.74	6.17%
	Road Bikes	$4,448,636.90	-6.51%
	Touring Bikes	$5,048,359.55	-3.87%
		$13,399,243.18	

The report shows only details for the Bikes category, although the query results include subtotals for other categories. Notice also the total row does not include a value for Reseller Gross Profit Margin.

3. Click the Design tab.

4. In the Report Data window, double-click DataSet1.

5. In the Dataset Properties dialog box, click Query Designer.

6. On the query designer toolbar, click the Execute Query button.

Category	Subcategory	Reseller Sales Amount	Reseller Gross Profit Margin	Reseller Total Product Cost
Accessories	(null)	161794.3332	0.367493657064622	102335.942
Bikes	Mountain Bikes	3902246.7399	0.0617062596626503	3661453.6893
Bikes	Road Bikes	4448636.8959	-0.0650547227099439	4738041.7356
Bikes	Touring Bikes	5048359.5478	-0.0386838664819554	5243649.6145
Clothing	(null)	386013.1626	0.0858505183522465	352873.7325
Components	(null)	2091011.9184	0.0660041707966957	1952996.4106

Here you can see the query actually returns subtotals for the Accessories, Clothing, and Component categories, and details for the Mountain Bikes, Road Bikes, and Touring Bikes subcategories for the Bikes category. Remember that the report displays only the subcategories for Bikes.

7. Click Cancel.

8. In the Dataset Properties dialog box, in the left pane, click Options.

9. In the Interpret Subtotals As Detail Rows drop-down list, select True, as shown here.

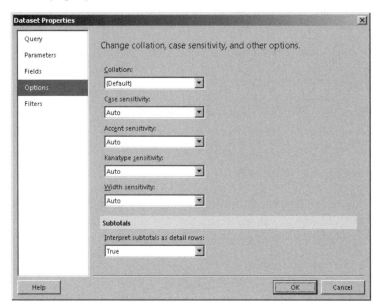

When the Interpret Subtotals As Detail Rows value is *Auto,* Reporting Services checks
to see if subtotal rows and detail rows are in the query results and adjusts the report
display to include the subtotal rows. However, if an *Aggregate* function is used in the
report, then the subtotal rows are ignored as you saw when viewing the report in a
previous step. By changing the value to *True,* Reporting Services instead includes the
subtotal rows and ignores only the *Aggregate* function instead.

10. Click OK, and then save and preview the report, as shown here.

Category	Subcategory	Reseller Sales Amount	Reseller Gross Profit Margin
Accessories		$161,794.33	36.75%
Bikes	Mountain Bikes	$3,902,246.74	6.17%
	Road Bikes	$4,448,636.90	-6.51%
	Touring Bikes	$5,048,359.55	-3.87%
Clothing		$386,013.16	8.59%
Components		$2,091,011.92	6.60%
		$16,038,062.60	

Now the subtotal rows appear in the report. To get the correct aggregate value in the
total row, you must create an expression that sums the constituent components of the
calculation first, and then calculates the percentage.

11. Click the Design tab.

12. Right-click the text box in the total row of the Reseller Gross Profit Margin column, and
click Expression.

13. In the Expression dialog box, construct the following expression:

```
=(Sum(Fields!Reseller_Sales_Amount.Value) - Sum(Fields!Reseller_Total_Product_Cost.
Value))/Sum(Fields!Reseller_Sales_Amount.Value)
```

This expression calculates the total Reseller Gross Profit Margin value by subtracting the sum of costs from the sum of sales and then dividing the result by the sum of sales.

14. Click OK, and then save and preview the report, as shown here. If necessary, click the Refresh button on the toolbar to display the values in the detail lines.

Category	Subcategory	Reseller Sales Amount	Reseller Gross Profit Margin
Accessories		$161,794.33	36.75%
Bikes	Mountain Bikes	$3,902,246.74	6.17%
	Road Bikes	$4,448,636.90	-6.51%
	Touring Bikes	$5,048,359.55	-3.87%
Clothing		$386,013.16	8.59%
Components		$2,091,011.92	6.60%
		$16,038,062.60	-0.08 %

The correct value for Reseller Gross Profit Margin now displays in the total row.

Designing Parameters

Working with linked report parameters and query parameters when using an Analysis Services dataset is quite different from the procedures you followed in Chapter 6, "Adding Interactivity," to set up linked parameters for a relational dataset. If you use dimension members from the Analysis Services cube to populate a list of available values for a report parameter, the process to create and configure the report parameter is quite easy. You're not limited to creating report parameters that are based on a cube, however. In this section, you learn how to work with both types of report parameters to filter a dataset and how to customize a query parameter linked to a report parameter.

Adding a Parameter to an Analysis Services Dataset

In Chapter 6, you learned how to create a report parameter using a dataset to provide the list of available values and how to link a report parameter to a query parameter. When you use an Analysis Services data source, these steps are simplified. You need only define the dimension on which the filter is based, specify a default value, and indicate that you want to create a parameter. The rest of the work required to build the report parameter and the query parameter is done for you.

In this procedure, you add a parameter to filter a dataset by calendar year.

Add a parameter to filter a dataset

1. In Solution Explorer, double-click Reseller Sales OLAP.rdl, and click the Design tab.

2. In the Report Data window, double-click DataSet1.

3. In the Dataset Properties dialog box, click Query Designer.

> **Note** A message box displays with a message regarding a syntax error in the calculated member. However, you can safely ignore this message. Just click OK to continue. You also need to drag Goal Variance from the Calculated Members pane to the Data pane.

4. In the Filter pane, select the Parameters check box to the right of {CY 2004}, and click OK.

5. In the Dataset Properties dialog box, click OK.

6. In the Report Data window, expand the Parameters folder, and double-click DateCalendarYear.

   After selecting the Parameters check box in the dataset, a new report parameter becomes available. Notice that the data type is Text and the option to allow multiple values is enabled.

7. In the left pane, click Available Values, as shown here.

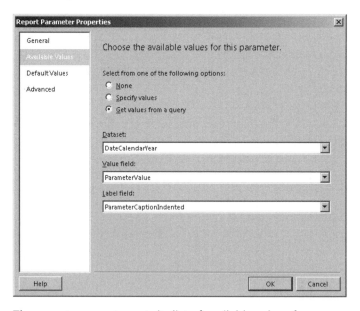

The report parameter gets its list of available values from a new dataset, DateCalendarYear, which includes a value field used to filter the query results in the dataset and a label field used to display the available choices to the user. This new dataset is created automatically for you.

8. In the left pane, click Default Values, as shown here.

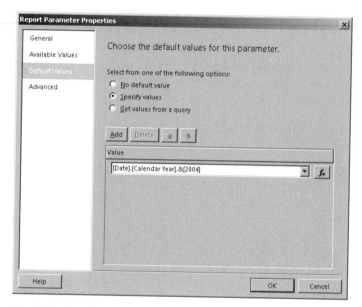

The default value defined for the report parameter is the same value you selected in the query designer, although the format of the value is not the same. When you supply a default value for a report parameter that is linked to an Analysis Services dataset, you must provide the unique name of a dimension member. The unique name includes the dimension, hierarchy, and member names. The key name can be used in place of the member name and is often preferred because the key doesn't usually change, whereas the member name might. In the current scenario, the label CY 2004 corresponds to the unique name [Date].[Calendar Year].&[2004] in the cube.

9. Click OK.

Now that you know the report parameter uses the DateCalendarYear dataset, you might want to review the new dataset. However, you probably don't see that dataset in the Report Data window right now because the dataset is hidden by default.

10. In the Report Data window, right-click anywhere in the window, and click Show All Hidden Datasets.

11. In the Report Data window, double-click DateCalendarYear, and then, in the Dataset Properties dialog box, click Query Designer to see the MDX generated by the query designer, as shown here.

```
WITH MEMBER [Measures].[ParameterCaption] AS [Date].[Calendar
Year].CURRENTMEMBER.MEMBER_CAPTION MEMBER [Measures].[ParameterValue] AS
[Date].[Calendar Year].CURRENTMEMBER.UNIQUENAME MEMBER [Measures].[ParameterLevel] AS
[Date].[Calendar Year].CURRENTMEMBER.LEVEL.ORDINAL SELECT {[Measures].[ParameterCaption],
[Measures].[ParameterValue], [Measures].[ParameterLevel]} ON COLUMNS , [Date].[Calendar
Year].ALLMEMBERS ON ROWS FROM [Adventure Works]
```

Notice that the fields used in the report parameter, *ParameterCaptionIndented* and *ParameterValue,* are defined in this query as calculations in the Measures dimension even though these values are not the numeric values that are normally found in the Measures dimension. Nonetheless, to create the proper query structure, which requires you to use only measures on the columns axis, you can create calculations that evaluate as string values and assign the result to a new member in the Measures dimension as shown in the previous query.

12. On the Query Designer toolbar, click the Execute Query button to view the query results, as shown here.

Calendar Year	ParameterCaption	ParameterValue	ParameterLevel
(null)	All Periods	[Date].[Calendar Year].[All Periods]	0
CY 2001	CY 2001	[Date].[Calendar Year].&[2001]	1
CY 2002	CY 2002	[Date].[Calendar Year].&[2002]	1
CY 2003	CY 2003	[Date].[Calendar Year].&[2003]	1
CY 2004	CY 2004	[Date].[Calendar Year].&[2004]	1
CY 2006	CY 2006	[Date].[Calendar Year].&[2006]	1

Notice that the query also includes a *ParameterLevel* field, which is used to determine how many spaces to include as a prefix when displaying the list of available values in the parameter drop-down list. The use of spaces in the list of available values helps the user easily identify the hierarchical relationship between items in the list when multiple levels of a hierarchy are included in the list.

13. Click OK twice, and then save and preview the report.

14. In the Date.Calendar Year drop-down list, clear the CY 2004 check box, select the CY 2003 check box, and click View Report.

The report data changes to reflect the current parameter selection.

Creating a Custom Query Parameter

The Parameter check box in the Filter pane makes it easy to create a report parameter and linked query parameter, but you might have a situation in which you create a report parameter independently of the Analysis Services dataset. As an example, when you require a report parameter that allows the user to select a specific day, you can use a calendar control instead of requiring the user to scroll through a list of date labels from the cube. However, when a date is selected by the user, the calendar control returns a string value that cannot be used in the MDX query as a query parameter value. You must convert the date string to the unique name of the date as it is represented in the Analysis Services cube, and then you can use the converted value as a filter on the dataset.

In this procedure, you add a report parameter that uses a calendar control and link it to a new query parameter to filter the dataset by date.

Create a custom query parameter to filter by date

1. In Solution Explorer, double-click Calendar Control.rdl to open the Report Designer.

   This report is similar to the Reseller Sales OLAP report you created earlier in this chapter, but it has no report parameter defined. Instead of using date labels from the cube in a report parameter, you want to use a calendar control to allow the user to filter the report by date.

2. In the Report Data window, double-click DataSet1.

3. In the Dataset Properties dialog box, click Query Designer.

4. On the query designer toolbar, click the Design Mode button to switch to Query Mode.

5. On the query designer toolbar, click the Query Parameters button.

6. In the Query Parameters dialog box, in the Parameter text box, type **Date**.

7. In the Dimension drop-down list, select Date, and then, in the Hierarchy drop-down list, select Date.Date.

8. In the Default drop-down list, expand All Periods, select July 1, 2001, and click OK. The Query Parameters dialog box now looks like this:

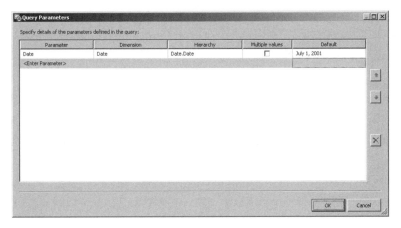

9. Click OK to close the Query Parameters dialog box, and then click OK to close the Dataset Properties dialog box.

10. Click Start, click Windows Explorer, navigate to the Microsoft Press\Rs2008sbs \Chap07folder in your Documents folder, double-click MDXQuery.txt, press CTRL+A to select the query text, and press CTRL+C to copy the text to the Clipboard.

11. On the query designer toolbar, click the Design Mode button to switch to Query Mode.

12. Highlight the query text, and press CTRL+V to replace the current query with the query text in the Clipboard.

The new MDX query looks like this:

```
SELECT NON EMPTY { [Measures].[Reseller Sales Amount] } ON COLUMNS, NON EMPTY {
([Product].[Category].[Category].ALLMEMBERS ) } DIMENSION
PROPERTIES MEMBER_CAPTION, MEMBER_UNIQUE_NAME ON ROWS FROM (SELECT (
STRTOSET(@Date)) ON
COLUMNS FROM [Adventure Works]) CELL PROPERTIES VALUE, BACK_COLOR, FORE_COLOR,
FORMATTED_VALUE, FORMAT_STRING, FONT_NAME, FONT_SIZE, FONT_FLAGS
```

This query replaces the FROM [Adventure Works] clause in the original query with the following expression:

```
FROM (SELECT ( STRTOSET(@Date)) ON COLUMNS FROM [Adventure Works])
```

In the new MDX query, you use a subcube subquery to retrieve all data from the cube filtered by the query parameter, *@Date*. These results are used by the main query to retrieve Reseller Gross Profit Margin and Reseller Sales Amount by Category.

13. Click OK to close the query designer, and then click OK to close the Dataset Properties dialog box.

You must close the Dataset Properties dialog box so that Reporting Services can create the new report parameter.

14. In the Report Data window, expand the Parameters folder, and double-click Date.

15. In the Data Type drop-down list, select Date/Time.

When you select the Date/Time data type, the parameter displays a calendar control.

16. In the left pane, click Available Values, and then select None.

By creating the parameter in the Query Parameters dialog box earlier in this procedure, a new dataset was created automatically to supply the list of available values for the report parameter. However, when you use a calendar control, you must disable this list.

17. In the left pane, click Default Values, select No Default Value, and click OK.

As you learned in Chapter 6, you can set a default value, such as *=Today()*, to allow the report to execute without forcing the user to make a date selection. However, because the cube does not contain data for current dates, the report will be empty if you set today as the default. Accordingly, you use the No Default Value option for this report parameter.

18. In the Report Data window, double-click DataSet1, and then, in the left pane, click Parameters.

19. To the right of the Parameter Value text box, click the expression button.

20. In the Expression dialog box, construct the following expression:

```
="[Date].[Calendar].[Date].[" + Format(CDate(Parameters!Date.Value), "MMMM d, yyyy") + "]"
```

Tip You can copy this expression from the ConvertDate.txt file in the Microsoft Press \Rs2008sbs\Chap07folder in your Documents folder.

This expression converts the parameter value, which is in date/time format, to a string that matches the structure of a unique name of a date member. In the Adventure Works cube, the unique name for the first day of July 2001 is [Date].[Calendar].[Date].[July 1, 2001].

> **Important** Be sure to use *MMMM* instead of *mmmm* in the expression to convert the month number to the full month name.

21. Click OK to close the Expression dialog box, and then click OK to close the Dataset Properties dialog box.

22. Save and then preview the report.

23. Click the calendar icon to the right of the Date parameter box.

24. In the calendar control, click the year, and then click the spinner control to decrease the year value to *2004*.

25. In the calendar control, click Previous to change the month to June, and then click day 1 in the month to select June 1, 2004. If your locale displays dates in *mm/dd/yyyy* format, the date parameter now contains 6/1/2004.

26. Click View Report, and you see the report as shown here.

Using Analysis Services as a data source allows you to deliver high-performance reports with ease. Even if you're not skilled in developing MDX queries, you can still retrieve data from an Analysis Services data source. Reporting Services even includes additional features to support working with data from Analysis Services, such as extended field properties, the *Aggregate* function, and simplified parameter creation.

Now that you know how to use both relational and OLAP data sources, you have expanded your options for building reports. There remains one more aspect of report development to learn. In Chapter 8, "Visualizing Data," you explore the data visualization features of Reporting Services.

Chapter 7 Quick Reference

To	Do This
Create an Analysis Services shared data source	In Solution Explorer, right-click the Shared Data Sources folder, select Add New Data Source, name the data source, select Microsoft SQL Server Analysis Services in the Type drop-down list, click Edit, provide a server name, and select an Analysis Services database name.
Use the MDX query designer in Design Mode to build a query	In the Report Data window, select New, Dataset, Query Designer, expand folders in the Metadata pane, and drag items from the Metadata pane to the Data pane.
Filter the Analysis Services dataset	In the MDX query designer, in the Filter pane, select a dimension in the Dimension drop-down list, select a hierarchy in the Hierarchy drop-down list, select an operator, and provide a filter expression.
Add a calculation to the MDX query in Design Mode	In the MDX query designer, click the Add Calculated Member button on the query designer toolbar, provide a name for the calculation, drag items from the Metadata pane to the Expression box or type an MDX expression directly in the Expression box, click OK, and drag the calculation from the Calculated Members pane to the Data pane.
Use the format string defined for a measure in the source cube	In the data region, right-click the text box containing the measure field, select Expression, and replace the *Value* property with the *FormattedValue* property, like this: `=Fields!Reseller_Sales_Amount.FormattedValue`
Display a server aggregate for a non-additive measure	In the data region, right-click the text box containing the aggregate expression for a measure field, click Expression, and replace the *Sum* function (or other aggregate function) with the *Aggregate* function, like this: `=Aggregate(Fields!Reseller_Sales_Gross_Profit_Margin.Value)`
Combine detail and subtotal rows in a data region	In the Report Data window, double-click the dataset, click Options, and then, in the Interpret Subtotals As Detail Rows drop-down list, select True.
Add a parameter to filter an Analysis Services dataset	In the Report Data window, double-click the dataset, click Query Designer, add a filter to the Filter pane, and select the Parameters check box to the right of the filter expression.
Create a custom query parameter	In the Report Data window, double-click the dataset, select Query Designer, click the Design Mode button on the query designer toolbar, click the Query Parameters button on the query designer toolbar, provide a parameter name, select a dimension in the Dimension drop-down list, select a hierarchy in the Hierarchy drop-down list, specify whether to allow multiple values, select a default value, click OK, and modify the MDX query to replace the FROM clause with a subcube subquery. Modify the report parameter as needed to set or remove available values and default values. Modify the dataset parameter properties to define an expression using the report parameter as needed.

Chapter 8
Visualizing Data

After completing this chapter, you will be able to:

- Choose a chart type or gauge type to present data visually.
- Create a column chart.
- Configure properties for chart elements.
- Add a calculated series to a chart.
- Move values to a secondary axis or a separate chart area.
- Combine chart types in a single chart.
- Create a linear gauge.

Users can often gain better insights into data when visualization methods are used to display summarized data. With Reporting Services, you can choose from many different types of charts and gauges to provide rich data visualization. In this chapter, you explore a variety of data visualization methods. The emphasis in this chapter is on chart development because charts are more commonly used than gauges in most organizations, but you also learn how to work with gauges to provide reports for key performance indicator information.

 Note Some of the charts that you create in this chapter depend on the Analysis Services sample database that you use in Chapter 7, "Using Analysis Services as a Data Source." If you have not installed this database yet, refer to the instructions in Chapter 7 to install the sample database so that you can successfully work with all of the charts in this chapter.

Creating Charts

Charts are a great way to summarize numerical information. If you apply good chart design principles, users can easily compare values, spot trends, and identify anomalies. You can create a report that contains only a chart, or you can combine a chart with other data regions to present data in multiple formats. You can even insert a chart inside a table, matrix, or list to repeat a chart within a data region. Reporting Services provides amazing flexibility in chart design. This section introduces you to the key charting features. After you master the fundamentals, you should spend some time exploring the many available properties for charts and chart elements to fully appreciate the scope of possibilities.

> **Tip** After you complete this chapter, download and install the AdventureWorksOffline Report Samples from *http://www.codeplex.com/MSFTRSProdSamples/Release /ProjectReleases.aspx?ReleaseId=18649* to view more examples of charts.

Understanding Chart Types

Although you can use many different chart types, most chart types share some common elements. Figure 8-1 illustrates these various chart elements.

- **Value axis**   The value axis is also called the y-axis in a column chart. The value axis is a scale that shows the numerical values in the chart and includes a title that you can choose to remove. You can change many properties of the value axis, including the appearance of gridlines, the minimum and maximum values of the scale, the intervals between values on the scale, and the font and formatting of axis labels.

- **Chart title**   The chart title is an element that appears by default, but you can remove it, move it to a new location, or change its properties by specifying visibility, font, fill, border, and shadow options. You can also associate an action with the chart title.

- **Category axis**   The category axis is also called the x-axis in a column chart. This axis displays the grouping of numerical values in the chart. The category axis has most of the same properties available for the value axis, allowing you to customize its appearance. By default, the category axis includes a title that you can choose to remove as the report author has done in Figure 8-1.

- **Series**   The chart series is an optional chart element that allows you to add another level of grouping. When you have multiple sets of numerical data in a chart, such as Sales Amount and Order Quantity, each set of data is a series. You can also add a field explicitly, such as *Calendar Year*, as a series or define an expression. You can apply a filter to a series group, specify a sort order, or define a group variable.

- **Legend**   The legend maps the colors in the chart to specific series values. You can configure the layout and position of the legend, set visibility properties, and specify font, fill, border, and shadow options.

When you add a chart to the report design surface, you must select a chart type. The chart type determines how the numerical data displays in the report. A preview of each chart type appears in the Select Chart Type dialog box to help you match a chart type to your report specifications. When selecting a chart type, you should consider which chart types are best suited for the type of data you plan to show in the chart.

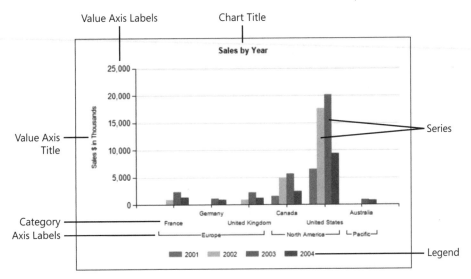

FIGURE 8-1 Chart elements

Charts to Display Linear Data

Most charts that you use in business reporting display linear data using a coordinate system along an x-axis and y-axis. Here are the available chart types used to display linear data:

- **Column chart**   The column chart is arguably one of the more common chart types that you'll use in your reports. Each series in the chart displays as a set of vertical bars. Use this chart type when you want to compare values in multiple series.

- **Line chart**   A line chart is also commonly used in business reports. A line represents the set of data points in a series with the categories on the x-axis determining the relative position of data points horizontally. Often, time periods are used as categories in a line chart. If a category has an empty point in a series, Reporting Services adds a placeholder line, but you can disable this behavior. You can combine a line chart with a column chart, but not with other chart types. You can create a sparkline chart by removing all axis titles, axis labels, and the legend from the chart. (A sparkline chart, popularized by Edward Tufte, is a small condensed line chart that is presented inline and intended to show trends and variation rather than precise details.)

- **Bar chart**   A bar chart is similar to a column chart because it displays each series as a set of bars. However, the bar chart displays bars horizontally. In effect, the vertical axis becomes the category axis and the horizontal axis becomes the value axis. This type of chart is useful when the category labels are too long to read easily in a column chart format.

- **Area chart**   The area chart displays the data points in each series as a connected line and fills in the area between the line and the axis. You can also use a variation called the 100% stacked area chart to show how each series contributes to the total of the dataset. You typically use the area chart type to display data for a continuous period of time as categories. If your data has empty data points, you should avoid using this chart type.

- **Scatter chart**   A scatter chart displays numerical data as a set of points. Each category displays as a different marker on the chart. This type of chart is good for comparing thousands of data points across categories. You shouldn't add series groupings to the chart because the chart then becomes too visually complex. When used properly, this type of chart allows you to see value distributions and clusters in your data more easily.

Charts to Display Ratio Data

When you want to compare values for individual categories to the value for all categories, you should choose a chart type designed to display ratio data. Here are the available types:

- **Pie chart and doughnut chart**   The pie chart and the doughnut chart are shape charts that show data as a proportion of the whole to facilitate comparisons between categories. Reporting Services calculates each category value as a percentage of the total and sizes the category segment in the shape proportionally. You simply provide the raw data in your dataset.

> **Tip** In general, you should use no more than seven categories when using the pie chart and doughnut chart types because too many categories make the chart difficult to read. Null, negative, or zero values in your dataset are excluded from the chart.

- **Funnel chart and pyramid chart**   The funnel chart and the pyramid chart are another variation of shape charts that also display each category as a percentage of whole, but Reporting Services orders categories in the shape from largest to smallest. For best results, you should sort your dataset and, as with the other shape charts, use seven or fewer categories.

- **Polar chart**   The polar chart displays each series as a set of points grouped by category in a 360-degree circle. Higher values are farther from the center of the chart than lower values. Categories display along the perimeter of the chart. A variation of the polar chart is the radar chart, which shows series data as a circular line or a filled area. The radar chart is useful for comparing multiple categories of data, while a polar chart is best for graphing data coordinates consisting of angle and distance values.

- **Scatter chart**   A scatter chart can also display ratio data as a set of points and is not restricted to linear data. Your must provide the ratio values in the dataset.

Charts to Display Multi-value Data

You can display multiple data points for each category and series combination in the chart by using the following chart types designed for multi-value data:

- **Range chart** A range chart must have a high and a low value for each category. The chart fills in the area between the two values for each data point. In addition to using this chart type to plot minimum and maximum values in a dataset by category, you can also use it to create a Gantt chart for tracking start and finish dates for a schedule.

- **Stock chart** A stock chart plots up to four values for each data point. For example, financial stock data has a high, low, open, and close value for each point in time.

Creating a Column Chart

You add a chart to a report just as you add a table or matrix—by dragging the control from the Toolbox to the report design surface. You add fields from your dataset to the data and category drop zones in the chart, and optionally to the series drop zone. As with a matrix, numeric values are aggregated automatically with an expression that uses the *Sum* function, but you can change the expression to use a different function. You can also drag a non-numeric field into the data drop zone, in which case the *Count* function is applied. You can think of a chart as behaving very much like a matrix. Categories are like columns in the matrix and series are like matrix rows.

> **Tip** If your dataset contains no rows of data, you can use the *NoDataMessage* property for the chart to display a message. If, on the other hand, your dataset contains rows of data but has no values for the fields you add to the chart's data drop zones, Reporting Services renders an empty chart and ignores the *NoDataMessage* property.

In this procedure, you create a column chart that displays sales by sales territory as a category and by year as a series.

Create a column chart

1. In SQL Server Business Intelligence Development Studio, on the File menu, point to Open and select Project/Solution.

2. In the Open Project dialog box, navigate to the Microsoft Press\Rs2008sbs \Chap08folder in your Documents folder and double-click Sales.sln.

3. In Solution Explorer, double-click Sales Summary.rdl.

4. From the Toolbox, drag the Chart control to the report design surface below the report title and the blue line.

5. In the Select Chart Type dialog box, click OK.

The default chart type is a column chart. The Select Chart Type dialog box shows a preview of each chart type and its variations to help you determine which chart type matches your requirements.

6. Click the chart to display the drop zones, as shown here.

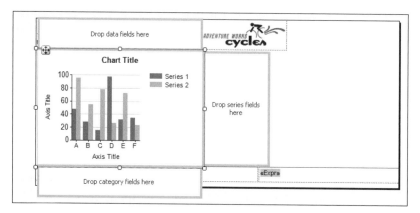

Notice the three drop zones for the chart. You use the data drop zone that appears above the chart to define the fields that represent the columns in the chart. You use the category drop zone that appears below the chart to define the groupings of data along the horizontal axis of the chart. The series drop zone that appears to the right of the chart is optional for adding another level of grouping to the chart.

7. From the Report Data pane, from the ResellerSales dataset, drag SalesAmount to the data drop zone.

8. In the category drop zone, click the Field List icon and select SalesTerritoryGroup.

The Field List icon provides an alternative method for adding fields to the chart's drop zones. You use the *SalesTerritoryGroup* field to group sales by sales territory in the column chart.

9. In the category drop zone, click the Field List icon and select SalesTerritoryCountry.

You use the *SalesTerritoryCountry* field to add a second grouping level to the column chart.

10. In the series drop zone, click the Field List icon and select CalendarYear.

Adding the *CalendarYear* field to the column chart produces a chart that displays one column per year for each sales territory country and sales territory group combination.

11. Save and then preview the report, as shown here.

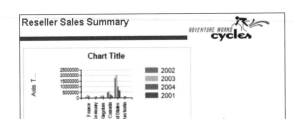

The column chart displays in the report, but it is difficult to read due to its size and lack of formatting. Whenever you create a chart, you must spend some additional time setting properties to improve the chart appearance.

Formatting a Chart

In addition to properties for the chart itself that define its size and visibility, each chart element has properties that can customize the overall appearance of your chart. For example, you can control the location of the legend or choose to exclude it from the chart altogether. You can also customize the appearance of the horizontal and vertical axes and their labels. Although you can use the Properties window in the development interface to configure properties for a selected chart element, you might find it easier to open the element's Properties dialog box.

In this procedure, you improve the appearance of a chart by changing the property values of selected chart elements.

Configure chart element properties

1. Click the Design tab.

2. Click the chart, and then, in the Properties window, expand the Size category.

3. In the Width text box, type **6in**, and then, in the Height text box, type **4in**.

4. Right-click the legend and select Legend Properties.

5. In the Legend Properties dialog box, in the Legend Position diagram, click the bottom center option button, as shown here, and then, in the Layout drop-down list, select Row.

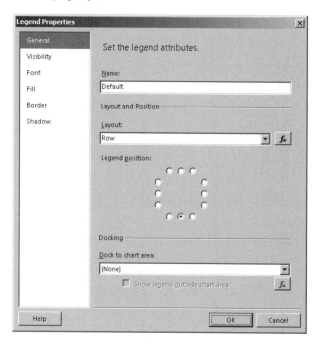

By default, the legend displays in a table and expands horizontally or vertically according to the chart space available. You can force the legend to expand vertically by choosing Tall Table or to expand horizontally by choosing Wide Table. You can also require the legend to display as a single column or row by choosing Column or Row, respectively.

Notice the other pages available in the Legend Properties dialog box to set properties for legend visibility, font appearance, the color and style of fill, border, and shadow effects.

6. Click OK.

7. On the vertical axis, right-click Axis Title and select Axis Title Properties.

8. In the Axis Title Properties dialog box, in the Title text box, type **Sales $ in Thousands** and click OK.

By default, the axis title alignment is set to Center. You can also choose Near to move the axis title closer to the intersection of the value and category axes, or Far to move the axis title farther from the axis intersection. You can also configure font properties for the axis title by using this dialog box.

9. Right-click any of the numeric labels on the vertical axis and select Axis Properties.

10. In the Value Axis Properties dialog box, in the left pane, click Number.

11. In the Category list, select Number, and then, in the Decimal Places text box, type **0**.

12. Select the Use 1000 Separator (,) check box.

13. Select the Show Values In check box, as shown here.

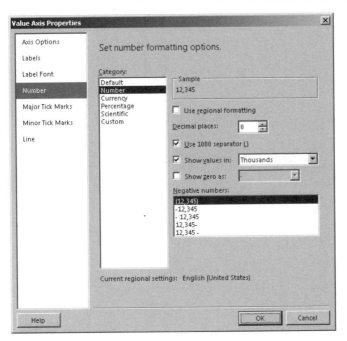

The default of Thousands converts the value *1,000* to *1* and the value *1,000,000* to *1,000* to avoid clutter on the vertical axis.

Notice the User Regional Formatting check box, which allows you to localize numerical formatting for the current user.

14. Click OK. The numeric values on the vertical axis now display 0, but when you preview the report, you see that the correct conversion of values is applied.

15. On the horizontal axis, right-click Axis Title and select Axis Title Properties.

16. In the Title Text box, clear the text and click OK.

17. Double-click the Chart Title, select the text Chart Title, and then type **Sales by Year**.

18. In the series drop zone, right-click CalendarYear and select Series Group Properties.

19. In the Series Group Properties dialog box, in the left pane, click Sorting.

20. Click Add.

21. In the Sort By drop-down list, select Calendar Year and click OK.

22. Save and then preview the report, as shown here.

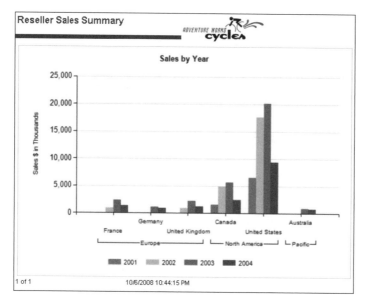

Now the chart information displays more clearly.

Using a Scale Break

When the range between high and low values in a chart is significant, you can use a scale break to cut out sections of the scale. You can also use properties to customize the appearance of the scale break further. For example, you can change the color and width of the lines representing the scale break.

> **Note** You cannot enable a scale break in a three-dimensional chart, with a logarithmic value axis, or when you have specified minimum or maximum values for the axis. You also cannot enable a scale break with the following chart types: polar, radar, pie, doughnut, funnel, pyramid, or a stacked chart of any type.

In this procedure, you create a column chart and enable scale breaks on the vertical axis.

Enable scale breaks

1. Click the Design tab.

2. In the Properties window, in the Report Item drop-down list at the top of the window, select Body.

3. Expand the Size category, and then, in the Height text box, type **8in**.

4. From the Toolbox, drag a Chart control to the report design surface below the existing chart.

5. In the Select Chart Type dialog box, click OK.

6. Drag the right edge of the chart to expand the width of the new chart to match the width of the chart above it.

   The blue snap line appears when the edges of each chart line up.

7. In the Properties window, in the Height text box, type **3in**.

8. Double-click the chart to display the drop zones.

9. In the data drop zone, click the Field List icon, point to AdventureWorksDW2008, point to EmployeeSales, and select SalesAmount.

   When multiple datasets are available in the report, you must specify a dataset before you can select a field. The next time you click the Field List icon only fields in the specified dataset appear because you can associate only one dataset with a data region.

10. In the category drop zone, click the Field List icon and select Employee.

    The Field List icon provides an alternative method for adding fields to the chart's drop zones.

11. Save and preview the report, and then scroll to the bottom of the report to view the second chart, shown here.

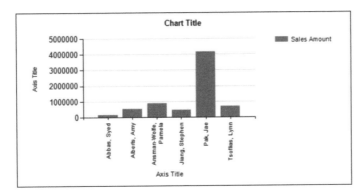

Here you can see that the value for Jae Pak is considerably higher than all other values in the chart. You can use a scale break to see more easily the relative values of all other employees in this dataset.

12. Click the Design tab.

13. On the vertical axis, right-click any axis label and select Axis Properties.

14. In the Value Axis Properties dialog box, select the Enable Scale Breaks check box, as shown here.

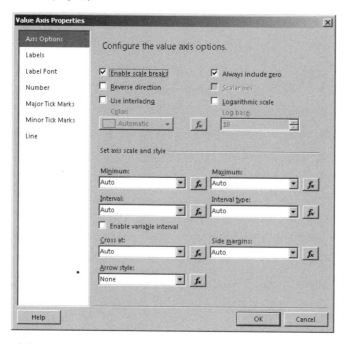

15. Click OK, save and preview the report, and scroll to the bottom of the report to view the second chart, as shown here.

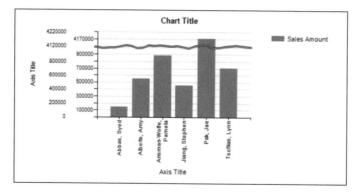

Notice the break in the scale between 900,000 and 4,120,000. You can now see more easily from the scale that Jae Pak has significantly higher sales than the other employees, and you can readily compare the differences between the other employees' sales.

Note You can access several properties for scale breaks in the Properties window. In the chart, click the vertical axis labels, and then in the Properties window, locate the ScaleBreakStyle category. Expand the category and review the various options available. For example, you can configure the maximum number of breaks permissible in the chart, the spacing between the break lines, and the color, style, and width of the break lines. You can even change the break line style from the default of Ragged, to Wave, Straight, or None.

Notice also that the labels on the horizontal axis display at a 90-degree angle. By default, the axis labels rotate to fit the chart. You can control the angle of the labels by setting the label angle explicitly.

16. Click the Design tab, right-click a horizontal axis label, and select Axis Properties.

17. In the Category Axis Properties dialog box, in the left pane, click Labels.

The default axis label options adjust the size and rotation of the labels automatically. For this chart, you force the labels to display at a 45-degree angle.

18. Select Disable Auto-fit, and then, in the Label Rotation Angle text box, type **-45**.

You can specify a rotation angle from –90 to 90 degrees. When you specify a negative value, the label angles upward and the end of the label is close to the horizontal axis. A positive value displays each label with a downward angle with the beginning of each label close to the horizontal axis.

19. Click OK, save and preview the report, and scroll to the bottom of the report to view the second chart, as shown here.

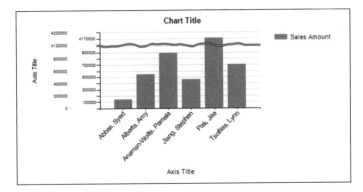

As you can see, using a 45-degree angle makes it easier to read the labels on the horizontal axis.

Note Many other properties are related to axis labels, including font type, size, color, and effects. You can also set the label interval to skip some labels and display the label at the specified interval. For example, if you define a category of days on the horizontal axis and you need to display a label only for every seventh day, you can set an interval of 7.

Adding a Calculated Series

In addition to using dataset fields and expressions based on dataset fields in the data drop zone of a chart, you can add a calculated series to display built-in formulas such as a moving average or median. Reporting Services includes several calculations for financial stock data, such as Bollinger bands and moving average convergence/divergence (MACD).

In this procedure, you add a moving average of three quarters as a calculated series to a report.

Add a moving average to a chart

1. In Solution Explorer, double-click Employee Sales Moving Average.rdl.

   This report displays sales for a single employee across quarters for multiple years. You add a moving average to the report.

2. Click the chart twice to display the drop zones.

3. Right-click [Sum(SalesAmount)] and select Add Calculated Series.

4. In the Calculated Series Properties dialog box, in the Period text box, type **3**.

5. Select the Start From First Point check box, as shown here.

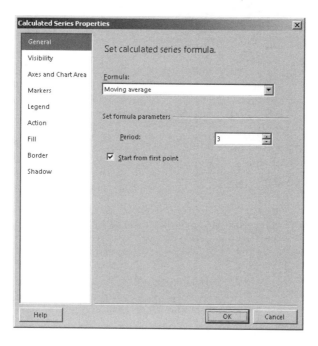

6. In the left pane, click Legend.

7. In the Custom Legend Text box, type **Moving Avg Sales**, as shown here.

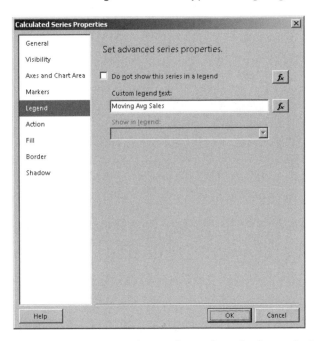

You can use an expression to determine whether to include the calculated series in the legend or customize the legend text by using an expression.

 Note The Calculated Series Properties dialog box provides access to many other properties for the moving average. You can set visibility, reassign the calculated series to a different value or category axis, move the calculated series to a separate chart area, assign the calculated series to an action, or configure appearance properties such as markers, fill, border, and shadow settings.

8. In the left pane, click Border.

9. In the Line Width text box, type **3pt**.

10. Click OK, and then save and preview the report, as shown here.

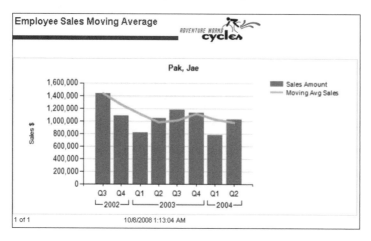

As you can see in the chart, a moving average smoothes out fluctuations in values within the number of periods specified for the calculated series and allows you to see whether values are trending up or down.

Using a Secondary Axis

When you want to compare values that use different units of measure, such as sales dollars versus order quantity, you can display the data in the same chart by placing each value on a separate axis. By default, a chart puts all items in the data drop zone on the primary value axis, but you can change the properties of any data item to assign it to the secondary value axis. Each axis has its own properties that you can use to apply formatting. Not only can you add a secondary axis for values, but you can also add a secondary axis for categories, although you will likely use the secondary value axis more often.

In this procedure, you modify a chart to display order quantity on the secondary value axis.

Move data to the secondary value axis

1. In Solution Explorer, double-click Sales And Order Quantity Summary.rdl.

2. Click the Preview tab to view the chart, as shown here.

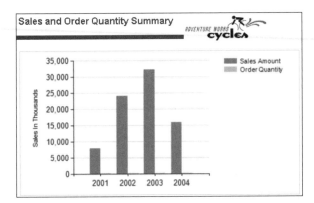

In this chart, the columns for the Order Quantity values are small compared to the Sales Amount values and are barely visible in the chart.

3. Click the Design tab, and then click the chart twice to display the drop zones.

4. In the data drop zone, right-click [Sum(OrderQuantity)] and select Series Properties.

5. In the Series Properties dialog box, in the left pane, click Axes And Chart Area.

6. Below Value Axis, select Secondary, as shown here.

7. Click OK, right-click any of the numeric values on the vertical axis to the right of the chart, and select Axis Properties.

8. In the Secondary Value Axis Properties dialog box, in the left pane, click Number.

9. In the Category list, select Number.

10. In the Decimal Places text box, type **0**.

11. Select the Use 1000 Separator (,) check box, select the Show Values In check box, and click OK.

12. Click Axis Title to the right of the chart and type **Order Qty In Thousands**.

13. Save and then preview the report, as shown here.

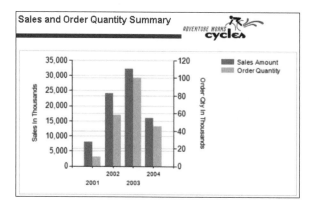

The Order Quantity values are visible in the chart now that they are associated with the secondary value axis.

Combining Chart Types

Another way to visualize data is to use different chart types within the same chart. For example, you can use a column chart to display the values of one series and a line chart to display the values of another series.

In this procedure, you add average sales as a calculation to the chart and display the result as a line.

Change the chart type for a data value

1. In Solution Explorer, select Sales And Order Quantity Summary.rdl, press CTRL+C, select the Reports folder, and press CTRL+V to create a copy of the report that you modified in the previous procedure.

2. Right-click Copy Of Sales And Order Quantity Summary.rdl, select Rename, and type **Sales and Average Sales.rdl**.

3. Double-click Sales And Average Sales.rdl to open this report on the design surface.

4. Click the chart twice to display the drop zones.

5. Right-click [Sum(OrderQuantity)] and select Series Properties.

6. In the Series Properties dialog box, to the right of the Value Field drop-down list, click the expression button.

7. In the Expression dialog box, modify the expression to look like this:

```
=Sum(Fields!SalesAmount.Value)/Sum(Fields!OrderQuantity.Value)
```

This expression calculates average sales.

8. Click OK to close the Expression dialog box, and then click OK to close the Series Properties dialog box.

An expression replaces Order Quantity as a data field.

9. In the data drop zone, right-click <<Expr>> and select Change Chart Type.

10. In the Select Chart Type dialog box, click Line and click OK.

The preview of the chart in the Report Designer now displays a line for the expression. You can make the line appear larger by changing the series properties. You already know that you can right-click a field or expression in the data drop zone to change its series properties, but another way to open the Series Properties dialog box is to right-click the series in the chart. This technique is useful when the drop zones aren't visible.

11. In the chart, right-click any point on the line and select Series Properties.

12. In the Series Properties dialog box, in the left pane, click Border.

13. In the Line Width text box, type **3pt** and click OK.

Next, you need to adjust the secondary value axis to remove the setting to display values in thousands.

14. Right-click any of the numeric values on the vertical axis to the right of the chart and select Axis Properties.

15. In the Secondary Value Axis Properties dialog box, in the left pane, click Number.

16. Clear the Show Values In check box and click OK.

Finally, adjust the title of the secondary axis.

17. Double-click Order Qty In Thousands to the right of the chart and replace the text title by highlighting the existing text and typing **Average Sales**.

18. Save and then preview the report, as shown here.

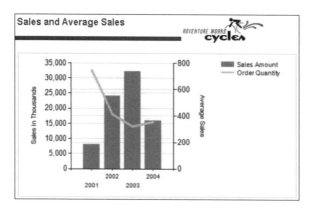

Adding a Second Chart Area

Instead of using a secondary axis, you might consider using separate chart areas for data that share categories but use a different scale for values. This approach is useful when you want to avoid visual comparisons of each series within a specific category and instead want to emphasize the series trend separately across a common set of categories, such as time periods. You can add as many chart areas as you need to display data, but you should resize the chart to ensure that each chart area has enough space to clearly view the data it contains.

In this procedure, you move Order Quantity data to a second chart area.

Add a new chart area

1. In Solution Explorer, double-click Sales And Order Quantity By Year.rdl.

2. Preview the report.

   This report starts with the same chart layout that you saw before modifying the Sales and Order Quantity Summary report. This time, instead of moving Order Quantity to a separate value axis, you move it to a separate chart area.

3. Click the Design tab.

4. Right-click any white space in the chart and select Add New Chart Area to update the chart, as shown here.

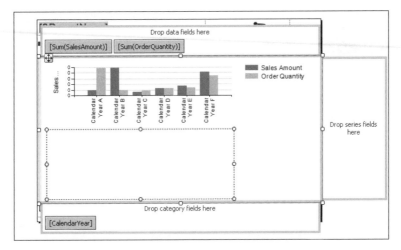

The chart divides into two chart areas of equal size.

5. In the data drop zone, right-click [Sum(OrderQuantity)] and select Series Properties.

6. In the Series Properties dialog box, click Axes And Chart Area.

7. In the Chart Area drop-down list, select ChartArea1.

The initial chart area in a chart is named Default and currently displays values for both Sales Amount and Order Quantity. The newly added chart area is named ChartArea1.

8. Click OK, and then save and preview the report, as shown here.

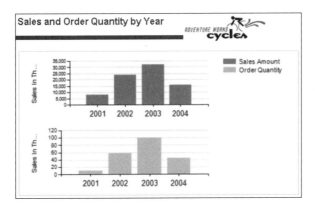

Now Sales Amount and Order Quantity display in separate chart areas, but notice that the columns in each chart area are not aligned because the axis labels in each chart area are different sizes. You can force alignment of the chart areas by setting properties.

9. Click the Design tab, right-click any white space in the chart, and select Chart Area Properties (ChartArea1).

10. In the Chart Area Properties dialog box, in the left pane, click Alignment.

11. In the Align With Chart Area drop-down list, select Default, as shown here.

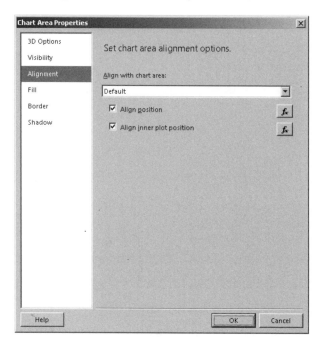

12. Click OK, and then save and preview the report, as shown here.

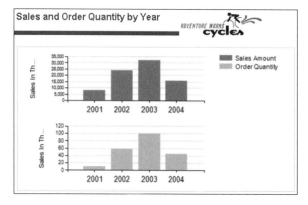

Now the columns line up properly.

Working with Gauges

A gauge is a special type of data visualization that you can use to display key performance indicators. You can place a gauge inside a table, matrix, or list when you want to repeat gauges.

In addition, you can place multiple gauges in a single gauge panel to compare data between fields. You can display gauges side by side in a gauge panel or you can nest a child gauge inside a parent gauge. You can use a gauge panel to apply common filtering, grouping, or sorting options to a set of gauges.

> **Tip** The AdventureWorksOffline Report Samples that you can download and install from *http://www.codeplex.com/MSFTRSProdSamples/Release/ProjectReleases.aspx?ReleaseId=16045* also includes examples of reports with gauges.

Understanding Gauge Types

Unlike a chart, which displays multiple data points, a gauge represents a single data value from your dataset that displays on a scale, much like a data point on a value axis. A gauge uses a pointer to indicate the position of the data value on the scale. You can also add one or more ranges to the scale to identify areas on the scale that represent a warning zone or a target zone. You can also use multiple scales in a gauge and assign a separate pointer to each scale.

You must select a gauge type when adding a gauge to the report. Both gauge types behave similarly. Radial gauges use a circular scale, whereas linear gauges use a horizontal or vertical scale. For both gauge types, you can use a marker or a bar as a pointer, but radial gauges also allow you to use a needle.

Creating a Linear Gauge

To create a gauge, you drag the control from the Toolbox into the report layout. A gauge has a single drop zone that you use to assign data fields to a pointer. You can then configure properties for the pointer and scale, and add a range, a label, an additional scale, or an additional gauge if you want.

In this procedure, you add a gauge to a matrix to compare the performance of each product category in a selected year visually.

Nest a gauge inside a matrix

1. In Solution Explorer, double-click Category Performance.rdl.

   This report contains a matrix that has been resized so that you can nest a linear gauge inside it.

2. From the Toolbox, drag the Gauge control to the text box in the last column of the detail row.

3. In the Select Gauge Type dialog box, in the Linear section, select Horizontal (the first gauge in the section) and click OK.

4. Click the gauge to display the drop zone, right-click LinearPointer1, and select Pointer Properties.

5. In the Linear Pointer Properties dialog box, click the expression button to the right of the Value box.

6. In the Expression dialog box, construct the following expression:

```
=Fields!Goal_Variance.Value
```

The goal variance represents the difference between the target gross profit margin percentage and the actual gross profit margin percentage.

7. Click OK to close the Expression dialog box and return to the Linear Pointer Properties dialog box, shown here.

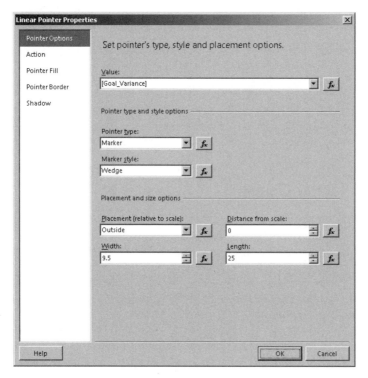

Several properties are available in this dialog box that you can use to customize the appearance of the pointer, and you can also associate the pointer with an action.

8. Click OK to close the Linear Pointer Properties dialog box.

9. In the gauge, click the scale to select it, right-click the scale, and select Scale Properties.

10. In the Minimum Value text box, type **-.5**, and then, in the Maximum Value text box, type **.5**. Click OK.

    Any value that is outside the minimum or maximum values that you configure displays at the applicable outside edge of the scale. For example, a value of –.7 will appear as –.5 on the scale.

11. Right-click the scale, select Add Range, right-click the red rectangle above the scale, and select Range Properties.

12. In the Linear Scale Range Properties dialog box, in the End Range At Scale Value text box, type **0** and click OK.

    In this example, any variance below 0 displays in a warning zone. You can create a target zone by setting the start and end range values appropriately and then changing the fill color to a value other than red. When you use color-coded zones that have meaning to the business user, the user can assess the qualitative meaning of the pointer position more easily.

13. Click OK to close the Linear Pointer Properties dialog box, and then save and preview the report, as shown here.

Category Performance CY 2004	Reseller Sales Amount	Reseller Gross Profit Margin	Goal Variance	
Accessories	$161,794.33	36.75%	15.25%	
Bikes	$13,399,243.18	-1.82%	3.38%	
Clothing	$386,013.16	8.59%	-0.59%	
Components	$2,091,011.92	6.60%	-3.40%	
	$16,038,062.60	-0.08 %	3.64 %	

Note The text boxes containing fields with the *FormattedValue* property might appear empty when you preview the report. If necessary, click the Refresh button on the toolbar to execute the report one more time to display the formatted values correctly.

14. In the Date.Calendar Year parameter drop-down list above the toolbar in Preview, select CY 2001 and click View Report.

    Notice the changes in the gauge pointers to reflect the goal variance in 2001.

You can do a lot more with charts and gauges in Reporting Services than I have described in this chapter, but space does not permit a full exploration of all the available features. However, you should now have a good understanding of the steps required to add data visualization to your reports. Furthermore, by completing the chapters in Part II to this point, you have learned all about the many aspects of managed report development in Reporting Services. In Chapter 9, "Developing Report Models," you learn how to develop a report model to support ad hoc report development by business users.

Chapter 8 Quick Reference

To	Do This
Create a column chart	From the Toolbox, drag a chart to the design surface, keep the default chart type, and drag fields from a dataset in the Report Data pane to the data and category drop zones. If you want, drag fields to the series drop zone.
Format a chart legend	Right-click the legend, select Legend Properties, and specify options in the Legend Properties dialog box.
Format an axis title	Right-click the axis title, select Axis Title Properties, and then, in the Title text box, type a new title. If you want, set options for font size, color, and effects.
Format an axis	Right-click an axis label and select Axis Properties. Set options as needed for axis scale, axis style, labels, label font settings, number formatting, major and minor tick marks, and axis line style.
Change the chart title	Double-click the chart title, highlight the existing text, and type a new title.
Sort series fields	Click the chart twice to display the drop zones, right-click a field in the series drop zone, select Series Group Properties, Sorting, Add, and select a field in the Sort By drop-down list.
Add a scale break	Right-click the value axis, select Axis Properties, and select the Enable Scale Breaks check box.
Rotate category labels to a specific angle	Right-click a horizontal axis label, select Axis Properties, Labels, Disable Auto-fit, and then, in the Label Rotation Angle box, type a value between −90 and 90.
Add a moving average to a chart	Click the chart twice to display the drop zones, right-click a field in the data drop zone, select Add Calculated Series, keep the default formula, specify a value for the number of periods to include in the moving average calculation, and, if you want, select the Start From First Point check box. On the Legend page of the Calculated Series Properties dialog box, type text in the Custom Legend Text box, if you want.
Move values to a secondary axis	Click the chart twice to display the drop zones, right-click a placeholder expression, select Series Properties, Axes and Chart Area, and then, below Value Axis, select Secondary.

To	Do This
Combine chart types in a single chart	Click the chart twice to display the drop zones, right-click a placeholder expression, select Change Chart Type, and then, in the Select Chart Type dialog box, select a chart type.
Add a second chart area	Right-click any white space in the chart, click Add New Chart Area, right-click a placeholder expression in the data drop zone, select Series Properties, Axes and Chart Area, and then, in the Chart Area drop-down list, select the new chart area.
Align chart areas	Right-click any white space in the chart, click Chart Area Properties for the chart area to align, click Alignment, and then, in the Align With Chart Area drop-down list, select the chart area to use for alignment.
Create a linear gauge	From the Toolbox, drag the Gauge control to the report design surface.
Configure the pointer in a linear gauge	Select a linear gauge, click the gauge to display the drop zone, right-click the pointer placeholder, select Pointer Properties, and select a field aggregation or provide an expression.
Configure the scale of a linear gauge	Click the gauge scale, right-click the scale, select Scale Properties, and adjust the values in the Minimum Value and Maximum Value text boxes as needed.

Chapter 9
Developing Report Models

After completing this chapter, you will be able to:

- Create a report model project.

- Create and modify a data source view to support ad hoc reporting.

- Generate a report model by using the Report Model Wizard.

- Refine the report model by adding, changing, and deleting objects in the Model Designer.

- Manage change in a report model.

- Deploy a report model to the report server.

As you worked through the procedures in the preceding chapters of Part II, "Developing Reports," you learned how to use Business Intelligence Development Studio (BI Dev Studio) to develop managed reports that you deploy to the report server in Part III, "Managing the Report Server." To support ad hoc reporting, you use BI Dev Studio to build report models that you also deploy to the report server. The report model is an intermediate layer between the business user and the source data that generates queries based on the objects that the users select. With this layer in place, the user does not need to know the query language to retrieve data successfully for a report. In this chapter, you learn how to start a report model project, how to generate and fine-tune a report model, and how to deploy a report model to the report server.

Preparing to Develop a Report Model

To develop a report model, you start by creating a new project in BI Dev Studio. You must then add two files to the project before you can start working on the report model. First, you create a data source file to provide the connection information for accessing the source data. Second, you create a data source view (DSV) file to describe the structure of the source data.

Adding a Report Model Data Source

You create a data source for a report model just as you create one for a report project. The data source provides the connection string and authentication information required to connect to the database hosting the data that you want users to access for their ad hoc reporting. You can use only one data source for each report model based on either the SqlClient Data Provider or the OracleClient Data Provider.

Note Although you can use Analysis Services cubes or a Teradata database as a data source, you cannot use BI Dev Studio to generate and customize the report model for either of these sources. Instead, you must use the report management tools to generate the report model. Refer to the sidebar "Using Report Management Tools to Generate a Report Model" later in this chapter, for more information.

In this procedure, you create a report model project and add a Microsoft SQL Server 2008 data source to the project.

Add a data source to a report model project

1. Click Start, point to Microsoft SQL Server 2008, and select SQL Server Business Intelligence Development Studio.

2. Click File, point to New, and select Project.

3. In the New Project dialog box, in the Templates pane, select the Report Model Project template.

4. In the name text box, type **Reseller Sales**.

5. Click Browse, and navigate to the Microsoft Press\Rs2008sbs folder in your Documents folder, select the Workspace folder, and then, in the Project Location dialog box, click OK.

6. In the New Project dialog box, click OK.

7. In Solution Explorer, right-click the Data Sources folder, and then select Add New Data Source.

8. In the Data Source Wizard, on the Welcome page, click Next.

9. On the Select How To Define The Connection page, click New.

10. In the Connection Manager dialog box, in the Server Name text box, type **localhost**, and then, in the Select Or Enter A Database Name drop-down list, select AdventureWorksDW2008. Click OK.

11. In the Data Source Wizard, click Next, and on the Completing The Wizard page, click Finish.

Adding a Data Source View

The DSV describes the structure of the data found in the data source file. You can reduce the amount of work required to make your report model user-friendly by adjusting object names and relationships in the DSV first. In addition, you should add to the DSV only tables or views that you intend to expose in the report model, to eliminate the need to delete these objects from the report model later. To minimize the complexity of a report model, you can consolidate multiple tables into a *named query*, which is a logical object in the report model that is analogous to a view in a relational database. You can also use a named query to add a derived column to the DSV or to limit the number of columns from a single table that you want available in the DSV. The changes you make in the DSV do not affect the source data; they create logical structures that better support reporting requirements in a user-friendly way.

In this procedure, you create a DSV using a subset of AdventureWorksDW2008 tables to support reporting of reseller sales data.

Create a DSV

1. In Solution Explorer, right-click the Data Source Views folder, and then select Add New Data Source View.

2. In the Data Source View Wizard, on the Welcome page, click Next, and then, on the Select A Data Source page, select Adventure Works DW2008. Click Next.

3. On the Select Tables And Views page, move the following Available Objects to the Included Objects list, as shown here: DimDate, DimEmployee, DimProduct, DimSalesTerritory, and FactResellerSales.

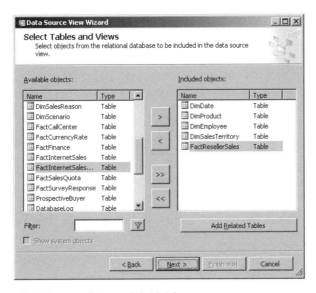

4. Click Next and then click Finish.

5. In Solution Explorer, double-click Adventure Works DW2008.dsv to view the DSV, as shown here.

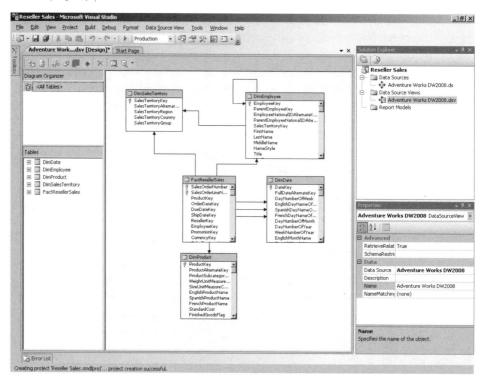

The Data Source View Designer automatically includes the foreign key relationships between the tables and identifies the primary key column(s) in each table.

> **Important** The Model Designer depends on the correct identification of primary keys and foreign key relationships to generate the report model correctly. If the DSV does not include a primary key, you can right-click a table column (or, for a composite key, first select multiple columns in the table), and select Set Logical Primary Key. To add a new relationship, right-click anywhere in the DSV, and select New Relationship. In the Specify Relationship dialog box, you can define the primary key table, the foreign key table, and the columns in each table that are included in the relationship.

6. In the Tables pane of the DSV, select DimDate, and then, in the Properties window, in the FriendlyName text box, delete "Dim" from the text string to change the property's value to *Date*.

7. Repeat the previous step for the remaining tables, removing the "Fact" and "Dim" strings from the *FriendlyName* property name.

Because the Model Designer uses the *FriendlyName* property of tables and columns in the DSV, you should make all name changes in the Data Source View Designer. You can make name changes in the Model Designer as well, but because you'll probably regenerate the report model several times before finalizing the model design, you'll find that making the changes once in the DSV saves you from making name changes in the model design after each regeneration of the model.

8. Locate the Product table in the design area, right-click the table header, select Replace Table, With New Named Query.

9. In the Create Named Query dialog box, on the Query Definition toolbar, click the Add Table button (the last button).

10. In the Add Table dialog box, select DimProductCategory and then, while pressing CTRL, select DimProductSubCategory.

11. Click Add and then click Close.

12. In the Diagram pane in the Query Definition section of the Create Named Query dialog box, you can rearrange the tables for easier viewing.

13. In the DimProductSubCategory table, select the EnglishProductSubCategoryName check box, and then, in the DimProductCategory table, select the EnglishProductCategoryName check box.

14. In the Grid pane (the center pane), in the Alias column, to the right of EnglishProductName, type **Product**.

15. To the right of EnglishProductSubCategoryName, type **Subcategory**, and then, to the right of EnglishProductCategoryName, type **Category**.

The Create Named Query dialog box looks like this:

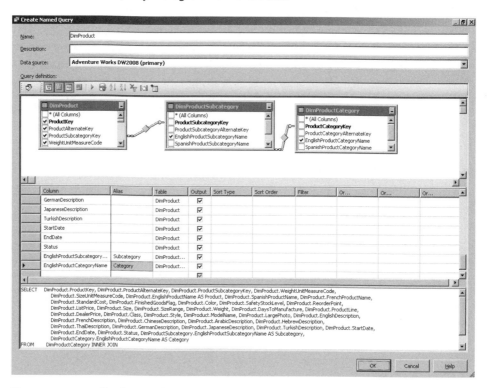

You can use an alias for a column in the named query instead of changing the *FriendlyName* property for the column in the DSV.

16. In the Create Named Query dialog box, click OK.

> **Tip** For the purposes of completing the procedures in this chapter, you keep all the columns in each table, but for a production report model, you delete any columns that you don't want to make available for ad hoc reports.

Generating a Report Model

With the data source and DSV files in place, you're ready to create a report model. You can create a model manually using the Model Designer, but you should know that doing so can be a very tedious, error-prone process. A better approach is to use the Report Model Wizard to generate a report model automatically. You can then modify the generated model to tailor it to your reporting needs.

Using the Report Model Wizard

The Report Model Wizard prompts you to select a DSV, to choose the report model generation rules to apply, and to specify whether to generate or update model statistics. You can use only one DSV as input for the wizard. In general, you should keep the default report model generation rules until you understand better how rules affect the structure of the report model. The wizard stores cardinality information and the distinct count of instances for each column in the DSV as model statistics and then uses the model statistics to set properties for model objects. For example, if a table has a high number of unique instances, the corresponding *InstanceSelection* property in the report model is set to a value that forces the user to specify a filter before viewing a list of instances for a table in the DSV.

In this procedure, you generate a report model by using the Report Model Wizard.

Run the Report Model Wizard

1. In Solution Explorer, right-click the Report Models folder, then select Add New Report Model.

2. In the Report Model Wizard, on the Welcome page, click Next, and then, on the Select Data Source View page, select Adventure Works DW2008.dsv. Click Next.

3. On the Select Report Model Generation Rules page, click Next.

   You can click Help on the Select Report Model Generation Rules page to view a description of each rule.

4. On the Collect Model Statistics page, verify that Update Model Statistics Before Generating is selected, and click Next.

   Because no statistics are available, you should update the model statistics now. If you use the Report Model Wizard to update an existing report model, you can select the Use Current Model Statistics Stored In The Data Source View option if the DSV has not changed since you last used the wizard. If you originally generated the report model when the data source was not fully populated, such as might occur with a new application or new data warehouse, and the volume of data has changed significantly since you last used the wizard, you should update the model statistics.

5. On the Completing The Wizard page, in the Name text box, type **Reseller Sales**, and then click Run.

   The model generation might take a few minutes. The time required to generate the model depends on the volume and complexity of data in the data source. When the Finish button is no longer dimmed, the model generation is complete.

6. On the Completing The Wizard page, click Finish.

7. In the Microsoft Visual Studio message box regarding file modification outside the source editor, click Yes to reload the file.

The report model displays in the Model Designer, as shown here.

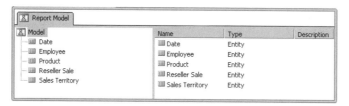

The report model is now part of the report model project as a Semantic Model Definition Language (SMDL) file, which is an Extensible Markup Language (XML) schema that applications such as the Report Builder client in Reporting Services can use to support ad hoc reporting. The report model is ready for deployment to the report server at this point, but first you should review the report model to determine if any changes are necessary. Your goal is to ensure the report model is as easy to use for your business users as possible.

Using Report Management Tools to Generate a Report Model

You can generate a report model and make it available for ad hoc reporting by using report management tools instead of BI Dev Studio. When you use this approach to create a new report model, you cannot edit the report model, but you can regenerate it if the underlying data source changes. You can download the report model file from the report server to edit it in BI Dev Studio only if the report model is based on a SQL Server or Oracle data source.

Regardless of which report server mode you are using, you must first have a data source deployed to the Data Sources folder (for native mode) or the Data Connections library (for SharePoint integrated mode). For more information about deploying a data source, refer to Chapter 10, "Deploying Reports to a Server."

To generate a report model for a native-mode server, follow these steps:

1. Open Windows Internet Explorer, and then navigate to a folder containing data sources in Report Manager, such as *http://<servername>/reports/data sources*.

> **Note** The default folder to which you can deploy data sources in a native-mode report server is the Data Sources folder accessible from the Home folder. You can deploy a data source to any folder, though.

2. Click the data source link, and then click Generate Model.

3. Type a name, and (if you want) a description, for the report model.

4. Click Change Location, and then, in the folder tree, select Models (or any other folder in which you want to store the report model), and click OK twice. The Properties page of the newly generated model displays and is now ready for use with Report Builder.

> **Note** The folder must exist before you generate the model. You can also move a model to another location later if necessary.

To generate a report model for a SharePoint integrated-mode server, follow these steps:

1. Open Internet Explorer, and then navigate to the document library in the Report Center site *http://<servername>/sites/ssrs/ReportsLibrary*, which you created in Chapter 2, "Installing Reporting Services."

> **Note** You can generate a report model in any SharePoint document library to which you have added the Report Builder Model content type, as described in Chapter 2.

2. On the New menu, choose Report Builder Model.

3. In the Name text box, type the name of the report model.

4. In the Data Source Link text box, type the path to a shared data source file on which to base the report model, or click the ellipsis button to open the Select An Item dialog box to navigate to a data connections library in your SharePoint site. For example, if you have deployed the AdventureWorksDW2008.rsds file to the Report Center's Data Connections library created in Chapter 2, the path you use in the Data Source Link box is *http://<servername>/sites/ssrs/Data Connections /AdventureWorksDW2008.rsds*.

5. On the Generate Model page, click OK. The new report model displays in the document library.

Reviewing a Report Model

The report model contains three types of objects: entities, attributes, and roles. An *entity* corresponds to a table in the DSV. Each entity contains a set of one or more *attributes*, each of which represents a column in the related table. A *role* defines the relationship between two entities. When reviewing the report model, you should ensure you have all the objects needed for reporting and note which objects should be removed.

In this procedure, you review the report model generated in the previous procedure.

Review a report model

1. Review the layout of the Report Model Designer.

   The left panel of the Model Designer is the tree view and contains the list of entities in the model. You can select an entity in the tree view to view its properties in the Properties window and to view the objects it contains in the detail view.

2. In the tree view, select Date, as shown here.

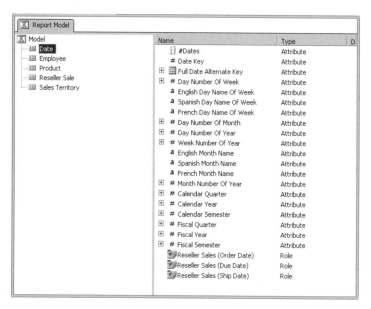

In most cases, the icon in front of each attribute identifies the data type. The # symbol indicates a numeric value, the letter *a* indicates a string value, and the calendar icon indicates a date value. In this example, you also see an icon with yellow cubes to indicate an aggregate value. By default, the report model includes an aggregate attribute to count the number of records associated with an entity.

The Date entity also includes three roles. These roles correspond to the three foreign key relationships between the Date table and the Reseller Sales table in the DSV for tracking three types of dates: Order Date, Due Date, and Ship Date. The multilayer icon for the role tells you that the relationship is one-to-many between Date and Reseller Sales. A single layer icon for a role would indicate a one-to-one relationship.

3. In the detail view, expand the Full Date Alternate Key attribute, as shown here.

When you use the default report generation rules, your report model includes multiple attributes for each date attribute. Here, you see the day, month, year, and quarter variations of the date attribute, as well as attributes to retrieve the first and last date value in the data source. You can change the names of these attributes to provide a friendlier name.

4. Expand the Day Number Of Week attribute, as shown here.

Another result of using the default report generation rules is the generation of Total, Avg, Min, and Max numeric aggregations for each numeric attribute. These aggregations are useful in the Reseller Sales entity for attributes like Order Quantity or Sales Amount, but they are illogical for numerical values like Day Number Of Week. Therefore, you should eliminate these aggregate attributes when you complete your review of the report model.

5. In the tree view, select the Reseller Sale entity, and then, in the detail view, select the Order Quantity attribute.

6. In the Properties window, shown here, locate the *DefaultAggregateAttribute* property.

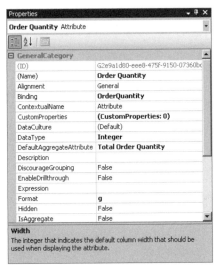

For numeric attributes for which you have aggregate attributes, you can specify the default aggregate attribute. This attribute is the first attribute visible to the user when building a report, but the user can access easily the other aggregate attributes, or even the base attribute for the aggregate attributes, when necessary.

You might find it necessary to change other properties for an attribute. For example, you might change the *Format* property for a numeric value or the *SortDirection* property for a string value. A user can define formatting and sort order when developing a report in Report Builder, but you can minimize the amount of extra work the user must do in each report if you set properties in the report model.

Refining a Report Model

If your report model is based on a SQL Server or Oracle data source, you can fine-tune the report model in the Report Designer in BI Dev Studio whether the report model was originally generated in BI Dev Studio or in the Web application for your server mode: Report Manager for native mode, or a SharePoint site for SharePoint integrated mode. Remember that the purpose of the report model is to help users build their own reports, so you should consider changes that improve the model structure to make it easier to find and recognize items to add to a report. You can also make changes to improve the appearance of objects in a report, such as alignment or formatting, or to better support the interactive experience when using filters or drillthrough reports when using Report Builder.

Organizing Model Objects

You can rearrange objects within the model to place more frequently accessed objects at the top of a list. When you have a lot of entities or attributes in the model, you can add folders to improve the organization of these objects. Another option to consider when you have a lot of objects in a model is to add a perspective to the model to limit the user to a subset of objects.

In this procedure, you reorganize objects in the report model.

Reorganize the report model

1. In the tree view, select Model. In the detail view, drag Reseller Sale to the top of the entity list, and then drag Product between Date and Employee to match the report model structure shown here.

Name	Type	Description
Reseller Sale	Entity	
Date	Entity	
Product	Entity	
Employee	Entity	
Sales Territory	Entity	

   You can use a drag-and-drop operation to rearrange objects in the detail view.

2. In the tree view, select Date. In the detail view, right-click anywhere and select New, Folder.

3. Right-click NewFolder, select Rename, and then type **Hidden Items**.

   You can create a folder to organize entities, attributes, or perspectives.

4. With the Hidden Items folder selected, in the Properties window, in the *Hidden* drop-down list, select True.

   You can create a hidden folder and move items into this folder before permanently deleting them from the report model. In this way, you can test the report model without the hidden items and then add them back to the report model more easily if you change your mind. If you delete items instead, then you must regenerate the report model when you want to restore them to the report model.

5. Drag the following items to the Hidden Items folder: French Day Name Of Week, Spanish Day Name Of Week, French Month Name, and Spanish Month Name.

6. Expand Day Number Of Week.

7. Select Total Day Number Of Week, press the Shift key, select Max Day Number Of Week, press the Delete key, and click OK.

8. Repeat step 7 to delete the aggregate attributes for Day Number Of Month, Day Number Of Year, Week Number Of Year, and Month Number Of Year.

> **Note** The aggregate attributes are unnecessary for these numeric attributes. You would want to delete other aggregate attributes in this entity if you were to use this report model in production, but you should understand the gist of the process now.

9. In the detail view, at the top of the list, select #Dates, press the Delete key, and click OK.

   Users do not require a count of dates in their ad hoc reports, so you can remove this aggregate attribute as well.

10. Right-click Model in the tree view and select New, Perspective.

    You can use a perspective to simplify a complex report model. In the current procedure, the report model is already basic, but you learn how to work with a perspective by performing the next five steps.

11. In the Edit Perspective dialog box, clear the following check boxes: Employee and Sales Territory.

    You can exclude entities from a perspective when you want to limit the number of entities from which the user can choose when building an ad hoc report.

12. Expand Product, clear the Product check box, and then select the following attributes: Color, Size, Weight, Model Name, Subcategory, and Category.

    You also can selectively include attributes for an entity.

13. Expand Date, clear the Date check box, and then select the following attributes: English Month Name, Calendar Quarter, and Calendar Year.

14. In the Edit Perspective dialog box, click OK.

15. In the detail view, right-click NewPerspective, select Rename, and type **Basic Reseller Sales**.

Changing Attribute Appearance Properties

Although changing properties related to an attribute's appearance is optional, you should determine at least whether the attribute name or its *Alignment*, *Format*, or *SortDirection* properties require adjustment. You can change the attribute name in the DSV as well, and then regenerate the model to reflect the new name, but the other properties can be configured only at the report model level.

In this procedure, you change attribute properties to define formatting, sorting, and alignment.

Change attribute properties

1. Select Reseller Sale in the tree view, select Sales Amount in the detail view, and then, in the Properties window, in the Format text box, type **C2**.

   This string formats the Sales Amount value as a currency value with two decimal places.

2. Expand Sales Amount, select Total Sales Amount, press the Shift key, select Max Sales Amount, and then, in the Properties window, in the Format text box, type **C2**.

   You can apply formatting in bulk when you select multiple attributes.

3. Select Order Quantity, and then, in the Properties pane, in the Format text box, type **N0**.

   This string formats the data as numeric, with no decimal places.

4. In the Alignment drop-down list, select Right.

   You can force the alignment direction of an attribute by using the *Alignment* property.

5. Expand Order Quantity, and then repeat steps 3 and 4 to apply the N0 formatting and the Right alignment to the aggregation attributes for Order Quantity.

6. In the tree view, select Date.

7. In the detail view, select Calendar Quarter, and then, in the Properties window, in the SortDirection drop-down list, select Ascending.

8. Repeat step 7 for the Calendar Year, Calendar Semester, Fiscal Quarter, Fiscal Year, and Fiscal Semester attributes.

> **Tip** To select all five attributes at once, you can select Calendar Year, and then while pressing the Shift key, select Fiscal Semester.

9. In the tree view, select Date, and then, in the detail view, right-click Full Date Alternate Key, click Rename, and type **Date**.

10. Expand Date, and rename the associated attributes as follows:

Rename This Attribute	To This
Full Date Alternate Key Day	Day
Full Date Alternate Key Month	Month
Full Date Alternate Key Year	Year
Full Date Alternate Key Quarter	Quarter
First Full Date Alternate Key	First Date
Last Full Date Alternate Key	Last Date

11. Drag Quarter above Year to rearrange the Data attributes into a natural sequence from Day to Year.

Adding Expressions

You can add an expression to the report model to store commonly used business logic in the centralized and managed report model. By keeping the expression in the report model, you ensure that the expression evaluates consistently no matter who uses the expression in a report.

In this procedure, you add an expression to the report model to concatenate string values.

Add a concatenation expression to the report model

1. In the tree view, right-click Employee and select New, Expression.

2. In the Define Formula dialog box, shown here, click the Functions tab, and then expand the folders to review the available functions.

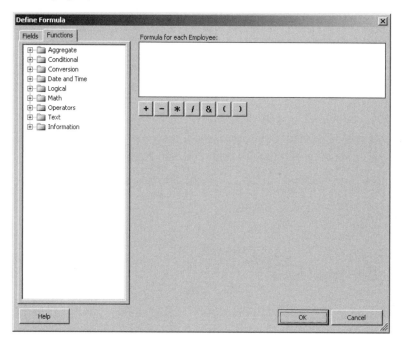

The Define Formula dialog box organizes functions by type into groups. You can expand a folder, and then double-click a function to add it to the formula box in the upper-right corner of the dialog box. Click Help to learn more about the available functions.

3. Click the Fields tab, as shown here.

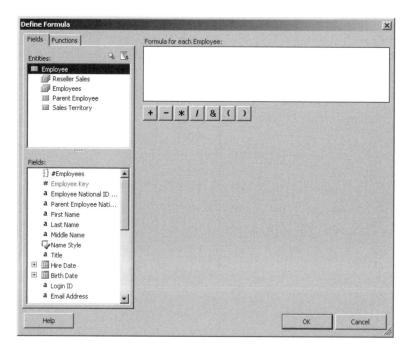

On the upper-left side is the Entities pane, which contains a list of entities available in the report model. Because you selected Employee in the tree view, the Employee entity displays above all the other entities in this list. The Fields pane in the lower left contains a list of attributes for the entity currently selected in the Entities pane. You can double-click a field to add it to the formula text box.

4. In the Fields pane, double-click Last Name to add it to the formula text box.

5. Click the concatenate button (marked with &) below the formula text box, type **", ",** click the concatenate button again, and then double-click First Name to create the following expression:

   `Last Name & ", ", & First Name`

6. In the Define Formula dialog box, click OK.

7. In the detail view, right-click NewExpression, select Rename, and type **Employee Name**.

Identifying an Entity Instance

When a user develops an ad hoc report using Report Builder, the user might want to filter by selecting an entity instance. One way to filter data is to create a list from which the user can select one or more instances for an entity. You can configure the *IdentifyingAttributes* property of an entity to display one or more attributes in the filter selection list to help the user identify unique instances.

> **Note**   The *IdentifyingAttributes* property is also used to identify instances when applying row-level security. You can learn more about model item security by searching for the topic "Applying Security Filters to Model Items" in SQL Server Books Online.

In this procedure, you review the *IdentifyingAttributes* property for the Reseller Sale and the Product entities and update the property for the Product entity.

Update the *IdentifyingAttributes* property

1. In the tree view, select Reseller Sale.

2. In the Properties window, in the IdentifyingAttributes text box, click the ellipsis button to open the AttributeReference Collection Editor dialog box, as shown here.

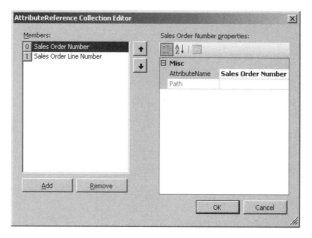

The AttributeReference Collection Editor dialog box displays the attributes used to identify each record in the Reseller Sales table uniquely for display in a list or a drop-down select. You can add or delete attributes from the collection as needed. If you use a hidden attribute, an error displays when you refresh the report model. The current settings are correct for the Reseller Sale entity, so you won't make any changes here.

3. In the AttributeReference Collection Editor, click Cancel to keep the current settings.

4. In the tree view, select Product.

5. In the Properties window, in the IdentifyingAttributes text box, click the ellipsis button.

Here the members are Product Alternate Key and Product. You can correct this property to use only the Product column in the table.

6. In the AttributeReference Collection Editor dialog box, select Product Alternate Key, click Remove, and click OK.

Configuring Properties for Drillthrough

In a well-designed report model, the user can generate a drillthrough report (which is also called a clickthrough report) automatically in Report Builder when the user clicks a field for which the *EnableDrillthrough* property is set to Yes. The query generator uses the model to determine how to retrieve the data and what to display in the drillthrough report. Therefore, you should spend some time considering what type of drillthrough reports might be useful in the ad hoc reporting environment. You can then specify which fields the user can click to start a drillthrough report by setting the *EnableDrillthrough* property on an attribute, and then you must also configure the *DefaultDetailAttributes* property on the entity to define the contents of the drillthrough report.

In this procedure, you configure a report model to support drillthrough.

Configure properties for drillthrough

1. In the tree view, select Reseller Sale.

2. In the Properties window, in the DefaultDetailAttributes text box, click the ellipsis button.

   You can see two members, Sales Order Number and Sales Order Line Number, in the AttributeReference Collection Editor dialog box. When a user clicks a field to generate a drillthrough report that displays multiple instances for the Reseller Sale entity, the user sees a list of one or more Sales Order Numbers and the respective Sales Order Line Numbers, but you can include more columns to provide the user with more context in the drillthrough report.

3. In the AttributeReference Collection Editor dialog box, click Add.

   You can select additional attributes from the same entity to display in the drillthrough report.

4. In the Default Detail Attributes dialog box, select Order Quantity, and while pressing the CTRL key, select Sales Amount. Click OK.

5. In the AttributeReference Collection Editor dialog box, click Add.

   You can also add attributes from other entities in the report model.

6. In the Default Detail Attributes dialog box, in the Entities pane, select Product, and then in the Fields pane, select Product. Click OK.

7. In the AttributeReference Collection Editor dialog box, click Add.

8. In the Default Detail Attributes dialog box, in the Entities pane, select Order Date, and then, in the Fields pane, select Date, and click OK.

   After adding attributes, you can rearrange the attributes to control the sequence in which the attributes appear in the drillthrough report.

9. In the AttributeReference Collection Editor dialog box, select Order Quantity, and then click the down arrow button to move Order Quantity below Date.

10. Select Sales Amount, and then click the down arrow button to move Sales Amount below Date, as shown here.

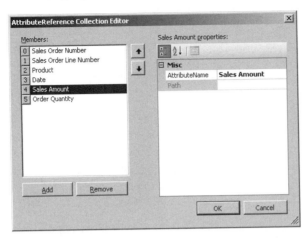

11. In the AttributeReference Collection Editor dialog box, click OK.

12. In the detail view, select Order Quantity, and then, in the Properties window, look for the *EnableDrillthrough* property.

    The value is set to *False* for Order Quantity because this attribute is a scalar value. That is, when you use Order Quantity to build a report, each individual record in the Reseller Sale entity displays. There is no way to drill to a lower level of detail because the use of Order Quantity in the report already returns the lowest level of detail.

13. Expand Order Quantity, select Total Order Quantity, and then, in the Properties window, look for the *EnableDrillthrough* property.

    Here you can see the property value is *True*. When using aggregate values in a report, you can always drill through to a lower level of detail.

14. In the tree view, select Product.

15. In the Properties window, in the DefaultDetailAttributes box, click the ellipsis button.

16. In the AttributeReference Collection Editor dialog box, select Spanish Product Name, press the Shift key, select French Product Name, and click Remove.

17. Click Add, and then, in the Default Detail Attributes dialog box, select Color. While pressing the CTRL key, select Subcategory and Category to add attributes, as shown here, and then click OK.

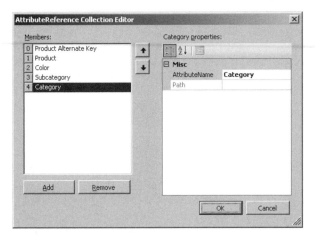

18. In the AttributeReference Collection Editor dialog box, click OK.

   Now the report model better supports drillthrough reports, which you will test when you build reports later in Chapter 14, "Creating Ad Hoc Reports." Much more work can be done to fine-tune this report model for drillthrough, but you should at this point understand the principles well enough to apply them to your own report model.

Managing a Report Model

When you have finished making changes to the report model, you are ready to deploy it to the report server. Before giving users access to the report model, you should test it thoroughly by creating reports using Report Builder. If you find further adjustments are necessary, you can return to your project in BI Dev Studio, edit the model, and redeploy it to the report server. Even after a report model has been released to production for a while, a change to the report model might be required. If you're careful with changes to a report model that has dependent reports, you can safely incorporate the changes and publish an update version of the report model to the report server.

Publishing a Report Model

To publish a report model to the report server from BI Dev Studio, you use the Deploy command. A copy of the data source file and the SMDL file is placed on the server during deployment. The Deploy command copies the data source file to the report server during the first deployment only by default, but copies the SMDL file to the server during each deployment.

Important If another report model with the same name already exists on the report server, that report model gets overwritten with the report model you are currently deploying. If the overwritten report model was truly a different report model rather than an earlier version of the report model you are deploying, any reports that were based on the overwritten report model fail to process. Therefore, be sure to check the target folder before deployment to eliminate any problems caused by having duplicate report model names.

The report model project properties contain the target folders for the data source and report model and the target URL for the report server. This target information varies based on whether you are deploying to a native-mode report server or to a SharePoint integrated-mode report server. The procedures in this section provide steps to deploy to either type of report server.

In this procedure, you deploy the Reseller Sales report model to a report server in native mode.

Deploy a report model project to a native-mode report server

1. In Solution Explorer, right-click Reseller Sales, and select Properties.

2. Review the default target settings.

   In native mode, the default target locations are provided for you as shown here. If the data source folder or model folder do not exist, the deployment process creates the missing folders.

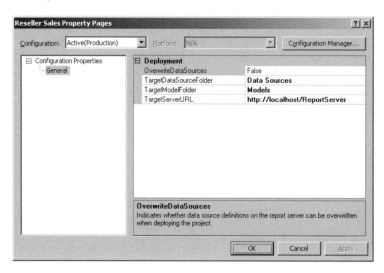

When deploying reports to a native-mode report server, the target server URL is always the virtual directory you defined for the Web Service URL in Reporting Services Configuration Manager, as you did in Chapter 2. If your target server is not your local computer, be sure to change the server name in the target server URL box.

3. In the Reseller Sales Property Pages dialog box, click OK.

4. Right-click the Reseller Sales report model in Solution Explorer, and then select Deploy.

5. When the Deploy is complete, open Internet Explorer, and then type the URL **http://localhost/reports/models** to open the Models folder in Report Manager, as shown here.

> **Note** This URL is based on the assumption that you followed the instructions in Chapter 2 to create a virtual directory called Reports for the Report Manager. If you created a different virtual directory, then use that URL instead.

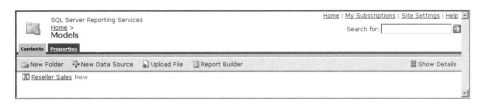

The Reseller Sales model is now available on the report server. You learn how to use the report model with Report Builder in Chapter 14.

6. Click the Home link in the upper-left corner of the browser window, and click the Data Sources link.

The Adventure Works DW2008 data source is also available on the server. Report Builder requires both the report model and the data source on the report server to support ad hoc reporting.

In this procedure, you deploy the Reseller Sales report model to a report server in SharePoint integrated mode.

Deploy a report model project to a SharePoint integrated-mode report server

1. In Solution Explorer, right-click Reseller Sales, and select Properties.

2. In the Reseller Sales Property Pages dialog box, in the TargetDataSourceFolder text box, type **http://<*servername*>/sites/ssrs/data connections**, replacing <*servername*> with **localhost** or the name of your server if you are deploying the report model to a remote report server. Be sure to include the port number with the server name if you have configured a port other than 80 for the Web Service URL.

In a typical SharePoint integrated-mode configuration, you store data sources in a data connections library, but you can use any document library to which the report data source content type has been added.

Note This URL is based on the assumption that you followed the instructions in Chapter 2 to create a Report Center site called SSRS. If you have an alternative site available, then use that URL.

Important Even if you are deploying to your local computer, you must specify the server name, rather than localhost, in the URL. Otherwise, the deployment fails with the following error: Report Server has encountered a SharePoint error.

3. In the TargetModelFolder text box, type
http://<*servername*>/sites/ssrs/ReportsLibrary.

The target report model folder can be any document library to which the report model content type has been added.

4. In the TargetServerURL box, type **http://<*servername*>/sites/ssrs**.

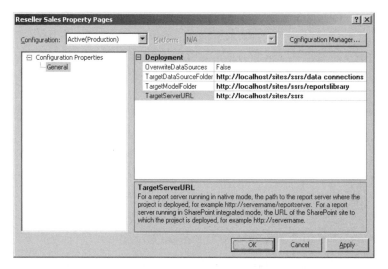

Notice the target server URL does not include a reference to the report server virtual directory, as it does when deploying to a native-mode report server. In this case, you deploy to a SharePoint site that is configured for reporting services. When you configured Reporting Services integration in Chapter 2, you provided the report server Web service URL in SharePoint's Central Administration application.

5. In the Reseller Sales Property Pages dialog box, click OK.

6. Right-click the Reseller Sales report model in Solution Explorer, and then select Deploy.

7. When the deployment is complete, open Internet Explorer, and then type the URL
http://localhost/sites/ssrs/ReportsLibrary to open the document library in the Report Center site created in SharePoint, as shown here.

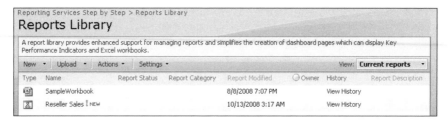

The Reseller Sales model now appears in the Reports Library. You learn how to use the report model with Report Builder in Chapter 14.

8. In the Navigation Link Bar on the left side of the page, click the Data Connections link.

The Adventure Works DW2008 data source is now added to the data connections library and the approval status is currently pending. At this point, you can use the report model and its associated data source because you are the owner of the files. When you're ready to grant access to other users, you must change the approval status of the data source. You learn how to do this, and to configure security for report models, in Chapter 11, "Securing Report Server Content."

Managing Change

Change inevitably happens, whether you need to add a new expression to the report model, a new column is added to a table in the data source that must be included in the report model, or another modification needs to be made. Your report model is built to withstand change within certain guidelines. For instance, you can change the data source for your report model so long as the new data source contains the same database objects with the same names used in the report model's DSV. Or, if no reports depend on the report model, you can run the Report Model Wizard and save the new report model by overwriting the previous report model file.

If, on the other hand, reports depend on the report model, you must use a different approach. When objects in the data source change or new objects are added to the data source, you should refresh your report model rather than replace it because a globally unique identifier (GUID) exists in the report model for each entity, attribute, and role. When you use Report Builder to create a report, the reports store GUIDs. To keep existing reports intact by preserving GUIDS in the report model, you can generate the report model automatically from the DSV or edit the report model manually so long as you don't change attribute data types or the *Inheritance* property of each entity.

You can use the Autogenerate command at the model, entity, or attribute level. Existing objects in the report model are not overwritten or deleted. Any new objects found in the DSV are added. If a column that is associated with an attribute is deleted from the DSV, an error message identifies the attribute that you must delete manually from the report model.

In this procedure, you update the DSV and use the Autogenerate command to refresh the report model.

Update a DSV and report model

1. Switch to Business Intelligence Development Studio, and then, in Solution Explorer, double-click Adventure Works DW2008.dsv.

2. Right-click the Product table header, and then select Edit Named Query.

3. In the SQL Query pane, type a comma after AS Category (before the FROM clause), and then type the following:

   ListPrice - StandardCost AS Margin

4. In the Edit Named Query dialog box, click OK.

   The DSV now has a new column that must be added to the report model as a new attribute for the Product entity.

5. Switch back to the Model Designer, in the tree view, right-click Product, select Autogenerate, and then click Yes to confirm your request to regenerate the selected item.

6. In the Report Model Wizard, click Next on each page to accept the default settings, and then, on the Completing The Wizard page, click Run.

7. When the wizard completes, click Finish.

8. In the detail view, scroll to the bottom of the attribute list, select Margin, and then, in the Properties pane, in the Format text box, type **C2**.

9. Expand Margin, and then update the *Format* property for each of the aggregation attributes by typing **C2**.

> **Note** New attributes are not added automatically to the report model's perspectives. If you want to add a new attribute to the perspective, you must add it manually.

10. Right-click the Reseller Sales report model in Solution Explorer, and then select Deploy to update the model on the report server.

You now have a good foundation for building report models. After deployment of a report model, you can implement security (which you learn to do in Chapter 11) to control which users can use the report model for ad hoc reporting. You should spend some time building reports with the report model (which you learn to do in Chapter 14) to discover additional refinements required in the report model before you allow users to begin using it.

Now that you have learned how to develop managed reports and create report models to support ad hoc reporting, you are ready to continue to the next phase of the reporting life cycle. In Part III, you learn about deploying reports and data sources to the report server, managing and securing report server content, and performing the many administrative tasks required to keep your reporting environment functioning properly.

Chapter 9 Quick Reference

To	Do This
Create a report model project	In BI Dev Studio, on the File menu, select New, Project, select the Report Model Project template, and then type a name and location for the project and click OK.
Add a data source to a report model project	In Solution Explorer, right-click the Data Sources folder, select Add New Data Source, click Next on the Welcome page of the Data Source Wizard, click New, type a server name in the Server Name box, select a database in the Select Or Enter A Database Name drop-down list, click OK, click Next, and then click Finish.
Add a DSV to a report model project	In Solution Explorer, right-click the Data Source Views folder, select Add New Data Source View, click Next on the Welcome page of the Data Source View Wizard, select a data source, click Next, add tables or views to the Included Objects list, click Next, and then click Finish.
Rename a table or column in the DSV	In the Data Source View Designer, in the Tables pane, select a table or column, and then, in the Properties window, in the FriendlyName text box, type a new name.
Replace a table with a named query in a DSV	In the Data Source View Designer, right-click a table header, select Replace Table, With New Named Query, modify the query in the Create Named Query dialog box, and click OK.
Use the Report Model Wizard to generate a report model	In Solution Explorer, right-click the Report Models folder, select Add New Report Model, click Next on the Welcome page of the Report Model Wizard, select a DSV, click Next, specify the report model generation rules, click Next, specify whether to update model statistics, click Next, name the model, and click Run.
Rearrange objects in the model	In the detail view, drag an entity, attribute, or role to the new location.
Rename a model object	In the detail view, right-click an entity, attribute, or role, select Rename, and type a new name.
Hide a model object	In the detail view, right-click the object, and then, in the Properties window, in the Hidden drop-down list, select True.
Delete a model object	In the detail view, select the object, press the Delete key, and click OK to confirm.

To	Do This
Add a folder	In the tree view, right-click the parent object, select New, and click Folder.
Add a perspective	In the tree view, right-click Model, select New, Perspective, clear check boxes to remove objects that you want to exclude from the perspective, and click OK. In the detail view, right-click NewPerspective, select Rename, and type a name for the perspective.
Change attribute properties	In the detail view, select an attribute, and then, in the Properties window, in the applicable property box, type a new value, such as C0 for Format, or use the property drop-down list to select Ascending for SortDirection, or Right for Alignment.
Add an expression to an entity	In the tree view, right-click an entity, select New, Expression, and double-click objects in the Fields and Functions list to construct an expression. In the detail view, right-click NewExpression, select Rename, and type a name for the expression.
Configure attributes to identify an entity instance in a selection list	In the tree view, select an entity, and then, in the Properties window, in the IdentifyingAttributes text box, click the ellipsis button. In the AttributeReference Collection Editor dialog box, add or remove attributes as necessary to create a list of attributes representing unique instances for the entity.
Configure entity properties for drillthrough reports	In the tree view, select an entity, and then, in the Properties window, in the DefaultDetailAttributes text box, click the ellipsis button. In the AttributeReference Collection Editor dialog box, add or remove attributes as necessary to create a list of attributes to display in a report that returns multiple instances for an entity.
Configure an attribute for drillthrough	In the detail view, select an attribute, and then, in the Properties window, in the EnableDrillthrough drop-down list, select True.
Configure the destination for a report model and its data source	In Solution Explorer, right-click the report model project, provide values for TargetDataSourceFolder, TargetModelFolder, and TargetModelFolder, and click OK.
Deploy a report model	In Solution Explorer, right-click the report model project, and select Deploy.

Part III
Managing the Report Server

In Part III, you learn how to deploy reports to the report server and how to manage the reporting environment. In Chapter 10, "Deploying Reports to a Server," you learn several ways to move reports from a report developer's computer to the report server. You also learn how to organize content on the report server and configure properties that control data source access and report execution behavior. You explore security options in detail in Chapter 11, "Securing Report Server Content." Then, in Chapter 12, "Performing Administrative Tasks," you review the management tools included in Reporting Services, explore the server configuration files that you can change, and learn about the tools that you can use to monitor report server performance. The procedures in these chapters give you hands-on experience with all aspects of managing the reporting life cycle.

Chapter 10
Deploying Reports to a Server

After completing this chapter, you will be able to:

- Deploy reports to the report server.

- Organize content on the report server by using folders.

- Create a linked report on a native-mode report server.

- Override report parameter settings.

- Manage authentication in data sources.

- Control report execution.

- Create and store report snapshots in history.

The process of deploying reports includes a variety of tasks that are covered in this chapter. At minimum, you place report definition files on the report server to make reports available to users. Typically, you also configure data sources to associate reports with a different test or production database. You might create alternate versions of a base report by setting up linked reports or generating report copies. You can also configure report properties, such as report parameter default values, execution options, or history management properties, to control what data displays in a report, the amount of time before the user request that the data is retrieved for the report, and the amount of time a snapshot of a report is saved on the report server.

 Important To complete the procedures in this chapter, you must be assigned to the Content Manager role on a native-mode report server or to the Owners role on an integrated-mode report server. If you are a local administrator on the server, you have the correct role assignment by default.

You learn more about assigning security permissions to control user activity on the report server in Chapter 11, "Securing Report Server Content."

Reviewing Deployment Options

The deployment process copies the report definition into the ReportServer database described in Chapter 1,"Introducing Reporting Services." A shared data source or a file that you want to store centrally for user access can also be deployed to the report server and is similarly stored in the ReportServer database. Report developers typically deploy a report directly from Business Intelligence Development Studio (BI Dev Studio), while report server administrators often deploy a report manually by using Report Manager or programmatically by using the Rs utility (described more fully in Chapter 16, "Programming Reporting Services").

Deploying a Report Project

A solution in BI Dev Studio can contain one or more report projects, each of which can contain one or more reports. Each project has a set of properties to define the target location for the reports and data sources that it contains. After you define these properties, you can deploy all reports in all report projects in the solution, all reports in a single report project, a selected set of reports, or a specific report.

In this procedure, you use BI Dev Studio to deploy a report server project.

Deploy a report project to a report server

1. Click Start, select Microsoft SQL Server 2008, and then select SQL Server Business Intelligence Development Studio.

2. On the File menu, select Open, and then select Project/Solution.

3. In the Open Project dialog box, navigate to the Microsoft Press\Rs2008sbs\Chap10 folder in your documents folder, select Sales.sln, and click Open.

> **Important** Although the reports in this project are similar to the reports that you created if you completed the previous chapters, you must use the report project in the Chap10 folder to complete all procedures in this chapter successfully.

4. In Solution Explorer, right-click Sales, and then select Properties.

> **Note** Many of the remaining steps to follow in this procedure depend on whether your target report server is native mode or SharePoint integrated mode. Each step includes instructions for both architectures.

5. In the Sales Property Pages dialog box, in the TargetDataSourceFolder text box, provide the target location for the shared data source in the project. You can create a hierarchy of folders also by including each folder name in the TargetDataSourceFolder box and separating each folder name with a forward slash (/).

   ❑ *Native mode:* Keep the default value, *Data Sources*. This folder will be created on the Home page of Report Manager if it doesn't already exist.

❏ *Integrated mode:* Type **http://<*servername*>/sites/ssrs/data connections**, replacing *<servername>* with the name of your server.

Note This URL for the integrated mode server assumes that you followed the instructions in Chapter 2, "Installing Reporting Services," to create a Report Center site called SSRS. Replace the example URL if you have an alternate site available.

Important Even if you are deploying to your local computer, you must specify the server name in the URL rather than localhost. Otherwise, the deployment fails with the following error: Report Server has encountered a SharePoint error.

In a typical SharePoint integrated-mode configuration, you store data sources in a data connections library, but you can use any document library to which the report data source content type has been added.

6. In the TargetReportFolder text box, provide the target location for the reports in the project.

❏ *Native mode:* Keep the default value, *Sales*.

❏ *Integrated mode:* Type **http://<*servername*>/sites/ssrs/ReportsLibrary**, replacing *<servername>* with the name of your server.

The target report folder can be any document library to which the report content type has been added as described in Chapter 2.

7. In the TargetServerURL text box, provide the URL for the target report server.

❏ *Native mode:* Type **http://localhost/ReportServer**, as shown here, and then click OK.

Note This procedure assumes that you followed the instructions in Chapter 2 to install Reporting Services on your local computer and to create a virtual directory called ReportServer for the Web service. Replace the server name or the virtual directory name in this URL as appropriate if your configuration differs from the environment described in Chapter 2.

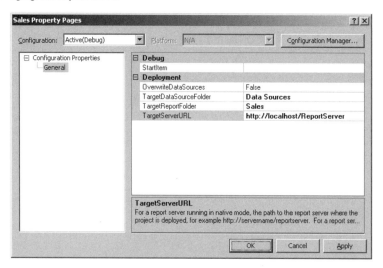

❏ *Integrated mode:* Type **http://<*servername*>/sites/ssrs**, replacing <*servername*>
with the name of your server, as shown here.

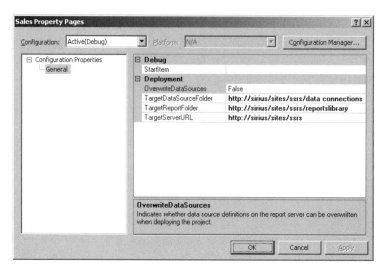

Note In this example, and throughout this chapter, the server name in the URL is fictitious
and is included for illustration purposes only.

Notice that the target server URL does not include a reference to the report server
virtual directory as it does when deploying to a native-mode report server. In this case,
you deploy to a SharePoint site that is configured for Reporting Services as described
in Chapter 2.

8. In Solution Explorer, right-click Sales, and select Deploy.

> **Tip** In this procedure, you deploy all reports in the project. In some cases, you might prefer to deploy a specific report or set of reports. To limit deployment to a set of one or more reports, select each report to include in the set, right-click one of the reports in the set, and then select the Deploy command from the shortcut menu.

9. Review the output of the deployment process in the Output window, which displays at the bottom of your screen in the default layout. The Output window shown here is for deployment to a native-mode report server. An integrated-mode report server deployment looks very similar and displays the report's URL reference as each report deploys.

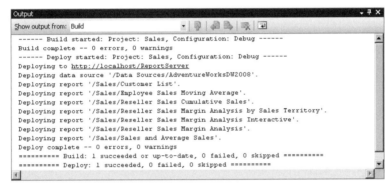

10. When deployment completes, open Windows Internet Explorer and navigate to the Web application hosting Reporting Services.

❑ *Native mode:* In the address bar, type **http://localhost/Reports** to open the Home page in Report Manager, and then click the Sales link to view the deployed reports, as shown here.

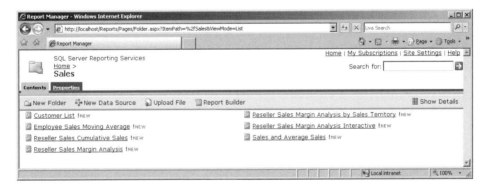

❑ *Integrated mode:* In the address bar, type **http://<*servername*>/sites/ssrs /ReportsLibrary** to open the Reports Library, replacing <*servername*> with the name of your server, as shown here.

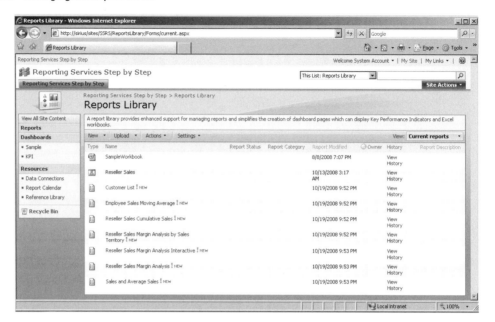

Note The SampleWorkbook appearing in the Reports Library is a Microsoft Office Excel 2007 workbook added to the Reports Library automatically when you created the site collection. The Reseller Sales item is the report model that is deployed at the end of Chapter 9, "Developing Report Models."

All files are physically stored as binary files in the Catalog table in the ReportServer database. For a native-mode report server, Report Manager queries this table to retrieve a list of the items for the current folder, Sales, and displays the results in two columns in alphabetical order. An integrated-mode report server also stores the report definition files in the SharePoint content database and displays the list of report definition files as a single column of report titles.

Uploading a Report

In some organizations, certain users might have permission to add content to the report server but might not be report developers and therefore won't have BI Dev Studio installed on their computers. These users can upload reports directly to the report server using the Web application interface.

In this procedure, you upload a report to the report server.

Upload a report to a report server

1. In Internet Explorer, open the target report folder.

- ❑ *Native mode:* If the Sales folder is not already open, in the address bar, type **http://localhost/Reports/Sales**.

- ❑ *Integrated mode:* If the reports library is not already open, type **http://<*servername*>/sites/ssrs/ReportsLibrary**, replacing *<servername>* with the name of your server.

2. Upload the Sales Summary report definition file.

- ❑ *Native mode:* On the Report Manager toolbar, click Upload File, click Browse, navigate to the Microsoft Press\Rs2008sbs\Chap10 folder in your documents folder, select Sales Summary.rdl, and click Open. In the Name text box, keep the default report name, as shown here, and click OK.

- ❑ *Integrated mode:* On the SharePoint toolbar, click the Upload button, click Browse, navigate to the Microsoft Press\Rs2008sbs\Chap10 folder in your documents folder, select Sales Summary.rdl, and click Open. On the Upload Document: Reports Library page, shown here, click OK.

Note By default, the uploaded document in SharePoint adds the report definition as new content to support the versioning feature in SharePoint. In-depth coverage of generic features of SharePoint such as this is beyond the scope of this book. However, you can learn more from the Help article "Introduction to Versioning," at *http://office.microsoft.com /en-us/help/HA100215761033.aspx?pid=CL100605171033*.

3. On a SharePoint integrated-mode report server, keep the default report name, as shown here, and then click OK.

 Important The upload process to a report server in native mode or integrated mode does not associate the report definition file with a data source, which prevents you from viewing the report at this time. Later in this chapter, you learn how to correctly associate a report with its data source.

Using the Rs Utility

A report administrator can use script files to manage many activities on a native-mode report server, including report deployment. When you want an administrator to deploy reports in bulk, you develop a script file using Microsoft Visual Basic .NET and save the file as a Unicode or UTF-8 text with an .rss file name extension. Then you provide the administrator with the script file and report definition files to be uploaded. The report administrator can then use the script file as an input file for the Rs utility (described in more detail in Chapter 16).

Important The Rs utility is not supported for use with an integrated-mode report server.

In this procedure, you execute the Rs utility with the DeploySalesReports.rss script to deploy reports.

Deploy reports to a native-mode report server by using the Rs utility

1. On a native-mode report server, open a command prompt window.

2. Type the command to navigate to the folder containing the script file. For example, if you're running Windows XP or Windows Server 2003, type **cd C:\Documents and Settings\<*username*>\My Documents\Microsoft Press\Rs2008sbs\Chap10**. If you're running Windows Vista or Windows Server 2008, type **cd C:\Users \<*username*>\Documents\Rs2008sbs\Chap10**.

3. To run the Rs utility, type **rs –i DeploySalesReports.rss –s http://localhost /ReportServer**, and press Enter. The results of executing the utility display in the command prompt window.

4. To confirm the successful deployment of the reports, switch to Internet Explorer, navigate to *http://localhost/Reports*, and click the Sales And Order Quantity Analysis link in Report Manager and view the list of reports.

Managing Content

One way to manage content on a report server is to store every report in a single location, such as the Home page, but before long, you'll find that the number of reports becomes so large that it is difficult to manage security and to find content. You can use folders to simplify report management and usage. You can move content to a new folder later and, on a native-mode server, use a linked report to set up variations of a single report for applying different properties such as security or parameters.

Using Folders to Organize Content

Folders are useful for organizing content into logical groups by subject matter, target audience, security, or any combination of these. Folders can be nested into a hierarchical structure, and you can provide a description for a folder to provide users with more information about the folder contents. On a native-mode report server, you can also hide a folder name from the list view in Report Manager.

In this procedure, you add folders to store reports.

Add a folder to a report server

1. In Internet Explorer, open the home folder for Reporting Services.

   ❏ *Native mode:* In the address bar, type **http://localhost/Reports** to open the Home folder in Report Manager or click the Home link at the top of the window.

   ❏ *Integrated mode:* Type **http://<*servername*>/sites/ssrs/ReportsLibrary**, replacing <*servername*> with the name of your server, to open the Reports Library folder in SharePoint.

2. Add a new folder.

   ❏ *Native mode:* On the Report Manager toolbar, click the New Folder button.

   ❏ *Integrated mode:* On the Reports Library toolbar, click the arrow on the New button, and select Folder.

3. Provide a name for the folder.

   ❏ *Native mode:* Replace the default name with **For Review**, and then, in the Description box, type **Reports in this folder are pending user review and acceptance**, as shown here. Click OK.

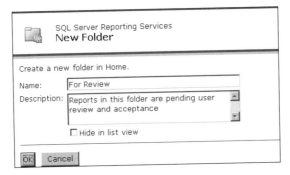

 Note On a native-mode report server, you can hide a folder in the list view. Hiding a folder is not a security measure because the user can switch to detail view and see the folder. However, you can use a hidden folder to store reports that users don't normally access. For example, you can use a hidden folder to store subreports that users don't need to view as individual reports.

   ❏ *Integrated mode:* In the Name text box, type **For Review**, and click OK.

Moving Content

Getting the right folder structure established for reports might take some time. After reports are deployed to a report server, you can move them from one folder to another folder.

In this procedure, you move selected reports from the Sales folder to the For Review folder.

Move content

1. In Internet Explorer, open the folder containing the Reporting Services reports that you deployed earlier in this chapter.

    ❑ *Native mode:* On the Home page of Report Manager, click the Sales link.

    ❑ *Integrated mode:* If the Reports Library folder is not already open, in the address bar, type **http://<*servername*>/sites/ssrs/ReportsLibrary**, replacing <*servername*> with the name of your server.

2. Open the view that allows you to select the reports to move.

    ❑ *Native mode:* On the Report Manager toolbar, click the Show Details button.

    When you click the Show Details button, the contents of the folder display as a single list with a check box to the left of each item, as shown here. You can move or delete one or more items in the list by selecting each item's check box and then clicking the Move or Delete button on the toolbar, respectively.

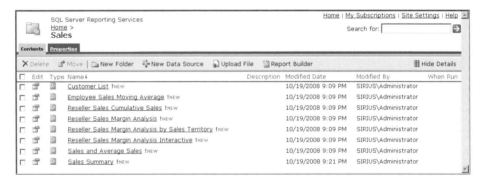

    ❑ *Integrated mode:* In the upper-right corner of the window, click Site Actions, select Manage Content And Structure, and then, in the tree view on the left, select Reports Library to view the library contents, as shown here.

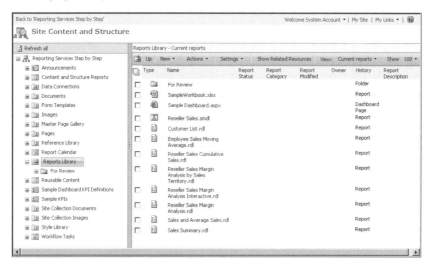

3. Select all reports except the Reseller Sales Margin Analysis by Sales Territory report to move to the For Review folder.

❑ *Native mode:* Select the uppermost check box (to the left of Edit) to select all reports, clear the Reseller Sales Margin Analysis By Sales Territory check box, and then click Move.

❑ *Integrated mode:* Select the uppermost check box (to the left of Type) to select all reports, clear the For Review, SampleWorkbook.xlsx, Sample Dashboard.aspx, Reseller Sales.smdl, and Reseller Sales Margin Analysis By Sales Territory check boxes, click the arrow on the Actions button, and select Move.

4. Select the For Review folder as the target location for the reports.

❑ *Native mode:* Select the For Review folder, as shown here, and then click OK.

❑ *Integrated mode:* In the Move... Webpage Dialog box, expand Reports Library, select the For Review folder, as shown here, and then click OK.

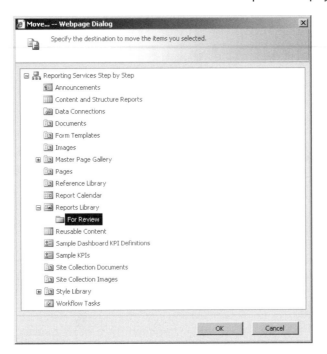

5. Open the For Review folder to confirm that the seven reports have been moved successfully.

   ❏ *Native mode:* In the upper-left corner of the browser window, click the Home link, and then, in the list view, click the For Review link.

   ❏ *Integrated mode:* In the address bar, type **http://<*servername*>/sites/ssrs /ReportsLibrary/For Review,** replacing <*servername*> with the name of your server.

Important When you move reports to a new folder on an integrated-mode report server, the link between the data source and the report breaks. You must reset the link on each report manually before users can view the reports. In the sections "Configuring Report Parameters," "Executing a Report on Demand," and "Saving Report Snapshots in History," later in this chapter, you perform the steps necessary to reset this link for three reports.

Creating a Linked Report

On a native-mode report server, you can create a variation of a report without the need to create and maintain multiple report definition files by creating a *linked report*. A linked report is a separate report item on the report server that uses a report definition file as a base but has separate execution, parameter, subscription, and security properties. A common reason to use a linked report is if you want to build a report that contains data for multiple departments and includes a parameter to filter the report content by department. You can then deploy the report to a folder that none of the users can access, create one linked report per department, set the report parameter default to a specific department, and configure security such that users can access only the linked report for their department.

In this procedure, you create a linked report for the Reseller Sales Margin Analysis by Sales Territory report.

Create a linked report

1. In Internet Explorer, click the Home link at the top of the window, and then click the Sales link.

> **Note** If you see the Hide Details button, then the list view is visible in Report Manager. You must be in list view to access the Properties page of a report directly, without viewing the report first. If Report Manager is not in list view, perform step 2 to switch modes. Otherwise, you can skip to step 3.

2. If necessary, click the Show Details button to switch the view to list view.

3. In the Edit column for the Reseller Sales Margin Analysis by Sales Territory report, click the Properties icon, as shown here.

Properties Icon

4. Click Create Linked Report.

5. In the Name text box, type **Pacific Reseller Sales Margin Analysis**, as shown here.

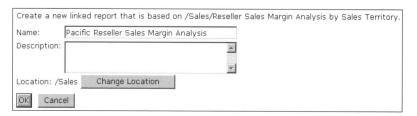

Note that, as with the base report, you can add a description to the linked report. By default, the linked report is created in the same folder as the base report. You can click Change Location and select a target folder for the linked report.

6. Click OK.

The linked report displays in the browser window. You can now change the properties of the linked report. For example, to display only data for the Pacific sales territory in the report, you must change the parameter properties, which you do in the next procedure.

Copying a Report

Although you cannot create linked reports on an integrated-mode report server, you can create a copy of a report to achieve a similar result. That is, you can reproduce the same report definition as a separate file on the report server and set different execution, parameter, subscription, and security properties on the new file. However, any changes to the base report definition do not update the copy.

> **Important** If you followed the steps in Chapter 2, you currently have a site collection at *http://<servername>/sites/ssrs*. To complete the following procedure successfully, you must also have a root site collection, *http://localhost*, on your SharePoint server. To create a root site collection, click Start, select All Programs, Administrative Tools, and SharePoint 3.0 Central Administration. Click the Application Management tab, and click the Create Site Collection link. In the Web Application drop-down list, select Change Web Application, and then select SharePoint – 80 in the list associated with the root URL, *http://<servername>*. On the Create Site Collection page, provide a title for the site, and then, in the Web Site Address section, make sure the URL looks like this: *http://<servername>/*, selecting / in the drop-down list to replace sites if necessary. Select a template of any type for the site. In the Primary Site Collection Administrator section, in the User Name box, type your login name, and click the Check Names icon to the right. Click OK to create the root site collection.

In this procedure, you create a copy of the Reseller Sales Margin Analysis by Sales Territory report on an integrated-mode server.

Create a report copy

1. In Internet Explorer, in the navigation bar on the left, click Reports.

2. Point to the Reseller Sales Margin Analysis by Sales Territory report, click the Edit button (which appears as an arrow to the right of the report title), point to Send To, and select Other Location.

3. On the Copy: Reseller Sales Margin Analysis By Sales Territory.rdl page, in the Destination Document Library Or Folder box, append **/ReportsLibrary** to the existing URL.

4. In the File Name For The Copy box, replace the default text by typing **Pacific Reseller Sales Margin Analysis**, as shown here.

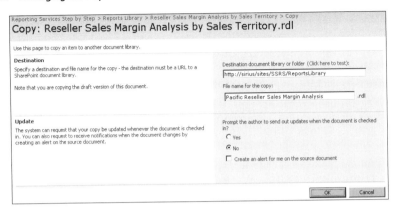

Note Because the Reporting Services deployment process does not depend on checking items in and out, setting the Prompt The Author To Send Out Updates When The Document Is Checked In? option to Yes does not lead to an update of the report copy when the base report changes.

5. Click OK.

6. In the Copy Progress message box, click OK, and then, when the copy operation completes, click Done.

7. In the Copy Progress message box, click OK.

   The report copy displays in the list of reports. You can now change properties for the report copy, which you do in the next procedure.

Configuring Report Parameters

Besides managing the location of reports on the report server, you can also manage the default values that are configured for the report parameters. In addition, you can remove the parameter prompt for a report so that a user cannot choose a different parameter value.

In this procedure, you configure the default value of a parameter in the Pacific Reseller Sales Margin Analysis report and remove the user prompt for the parameter.

Configure parameter properties

1. In Internet Explorer, open the parameter properties page of the Pacific Reseller Sales Margin Analysis report that you created earlier in this chapter.

   ❑ *Native mode:* Open the report if necessary, click the Properties tab above the report, and then click the Parameters link.

❑ *Integrated mode:* Open the reports library folder for the report, if necessary, point to the report in the list, click the Edit button (which appears to the right of the report title), and select Manage Parameters.

2. Change the default value for the *SalesTerritoryGroup* parameter to *Pacific*.

❑ *Native mode:* On the SalesTerritoryGroup row, in the Default Value drop-down list, clear the rows containing Europe and North America, as shown here.

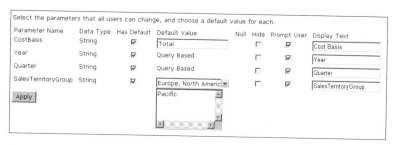

❑ *Integrated mode:* Click the SalesTerritoryGroup link, and then, in the Use This Value drop-down list, clear the check boxes for the rows containing Europe and North America.

3. Remove the user prompt for SalesTerritoryGroup.

 Important When a default value is missing for a report parameter, the report cannot execute until the user provides a parameter value. For this reason, be sure not to remove the user prompt for a report parameter without also specifying a default value, or else the report can never execute.

❑ *Native mode:* On the SalesTerritoryGroup row, clear the Prompt User check box, and then click Apply.

❑ *Integrated mode:* Select the Hidden option, click OK, and then, on the Manage Parameters: Pacific Reseller Sales Margin Analysis page, click Close.

 Note The Hidden option allows you to specify a default value for a report parameter without allowing the user to view or change the report parameter value. The Internal option also hides the parameters, but it requires an expression in the report definition to evaluate at run time.

4. View the report.

❑ *Native mode:* Above the parameter properties, click the View tab to render the report, as shown here.

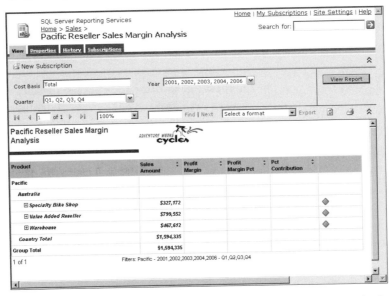

Notice that the prompt for the sales territory selection does not appear in the parameter toolbar above the report and that the report displays data only for the Pacific sales territory.

❑ *Integrated mode:* In the Reports Library list, point to the Pacific Reseller Sales Margin Analysis report, click the Edit button (which appears to the right of the report title), and select Manage Data Sources. Click the AdventureWorksDW2008 link, and then click the ellipsis button to the right of the Data Source Link box. In the Select An Item dialog box, click Up, click the Data Connections link, select AdventureWorksDW2008, click OK twice, and click Close. Now that the data source information has been linked to the report, click the Pacific Reseller Sales Margin Analysis link to view the report, shown here.

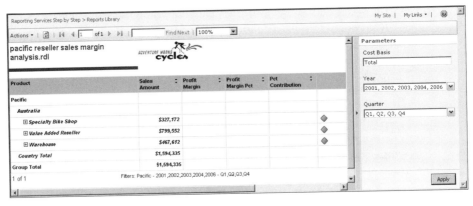

Enabling Personalized Folders

On a native-mode report server, you can enable My Reports to give each user a personal workspace in which the user can store reports created using one of the report development tools for personal use. A user with appropriate permissions can also create a linked report to personalize a report, such as setting a specific parameter value when the report opens. To enable My Reports using SQL Server Management Studio, connect to Reporting Services, right-click the server in Object Explorer, select Properties, and then select the Enable A My Reports Folder For Each User check box. The tasks that a user can perform in this folder are controlled by the role settings that are described in Chapter 11.

On an integrated-mode server, you can also provide a personal workspace for report storage, by creating a Shared Services Provider and configuring a My Site Location and personalization on the SharePoint server. (For more information, see the article "Create and Configure Shared Services Providers," at *http://technet.microsoft.com/en-us/library /cc303421.aspx*.) A user with appropriate permissions can then click the My Site link at the top of the SharePoint site to create a personal site, and then use the Send To command (as described in the procedure entitled "Create a report copy" earlier in this chapter) to copy a report and personalize the parameter settings.

Configuring Data Source Properties

You will likely design and test reports in BI Dev Studio by using a local data source that contains a representative subset of production data. By limiting the data used for report development, you can avoid long waits for report execution. On the server, however, you want reports to retrieve data from the production data sources. You can maintain one data source for your development environment and another for your server environment. The *OverwriteDataSources* property for the project controls whether the data source in your project gets copied to the server. By default, deployment copies the data source file the first time, but subsequent deployments ignore the data source file, allowing you to change the properties on the server without affecting the data source on your development computer.

Prompting the User for Credentials

The simplest type of security to implement is Windows integrated security, which passes the user's credentials to the data source, but you might have data sources that don't use Microsoft Windows credentials for authentication. For these situations, you can prompt the user for credentials, which then pass to the data provider for authentication at the data source. You should use this authentication method only for reports that the user can access on demand because the report cannot execute without user input.

In this procedure, you create a report-specific data source to prompt the user for credentials before executing the report.

Configure prompted credentials

1. In Internet Explorer, open the Sales Summary report that you created earlier in this chapter.

   ❑ *Native mode:* In Report Manager, click the Home link at the top of the window, click the For Review link, and then click the Sales Summary link.

   ❑ *Integrated mode:* In the address bar, type **http://<servername>/sites/ssrs /ReportsLibrary/For Review** (replacing *<servername>* with the name of your server), or if viewing a report, click the Reports Library link at the top of the window and then click the Sales Summary link.

   A message displays explaining that the current data source connection information has been deleted. Remember that this report was uploaded directly to the report server and independently of any shared data source described in the report definition. You must either associate the report with shared data sources on the report server, or configure a report-specific data source. In this procedure, you create a report-specific data source to learn the proper steps.

2. Open the data source properties page for the report.

   ❑ *Native mode:* Above the report, click the Properties tab, and then click the Data Sources link. A message displays explaining that the data source reference is no longer valid.

   ❑ *Integrated mode:* At the top of the window, click the For Review link, point to the Sales Summary report, and click the Edit button to the right of the report title, select Manage Data Sources, and click the AdventureWorksDW2008 link. A message displays explaining that the linked data source could not be found.

3. Create a report-specific data source to connect to the AdventureWorksDW2008 data source.

   ❑ *Native mode:* Select A Custom Data Source, and then, in the Connection String text box, type **Data Source=localhost;Initial Catalog=AdventureWorksDW2008;**.

   The default authentication when creating a new data source on the report server is Credentials Supplied By The User Running The Report, as shown here.

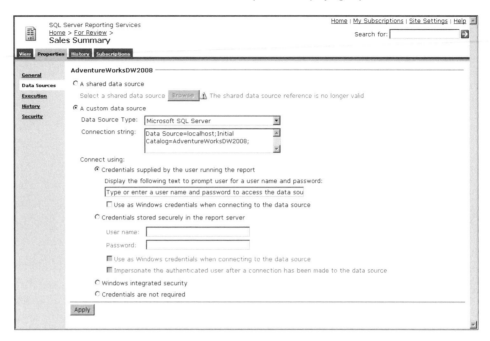

❑ *Integrated mode:* Select Custom Data Source, and then, in the Connection String box, type **Data Source=localhost;Initial Catalog=AdventureWorksDW2008;**, and then select Prompt For Credentials.

Before the user can view the report, the user must enter a user name and password. You can change the prompt that is displayed to the user in the Display The Following Text To Prompt User For A User Name And Password text box in native mode, or in the Provide Instructions Or Example box in integrated mode.

Important If the user must supply a Windows user account, be sure to select the Use As Windows Credentials When Connecting To The Data Source check box in native mode, or select Use As Windows Credentials in integrated mode.

4. Apply the change to the data source properties.

❑ *Native mode:* Click Apply.

❑ *Integrated mode:* Click OK, and then click Close.

5. View the report.

❑ *Native mode:* Above the data source properties, click the View tab. The prompt for credentials displays, as shown here. Type your user name and password, and then click View Report to display the report.

Type or enter a user name and password to access the data source:

Log In Name: [   ]   Password: [   ]

❑ *Integrated mode:* Click the Sales Summary link. The prompt for credentials displays. Type your user name and password, and then click Apply to display the report.

Important If you have configured Windows authentication for your SQL Server database engine, which is the default, be sure to include the domain name with your user name in the Log In Name box, using the Domain\User format.

Using Stored Credentials

Several execution methods require the data source to use stored credentials when the report runs on a scheduled basis or produces a report snapshot. The stored credentials are stored in the ReportServer database using reversible encryption. The account used for stored credentials must be granted Read permission on the source database.

In this procedure, you configure a shared data source to use stored credentials.

Configure stored credentials

1. In Internet Explorer, open the AdventureWorksDW2008 data source that was deployed with your report project earlier in this chapter.

Important If you deployed the report model project in Chapter 9, you also see the Adventure Works DW2008 data source for the report model in the Data Sources folder. Be sure to select the correct data source.

❑ *Native mode:* In Report Manager, click the Home link at the top of the window, click the Data Sources link, and then click the AdventureWorksDW2008 link.

❑ *Integrated mode:* Type **http://<*servername*>/sites/ssrs/data connections** (replacing *<servername>* with the name of your server), and then click the AdventureWorksDW2008 link.

2. Configure the stored credentials option.

❑ *Native mode:* Select Credentials Stored Securely In The Report Server, type your user name and password in the applicable text boxes, select the Use As Windows Credentials When Connecting To The Data Source check box if you are using Windows authentication in your SQL Server database, and then click Apply. The updated properties page for the data source is shown here.

Note In this example, the server name in the User Name string is fictitious and is included for illustration purposes only.

❑ *Integrated mode:* Select Stored Credentials, type your user name and password in the applicable boxes, select the User As Windows Credentials check box if you are using Windows authentication in your SQL Server database, and click OK.

Important If you type an incorrect user name and password for a data source's stored credentials, no error message displays. You must test a report using this data source to confirm the user name and password are correct, which you do in the next procedure.

Configuring Report Execution Properties

Report execution transforms a report stored in the ReportServer database into a rendered report that the user views. As part of the execution process, the queries defined in the report's datasets execute and return data to the report server, which then uses the report definition file to determine how to construct the report with the retrieved data. At this point, the report is in an intermediate format that is sent to the applicable rendering extension to produce the final rendered report.

Report performance is determined largely by how much data is retrieved by the report and how much processing is required to produce the rendered report. If the users don't need the most current data in the database each time the report executes, you should consider any execution option that generates the report's intermediate format in advance of the user viewing the report to achieve optimal performance. The following sections in this chapter explain the relationship between each execution option and generation of the intermediate format.

Executing a Report on Demand

When a user clicks the link for a report, the report executes on demand, returning the most current data to the report server which then produces an intermediate format. The intermediate format is stored in the ReportServerTempDB database in a session cache to speed up subsequent requests by the same user for the same report during the current session. For example, after the user views the report online, the user might export the report to an Excel format. By having the intermediate format in session cache, the online version and the Excel version of the report match. Furthermore, the Excel version renders very quickly from the intermediate format of the report because the report server does not need to wait for the query to execute again.

In this procedure, you configure the execution properties of the Employee Sales Moving Average report to execute on demand with a 60-second timeout.

Configure report execution on demand with a 60-second timeout

1. In Internet Explorer, open the execution properties page of the Employee Sales Moving Average Report.

   ❑ *Native mode:* In Report Manager, click the Home link at the top of the window, click the For Review link, click the Employee Sales Moving Average link, click the Properties tab, and then click the Execution link to view the execution properties, as shown here.

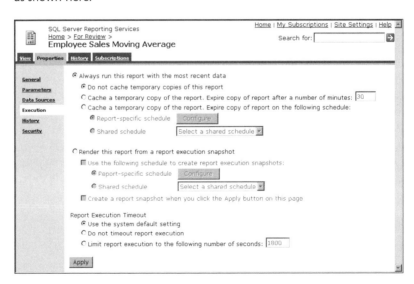

❑ *Integrated mode:* In the navigation bar, click Reports, click the For Review link, point to Employee Sales Moving Average, click the Edit button appearing to the right of the report title, and select Manage Data Sources. Click the AdventureWorksDW2008 link, and then click the ellipsis button to the right of the Data Source Link box. In the Select An Item dialog box, click Up twice, click the Data Connections link, select AdventureWorksDW2008, click OK twice, and click Close. Now the link to the data source, which was broken when you moved the report to the For Review folder, is fixed, and you can proceed to set the execution properties. Point to Employee Sales Moving Average, click Edit, and then select Manage Processing Options.

The two execution properties for a report are the type of execution and the report execution timeout, as shown in the following table.

For This Property Type	On a Native-Mode Report Server, the Default Property Is	On an Integrated-Mode Report Server, the Default Property Is
Execution type	Do Not Cache Temporary Copies Of The Report	Use Live Data
Execution timeout	Use The System Default Setting	Use Site Default Setting

You learn how to configure the System/Site default setting in Chapter 12, "Performing Administrative Tasks," if you want to use a value other than the 1,800-second default for all reports. Alternatively, you can override this value, as shown in the next step.

2. Change the report execution timeout value to *60*.

❑ *Native mode:* In the Report Execution Timeout section, select Limit Report Execution To The Following Number Of Seconds, and then, in the text box to the right, type **60**, and click Apply.

❑ *Integrated mode:* In the Processing Time-out section, select Limit Report Processing (In Seconds), and then, in the text box to the right, type **60**, and click OK.

3. View the report to confirm execution on demand.

❑ *Native mode:* Click the View tab and note the date-time stamp below the chart.

❑ *Integrated mode:* Click the Employee Sales Moving Average link and note the date-time stamp below the chart.

4. Above the report title, click the For Review link, click the Employee Sales Moving Average link, and then note the new date-time stamp below the chart.

Caching Reports

Caching a report is helpful when you want to strike a balance between having current data in the report and having faster access to the online report. The first time a user clicks the link for a report configured to cache, the report execution process is identical to the on-demand process. However, the intermediate format is flagged as a cached instance and stored in ReportServerTempDB until the time specified by the cache settings expires. Meanwhile, if any user requests the report during the time that it still resides in cache, then the report server retrieves the intermediate format and renders the report so long as the user requests the same combination of parameter values. This process is much faster than retrieving the data, producing the intermediate format, and then rendering the report.

If a user requests a different set of parameter values for a cached report, then the report processor treats the request as a new report executing on demand, but flags it as a second cached instance. If users are constantly looking at different parameter combinations and not reusing parameter values, then using cached reports is not helpful.

In this procedure, you configure the execution properties of the Employee Sales Moving Average report to cache the report and expire the cached instance after 60 minutes.

Configure caching with expiration after 60 minutes

1. In Internet Explorer, open the execution properties page of the Employee Sales Moving Average report.

   ❑ *Native mode:* Open the report, if necessary, click the Properties tab, and then click the Execution link to view the execution properties.

   ❑ *Integrated mode:* If the report is open, click the For Review link. Otherwise, type **http://<*servername*>/sites/ssrs/ReportsLibrary/For Review** (replacing <*servername*> with the name of your server), point to Employee Sales Moving Average, click the Edit button (located to the right of the report title), and then select Manage Processing Options.

2. Set the execution type to caching with an expiration after 60 minutes.

   ❑ *Native mode:* Select Cache A Temporary Copy Of The Report, and then, in the Expire Copy Of The Report After A Number Of Minutes text box, type **60**. Click Apply.

   ❑ *Integrated mode:* Select Use Cached Data, and then, in the Elapsed Time In Minutes text box, type **60**, as shown here, and click OK.

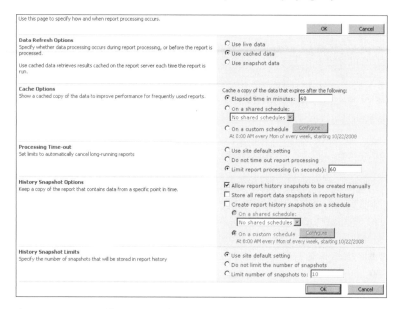

3. View the report to confirm execution.

   ❑ *Native mode:* Click the View tab and note the date-time stamp below the chart.

   ❑ *Integrated mode:* Click the Employee Sales Moving Average link.

4. Above the report title, click the For Review link, click the Employee Sales Moving Average Report link, and then note the date-time stamp below the chart has not changed to reflect the current time.

5. In the Employee drop-down list, select Campbell, David, click View Report or Apply (as applicable to your report server), and then note the new date-time stamp.

6. In the Employee drop-down list, select Pak, Jae, click View Report or Apply as applicable, and then note the date-time stamp for the first cached instance of the report.

Creating Report Snapshots

When users don't need up-to-the minute data from the data source, and also need fast report performance, you can use report snapshots. A report snapshot executes the query and produces the intermediate format in advance of the user's request to view the report. You can configure a report to generate a snapshot on demand, or you can set up a recurring schedule to replace a snapshot periodically with a more current version. The intermediate format of the report has no expiration time like a cached instance, and is stored in the ReportServer database as part of permanent storage. If you have limited disk space, you should monitor the growth in your ReportServer database, as described in Chapter 12.

If you decide to create a report snapshot on a recurring schedule, you can choose between a report-specific schedule and a shared schedule. The benefit of using a shared schedule is the ability to apply the schedule to several different activities, such as creating snapshot, expiring caches, or delivering subscriptions.

In this procedure, you configure the Sales and Average Sales report to execute as a report snapshot on a weekly schedule.

Configure a report as a scheduled snapshot

1. Click Start, select All Programs, Microsoft SQL Server 2008, Configuration Tools, and click SQL Server Configuration Manager. Then select SQL Server Services in the tree view on the left, right-click SQL Server Agent in the detail view on the right, and, if the state of the SQL Server Agent is stopped, select Start. Close SQL Server Configuration Manager.

> **Important**   The SQL Server Agent must be running to create and execute schedules. If you later stop or disable the SQL Server Agent, any schedules that were missed do not execute.

2. Switch to Internet Explorer, and open the execution properties page of the Sales and Average Sales report.

   ❑ *Native mode:* In Report Manager, click the Home link at the top of the window, click the For Review link, click the Sales And Average Sales link, click the Properties tab, and then click the Execution link to view the execution properties.

   ❑ *Integrated mode:* If the report is open, click the For Review link. Otherwise, type **http://<*servername*>/sites/ssrs/ReportsLibrary/For Review** (replacing <*servername*> with the name of your server), point to Employee Sales Moving Average, click the Edit button (located to the right of the report title), and then select Manage Processing Options.

3. Set the execution type to a report execution snapshot using a report-specific schedule.

   ❑ *Native mode:* Select Render This Report From A Report Execution Snapshot, select the Use The Following Schedule To Create Report Execution Snapshots check box, and then click Configure.

> **Note**   If a shared schedule exists, you can select the Shared Schedule option, and select the shared schedule in the corresponding drop-down list. You can configure server-wide schedules by clicking the Site Settings link at the top of the window, clicking the Schedules link, and then clicking New Schedule. You then specify the schedule details on the Scheduling page, which looks very similar to the page that you configure in the next step.

❑ *Integrated mode:* Select Use Snapshot Data, select the Schedule Data Processing check box, and then click Configure.

Note If a shared schedule exists, you can select the On A Shared Schedule option, and select the shared schedule in the corresponding drop-down list. You can configure server-wide schedules by clicking the Site Actions button at the top of the window. Click Site Settings, click Modify All Site Settings, click Manage Shared Schedules in the Reporting Services section, and click Add Schedule. You then specify the schedule details on the Scheduling page, which looks very similar to the page that you configure in the next step.

4. Configure a weekly schedule to create the snapshot each Monday at 6:00 AM, ending in two weeks.

❑ *Native mode:* Select Week, and then, in the first Start Time text box, replace the current value with **06**. Select the Stop This Schedule On check box, click the Calendar icon, and select a date two weeks into the future, as shown here. Click OK.

❑ *Integrated mode:* Select Week, and then, in the Start Time box, replace the current value with **6:00**. Select Stop Running This Schedule On, click the Calendar icon, select a date two weeks into the future, and click OK.

> **Note** In this procedure, a specific end date for the schedule is specified to limit the number of times the report executes on a schedule. In a production system, you are more likely to omit specifying an end date for the schedule to keep creating the report snapshot on an ongoing basis.

5. Apply the new execution properties.

❑ *Native mode:* On the execution properties page, shown here, click Apply.

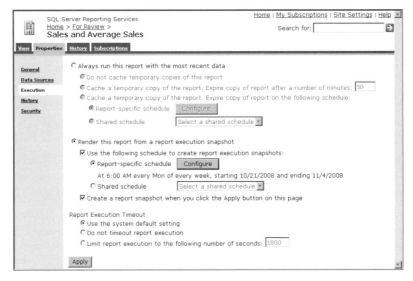

❑ *Integrated mode:* On the Manage Processing Options: Employee Sales Moving Average page, click OK.

Notice that the Create A Report Snapshot When You Click The Apply Button On This Page check box is selected by default on this page on a native-mode report server. On an integrated-mode server, the equivalent option is the Create Or Update The Snapshot When This Page Is Saved check box. You can create a snapshot on demand without waiting for the scheduled snapshot by opening this page, selecting this check box, and saving the page by clicking Apply on a native-mode report server or by clicking OK on an integrated-mode report server.

6. View the report snapshot label in the For Review folder.

❑ *Native mode:* Above the execution properties, click the For Review link to view the snapshot label, shown here.

> Sales and Average Sales !NEW
> *Last Run: 10/21/2008 5:06 AM*

❑ *Integrated mode:* After you click OK in the previous step, the contents of the For Review folder displays. However, there is no indicator that the report is now a snapshot report. The Report Modified date-time stamp displays the execution time of the snapshot after you refresh the browser.

Each time you click the report link to view the report snapshot, the execution date-time reflects the execution time of the snapshot. Note that the user cannot change any report parameter that passes a value to a query parameter. The report parameter is visible in the toolbar, but it is disabled.

When a new snapshot is created according to the defined schedule, the former snapshot is removed. Only the most current snapshot is available for viewing unless you configure report history, which you learn how to do in the next procedure.

Saving Report Snapshots in Report History

By default, a new report snapshot replaces the previous report snapshot. You can choose to accumulate report snapshots in report history to preserve a record of the report contents at specific points in time. To add a report snapshot to report history, you can click a button to add it manually, or you can add to report history each time a new report snapshot is created according to the defined schedule.

Because snapshots can require a lot of storage space, you might want to impose a serverwide limit to the number of snapshots that can accumulate for a report, or you can set a limit specific to each report.

In this procedure, you configure report history and manually add a report snapshot to report history.

Configure report history

1. Open the History page of the Sales and Average Sales report.

   ❑ *Native mode:* In Report Manager, click the Sales And Average Sales link, click the Properties tab, and then click the History link to view the history properties, as shown here.

❑ *Integrated mode:* In the For Review folder of the Reports Library, point to the Sales And Average Sales report, click the Edit button (which appears to the right of the report title), and select Manage Data Sources. Click the AdventureWorksDW2008 link, and then click the ellipsis button to the right of the Data Source Link box. In the Select An Item dialog box, click Up twice, click the Data Connections link, select AdventureWorksDW2008, click OK twice, and click Close. Now, to view the history properties, select the Sales And Average Sales report, click Edit, and then click Manage Processing Options.

Select the Allow Report History To Be Created Manually check box to enable the user to create a report history snapshot on demand. The report history snapshot is different from the snapshot you created in the previous procedure because it is accessible only on the History tab of the report on a native-mode report server, and on the View History page on an integrated-mode server, where you can accumulate multiple snapshots in report history. The New Snapshot button appears on the History tab when this option is enabled.

As an alternative to creating report history manually, you can select the Use The Following Schedule To Add Snapshots To Report History check box on a native-mode report server. On an integrated-mode report server, select the Create Report History Snapshots On A Schedule check box.

2. Configure the option to store each report execution snapshot in report history.

❑ *Native mode:* Select the Store All Report Execution Snapshots In History check box, and click Apply.

❑ *Integrated mode:* Select the Store All Report Data Snapshots In Report History check box, and click OK.

Note Only report execution snapshots created after you enabled this option are stored in report history.

Because report history consumes storage space in the ReportServer database, you should carefully manage the number of snapshots that accumulate in report history. You learn more about how to change the server-wide defaults in Chapter 12. The options for applying a snapshot limit are described in the following table.

To Set This Type of Snapshot Limit	On a Native-Mode Report Server, Use This Option	On an Integrated-Mode Report Server, Use This Option
Default	Default Setting	Use Site Default Setting
Specific number	Limit The Copies Of Report History	Limit Number Of Snapshots To
No limit	Keep An Unlimited Number Of Snapshots In Report History	Do Not Limit the Number Of Snapshots

3. Create a report snapshot manually.

- ❑ *Native mode:* Click the History tab, and then click the New Snapshot button. The report snapshot appears in a list on the History tab.

- ❑ *Integrated mode:* Select the Sales And Average Sales report, click Edit, click View Report History, and click New Snapshot.

The list of report snapshots in history includes the date and time the report snapshot was created and the total size of the report. You can delete a report by selecting its check box, and clicking the Delete button on the toolbar.

Managing Change in the Reporting Life Cycle

When report modifications are required to fix issues during testing or to accommodate changing business requirements, you must edit the report definition file and then redeploy the report. You can redeploy the report using any of the methods described previously in this chapter. The deployment process replaces the original report definition in the ReportServer database with the new report definition. All existing report properties are preserved, so you won't need to change execution settings or security permissions when you redeploy a report, for example. However, be aware that because parameter properties are preserved, any changes you make to report parameters in the report definition are visible when you view the report on the report server after deployment. You must first delete the report from the report server and then deploy the report to enable access to report parameter settings in the report definition.

Chapter 10 Quick Reference

To	Do This
Set report server project properties	In Solution Explorer, right-click the project, select Properties, and then specify a target data sources folder, a target report folder, and the target report server URL.
Deploy a report server project	In Solution Explorer, right-click the project, and select Deploy.
Upload a report to the report server	*Native mode:* In Internet Explorer, open Report Manager, navigate to the folder in which to store the report, click the Upload File button on the Report Manager toolbar, click Browse, navigate to the report on the file system, and select the report definition file. *Integrated mode:* In Internet Explorer, open the reports library on the SharePoint site, click the Upload button on the reports library toolbar, click Browse, navigate to the report on the file system, and select the report definition file.
Deploy reports with the Rs utility on a native-mode report server	Create a script file that uses the *CreateFolder* and *CreateReport* methods, and provide the path to this script file as an input argument for the Rs utility by using the following syntax: rs –i inputfile –s http://<*servername*>/ReportServer.
Add a folder to a report server	*Native mode:* In Report Manager, navigate to an existing folder, and click the New Folder button on the Report Manager toolbar. *Integrated mode:* In the SharePoint reports library, on the reports library toolbar, click the arrow on the New button, and select Folder.
Move a report to a new folder	*Native mode:* In Report Manager, navigate to the report's parent folder, click the Show Details button on the Report Manager toolbar, select the report's check box, click the Move button, and select a target folder. *Integrated mode:* In the upper-right corner of a page in the SharePoint site, click Site Actions, select Manage Content And Structure, select Reports Library in the tree view, select the report's check box, click the arrow on the Actions button, select Move, and select a target folder.
Create a linked report on a native-mode report server	In Report Manager, open the base report, click the Properties tab, click Create Linked Report, provide a name for the linked report, and then, if you want, click Change Location and select a target location.
Create a report copy on an integrated-mode report server	In a SharePoint site, in the navigation bar, click Reports, point to a report in the library, click the Edit button appearing to the right of the report title, select Send To, click Other Location, type the name of a target document library or folder, and type a name for the report copy.

To	Do This
Configure report parameter properties	*Native mode:* In Report Manager, open the report, click the Properties tab, click the Parameters link, and, if you want, clear the Has Default check box, provide an alternate default value, select the Hide check box, clear the Prompt User check box, or change the Display Text for the report parameter prompt.
	Integrated mode: In the SharePoint reports library, point to the report, click the Edit button appearing to the right of the report title, select Manage Parameters, click a parameter link, and, if you want, select a new default value, select Do Not Use A Default Value, change the Prompt text, or hide the parameter by selecting Hidden or Internal.
Configure a data source	*Native mode:* In Report Manager, open the shared data source or open a report, click the Properties tab, click the Data Sources link, select A Custom Data Source, select a data source type, and provide a connection string. Select the applicable Connect Using option to configure one of the following authentication methods: prompted credentials, stored credentials (which requires supplying the login name and password), Windows integrated security, or no credentials.
	Integrated mode: In SharePoint, open the Data Connections folder on the site, and select a data source link or, in a reports library, point to a report, click the Edit button appearing to the right of the report title, select Manage Data Source, click the data source link, and select Custom Data Source. Select a data source type, and provide a connection string. Select the applicable Credentials option and configure one of the following authentication methods: Windows integrated security, prompted credentials, stored credentials (which requires supplying the login name and password), or the unattended report processing account.
Configure report execution properties	*Native mode:* In Report Manager, open the report, click the Properties tab, click the Execution link, and then specify an execution type (on demand, caching, or snapshot) and a report execution timeout setting.
	Integrated mode: In SharePoint, open the reports library, point to a report, click the Edit button located to the right of the report title, select Manage Processing Options, and then specify an execution type (on demand, caching, or snapshot) and a report execution timeout setting.
Enable report history	*Native mode:* In Report Manager, open the report, click the Properties tab, click the History link, and select a method for adding snapshots to report history and a limit to the number of snapshots to keep in report history.
	Integrated mode: In SharePoint, open the reports library, point to a report, click the Edit button located to the right of the report title, select Manage Processing Options, and select a method for adding snapshots to the report history and a limit to the number of snapshots to keep in report history.

Chapter 11
Securing Report Server Content

After completing this chapter, you will be able to:

- Assign groups or individual users to security roles.

- Secure folders or individual items on the report server by using role assignments.

- Configure system security roles.

- Restrict access to data by using role and query parameters, permissions tables, or dataset filters.

Whether everyone in your organization can access all reports on the report server freely or groups of users are restricted to viewing specific sets of reports, you must implement security to allow access to the content that you deployed to the report server in Chapter 10, "Deploying Reports to a Server." In this chapter, you learn how to use security to manage user access to folders, reports, and report models and to grant specific administrative privileges for managing the report server. You also learn how to restrict the data that displays in a report based on the current user.

Important To complete the procedures in this chapter, you must be a local system administrator on the report server. You also must have completed Chapter 10 successfully so that you have content available on the report server to secure.

Configuring Report Server Security Policies

Before a user can access content on the report server, Reporting Services uses *authentication* to confirm the user's identity through the use of a login name and password. In this chapter, you use the default authentication method, Windows integrated security. This authentication method requires you to create a Microsoft Windows account for each user who will access the report server. If you want, you can organize these user accounts into Windows groups.

Tip Reporting Services also supports basic authentication in native mode and custom forms authentication in both native mode and SharePoint integrated mode. To learn more about implementing alternate authentication methods, refer to "Security and Protection (Reporting Services)" in SQL Server Books Online.

After authentication, the process of *authorization* grants permissions to the user to access content on the report server and to perform specific actions. In native mode, Reporting Services uses a role-based authorization system to control what users can see and do on the report server. In SharePoint integrated mode, all authorization is managed through Microsoft SharePoint security policies, but it is conceptually similar to the role-based system in native mode. To implement authorization, you map Windows users or groups to a set of tasks that they can perform on the server. This set of tasks is called a *role* in native mode and a *permission level* in SharePoint integrated mode.

Preparing to Implement Security

Before you can implement security on the report server using Windows integrated security, you must create Windows user accounts. You can also create Windows groups to combine many users that require the same role or permissions level assignments into a set.

 Important Do *not* create these accounts on a production server. The procedures in this book are intended only for use on a test or development server.

In this procedure, you add Windows group and user accounts to the report server.

Add Windows group and user accounts

1. Click Start, right-click My Computer (or, if using Windows Vista, right-click Computer), and select Manage.

2. In the Computer Management console, expand Local Users And Groups, right-click the Users folder, and select New User.

3. Type **VP** in the User Name, Password, and Confirm Password boxes, clear the User Must Change Password At Next Login check box, and then click Create.

4. Repeat the previous step to create accounts for **PacificMgr, EuropeMgr,** and **Analyst**.

5. Click Close.

6. Right-click the Groups folder and select New Group.

7. In the Name box, type **SalesAnalysts,** and click Add.

8. In the Enter The Object Names To Select (Examples): text box, type **Analyst**, click Check Names, click OK, and then click Create.

9. In the Name box, type **Managers**, and click Add.

10. In the Enter The Object Names To Select (Examples): text box, type **VP;EuropeMgr;PacificMgr**, click Check Names, click OK, and then click Create.

Reviewing Default Authorization Policies

The authorization policy that you implement depends on your report server topology. A native-mode report server uses roles to restrict the activities of users, while a SharePoint integrated-mode server uses SharePoint groups. Table 11-1 compares the default authorization policies defined by roles and SharePoint groups.

TABLE 11-1 Comparison of Default Authorization Policies

Native-Mode Roles	SharePoint Groups
Content Manager	**Owners**
Permission to perform all content management tasks, including security configuration	Full Control permission to change site content, pages, or functionality
Publisher	**Members**
Permission only to view and manage all content except subscriptions and security	Contribute permission to view and manage content and submit changes for approval
Browser	**Visitors**
Permission only to view reports and manage individual subscriptions	Read permission to view content and create subscriptions
Report Builder	No equivalent group—Owners and Members can start Report Builder
Permission only to view reports, manage individual subscriptions, and start Report Builder	
My Reports	No equivalent group—Enable the My Site features of SharePoint to support similar functionality within My Site
Permission to perform all content management tasks within the My Reports folder only	

You can change the activities associated with each role or SharePoint group or add new roles or SharePoint groups to customize the authorization policies. The activities that users can perform are called *tasks* on a native-mode report server and *permissions* on a SharePoint integrated-mode server. Table 11-2 compares the native-mode tasks to SharePoint permissions.

TABLE 11-2 Comparison of Activities

Use This Native-Mode Task	Or This SharePoint Permission or Permissions	To Allow This Activity
Consume reports	Edit Items, View Items	Open a report
Create linked reports	Not applicable	Create a copy of a report that remains linked to a base report
Manage all subscriptions	Manage Alerts	View and manage all users' subscriptions
Manage data sources	Add Items, Edit Items, Delete Items, View Items	Add, change, or delete data sources
Manage folders	Add Items, Edit Items, Delete Items, View Items	Add, change, or delete folders

TABLE 11-2 Comparison of Activities

Use This Native-Mode Task	Or This SharePoint Permission or Permissions	To Allow This Activity
Manage individual subscriptions	Create alerts	Add, change, or delete subscriptions owned by the user
Manage models	Add Items, Edit Items, Delete Items, View Items	Add, change, or delete report models
Manage report history	Edit Items, View Versions, Delete Versions	Add or delete report history snapshots and change report history properties
Manage reports	Add Items, Edit Items, Delete Items, View Items	Add or delete reports and change report properties
Manage resources	Add Items, Edit Items, Delete Items, View Items	Add, change, or delete resources and change resource properties
Set security for individual items	Not applicable	View and change security properties for folders, data sources, reports, report models, and resources
View data sources	View Items, Edit Items	View data sources in a folder and view the data source properties
View folders	View Items	View folders in the folder hierarchy and view folder properties
View models	View Items	View report models and report model properties and use report models as data sources
View reports	View Items	View reports in a folder
View resources	View Items	View resources in a folder and view resource properties

Native Mode

Reporting Services in native mode includes five default roles that will likely satisfy most of your authorization requirements. For example, the Browser role lets users view reports, but they cannot add or delete reports. Each default role definition includes a predefined group of tasks that the user can perform. You can modify a default role to add or remove tasks, or you can create a new role to define a customized set of tasks.

In this procedure, you review the default role definitions by using SQL Server Management Studio.

Review default role definitions

1. Click Start, select All Programs, select Microsoft SQL Server 2008, and select SQL Server Management Studio.

2. In the Connect To Server dialog box, in the Server Type drop-down list, select Reporting Services.

3. In the Server Name text box, if necessary, type **localhost** or the name of your report server, and then, in the Authentication drop-down list, select Windows Authentication. Click Connect.

4. In Object Explorer, expand the Security folder, and then expand the Roles folder to view the current roles, shown here.

After installing Reporting Services, five roles are available: Browser, Content Manager, My Reports, Publisher, and Report Builder. To add your own role or delete a role, use the shortcut menu on the Roles folder, which you access by right-clicking the Roles folder.

5. Double-click Browser to open the User Role Properties – Browser dialog box, as shown here, and review the selected tasks for the Browser role.

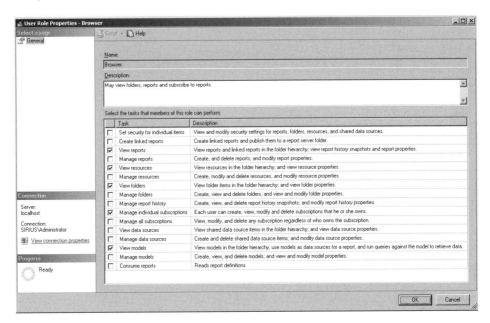

You can add permissions to the role by selecting the applicable check boxes, or remove permissions by clearing the check boxes. However, you cannot add custom tasks to the role.

6. Click Cancel to close the dialog box.

7. Repeat the previous two steps to review the other roles.

SharePoint Integrated Mode

If you have a SharePoint integrated-mode report server, you can use the three default SharePoint groups to manage authorization. You assign most users to the Visitor group to let them view reports and prevent them from adding or removing content. The default SharePoint groups are associated with specific permission levels that you can change, or you can add new SharePoint groups.

In this procedure, you review the default SharePoint groups and permission levels for the Report Center site.

Review default SharePoint groups and permissions levels

1. Open Windows Internet Explorer, and open the Report Center site at *http://localhost/sites/ssrs*.

2. Click Site Actions, select Site Settings, select People And Groups, and in the navigation bar on the left, click Site Permissions to view the current permission level assignments, similar to the page shown here.

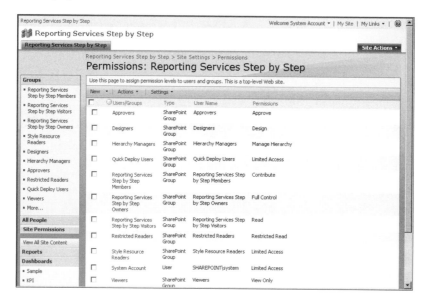

When the Report Center site was created, many SharePoint groups were created automatically for it, but the three groups that you use for managing Reporting Services activities are Reporting Services Step by Step Members, with Contribute permissions, Reporting Services Step by Step Owners, with Full Control permissions, and Reporting Services Step by Step Visitors, with Read permissions.

> **Note** The default group names for a site always include the name of the site (in this case, Reporting Services Step by Step) and the type of group, such as Members, Owners, or Visitors.

3. Click the Reporting Services Step By Step Visitors link to open the Edit Permissions: Reporting Services Step By Step page, shown here.

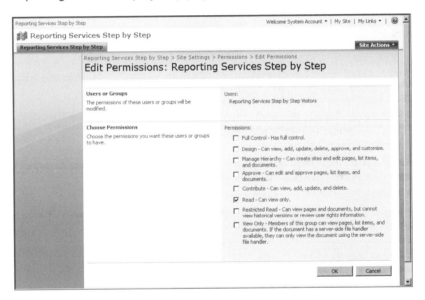

A group can have one or more permission levels assigned. In this example, the group has Read permission only. The specific activities that are associated with the Read permission are defined on the Permission Level page, which you explore next.

4. Click Cancel.

5. Click Settings, and then select Permission Levels to open the Permission Levels page, where you can review the available permission levels or create a new permission level.

6. Click the Read link to open the Edit Permission Level page, and select the Edit Items check box, as shown here.

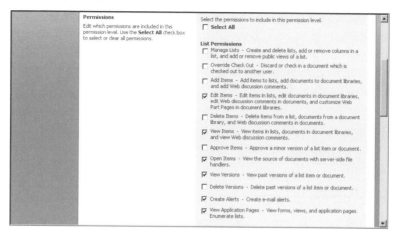

Users must have the Edit Items permission to open reports. The View Items permission allows users only to see the report in the document library list.

7. Click Submit.

Assigning User Permissions

The report server content is secure by default. You must grant access to the report server content before users can use the reports that you have deployed. You can then implement item-level security for more specific control over which reports that users can access and what activities they can perform.

Granting Access to Report Server Content

The procedure that you follow to grant access to report server content depends on your server architecture. Conceptually, the process is similar for both server types. You map users or groups to the activities they can perform at the upper-level folder for report server content. The upper-level folder is the Home page on a native-mode report server, and the Reports Library folder on a SharePoint integrated-mode server.

Creating Role Assignments

A *role assignment* is the mapping of a Windows user or group to a role for a selected item on the native-mode report server. An item can be a folder, a report, a report model, or any other resource uploaded to the report server, such as image or spreadsheet files. Although you can specify a role assignment on each individual item for each user, most administrators use role assignments for Windows groups at the folder level to simplify administration. Even if you want everyone to have access to all report server content, you must configure a role assignment on the Home folder that allows users to view reports. All folders below the Home folder inherit its role assignments, but you can override inheritance for any item to specify a new role assignment for that item.

In this procedure, you assign the SalesAnalysts and Managers groups to the Browser role on the Home folder.

Assign Windows groups to a role on a native-mode report server

1. Open Internet Explorer and navigate to Report Manager at *http://localhost/Reports*.

2. Click the Properties tab to view the Security page of the Home folder, as shown here.

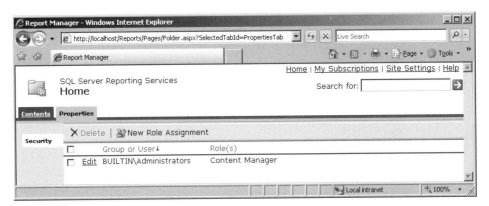

By default, the local Administrators group is assigned to the Content Manager role on the Home folder. Only local administrators have access to the report server after installing Reporting Services and must grant access to other nonadministrators through role assignments before these other users can deploy reports or access deployed content.

3. Click New Role Assignment.

4. In the Group Or User Name text box, type **SalesAnalysts**.

5. Select the Browser check box, as shown here, and then click OK.

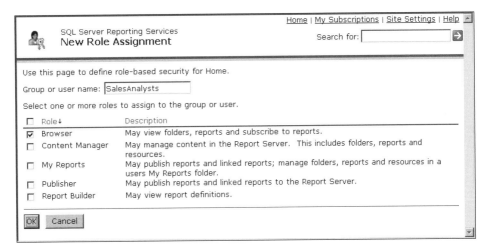

6. Repeat steps 3-5 to assign **Managers** to the Browser role. When finished, the Security page of the Home folder looks like this:

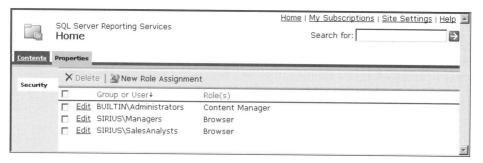

At this point, only local administrators and members of the Managers and SalesAnalysts groups have access to the report server. Local administrators can add and delete content, among other tasks, but the other users can only browse the folders and open reports. Because security of the Home folder is inherited by all other folders, all users have access to the other folders, such as the For Review or Sales folders.

Assigning SharePoint Permission Levels

You can use SharePoint groups to map a Windows user or group to a permission level. You then define the SharePoint groups that can access the Reports Library in your Report Center site (or any document library for which you have enabled Reporting Services content types). All folders below the upper-level folder inherit its role assignments, but you can override inheritance for any item to specify different users or groups with permission to access that item.

In this procedure, you assign the SalesAnalysts and Managers groups to the Reporting Services Step by Step Visitors group in the Report Center site.

Assign Windows groups to SharePoint groups

1. In Internet Explorer, navigate to the Report Center site at *http://localhost/sites/ssrs*, click Site Actions, select Site Settings, and select People And Groups.

2. In the navigation bar, click the Reporting Services Step By Step Visitors link.

3. Click New.

4. On the Add Users: Reporting Services Step By Step page, in the Users/Groups text box, type **SalesAnalysts;Managers**, and then click the Check Names icon below the text box to validate the group names, as shown here.

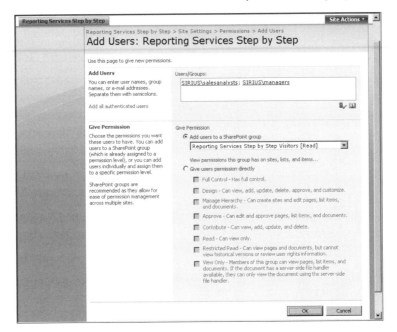

The Web application prefixes each group name with the domain or server name applicable to the Windows group names that you entered.

The default permission, Read, displays in the Add Users To A SharePoint Group drop-down list next to the SharePoint group name. You can use the drop-down list to assign the Windows groups to a different SharePoint group. You can click the View Permissions This Group Has On Sites, Lists, And Items link to confirm the permissions level that the group has for the current site collection.

If you want to assign the permissions level for the groups that you entered, rather than assign them to a SharePoint group, you can select Give Users Permissions Directly and then select the check box applicable to the desired permission level.

5. Click OK to save the assignment, and return to the view of users and groups assigned to the Reporting Services Step by Step Visitors group, as shown here.

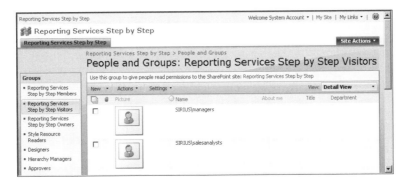

Configuring Item-Level Security

After granting access to the report server content, you then configure security to control which items each user can see and open. If a user's role does not permit access to an item, the item is not visible to the user. Similarly, if the user cannot perform a certain task, the user interface does not include the option or buttons required to perform that task. Because security is inherited from the parent folder, you change the security settings only for those items requiring a different role assignment than the one configured for the upper-level folder.

> **Note** Many of the steps described in the procedures in the following section depend on whether your report server is native mode or SharePoint integrated mode. Where applicable, steps include instructions for both architectures.

Securing a Folder

Folder-level security is easier to implement and maintain than report-level security because you can then take advantage of security inheritance. At minimum, you should secure the folder containing data sources to control who can add, change, or delete them. Then, you need to consider on a folder-by-folder basis how to manage access and configure user permissions accordingly.

In this procedure, you restrict access to the Data Sources and the For Review folders to local administrators.

Restrict access to a folder

1. Open the upper-level folder for report server content.

   ❑ *Native mode*: In Report Manager, return to the Home page by clicking the Contents tab.

   ❑ *Integrated mode*: In the Report Center site, click the Reporting Services Step By Step tab.

2. Open the security page for the data sources folder.

   ❑ *Native mode*: Click the Data Sources folder, click the Properties tab, and then click the Security link. The same role assignments that you configured for the Home folder appear in the Data Sources folder because security is currently inherited.

❑ *Integrated mode*: In the navigation bar, click the Data Connections link, and then, on the Settings menu, select Data Connection Library Settings. In the Permissions And Management section, click the Permissions For This Data Connection Library link. The same permissions that you saw at the site level appear in the Data Connections folder because security is currently inherited.

3. Disable security inheritance.

❑ *Native mode*: Click Edit Item Security, and then click OK to confirm that you want to apply different security settings for this item.

❑ *Integrated mode*: On the Actions menu, select Edit Permissions, and then click OK to confirm that you want to create unique permissions for this document library.

Now that you have disabled security inheritance, any permissions changes made to the upper-level folder are not applied to the folder containing data sources.

4. Set permissions to allow only content managers or SharePoint owners to access the folder containing data sources.

❑ *Native mode*: Select the check boxes to the left of the Managers and SalesAnalysts groups, as shown here, click Delete, and then click OK in the message box to confirm the deletion.

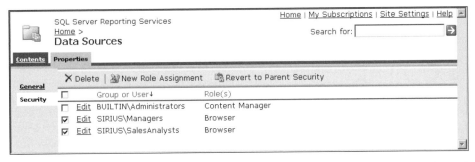

Notice the Revert To Parent Security button on this page, which allows you to discard the item-level role assignments and restore security inheritance from the Home folder.

❑ *Integrated mode*: Select the check box to the left of the Users/Groups column label to select all SharePoint groups, clear the Reporting Services Step By Step Owners check box, as shown here, and then on the Actions menu, select Remove User Permissions. Click OK to confirm the deletion. The Permissions page now includes a note explaining that the library no longer inherits permissions from its parent Web site.

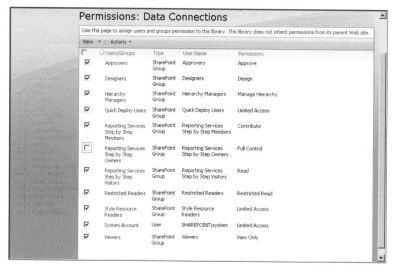

5. Return to the upper-level folder.

   ❏ *Native mode*: Click the Home link in the upper-left corner of the window.

   ❏ *Integrated mode*: On the Actions menu, select Edit Permissions, and then click OK to confirm that you want to create unique permissions for this document library.

6. Remove all but the content managers from the For Review folder.

   ❏ *Native mode*: Repeat steps 2 to 5 to open the For Review folder, disable security inheritance, and remove Managers and SalesAnalysts from the For Review folder.

   ❏ *Integrated mode*: In the navigation bar, click the Reports link, point to the For Reviewer folder, click the Edit button that appears to the right of the folder name, and select Manage Permissions. Repeat steps 3 to 5 to disable security inheritance, and remove all but the Reporting Services Step by Step Owners from the For Review folder.

> **Tip** In a real-world situation, you would limit access to the For Review folder to the groups or users with responsibility for validating and approving reports. After the reports are approved, you follow the steps you learned in Chapter 10 to move the reports to a folder that is configured for access by the target user community.

7. Test the security by opening Internet Explorer as a member of one of the removed groups. If your computer runs Windows Vista or Windows Server 2008, you must log off and then log in using VP as both the user name and password, and then open Internet Explorer. If your computer runs Windows XP, Windows Server 2000, or Windows Server 2003, click Start, select All Programs, right-click Internet Explorer, and select Run As. Select The Following User, type **VP** in the User and Password text boxes, and then click OK.

8. In Internet Explorer, navigate to the upper-level folder for report server content.

Note You might be prompted to provide credentials again when you open the Web application. After you type the user name and password, click OK. At the top of the browser window, click the yellow bar containing the message that Intranet settings are turned off by default, select Enable Intranet Settings, and then click Yes to confirm. The site is then added to the Local Intranet zone and you can access Report Manager without providing credentials. You can also eliminate the credentials prompt in Internet Explorer by following these steps if your computer is part of a domain: click Tools, select Internet Options, click the Security tab, select Local Intranet, click Sites, click Advanced, type **http://localhost** in the Add This Website To The Zone text box, click Close, and click OK twice. If your computer is not part of a domain, then you cannot adjust the intranet settings and must type the user name and password each time you open Report Manager.

❑ *Native mode:* Open Report Manager at *http://localhost/reports*, as shown here.

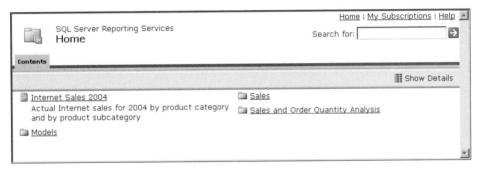

Notice that the Data Sources and For Review folders are not visible.

❑ *Integrated mode:* Open the Reports library at *http://localhost/sites/ssrs /ReportsLibrary*, as shown here.

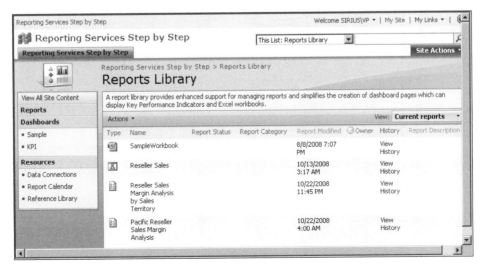

Notice that the For Review folder is not visible. The Data Connections link still appears in the navigation bar, but an Access Denied error displays if you click it.

9. Close the Internet Explorer window. If necessary, log off your computer and then log in again using your administrator credentials.

Approving Data Sources in SharePoint Integrated Mode

When you deploy data sources from SQL Server Business Intelligence Development Studio to the report server, the data source is put into a pending state. As the owner of the data source, you can view reports that use the data source. Users with the Manage Lists permission can also view reports associated with the data source, but all other users receive an Access Denied message when they try to view the report. To enable the data source for all users, you must change its status to Approved.

In this procedure, you approve the AdventureWorksDW2008 data source.

Approve a data source

1. Click the Reporting Services Step By Step tab, and then click the Data Connections link.

   Notice the status of the AdventureWorksDW2008 data source is currently pending.

2. Point to the AdventureWorksDW2008 link, click the Edit button, and select Approve/Reject.

3. On the Data Connections: AdventureWorksDW2008 page, select Approved, as shown here, and click OK.

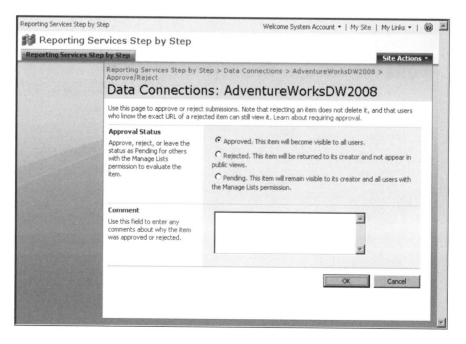

Securing a Report

The process of securing a report is similar to securing a folder. By default, the report inherits the security settings of its parent folder. You can disable inheritance and configure different role assignments for an individual report when necessary. Any changes to the parent folder security do not change the report's security settings.

In this procedure, you restrict access to the Reseller Sales Margin Analysis By Sales Territory report to the VP account and content managers or owners.

Restrict access to a report

1. Open the folder containing the Reseller Sales Margin Analysis By Sales Territory report.

   ❑ *Native mode:* In Report Manager, on the Home page, click the Sales folder link.

   ❑ *Integrated mode:* In the Report Center site, in the navigation bar, click the Reports link.

2. Open the security page for the Reseller Sales Margin Analysis By Sales Territory report.

   ❑ *Native mode:* Click the Reseller Sales Margin Analysis By Sales Territory link, click the Properties tab, and click the Security link.

   ❑ *Integrated mode:* Point to the Reseller Sales Margin Analysis By Sales Territory report, click the Edit button, and select Manage Permissions.

   You can see that the page to configure security for a report is similar to the security page for a folder.

3. Disable security inheritance.

   ❑ *Native mode:* Click Edit Item Security, and then click OK to confirm that you want to apply different security settings for this item.

   ❑ *Integrated mode:* On the Actions menu, select Edit Permissions, and then click OK to confirm that you want to create unique permissions for this document library.

4. Set permissions to allow only the content managers or SharePoint owners to access the report.

   ❑ *Native mode:* Select the check boxes to the left of the Managers and SalesAnalysts groups, click Delete, and then click OK in the message box to con-firm the deletion.

   ❑ *Integrated mode:* Select the check box to the left of the Users/Groups col-umn label to select all SharePoint groups, clear the Reporting Services Step By Step Owners check box, and then, on the Actions menu, select Remove User Permissions. Click OK to confirm the deletion.

5. Set permissions to allow the VP account to access the report.

   ❏ *Native mode:* Click New Role Assignment. In the Group Or User Name text box, type **VP**, select the check box next to Browser, and click OK.

   ❏ *Integrated mode:* Click New. In the Users/Groups text box, type **VP**, click the Check Names icon, select the Read check box, and click OK.

6. Test the security by opening the Web application as a member of one of the removed groups, such as Analyst, to confirm that the report is no longer available, and then open the Web application as VP to confirm that you can access the report.

7. Close the Internet Explorer window. If necessary, log off your computer and then log in again using your administrator credentials.

Assigning a System Role

System role assignments are used to assign users to tasks related to system administration tasks on the report server. Assigning a user to a system role does not grant access to report server content. Two default system roles, System Administrator and System User, are defined with different sets of administrative tasks. You can change the system role definitions or create a custom system role definition using Management Studio. The set of administrative tasks that you can use in a system role definition are shown in Table 11-3. To assign users or groups to the system role, you use Report Manager.

> **Note** System roles apply only to a native-mode report server. The capabilities authorized by System Administrator and System User roles are available to SharePoint farm administrators and to other users as defined by permissions at the Web application level.

TABLE 11-3 System Roles

Use This Task	To Allow This Activity
Execute Report Definitions	Execute a report independently of a report server, such as in Report Builder
Generate Events	Generate events in the report server namespace (applicable to applications, not to users)
Manage Jobs	View and cancel running jobs
Manage Report Server Properties	Change report server properties
Manage Report Server Security	Add or delete users assigned to system roles
Manage Roles	Add, change, or delete role definitions
Manage Shared Schedules	Add, change, or delete shared schedules used to execute reports or subscriptions
View Report Server Properties	View report server properties
View Shared Schedules	View shared schedules used to execute reports or subscriptions

In this procedure, you create a system user role to allow the SalesAnalysts group to manage shared schedules.

Create a system user role on a native-mode report server

1. In Management Studio 2008, connect to Reporting Services as described in the section entitled "Reviewing Default Authorization Policies" earlier in this chapter.

2. In Object Explorer, expand Security, and then expand System Roles.

3. Right-click System User and then select New System Role.

4. In the Name text box, type **Shared Schedule Manager**.

   Three default tasks for system users are selected automatically for you: View Report Server Properties, View Shared Schedules, and Execute Report Definitions.

5. Clear the Execute Report Definitions check box, select the Manage Shared Schedules check box, as shown here, and then click OK.

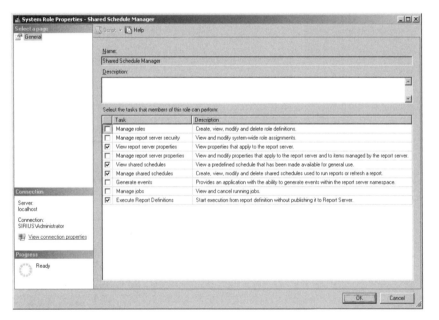

6. Switch to Report Manager, and click the Site Settings link in the upper-right corner.

7. Click the Security link, and then click New Role Assignment.

8. In the Group Or User Name text box, type **SalesAnalysts**, select the Shared Schedule Manager check box, as shown here, and click OK.

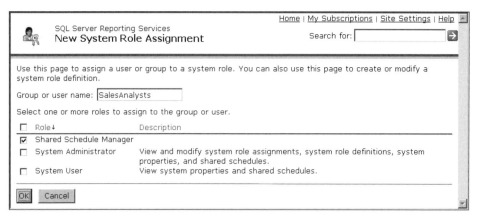

9. Test the security by opening Report Manager as Analyst, and click the Site Settings link. The Schedules page displays, as shown here.

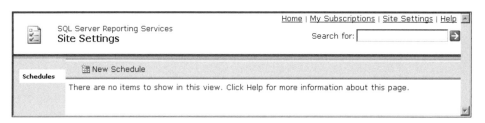

 Note You learn how to configure schedules in Chapter 15, "Working with Subscriptions."

10. Close the Internet Explorer window. If necessary, log off your computer and then log in again using your administrator credentials.

Securing a Report Model

You can control who can access a report model through role assignments or permissions just as you can control access to folders and reports. On a native-mode report server, users must first be assigned to the System User and Report Builder roles to use the report model in Report Builder. In addition to securing access to the report model, you can secure entities, attributes, and roles in the report model to limit access to specific items in the report model. Refer to Table 11-4 to learn which role assignments are required on a native-mode report server to deploy or use a report model. If you're using a SharePoint integrated-mode server, a user must have Full Control or Contribute permissions to work with a report model.

TABLE 11-4 Role Assignments Required for Using Report Models

Assign These Roles	To Allow This Activity
System User, Browser	View reports created with Report Builder (but the user is not able to start Report Builder to create ad hoc reports)
System User, Report Builder	View reports created with Report Builder, start Report Builder to create ad hoc reports, and save reports to the report server
System User, Publisher	Deploy a report model to the report server

Important The following procedure assumes that you have created and deployed a report model by completing the procedures in Chapter 9, "Developing Report Models."

In this procedure, you set permissions to allow all users to start Report Builder, grant access to the report model to everyone, and restrict access to the Employee entity in the Reseller Sales report model to the Managers group.

Configure Report Builder access and report model security

1. Configure permissions to allow all users to access Report Builder.

Important In a production system, you should grant access to Report Builder to specific groups, but for testing purposes, using the Everyone group allows you to complete the procedures in this book successfully.

   ❏ *Native mode:* In the upper-right corner of Report Manager, click Site Settings, click the Security link, and then click New Role Assignment. In the Group Or User Name text box, type **Everyone**, select the System User check box, and click OK.

   ❏ *Integrated mode:* Click the Reporting Services Step By Step tab, click the Reports link in the navigation bar, and then, on the New menu, click Folder. In the Name box, type **Ad Hoc Reports**, and click OK. Point to the Ad Hoc Reports folder, click the Edit button, and select Manage Permissions. On the Actions menu, select Edit Permissions, and click OK to confirm. Click New, click the Add All Authenticated Users link, select the Contribute check box, and click OK.

2. Open the security page of the report model.

   ❏ *Native mode:* Click the Home link at the top of the page, click the Models folder link, click the Reseller Sales link, and click the Security link. Notice that the Managers and SalesAnalysts groups currently have browser access to the report model.

❑ *Integrated mode:* Click the Reporting Services Step By Step tab, click the Reports link in the navigation bar, point to the Reseller Sales link, click the Edit button, and select Manage Permissions. The Reporting Services Step by Step Visitors group, which contains the Managers and SalesAnalysts groups, currently has Read permission on the report model, which is sufficient. The Contribute permission that you set in the previous step is necessary only to start Report Builder and to save reports, but not to use the report model as a data source.

3. Open the model item security page.

❑ *Native mode:* Click the Model Item Security link.

❑ *Integrated mode:* Click the Reporting Services Step By Step tab, click the Reports link in the navigation bar, point to the Reseller Sales link, click the Edit button, and select Manage Model Item Security.

4. Select the Secure Individual Model Items Independently For This Model check box. In the model item tree, select Reseller Sales, and then, in the Assign Read Permission To The Following Users And Groups text box, type **<*servername*> \Managers;<*servername*>\SalesAnalysts**, replacing <*servername*> with your computer name or the domain name for your Windows groups. In SharePoint integrated mode, click the Check Names icon.

The Model Item Security page in Report Manager in native mode looks like this:

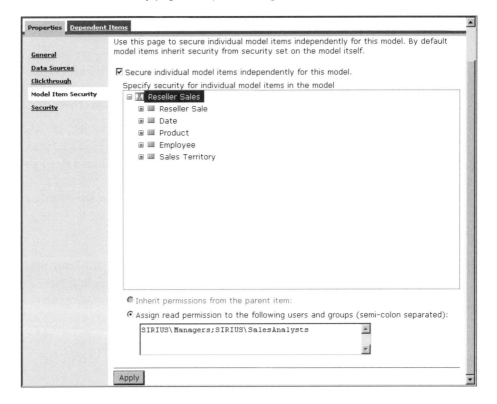

> **Note** The Model Item Security page in SharePoint integrated mode looks similar to the page shown here.

5. Click Apply in native mode. (You don't need to do anything in integrated mode; just skip to step 6.)

6. In the model item tree, select Employee, select Assign Read Permission To The Following Users And Groups, and then, in the text box, type **<*servername*>** **\Managers**. Click Apply.

Managers can create ad hoc reports using any item in the model, but Analysts cannot use any item in the Employee entity.

7. Save the model item security settings.

❑ *Native mode:* Click Apply.

❑ *Integrated mode:* Click OK.

8. Test the security by opening the Web application as VP.

> **Note** At this point, you are simply testing access to the Report Builder application. Later, in Chapter 14, "Creating Ad Hoc Reports," you test model item security as you learn how to use Report Builder. Note that this application is different from the Report Builder 2.0 application that you learned to use in Chapter 3, "Exploring Reporting Services."

❑ *Native mode:* In Internet Explorer, open Report Manager. You should see the Report Builder button on the Report Manager toolbar, as shown here.

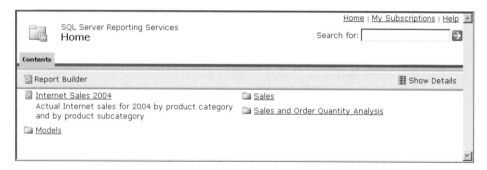

❑ *Integrated mode:* In Internet Explorer, open the Reports Library, click the Ad Hoc Reports folder link, and open the New menu to confirm that the Report Builder option is available, as shown here.

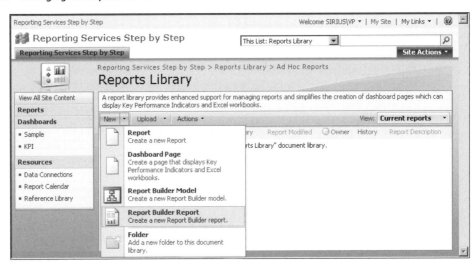

9. Close the Internet Explorer window. If necessary, log off your computer and then log in again using your administrator credentials.

Implementing Data Security

It's important to remember that giving a user access to a report does not necessarily mean that a user has access to the data retrieved by the dataset queries. If you're using Windows integrated security, then you must also give users Read permission on the source data.

Furthermore, when you need to give users access to the same report but must manage how much data displays in the report for each user, you must implement data security. There are several ways to implement data security, but all methods achieve the same result. Consider, for example, the Reseller Sales Margin Analysis By Sales Territory report in the Sales folder. This report includes a parameter that allows the user to view data for all sales territories or to select one or more specific sales territories. You can configure security to allow the VP to view all sales territories, and then limit the data in the report to the Europe sales territory data for the EuropeMgr and to the Pacific sales territory data for the PacificMgr. In this section, you explore three different ways to restrict data to specific sales territories by user.

Important Local administrators on the report server always have access to the report server, even if you remove the built-in administrators' role assignments on folders and reports. If you need to prevent local administrators from viewing reports, you need to implement data security.

Using a Query Parameter and a Role to Secure Data

One way to implement data security is to create a linked report, set the parameter value used to filter the report, hide the parameter, and then to use role assignments to control access to each linked report. In Chapter 10, you created a linked report for the Reseller Sales Margin Analysis By Sales Territory report (or a copy of the report if you're using SharePoint integrated mode), and configured the *SalesTerritoryGroup* parameter to default to Pacific. To build on this concept of using linked reports for data security, you would secure this linked report to allow only PacificMgr to view the report. Then you would repeat the entire process with linked reports for Europe and North America.

> **Note** Although a SharePoint integrated-mode server does not support linked reports, you can achieve similar results by creating a copy of a report, as explained in Chapter 10. Similarly, you can create report copies for each parameter value and secure each copy individually.

The benefit of using this approach is that you can implement data security for any report that uses parameters to filter content. The other approaches require you to modify the report definition in Report Designer and maintain a permissions table.

In this procedure, you finish implementing data security on the Pacific Reseller Sales Margin Analysis report by restricting the report to PacificMgr.

Secure a native-mode linked report or report copy in SharePoint integrated mode

1. Open the folder containing the Pacific Reseller Sales Margin Analysis report.

   ❑ *Native mode:* In Report Manager, on the Home page, click the Sales folder link.

   ❑ *Integrated mode:* In the Report Center site, in the navigation bar, click the Reports link.

2. Review the parameter settings for the report.

   ❑ *Native mode:* Click the Pacific Reseller Sales Margin Analysis link, click the Properties tab, and then click the Parameters link.

   ❑ *Integrated mode:* Point to the Pacific Reseller Sales Margin Analysis report, click the Edit button, click Manage Parameters, review the parameter settings, and then click Close.

   Remember that in Chapter 10, you changed the *SalesTerritoryGroup* default parameter value to *Pacific* and then cleared the Prompt User check box. The user cannot use the parameter drop-down list to select a different sales territory group.

   3. Disable security inheritance.

   ❑ *Native mode:* Click the Security link, click Edit Item Security, and then click OK to
       confirm that you want to apply different security settings for this item.

   ❑ *Integrated mode:* Point to the Pacific Reseller Sales Margin Analysis report, click
       the Edit button, and click Manage Permissions. On the Actions menu, select Edit
       Permissions, and then click OK to confirm that you want to create unique permis-
       sions for this document library.

   4. Set permissions to allow only the content managers or SharePoint owners to access the
       report.

   ❑ *Native mode:* Select the check boxes to the left of the Managers and
       SalesAnalysts groups, click Delete, and then click OK in the message box to
       confirm the deletion.

   ❑ *Integrated mode:* Select the check box to the left of the Users/Groups col-
       umn label to select all SharePoint groups, clear the Reporting Services Step By
       Step Owners check box, and then on the Actions menu, select Remove User
       Permissions. Click OK to confirm the deletion.

   5. Set permissions to allow the PacificMgr account to access the report.

   ❑ *Native mode:* Click New Role Assignment. In the Group Or User Name text box,
       type **PacificMgr**, select the check box next to Browser, and click OK.

   ❑ *Integrated mode:* Click New. In the Users/Groups text box, type **PacificMgr**, click
       the Check Names icon, select the Read check box, and click OK.

   6. Test the security by opening the Web application as a member of one of the removed
       groups, such as Analyst, to confirm that the report is no longer available, and then
       open the Web application as VP to confirm that you can access the report.

   7. Close the Internet Explorer window. If necessary, log off your computer and then log in
       again using your administrator credentials.

Using a Permissions Table to Secure Data

Another approach to implementing data security is to modify the dataset query to join to
a permissions table that maps the current Windows user to a value that filters the dataset
results. The user mapping is made possible by the use of a query parameter to which you
assign the expression =**User!UserID** to get the current user from the operating system. This
approach ensures that even local administrators on the report server, who always have access
to report server content, cannot view confidential data. The disadvantage of this approach is
the requirement to maintain the permissions table, which at minimum must include a column
for the user's Windows account and a column for the value filter. Your report must also use

a data source that uses Windows integrated security (and specifically does not use stored credentials) to get the proper user context when the report executes.

In this procedure, you modify a dataset query to use a query parameter and a join to a permissions table to secure data.

Secure data by using a query parameter and a permissions table

1. In Management Studio, connect to the Database Engine.

2. On the File menu, select Open, and then select File.

3. Navigate to the Microsoft Press\Rs2008sbs\Chap11 folder in your Documents folder, and double-click SecuritySetup.sql.

   This script grants the EuropeMgr and PacificMgr accounts read permission to the AdventureWorksDW2008 data source. It also creates and populates the permissions table, PermissionsSalesTerritory, to map these accounts to the applicable *SalesTerritoryGroup* parameter values for each user. The script also adds a mapping for the Administrator account to all parameter values.

   Important This script assumes that you are logged onto your computer as Administrator. You must replace Administrator in the script with your login name before executing the script. Press CTRL+H, type **Administrator** in the Find What text box, type your login name in the Replace With text box, and click Replace All.

4. On the toolbar, click the Execute button.

   Note You will see error messages stating that logins could not be dropped, which you can safely ignore if this is the first time that you have executed the script.

5. In Object Explorer, expand the Databases folder, expand the AdventureWorksDW2008 folder, expand the Tables folder, right-click dbo.PermissionsSalesTerritory, and select Select Top 1000 Rows to view the new table and its contents, shown here:

	UserId	SalesTerritoryGroup
1	SIRIUS\Administrator	Europe
2	SIRIUS\EuropeMgr	Europe
3	SIRIUS\Administrator	North America
4	SIRIUS\PacificMgr	Pacific
5	SIRIUS\Administrator	Pacific

   The script creates the user accounts listed in the UserId column with your server name to ensure that Windows integrated security works correctly in this procedure. Notice that only two of the Windows accounts that you created at the beginning of this chapter are included in the table because you will test only two accounts in this procedure. The table also includes rows that map the Administrator account (or your login if you changed the script) to each *SalesTerritoryGroup* value.

6. Start SQL Server Business Intelligence Development Studio, and then, on the File menu, point to Open, and select Project/Solution.

7. In the Open Project dialog box, navigate to the Microsoft Press\Rs2008sbs\Chap11 folder in your Documents folder, and double-click Data Security.sln.

8. In Solution Explorer, double-click Securing Source Query.rdl to open the report.

   This report is almost identical to the Reseller Sales Margin Analysis By Sales Territory report. In this case, the data source is embedded in the report instead of using the AdventureWorksDW2008 data source on the report server. The data source on the report server is configured to use stored credentials and consequently ignores the current user's credentials.

9. In the Report Data pane, right-click ResellerSales, and select Query.

10. In the Query Designer, on the toolbar, click Add Table (the last button).

11. In the Add Table dialog box, select the PermissionSalesTerritory table, click Add, and then click Close.

12. From the DimSalesTerritory table (which displays in the diagram pane with *st* as the caption), drag the *SalesTerritoryGroup* field to the *SalesTerritoryGroup* field in the PermissionSalesTerritory table to create a join between the two tables.

 Tip You might need to drag the PermissionsSalesTerritory table to a new location to make it easier to create the join.

Your diagram pane in the Query Designer should look similar to this:

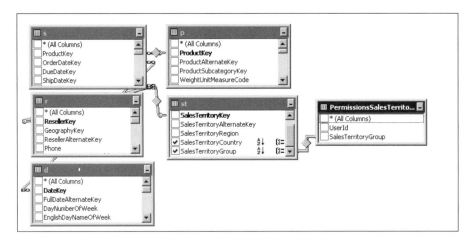

13. In the SQL pane, add the following expression to the end of the WHERE clause:

    ```
    and PermissionsSalesTerritory.UserID = @UserID
    ```

14. Click OK to close the Query Designer dialog box.

15. In the Report Data pane, right-click the ResellerSales dataset, and select Dataset Properties.

16. In the Dataset Properties dialog box, select Parameters.

    Adding the *@UserID* query parameter to the dataset query automatically adds a new report parameter and links it to the query parameter. You must change the value assignment for the query parameter to an expression that evaluates as the current user.

17. Click the Expression button to the right of [@UserID].

18. In the Expression dialog box, replace the existing expression by typing **=User!UserID**, and click OK twice to exit all the dialog boxes.

    Now you must delete the report parameter that was linked to the *@UserID* query parameter because it's not needed in the report.

19. In the Report Data pane, expand the Parameters folder, right-click UserID, select Delete, and click OK to confirm the deletion.

20. Save and preview the report to confirm that the report executes successfully before deployment.

    Because your Windows account is in the permissions table and maps to all three sales territory group values, the report executes for all sales territory groups. If someone whose account is not in the permissions table opens the report, no data displays.

21. Right-click the Securing Source Query.rdl report, then select Deploy.

> **Important** If you are deploying to a remote native-mode report server or to a SharePoint integrated-mode report server, you must change the values in the TargetDataSourceFolder, TargetReportFolder, and TargetServerURL text boxes in the Project Properties dialog box to match the applicable values for your server, as described in Chapter 10. For example, use *http://<servername>/sites/ssrs/ReportsLibrary/DataSecurity* for the TargetReportFolder.

22. Test the security by opening the Web application as EuropeMgr, clicking the Data Security folder, and opening the Security Source Query report to confirm that the report displays only Europe data, and then open the Web application as PacificMgr to confirm that the report displays only Pacific data.

23. Leave the Internet Explorer window open for the next procedure.

Using a Dataset Filter to Secure Data

The third way to implement data security also uses the =User!UserID expression to filter the dataset, but it uses the expression in the dataset filter property rather than as a value assigned to a query parameter. You also add a join to a permissions table in the dataset query, but you select the UserId column from the permissions table and compare its value to the current user to filter the dataset. The benefit of using this approach as compared to using the query parameter is the ability to use a data source configured to use stored credentials. Because the user expression is evaluated only when the filter is applied, all data is retrieved during report execution, which allows you to set up the report as a scheduled snapshot.

In this procedure, you add a filter to the dataset to apply data security based on the current user.

Secure data by using a dataset filter

1. Switch to SQL Server Business Intelligence Development Studio, and then, in Solution Explorer, double-click Securing Report Data.rdl to open the report.

2. In the Report Data pane, double-click ResellerSales, and then click Query Designer.

3. In the Query Designer, on the toolbar, click Add Table (the last button).

4. In the Add Table dialog box, select the PermissionSalesTerritory table, click Add, and then click Close.

5. From the DimSalesTerritory table (which displays in the diagram pane with *st* as the caption), drag the *SalesTerritoryGroup* field to the *SalesTerritoryGroup* field in the PermissionSalesTerritory table to create a join between the two tables.

6. In the PermissionSalesTerritory table, select the UserID check box to add the column to the query, and click OK.

7. In the Dataset Properties dialog box, select Filters.

8. Click Add, and then, in the Expression drop-down list, select [UserID].

9. In the Value text box, type **=User!UserID**, as shown here, and click OK.

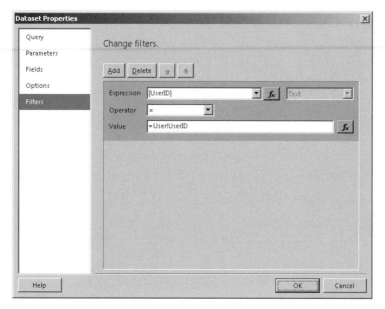

10. Save and preview the report.

   As you saw in the previous procedure, your account grants permission to view all sales territories in the report.

11. In Solution Explorer, right-click the Securing Report Data.rdl report, and then click Deploy.

12. Test the security by opening Report Manager as EuropeMgr, clicking the Data Security folder, and opening the Securing Report Data report to confirm that the report displays only Europe data, and then open Report Manager as PacificMgr to confirm that the report displays only Pacific data.

13. Close the Internet Explorer window. If necessary, log off your computer and then log in again using your administrator credentials.

As you have learned in this chapter, Reporting Services allows you a great deal of flexibility in your approach to implementing security. You can implement the simplest security configuration by defining permissions on the upper-level folder and using security inheritance to cascade these permissions across the folder hierarchy. You can also override inherited security on folders, reports, report models, and even report model items. The strongest security you can implement is to restrict the data in the report by user by using linked reports in combination with roles or by using the UserID item to pass the current user's Windows account as a value to a query parameter or a dataset filter. To complete your learning about managing the report server, you learn how to use SQL Server management tools to configure and maintain the report server in Chapter 12, "Performing Administrative Tasks."

Chapter 11 Quick Reference

To	Do This
Review role definitions on a native-mode report server	In Management Studio, connect to Reporting Services, expand the Security folder in Object Explorer, expand the Roles folder, and double-click a role.
Review SharePoint group permissions	In Internet Explorer, open the Report Center site, click Site Actions, select Site Settings, select People And Groups, click Site Permissions, and click a SharePoint group link.
Review SharePoint permission levels	In Internet Explorer, open the Report Center site, click Site Actions, select Site Settings, select People And Groups, click Site Permissions, click Settings, and select Permission Levels.
Grant access to report server content	*Native mode:* In Report Manager, on the Home page, click the Properties tab, select New Role Assignment, type a Windows user or group in the Group Or User Name box, and select a role check box.
	Integrated mode: In SharePoint, open the Report Center site, click Site Settings, select People And Groups, click a SharePoint group link in the navigation bar, click New, type a user or group in the Users/Groups text box, click Check Names, and specify permissions.
Secure a folder by removing permissions	*Native mode:* In Report Manager, open the folder, click the Properties tab, click the Security link, select Edit Item Security, click OK to confirm, select role check boxes, and click Delete to remove roles.
	Integrated mode: In SharePoint, open the parent folder of the folder that you want to secure, point to the folder that you want to secure, click Edit, select Manage Permissions, select Actions, Edit Permissions, click OK to confirm, select the check boxes for users or groups to remove, select Actions, Remove User Permissions, and click OK to confirm.
Secure the Data Connections library in SharePoint integrated mode	In SharePoint, open the Report Center site, click the Data Connections link in the navigation bar, select Settings, Data Connection Library Settings, click the Permissions For This Data Connection Library link, select Actions, Edit Permissions, click OK to confirm, select the check boxes for the users or groups to remove, select Actions, Remove User Permissions, and click OK to confirm.
Approve a data source on a SharePoint integrated-mode server	In SharePoint, open the Report Center site, click the Data Connections link in the navigation bar, point to the data source link, click Edit, select Approve/Reject, and select Approved.

To	Do This
Grant access to a report or report model	*Native mode:* In Report Manager, open the report or report model, click the Properties tab, click the Security link, select Edit Item Security, click OK to confirm, select New Role Assignment, type a Windows user or group in the Group Or User Name text box, and select one or more roles. *Integrated mode:* In SharePoint, point to the report or report model link, click Edit, select Manage Permissions, Actions, Edit Permissions, click OK to confirm, click New, type a Windows user or group in the User/Groups text box, select Check Names, and select the Read check box.
Create a system user role on a native-mode report server	In Management Studio, connect to Reporting Services, expand the Security folder in Object Explorer, expand System Roles, right-click System User, select New System Role, type a name, and select tasks.
Create a system role assignment on a native-mode report server	In Repot Manager, click the Site Settings link, click the Security link, select New Role Assignment, type a Windows user or group in the Group Or User Name text box, and select a role.
Allow users to start Report Builder	*Native mode:* In Report Manager, click Site Settings, click the Security link, type a Windows user or group in the Group Or User Name text box, and select the System User role. *Integrated mode:* In SharePoint, point to the folder in which users save Report Builder reports, click Edit, select Manage Permissions, select Actions, Edit Permissions, click OK to confirm, click New, type a Windows user or group in the Users/Groups text box, select Check Names, and select the Contribute check box.
Manage model item security	*Native mode:* In Report Manager, open the report model, click the Model Item Security link, select Secure Individual Model Items Independently For This Model check box, select a model item, select Assign Read Permission To The Following Users And Groups, and type a Windows user or group. *Integrated mode:* In SharePoint, point to the report model, click Edit, select Manage Model Item Security, select Secure Individual Model Items Independently For This Model check box, select a model item, select Assign Read Permission To The Following Users And Groups, and type a Windows user or group.

To	Do This
Restrict data using a linked report (or report copy) with a query parameter and item-level security	*Native mode:* In Report Manager, create a linked report as described in Chapter 10, open the linked report, click Properties, click the Parameters link, enter a default value for the parameter, clear the Prompt User check box, and click Apply. Click the Security link, select Edit Item Security, and set role assignments as needed.
	Integrated mode: In SharePoint, create a report copy as described in Chapter 10, open the folder containing the report copy, point to the report link, click Edit, select Manager Parameters, click a parameter link, and, if you want, select a new default value, select Do Not Use A Default Value, and hide the parameter by selecting Hidden or Internal. Point to the report link, click Edit, select Manage Permissions, and set permissions as needed.
Restrict data using a query parameter and a permissions table	Create a permissions table with user accounts and filter values, join the permissions table to a table in the dataset query, add a query parameter to the WHERE clause to filter the dataset on the user column in the permissions table using a query parameter, edit the dataset query parameter to **=User!UserID**, and remove the report parameter that was created for the query parameter.
Restrict data using a dataset filter	Create a permissions table with user accounts and filter values, join the permissions table to a table in the dataset query, add the permission table's user account column to the SELECT clause, add a filter to the dataset using **[UserID]** (or the applicable column name for the user account column) as the Expression value, and type **=User!UserID** in the Value text box.

Chapter 12
Performing Administrative Tasks

After completing this chapter, you will be able to:

- Use SQL Server Management Studio to update report server properties.

- Suspend report execution by disabling a shared data source.

- Edit configuration files to update report server settings for connections, authentication, and memory management.

- Use logs and performance counters to monitor conditions on the report server.

In addition to managing and securing content, which you learned how to do in the previous two chapters, you perform administrative tasks on the report server from time to time to modify the report server's configuration or to monitor the status of the report server. This chapter shows you how to use Reporting Services management tools to enable features, suspend report execution during server maintenance, and optimize performance. You also learn how to use monitoring tools to assess how the report server responds to changes in the workload for on-demand and scheduled operations.

Using Management Tools

Reporting Services provides three tools for managing your report server: SQL Server Management Studio (SSMS), a Web application interface (Report Manager or a Microsoft SharePoint site), and Reporting Services Configuration Manager. In most cases, there is no overlap in functionality between the tools, unlike previous versions of Reporting Services. You learned how to use the Reporting Services Configuration Manager in Chapter 2, "Installing Reporting Services." In Chapter 10, "Deploying Reports to a Server," you learned how to use Report Manager and the SharePoint site to manage data source authentication and to configure report properties. Then, in Chapter 11, "Securing Report Server Content," you learned how to set up roles by using SSMS. You also learned how to set up role assignments by using Report Manager and to assign permissions in the SharePoint site in the same chapter. In this section, you add to your understanding of how to use the management features in SSMS, Report Manager, and SharePoint to perform administrative tasks on your report server.

Using SSMS

SSMS allows you to configure properties for a report server that runs in either native mode or SharePoint integrated mode. Some properties enable specific features, such as My Reports, report execution logging, and client-side printing. Other properties define global values for report execution time-out or the amount of report history that can accumulate for a report.

> **Note** If you are familiar with previous versions of Reporting Services, you should be aware that you no longer use SSMS to manage the folder hierarchy or report server content. You cannot use this tool to assign permissions, nor can you manage reports, models, resources, shared data sources, or data-driven subscriptions. All content management is now performed by using Report Manager or a SharePoint site.

> **Note** The steps in several of the procedures in this chapter depend on whether you are running the report server in native mode or SharePoint integrated mode. When appropriate, each step includes instructions for both architectures.

In this procedure, you enable the My Reports folder in SSMS and review other report server properties.

Update and review server properties

1. Click Start, select All Programs, select Microsoft SQL Server 2008, and select SQL Server Management Studio.

2. In the Connect To Server dialog box, in the Server Type drop-down list, select Reporting Services.

3. In the Server Name text box, if necessary, type the name of your report server, or **localhost** if you are connecting to a native-mode server. If you are connecting to a SharePoint integrated-mode server, type **http://<*servername*>/sites/ssrs** (or the address of your Report Center site), replacing <*servername*> with your computer name. In the Authentication drop-down list, select Windows Authentication. Click Connect.

> **Important** You cannot use localhost as the server name even if you are connecting to a report server on your local machine. SSMS requires you to name the server to connect successfully to the report server.

4. In Object Explorer, right-click the server node, and select Properties to open the Server Properties dialog box, as shown here for a native-mode server.

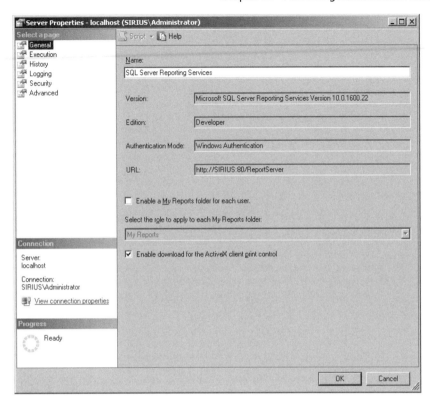

Note The My Reports folder feature is not supported for a SharePoint integrated-mode server. The Enable A My Reports Folder For Each User check box is disabled in the Server Properties dialog box.

The General page of the Server Properties dialog box provides important information about the version and edition of Reporting Services you have installed. The report server's authentication mode and the URL for the Web service also display on this page.

By default, the My Reports folder feature is disabled, but the ActiveX client print control is enabled. The My Reports folder feature allows users of a native-mode report server to create a personalized folder on the report server where they can store reports and other resources. The ActiveX client print control adds a button to the toolbar in Report Manager that permits users to print the report they are viewing without first downloading the report to their computers.

5. If you are working on a native-mode report server, select the Enable A My Reports Folder For Each User check box, and then, in the Select The Role To Apply To Each My Reports Folder drop-down list, select My Reports.

In Chapter 13, "Accessing Reports Online," you learn how to use the My Reports folder for a native-mode implementation. The My Reports folder feature gives users the functional equivalent of the Content Manager role, but only for the user's My Reports folder. This permission allows users to add or delete content in a folder that only they can access.

6. In the left pane, click Execution.

Notice that the default setting is to limit report execution to 1800 seconds. You can select Do Not Timeout Report Execution if you anticipate that some reports could require a long time to execute and prefer not to impose a static limit on the execution time required by the report server.

> **Tip** The report execution time-out setting here applies globally to all reports on the report server, unless you specify a time-out setting in the execution properties of an individual report. Report time-out may be a result of a long-running query at the source or complex processing and rendering by the report server. You can place a time-out on the dataset query only by modifying the report and editing the dataset properties.

7. In the left pane, click History.

The History page of the Server Properties dialog box gives you the option of allowing an unlimited number of snapshots to accumulate in report history or to define a limit. This setting is a global default only. You can override the value for an individual report, as you learned in Chapter 10.

8. In the left pane, click Logging.

By default, report execution logging is enabled, but log entries are removed automatically after 60 days.

> **Tip** The report execution log is a different mechanism from the trace logging that you learn about in the section entitled "Using the Trace Log," later in this chapter. As reports are executed, information about the execution, such as query processing time, report rendering time, parameter selections, and user name, are collected in a log. The format of the log in the ReportServer database does not lend itself well to reporting, so Microsoft has created a sample Integration Services package to illustrate how to extract data from the ReportServer database and load the data into a log database that is much better suited for reporting. Sample reports are also available to help you get started quickly with analyzing the log data. You can download the samples at *http://www.codeplex.com /MSFTRSProdSamples/Wiki/View.aspx?title=SS2008%21Server%20Management%20Sample %20Reports&referringTitle=Home.*

9. In the left pane, click Security.

The settings on this page allow you to enable Microsoft Windows integrated security for report data sources and ad hoc report execution. Both settings are enabled by default.

10. In the left pane, click Advanced.

This page provides access to many of the properties that you can set on other pages of the Server Properties dialog box. There are several additional properties on this page that you can change, such as *EnableRemoteErrors*. By default, this property is set to False, which means error information is captured only by the trace log and details do not display to the user. That is, the user sees only a general message that remote error information is not available and does not see the actual text of the error.

11. Click OK to close the Server Properties dialog box.

12. In Object Explorer, right-click the Jobs folder and notice the Cancel All Jobs command on the menu.

As an alternative to using time-outs to stopping a report that is taking too long to process, you can cancel an executing report, also known as a *job*, here manually. If jobs were running currently, you could cancel all the jobs in one step by using the Cancel All Jobs command. If you expand the Jobs folder, you can see all running jobs. To cancel an individual job, right-click the job, and then select Cancel Job(s).

Important Cancelling a job on the report server does not necessarily stop the corresponding process for a dataset query on the source data server.

Suspending Report Execution

When you need to stop users from executing reports, such as when you are performing maintenance tasks on a source database, you can disable the shared data source. Not only are users prevented from executing reports, but scheduled snapshots and subscriptions for reports that depend on the disabled shared data source cannot execute reports. You can use this technique only for reports that depend on a shared data source. There is no way to stop users or other jobs from executing a report with a dataset that uses an embedded connection.

Tip Another way to suspend snapshot and subscription jobs temporarily is to pause a shared schedule on which these jobs are dependent. You learn how to work with a shared schedule in Chapter 15, " Working with Subscriptions."

> **Important** To complete the following procedures, you must have successfully completed Chapter 10 so that you have a data source available on the report server.

In this procedure, you disable the AdventureWorksDW2008 shared data source.

Disable a shared data source

1. Open the data source folder for report server content.

    ❑ *Native mode:* In Report Manager, click the Home link at the top of the window, and click the Data Sources folder.

    ❑ *Integrated mode:* In Windows Internet Explorer, navigate to the Report Center site at *http://localhost/sites/ssrs*. In the navigation bar, click the Data Connections link.

2. Open the properties page for the data source.

    ❑ *Native mode:* Click the AdventureWorksDW2008 link.

    ❑ *Integrated mode:* Point to the AdventureWorksDW2008, click the Edit button located to the right of the data source name, and select Edit Data Source Definition.

3. Disable the data source.

    ❑ *Native mode:* Click the Properties tab (if necessary), clear the Enable This Data Source check box, type the password for the stored credentials in the Password text box, and click Apply.

    ❑ *Integrated mode:* Clear the Enable This Data Source check box, type the password for the stored credentials, and click OK.

> **Note** Because this data source uses stored credentials, you must type the password each time you make changes to the data source properties.

4. Review the dependent items.

    ❑ *Native mode:* Click the Dependent Items tab to view the reports using the AdventureWorksDW2008 shared data source, as shown here.

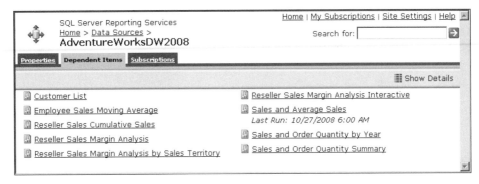

- ❏ *Integrated mode:* Point to AdventureWorksDW2008, click the Edit button located to the right of the data source name, and select View Dependent Items to view the list of reports, as shown here.

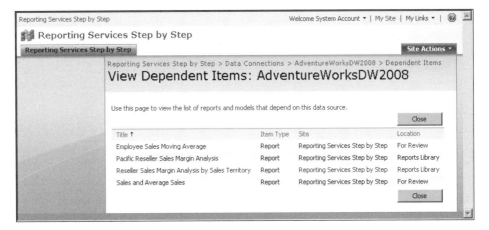

5. Test the data source by opening a dependent report.

- ❏ *Native mode:* Click the Customer List link to review the error message, as shown here.

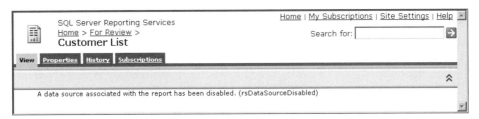

- ❏ *Integrated mode:* On the View Dependent Items: AdventureWorksDW2008 page, click the Reseller Sales Margin Analysis By Sales Territory link, and then, on the Reports Library: Reseller Sales Margin Analysis By Sales Territory page, click the Reseller Sales Margin Analysis By Sales Territory link to confirm that an error displays, as shown here.

6. Open the snapshot report.

   ❏ *Native mode:* Click Back to return to the list of Dependent Items, and then click the Sales And Average Sales link to view the report.

   ❏ *Integrated mode:* Click Back twice to return to the list of Dependent Items, click the Sales And Average Sales link, and click the Sales And Average Sales link on the Reports Library: Sales And Average Sales page.

   Because a snapshot report does not execute the report on demand, you can still view it even though the data source is disabled. However, if the snapshot is created on a schedule and the data source remains disabled at the next scheduled execution of the report snapshot, the job fails.

7. Enable the data source.

   ❏ *Native mode:* Click the Home link, click the Data Sources folder, click the AdventureWorksDW2008 link, select the Enable This Data Source check box, type the password for the stored credentials, and click Apply.

   ❏ *Integrated mode:* At the top of the page, click the Reporting Services Step By Step link, click the Data Connections link in the navigation bar, point to AdventureWorksDW2008, click the Edit button located to the right of the data source name, select Edit Data Source Definition, select the Enable This Data Source check box, type the password for the stored credentials, and click OK.

Configuring the Report Server

As you learned in Chapter 2, you use the Reporting Services Configuration Manager to set the values required to run the report server. In that chapter, you configured the service account, the virtual directories and URLs for the Web service and Report Manager (if you're running Reporting Services in native mode), database connection information, Simple Mail Transfer Protocol (SMTP) server information, and execution account. The settings you specify by using the Configuration Manager are stored in the Rsreportserver.config file, which you can find in the Program Files\Microsoft SQL Server\MSRS10.*<Instance>*\Reporting Services \ReportServer folder, where *<Instance>* is the instance identifier for your report server. (If you followed the instructions in Chapter 2 to use the default instance, the default instance identifier is MSSQLSERVER.)

The Rsreportserver.config file is an Extensible Markup Language (XML) file that contains settings used to run the report server, to control options in Report Manager, and to manage scheduled operations. In most cases, you use the Configuration Manager to update the setting that you want to change because there may be other updates required on the report server apart from the configuration file that the Configuration Manager performs for you. Furthermore, you must use the Configuration Manager or command-line utilities to update connection information because that information is encrypted and cannot be edited directly in the configuration file. Although you can manage many settings by using the Configuration Manager, you might need to change some default settings in the configuration file, such as authentication or memory management settings, by editing the file directly. To edit the configuration file, you can use Notepad, an XML editor, or Business Intelligence Development Studio (BI Dev Studio).

Note For a full description of each element in the Rsreportserver.config file, refer to the topic "RsReportServer Configuration File" in SQL Server Books Online.

Managing Encrypted Information

The Rsreportserver.config file contains the connection information that the report server uses to connect to the application databases (ReportServer and ReportServerTempDB), but encrypts the information to protect the security of the database. You must update this connection information when you need to change the credentials used to connect to the application databases, change the name of the databases, or relocate the databases to a new server. The configuration file also includes the domain user account and password defined as the execution account in the Reporting Services Configuration Manager (described in Chapter 2). You might need to update this information if you want to use a different account or update an expired password. Many administrators prefer to use command-line utilities to perform administrative tasks like these. To meet this need, Reporting Services includes the Rsconfig command-line utility to update encrypted information in the configuration file.

To use the Rsconfig utility, you must be a member of the local Administrators group on the report server. To view the syntax help, use the /? argument after the utility name like this: rsconfig /?.

In this procedure, you use the Rsconfig utility to update encrypted connection and execution account information in the configuration file.

Use the Rsconfig utility to manage encrypted information

1. If necessary, start BI Dev Studio.

2. On the File menu, select Open, and then select File.

3. Navigate to the Program Files\Microsoft SQL Server\MSRS10.MSSQLSERVER\Reporting Services\ReportServer folder, and double-click Rsreportserver.config to view the configuration file, as shown here.

> **Note** If you installed Reporting Services as a named instance, replace MSSQLSERVER with the correct instance name in the folder path.

```
<Configuration>
    <Dsn>AQAAANCMnd8BFdERjHoAwE/Cl+sBAAAAjpoT2/OovUmFauHyHR8j/AQAAAA
AHQAaQBuAGcAIABTAGUAcgB2AGUAcgAAAANmAACoAAAAEAAAAHnw8a1vO2DO9uvbrEd/
BIAAAKAAAAAQAAAArKt3AJCpXuCPkXkNdfpn8vgAAADHuCtYoE58wa+cF29kGpqvXn7L
wOT6qsqvQgueU2wwrvs/gMP2hmCm51ZbAyRwOQfAB4REOaf7MwUzH3N6DIX55S6MptcR
2eDxH+W7KFm/OV/y+DFHgSGR63q6ry87WSYvdTURNO+TOiJUWJpjvjX+KA71PvlgfHGY
4Bk3z1xS/AtFDzCVVQsewQ+Jbj9hybQPwarrzoVHnjFy6rjoGZvdBiW3VD2SDx5TI3y+
kz/wMnX11EfW2cAvWLKv/xQ2XXQzPs7hF2LT4RZr322SmnjEnLm4GsL1k/MrPfFfHiPt
KcNvmKZbxbZNjrt3ZHI+zOpeGw==</Dsn>
    <ConnectionType>Default</ConnectionType>
    <LogonUser></LogonUser>
    <LogonDomain></LogonDomain>
    <LogonCred></LogonCred>
    <InstanceId>MSRS10.MSSQLSERVER</InstanceId>
```

The *<Dsn>* element in the configuration file contains encrypted information required by the report server to connect to the application databases, such as the server name and credentials for authentication. Because this information is encrypted, you cannot edit the file directly when connection information changes.

Notice the *<ConnectionType>*, *<LogonUser>*, *<LogonDomain>*, and *<LogonCred>* elements in the configuration file.

4. Scroll to locate the *<UnattendedExecutionAccount>* element, as shown here.

```
    </UrlRoot>
    <UnattendedExecutionAccount>
        <UserName></UserName>
        <Password></Password>
        <Domain></Domain>
    </UnattendedExecutionAccount>
    <PolicyLevel>rssrvpolicy.config</PolicyLevel>
    <IsWebServiceEnabled>True</IsWebServiceEnabled>
```

The execution account information is not currently stored in the execution file. Notice the *<UserName>*, *<Password>*, and *<Domain>* elements in the configuration file have no values.

5. On the File menu, select Close to close the file, but leave BI Dev Studio open.

6. Open a command prompt window, type **rsconfig -c -d reportserver -a windows -u *<domain\account>* -p *<password>*** (where *<domain\account>* is your login domain and Windows account and *<password>* is the password that you use to log in), and press Enter. If you are running multiple report server instances , type the command using the following syntax instead: **rsconfig -c -s *<servername>**<instancename>* -d reportserver -a windows -u *<domain\account>* -p *<password>*.**

This command changes the account used to connect to the report server database to your own login account so that you can try the Rsconfig utility successfully.

> **Important** In a production environment, you should use only a least-privilege Windows account created for the purpose of creating a connection to the Reporting Services database in this procedure. You use your own account in this step just for demonstration purposes.

Here is the complete syntax for using this utility on the Report Server using Windows authentication:

```
rsconfig -c -m computername -s SQLServername -d ReportServerDatabaseName -a windows -u
[domain\]username -p password
```

The –c argument specifies that the utility will update the report server connection information. You use the –m argument when you run the utility on your local computer for a remote report server. You use the –s argument when the ReportServer database is not located in a default SQL Server instance, when you are running multiple instances of SQL Server, or when the database is located in a named instance. When you use the –s argument, you specify *<servername>\<instancename>* for the instance. For the –d argument, you include the name of the report server database, which by default is ReportServer. (Note that the Rsconfig utility is not case-sensitive when you type this name as an argument at the beginning of this step.) The –a argument specifies the authentication method. In this example, you are using Windows authentication, but you could also specify `sql` rather than `windows` with the –a argument if you prefer to use a SQL login to connect to the server. You can add an additional –t argument (with no value) to add trace information to error messages when the utility executes.

7. Open a command prompt window, type **rsconfig -e -u *<domain\account>* -p *<password>*** (where *<domain\account>* is your login domain and Windows account and *<password>* is the password that you use to log in), and press Enter.

This command changes the account specified to the unattended execution account.

> **Important** In a production environment, you should use only a least-privilege Windows account as the execution account in this procedure. You use your own account in this step just for demonstration purposes.

Here is the complete syntax for adding credentials for the execution account:

```
rsconfig -e -m computername -s SQLServername -u [domain\]username -p password
```

Notice that this syntax uses the –e argument in place of the –c argument that you used in step 6. In this step, the –e argument indicates that the utility updates execution account information.

As explained in step 6, you can omit the –m and –s arguments if you are executing this utility for a Reporting Services instance running on your local computer with its application databases stored on a local SQL Server default instance. Also, you can add the –t argument to add trace information if errors occur during execution of the utility.

8. Switch to BI Dev Studio. On the File menu, select Recent Files, and then select C:\... \Reporting Services\ReportServer\Rsreportserver.config to review the changes to the configuration file, as shown here.

```
<Configuration>
    <Dsn>AQAAANCMnd8BFdERjHoAwE/Cl+sBAAAAd7hdGOxnfkSNzQtby6PCMAQAAAAiAAAAUgBlAHAAbwBy
AHQAaQBuAGcAIABTAGUAcgB2AGUAcgAAAANmAACoAAAAEAAAANcMflKyz3CWHoJDWTq3EBEAAAAA
BIAAAKAAAAAQAAAAsx6MVNEI+xTS+Fkfmw4/+AABAACIUTkmv2yssR6rxV8na8wA3WkMBbSkVsVe
ElzYJC05701cawGVRa/wK8liIX6mGYEtI3HqAZBB/0i5keBVtxkbcfwE/8UeMrfEhr0RnZFM49Ih
mMIOIeGnNKhFRKmpNkKDVfwiJlvnzQGBbFE2tL+EmHTswlAyJXI2wNYBM8ipQgeVWaugZxK56+eM
oSoyCaehiELRpQ4w+ewYExTVof2jISBbJmFBxkl9c7iVBiSvoRllc4rdIsanj8wy84r9dXebdXTx
Al4syJKyNfrcmmNv1DhsQUwR1spbem+VjXw2JknKqN+soFSCHULr15eDWMz5wS4zx/VX/7hK7rr9
+H8uFAAAAErgv343YoPsHWohaxATN6oG4nde
    </Dsn>
    <ConnectionType>Impersonate</ConnectionType>
    <LogonUser>AQAAANCMnd8BFdERjHoAwE/Cl+sBAAAAd7hdGOxnfkSNzQtby6PCMAQAAAAiAAAAUgBlAHAAbwBy
AHQAaQBuAGcAIABTAGUAcgB2AGUAcgAAAANmAACoAAAAEAAAAGxb3OvSHTfhpyDIPMi/QmYAAAAA
BIAAAKAAAAAQAAAA6Ymb79c+AMq69+GS3AKCiAAAACPRo+q8CigBsg3Wm4WZb6Fn6YGgDWqoAzy
svKOmlcCWBQAAAD4jOqpEHcWS2dbIxnzeY8sHa5xXw==</LogonUser>
    <LogonDomain>AQAAANCMnd8BFdERjHoAwE/Cl+sBAAAAd7hdGOxnfkSNzQtby6PCMAQAAAAiAAAAUgBlAHAAbwBy
AHQAaQBuAGcAIABTAGUAcgB2AGUAcgAAAANmAACoAAAAEAAAAEAAAAFVXL3pU1zuTZXUxGmwe97QAAAAA
BIAAAKAAAAAQAAAAbknvYuHQgbRPsJOJAdHFThAAAACveyAf8ZcIhsS3XUSZOacWFAAAAIR9CeZl
13ZZa+1usZd8Tk9fyf0f
    </LogonDomain>
    <LogonCred>AQAAANCMnd8BFdERjHoAwE/Cl+sBAAAAd7hdGOxnfkSNzQtby6PCMAQAAAAiAAAAUgBlAHAAbwBy
AHQAaQBuAGcAIABTAGUAcgB2AGUAcgAAAANmAACoAAAAEAAAAEAAAAAOuLC4f+8SP4AEvRyTs0aAAAAA
BIAAAKAAAAAQAAAAqUnPs6zwPw2VJu+n4XZhrBgAAAAMCH/AclyyCIEApvZtaZRbh+mtkT4RYewU
AAAA4MYMq4tFd304yzoqEiFT1x7wwM4==</LogonCred>
    <InstanceId>MSRS10.MSSQLSERVER</InstanceId>
    <InstallationID>{bc63afb0-08a4-4608-9139-fe2a81c53a73}</InstallationID>
```

Notice the value of the *ConnectionType* element is now *Impersonate*. And the *LogonUser*, *LogonDomain*, and *LogonCred* elements have encrypted values.

9. Scroll to locate the *UnattendedExecutionAccount* element and confirm the execution account information in the *UserName*, *Password*, and *Domain* elements now exists and is encrypted.

10. On the File menu, select Close to close the file, but leave BI Dev Studio open.

11. Open a command prompt window, type **rsconfig -c -d reportserver -a windows**, and press Enter. If you are running multiple report server instances, type the command using the following syntax instead: **rsconfig -c -s *<servername>\<instancename>* -d reportserver -a windows**.

This command sets the connection information in the configuration file to the service account, which was the original setting if you followed the installation instructions in Chapter 2.

> **Tip** If you change your mind later and want to remove the configuration settings for the execution account, you must edit the configuration file directly by removing the values from the *UserName*, *Password*, and *Domain* elements. However, you must retain the element tags in the file.

12. Switch to BI Dev Studio. On the File menu, select Recent Files, and then select C:\...
\Reporting Services\ReportServer\Rsreportserver.config to confirm the *<UserName>*,
<Password>, and *<Domain>* elements in the configuration file now appear as they did
after step 4.

Managing Encrypted Keys

Reporting Services uses a symmetric key and a public key to encrypt and decrypt the
connection information in the configuration file. After completing the installation in
Chapter 2, you used the Reporting Services Configuration Manager to back up the
encryption keys. If you move the application databases to a new server, the encryption
keys are invalidated as a security measure to prevent someone from opening an unauthorized copy of the databases. Invalidation of the encryption keys also occurs when
you rename the report server or change the service account running the Reporting
Services Windows service. In addition to the commands in the Reporting Services
Configuration Manager to manage the encryption keys, Reporting Services includes the
Rskeymgmt command-line utility. You must be a member of the local Administrators
group on the report server to use this utility.

Recall that you extracted the encryption key by using the Reporting Services
Configuration Manager in Chapter 2. To extract the encryption key using the
Rskeymgmt utility, use the following syntax:

```
rskeymgmt -e -f [drive:][folder\]filename -p password
```

The −e argument indicates that the operation extracts the encryption key. You identify
a target location and file for the encryption key in the −f argument. If you exclude
this argument, the encryption key is stored in the folder in which you execute the
command. Use the −p argument to apply a password to the file. You must use this
password if you later need to restore the encryption key to the report server. After you
store the encryption key in an external file, you can move it to a secure location.

> **Important** You must run the Rskeymgmt utility locally on the report server and you must
> be a member of the local Administrators group.

To restore the encryption key using the Rskeymgmt utility, use the following syntax:

```
rskeymgmt -a -f [drive:][folder\]filename -p password
```

If you forget the password for the encryption key, or if you lose the file to which you
extracted the encryption key, you can delete encrypted information from the report
server by using `rskeymgmt -d`. You must then update each data source with the applicable connection string information and authentication method.

Configuring Authentication

The Rsreportserver.config file also contains settings to control how the report server authenticates users. If you are using Reporting Services in SharePoint integrated mode, you must keep the default authentication settings.

If you followed the installation instructions in Chapter 2, your Reporting Services instance runs under the built-in Network Service account, which is compatible with the default RSWindowsNegotiate authentication type. Reporting Services tries to use Kerberos authentication first. If Kerberos is not enabled in your network, Reporting Services then reverts to NTLM security automatically. You can force Kerberos authentication by using the RSWindowsKerberos authentication type or force NTLM authentication by using the RSWindowsNTLM authentication type. Another option is to use RSWindowsBasic authentication if you are using client applications connecting to the report server using Basic authentication.

> **Important** If you configure a domain account as the Reporting Services service account, RSWindowsNegotiate authentication fails if Kerberos is not enabled on your network or a service principal name (SPN) has not been registered for the Reporting Services service. A user attempting to open Report Manager is prompted for credentials several times and then fails to authenticate. To solve this problem, you can either change the authentication type in the configuration file or register the SPN. To change authentication, you edit the configuration file to include only RSWindowsNTLM in the Authentication section. To register the SPN, have your domain administrator execute the following two commands:
>
> ```
> setspn -a http://<servername> <domain>\<accountname>
> setspn -a http://<fully qualified domain name> <domain>\<accountname>
> ```

The authentication type determines only whether a user can access the report server. It does not directly affect whether a user is able to authenticate on the server hosting the data source if the data is hosted on an external server. However, the type of authentication that you choose to implement can affect data source authentication as follows: If you configure the report server to use either RSWindowsNegotiate or RSWindowsKerberos, and if Kerberos and delegation is enabled in the domain, the report server can connect to the external data source by impersonating the user. If you implement RSWindowsNTLM, you must configure data sources to use stored credentials because the report server cannot forward the user's credentials or impersonate the user.

> **Important** The browser that you use to access report server content must support Kerberos if you implement the RSWindowsKerberos authentication type. If you are using Internet Explorer, you must use RSWindowsNegotiate. You must also configure Internet Explorer to use Windows integrated security.

You can also implement ASP.NET forms authentication by specifying the Custom authentication type in the configuration file. However, you cannot use Custom authentication in combination with either of the Windows authentication types. Custom authentication requires you to change the Web.config file (found in the same folder as the Rsreportserver.config file) by setting the authentication mode to Custom and the impersonation flag to False.

> **Important** Because there is no validation of the authentication settings that you define in the configuration file, you should take care to test security before allowing users to access the report server. If you incorrectly configure authentication, attempts to open Report Manager fail with the HTTP 401 Access Denied error. For more information about authentication, refer to "Configuring Authentication in Reporting Services" in SQL Server Books Online.

In this procedure, you review the Authentication section of the configuration file.

Review authentication configuration on a native-mode report server

1. In BI Dev Studio, on the File menu, select Open, and then select File.

2. Navigate to the Program Files\Microsoft SQL Server\MSRS10.MSSQLSERVER\Reporting Services\ReportServer folder, and double-click Rsreportserver.config.

3. Scroll to locate the Authentication section in the configuration file, as shown here.

```
<Authentication>
    <AuthenticationTypes>
        <RSWindowsNegotiate/>
        <RSWindowsNTLM/>
    </AuthenticationTypes>
    <EnableAuthPersistence>true</EnableAuthPersistence>
</Authentication>
```

Notice that it's possible to configure multiple authentication types. Your configuration file might not include the *<RSWindowsNegotiate />* element if you configured the Reporting Services service account as NetworkService or LocalSystem.

Managing Memory

Report rendering can be a very memory-intensive process on the report server. Reports that must render a high volume of data require more RAM and increase the memory pressure on the report server. As memory pressure increases, the operating system must resort to paging to continue operations. If the memory requirements exceed the page file size, an out-of-memory exception occurs and report execution stops. Other processes that put memory pressure on the report server are model processing and background operations such as snapshots and subscriptions.

To reduce the possibility of out-of-memory exceptions, you can configure memory management settings in the Rsreportserver.config file to establish thresholds defining low, medium, and high memory pressure. Reporting Services uses the Memory Broker in SQL Server to detect memory pressure and responds to changes in memory pressure, as follows:

- **Low memory pressure**   All current requests made to the report server continue, new requests are accepted, and background processing is given lower priority than on-demand report rendering.

- **Medium memory pressure**   All current requests continue processing, new requests are accepted if existing reports can continue executing with reduced memory, and memory allocated to background processing is reduced most.

- **High memory pressure**   Current requests continue more slowly, new requests are denied, memory is reduced further across all running operations, and memory switches from RAM to the paging file.

The configuration file includes two settings that define the boundaries of medium memory pressure expressed as a percentage of memory. The lower boundary of medium memory pressure is defined by the *<MemorySafetyMargin>* element, which has a default value of *80*. The *<MemoryThreshold>* element defines the upper boundary of medium pressure and has a default value of *90*. Therefore, high memory pressure occurs when running processes consume more than 90 percent of server memory and low memory pressure exists when processes require less than 80 percent of memory.

You can tune the memory management settings by changing the boundaries of medium pressure and by adding two more settings to the configuration file to specify the minimum and maximum memory available to report server processes. These elements, *<WorkingSetMinimum>* and *<WorkingSetMaximum>*, are expressed in kilobytes. If you don't include *<Working SetMinimum>* in the configuration file, Reporting Services assumes that its processes can be allocated 60 percent of the available memory and does not release memory below this threshold. If you don't explicitly assign a value in the configuration file, the default value for *<WorkingSetMaximum>* is the total server memory.

In this procedure, you review the default memory configuration.

Review memory configuration

1. If the Rsreportserver.config file is not still open, in BI Dev Studio, on the File menu, select Open, and then select File. Navigate to the Program Files\Microsoft SQL Server \MSRS10.MSSQLSERVER\Reporting Services\ReportServer folder, and double-click Rsreportserver.config.

2. Scroll to locate the Service section in the configuration file, as shown here.

```
<Service>
    <IsSchedulingService>True</IsSchedulingService>
    <IsNotificationService>True</IsNotificationService>
    <IsEventService>True</IsEventService>
    <PollingInterval>10</PollingInterval>
    <WindowsServiceUseFileShareStorage>False</WindowsServi
    <MemorySafetyMargin>80</MemorySafetyMargin>
    <MemoryThreshold>90</MemoryThreshold>
    <RecycleTime>720</RecycleTime>
    <MaxAppDomainUnloadTime>30</MaxAppDomainUnloadTime>
    <MaxQueueThreads>0</MaxQueueThreads>
```

Notice that only the *<MemorySafetyMargin>* and *<MemoryThreshold>* elements are configured by default. You must manually add the other settings to the configuration file. For example, you can reduce the minimum allocation of memory to Reporting Services to 50 percent instead of the default value of 60 percent. For a server with 4 gigabytes (GB) of available memory, the minimum allocation should be 2 GB. In this scenario, you would change the configuration file to look like this:

```
<MemorySafetyMargin>80</MemorySafetyMargin>
<MemoryThreshold>90</MemoryThreshold>
<WorkingSetMaximum>4000000</WorkingSetMaximum>
<WorkingSetMinimum>2000000</WorkingSetMinimum>
```

> **Note** Regardless of the total memory available on a server, Reporting Services is unable to use more than 4 GB of memory.

Disabling Report Server Features

If you aren't using all report server features, you can disable those features as part of a lockdown strategy to reduce the surface area of a production report server that is at risk for attack. For example, if all report processing is performed as scheduled operations, you can disable all features except background processing. On the other hand, if you use interactive reporting only, disable all features except the Report Server Web service. Refer to Table 12-1 to learn how to disable report server features.

> **Note** Background processing cannot be fully disabled because it must provide database maintenance functions.

TABLE 12-1 Disable Report Server Features

To Disable This Feature	Do This
Report Manager	In the Rsreportserver.config file, set *IsReportManagerEnabled* to False.
On Demand Processing	In the Rsreportserver.config file, set *IsWebServicerEnabled* to False.
Scheduled Events and Report Delivery	In the Rsreportserver.config file, set the following elements to False: *IsSchedulingService, IsNotificationService,* and *IsEventService.*
Report Builder	In SSMS, open the Security page of the Server Properties dialog box, and clear the Enable Ad Hoc Report Execution check box.
Report Server Windows service	In SQL Server Configuration Manager, open the Service page of the SQL Server Reporting Services (MSSQLServer) Properties dialog box, and change Start Mode to Disabled.

Monitoring the Report Server

Administration of a report server includes monitoring the server to ensure adequate system resources are available and operations are running smoothly and error-free. You can use built-in reports in SSMS to track the size of the Reporting Services application databases and take action to reduce the database size or add disk space as needed. You can review Reporting Services log files to monitor and troubleshoot activity on the report server. Finally, you can use performance counters to assess the impact of Reporting Services operations on server resources and to monitor trends over time.

Checking the Application Database Size

Reporting Services uses two application databases, ReportServer and ReportServerTempDB. The ReportServer database is the primary storage used by Reporting Services to store the content, subscription, and schedule information, snapshots, and report history. Report definition files and most information stored on the server don't require a lot of space. However, if your reporting requirements depend on the availability of snapshots and report history, then you should periodically check the size of the ChunkData table in the ReportServer database. Recall from Chapter 10 that snapshots and report history are stored in the intermediate format, which can include a large volume of data.

 Note Although the SharePoint Web application stores reports, models, data sources, permissions, and properties in its content database, report snapshots and history continue to be stored in the ReportServer database.

The ReportServerTempDB database is used only for temporary storage of session and caching information and therefore fluctuates in size frequently based on user activity. Nonetheless, if users frequently request large reports, the session cache and cached instances can require a lot of space to store these reports in intermediate format. These temporary intermediate formats are found in the ChunkData table of the ReportServer TempDB.

In this procedure, you use SSMS to review disk usage by table in the ReportServer database.

Check the size of the report server content tables

1. Open SSMS and connect to the Database Engine on the server hosting the Reporting Services application databases.

2. In Object Explorer, expand the Databases folder, right-click ReportServer, select Reports, select Standard Reports, and select Disk Usage By Top Tables.

   If you installed Reporting Services to follow the procedures in this book and have deployed only the content you developed while working through this book, the ChunkData table at this time is insignificant. In a production environment, this table grows at a faster pace than other tables in the database as snapshots and report history are added to the server. You can use the Disk Usage By Top Tables report to monitor its size periodically. If you have disk space constraints that require that you prevent un-limited growth, work with your users to decide how best to limit the amount of report history or the number of reports with snapshots.

Using the Trace Log

When you need to troubleshoot report server operations, you can review the trace log generated by Reporting Services. After midnight each day, the first traceable activity triggers creation of a new file for the trace log in the Program Files\Microsoft SQL Server \MSRS10.MSSQLSERVER\Reporting Services\ReportServer folder (assuming that you installed Reporting Services to the default MSSQLSERVER instance). A new file is also created when Reporting Services is restarted. The trace log records application log events, errors and ex-ceptions, low resource warnings, report delivery details, and other details about Reporting Services operations.

You can configure the level of detail available in the trace log in addition to the maximum file size per log file and the number of days to persist a log file on the report server. You can even disable the trace log if you want. The configuration settings for the trace log are stored in the ReportServerService.exe.config file, which is in the Program Files\Microsoft SQL Server \MSRS10.MSSQLSERVER\Reporting Services\ReportServer\Bin folder.

In this procedure, you review the trace log configuration file and examine one of the trace log files on your computer.

Review the trace log configuration settings and trace log contents

1. In BI Dev Studio, on the File menu, select Open, and then select File.

2. Navigate to the Program Files\Microsoft SQL Server\MSRS10.MSSQLSERVER\Reporting Services\ReportServer\Bin folder, and double-click ReportingServicesService.exe.config.

3. Locate the DefaultTraceSwitch setting in the Switches section of the configuration file, as shown here.

```
<system.diagnostics>
  <switches>
    <add name="DefaultTraceSwitch" value="3" />
  </switches>
</system.diagnostics>
<RStrace>
  <add name="FileName" value="ReportServerService_" />
  <add name="FileSizeLimitMb" value="32" />
  <add name="KeepFilesForDays" value="14" />
  <add name="Prefix" value="appdomain, tid, time" />
  <add name="TraceListeners" value="file" />
  <add name="TraceFileMode" value="unique" />
  <add name="Components" value="all:3" />
</RStrace>
```

The DefaultTraceSwitch setting has a default value of 3, which logs most report server operations. You can add more information by changing this value to 4 for Verbose mode, or log less information by using a lower value. For example, a value of 2 means that the log stores exceptions, restarts, and warnings, but a value of 1 means that the log stores only exceptions and restarts. To disable logging altogether, set the value to 0.

The name of the log file is determined by two of the settings found in the RStrace section of the configuration file, FileName and Prefix. By default, all trace log files begin with ReportServerService_ and end with a date and time stamp as indicated by the *tid* and *time* values for the Prefix setting. The appdomain is included in the file name when you configure the Components setting to use specific component categories. You see an example of configuring the http component category and the resulting file name in the next procedure.

The default file size limit, specified by the FileSizeLimitMb setting, is 32 megabytes (MB). You can increase or decrease this limit as needed. Reporting Services creates a new log file after server activity logging exceeds the file size limit.

Typically, you use the most current log files for troubleshooting. Consequently, Reporting Services includes a mechanism to remove log files once an age threshold has been crossed. The KeepFilesForDays setting uses a default value of 14, but you can change this value to a more suitable value for your environment.

In addition to logging trace information to a file, which is the default behavior as defined by the TraceListeners setting, you can specify additional output modes, such as DebugWindow or StdOut, for the trace listener by using a comma separator in the value list.

Finally, the TraceFileMode setting of *unique* requires Reporting Services to generate one unique trace file per day. Microsoft recommends that you don't change this
setting.

Adding the HTTP Log

Hypertext Transfer Protocol (HTTP) activity is not logged by default. You can create a second
type of trace log by modifying the ReportingServicesService.exe.config to include settings
for HTTP logging. After this capability is enabled, all HTTP requests to the report server are
recorded in the trace log. You must also specify which fields to log, such as client Internet
Protocol (IP) address or HTTP status. You can use many of the same fields found in the World
Wide Web Consortium (W3C) extended log file that is managed by Internet Information
Services (IIS), which means that you use IIS log viewers to read the HTTP log file generated
by Reporting Services.

In this procedure, you modify the ReportingServicesService.exe.config file to enable HTTP
logging.

Update the trace configuration to include a log file for HTTP activity

1. If necessary, in BI Dev Studio, on the File menu, select Open, select File, navigate to
    the Program Files\Microsoft SQL Server\MSRS10.MSSQLSERVER\Reporting Services
    \ReportServer\Bin folder, and double-click ReportingServicesService.exe.config.

2. In the Rstrace section, above the `<add name="Components" value="all:3"` line, type
    the following code:

    ```
    <add name="HTTPLogFileName" value="ReportServerService_HTTP_" />
    <add name="HttpTraceSwitches" value="date,time,activityid,sourceactivityid
    ,clientip,username,serverip,serverport,host,method,uristem,uriquery,protocolstatus
    ,bytessent,bytesreceived,timetaken,protocolversion,useragent,cookiereceived,cookiesent
    ,referrer" />
    ```

    > **Tip** You can copy this code from the HttpLog.txt in Microsoft Press\Rs2008sbs\Chap12
    > folder in your Documents folder, and paste it into the applicable section of the configura-
    > tion file.

    This code defines part of the trace log file name using the HTTPLogFileName setting.
    As you can see by reviewing the HttpTraceSwitches settings, the information in the
    trace log includes many fields related to an HTTP request. You have the option to
    customize the log by removing fields from the HttpTraceSwitches folder.

3. Modify the Components setting to look like this:

    ```
    <add name="Components" value="all:3,http:4" />
    ```

This setting produces a log for all components using the default trace level and a separate log for HTTP activity using the verbose level.

4. Save the file.

5. Click Start, select All Programs, select Microsoft SQL Server 2008, select Configuration Tools, and select Reporting Services Configuration Manager.

6. In the Reporting Services Configuration Connection dialog box, click Connect.

7. On the Report Server Status page, click Stop, and then click Start.

Now that HTTP logging is enabled, you can generate some trace log updates by clicking folder and report links.

8. Switch to Internet Explorer, and then open the top-level folder for report server content *(http://localhost/reports* for native mode or *http://localhost/sites/ssrs* for integrated mode).

9. Navigate through the report server content to generate HTTP log activity.

❑ *Native mode:* In Report Manager, click each folder link on the Home page, and then click the Back button on the Internet Explorer toolbar to return to the Home page.

❑ *Integrated mode:* In Internet Explorer, navigate to the Report Center site at *http://localhost/sites/ssrs*. In the navigation bar, click the Reports link, and click folder links on the Reports Library page, clicking the Back button on the Internet Explorer toolbar to return to the Reports Library page.

10. Switch to Windows Explorer and navigate to Program Files\Microsoft SQL Server \MSRS10.MSSQLSERVER\Reporting Services\LogFiles.

11. Double-click the most recent ReportServerService_HTTP_ log file and review the log entries.

In the fifth row, you can see the list of fields included in the HTTP log file. You can use this list to interpret the data in the subsequent data rows even though the labels are not aligned with the columns. You must match the sequence of the field labels with the sequence of fields in the data rows. Each field is separated by a single space.

A common reason to review this file is to troubleshoot a client connectivity issue. You can confirm whether a client is communicating with the server by checking the client's IP address in the third column (labeled *c-ip*). You can also confirm the user identity used to connect to the report server by checking the user name in the fourth column (labeled *cs-username*). The *sc-status* field (in the eleventh column) shows the HTTP status code, such as 200 for OK or 401 for unauthorized, which helps you determine whether the client connectivity issue is related to the HTTP request.

Tip You can find a list of definitions for HTTP status codes at *http://www.w3.org/Protocols /rfc2616/rfc2616-sec10.html.*

Using Performance Counters

You can use the Windows Performance Console (in Windows XP and Windows Server 2003) and the Windows Reliability and Performance Console (in Windows Vista and Windows Server 2008) to monitor report server activity. The Reporting Services installation adds several ASP.NET performance counters to monitor the current state of the server, the trend of report server operations over time, and the cumulative total of a counter since the service was last started. These counters can help you understand how Reporting Services is using system resources during on-demand or scheduled report execution.

Reporting Services includes the following three performance objects:

- The MSRS 2008 Web Service object includes performance counters for activity related to online interactive viewing.

- The MSRS 2008 Windows Service object includes performance counters for report processing by scheduled operations such as subscriptions, snapshots, and report history.

- The ReportServer:Service object includes performance counters for HTTP activity related to Reporting Services and for memory management.

Tip A useful resource for learning how to run performance tests is "Planning for Scalability and Performance with Reporting Services," which you can view at *http://www.microsoft.com/technet /prodtechnol/sql/2005/pspsqlrs.mspx.* Although this white paper was written for use with Reporting Services 2005, much of the information is still applicable to Reporting Services 2008. However, the ReportServer:Service object is new to Reporting Services 2008 and is not discussed in the white paper. You can learn more about the performance counters included in that collection in the SQL Server Books Online topic "Performance Counters for the ReportServer:Service Performance Object."

In this procedure, you use performance counters to monitor activity on the report server.

Use performance counters to monitor a report server

1. Click Start, select Administrative Tools, and select Performance.

> **Note** These instructions are written for Windows Server 2003. To locate the applicable performance console on a different operating system, search the help file for your operating system.

2. In the Performance window, click the chart, and press CTRL+E to clear the current set of performance counters.

3. Right-click the chart, and select Add Counters.

4. In the Add Counters dialog box, change the server name to the report server name if it is located on a separate computer using the format \\<*servername*>.

5. In the Performance Object drop-down list, select ReportServer:Service, and then, in the Select Counters From List list, select Memory Pressure State, as shown here, and click Add.

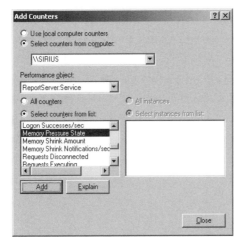

You can continue adding other counters if you want to monitor multiple counters in the same session.

6. Click Explain to view a description of the selected counter, as shown here.

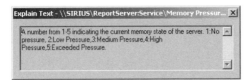

7. In the list of counters, select Requests/sec, click Add, and then click Close.

The maximum value of the Memory Pressure State counter is 5, but the chart displays a scale of 0 to 100. Although the number of requests per second would likely be much higher than 5 on a production system, you can reconfigure the chart scale to view changes to the counters using a scale of 0 to 5 for this procedure better.

8. Right-click the chart, and select Properties.

9. In the System Monitor Properties dialog box, click the Graph tab.

10. In the Maximum text box, type 5, and click OK.

Both counters display using the same color. You can adjust the color scheme if necessary to distinguish between the counters better.

11. In list of counters below the chart, right-click the row containing Requests/sec, and select Properties.

12. In the System Monitor Properties dialog box, in the Color drop-down list, select a different color, and in the Style drop-down list, select a different line style. Click OK.

The current state of memory pressure and the number of requests per second on the report server display in the chart. If no one is executing reports on the server, the chart shows the memory pressure state is 1 to indicate no pressure and the number of requests per second is 0, like this:

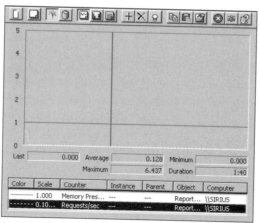

13. Open Internet Explorer, and navigate to the top-level report content folder of Report Manager (at *http://localhost/reports*) or the SharePoint Report Center site (at *http://localhost/sites/ssrs/ReportsLibrary*).

14. Click the For Review folder, and click any report link. Return to the For Review folder and click another report link.

15. Switch to the performance monitor, which now looks similar to this:

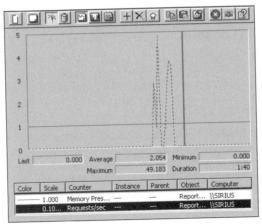

You can see the values of each performance counter display in the chart. Below the chart are statistics for the performance counter that is currently selected.

On a production system with many users frequently accessing reports, the statistics you see here would be considerably different. You can use the performance counters to establish a baseline of performance statistics, and then monitor these statistics over time to assess how increasing demand affects the report server. If the report server is frequently in the high pressure or exceeded pressure state, you can tune the memory configuration settings and then reassess the performance statistics after making the configuration change.

At this point, you have a good foundation of knowledge for managing the report server environment. In Chapter 10, you learned how to deploy report server content which you then learned how to secure in Chapter 11. In this chapter, you focused on the operational aspects of managing the report server. You're now ready to continue to the next phase of the reporting life cycle in Part IV, "Viewing Reports," where you learn how to access and interact with reports from a user's perspective.

Chapter 12 Quick Reference

To	Do This
Access server properties for review or update	In SSMS, connect to Reporting Services using the server name (or localhost) for a native-mode server or *http://*<servername> */sites/*<sitename> (or *http://*<servername>/<sitename>) for an integrated-mode server, right-click the server node in Object Explorer, and select Properties.
Suspend report execution by data source	*Native mode:* In Report Manager, open the Data Sources folder, click the data source link, click the Properties tab, clear the Enable This Data Source check box, type the password for the stored credentials if applicable, and click Apply. *Integrated mode:* In Internet Explorer, open the Data Connections folder, point to the data source, click Edit, select Edit Data Source Definition, clear the Enable This Data Source check box, type the password for the stored credentials if applicable, and click OK.
Change the account used to connect to the ReportServer database	*Windows account*: In a command prompt window, type **rsconfig -c reportserver -a windows -u <*domain \account*> -p <*password*>** (or **rsconfig -c -s <*servername*> \<*instancename*> -d reportserver -a windows -u <*domain \account*> -p <*password*>** if running a named instance or multiple instances), and press Enter. *Service account:* In a command prompt window, type **rsconfig -c -d reportserver -a windows** (or **rsconfig -c -s <*servername*>\<*instancename*> -d reportserver -a windows** if running a named instance or multiple instances), and press Enter.
Change the execution account	In a command prompt window, type **rsconfig -e -u <*domain \account*> -p <*password*>** (or **rsconfig -e -s <*servername*> \<*instancename*> -u <*domain\account*>** if running a named instance or multiple instances), and press Enter.
Review the server configuration settings in the Rsreportserver .config file	In BI Dev Studio, on the File menu, select Open, select File, navigate to Program Files\Microsoft SQL Server \MSRS10.MSSQLSERVER\Reporting Services\ReportServer folder, and double-click Rsreportserver.config.
Review the authentication type settings	In the Rsreportserver.config file, locate the Authentication section and review the settings.
Review the memory configuration	In the Rsreportserver.config file, locate the Service section and review the values for MemorySafetyMargin, MemoryThreshold, WorkingSetMaximum (optional), and WorkingSetMinimum (optional).
Check the size of report server content tables	In SSMS, connect to the Database Engine hosting the application databases, expand the Databases folder in Object Explorer, right-click ReportServer, select Reports, select Standard Reports, and select Disk Usage By Top Tables.

To	Do This
Review trace log configuration settings in the ReportingServicesService.exe .config file	In the ReportingServicesService.exe.config file, locate the system.diagnostics and RStrace sections.
Modify the trace configuration to include a log file for HTTP activity	In the Rsreportserver.config file, add the following code above the line that begins with Components:

```
<add name="HTTPLogFileName" value="ReportServerService_
HTTP_" />
```

```
<add name="HttpTraceSwitches" value="date,time,activityid
,sourceactivityid,clientip,username,serverip,serverport
,host,method,uristem,uriquery,protocolstatus,bytessent
,bytesreceived,timetaken,protocolversion,useragent
,cookiereceived,cookiesent,referrer" />
```

Update the line that begins with Components as follows:

```
<add name="Components" value="all:3,http:4" />
```

Save the file.

To	Do This
Review trace log and HTTP log files	In Windows Explorer, navigate to Program Files\Microsoft SQL Server\MSRS10.MSSQLSERVER\Reporting Services\LogFiles.
Monitor performance counters in the Performance console	On a Windows Server 2003 system, open the Performance console by clicking Start, selecting Administrative Tools, and selecting Performance. Search the help file for your operating system if using an operating system other than Windows Server 2003.
	In the Performance window, click the chart, press CTRL+E, right-click the chart, select Add Counters, change the server name to the report server name using the format \\<servername> if working remotely, select a performance object, such as ReportServer:Service, select a performance counter in the Select Counters Form List list, and click Add.

Part IV
Viewing Reports

The third and final stage of the reporting life cycle is report access. In Chapter 13, "Accessing Reports Online," you learn how to use a browser to locate and open managed reports from a central repository, how to export reports to alternate formats, and how to create and manage a personalized folder for selected reports. Then, in Chapter 14, "Creating Ad Hoc Reports," you learn how to use Report Builder 1.0 to build a report quickly based on a report model and how to work with the interactive features of published Report Builder reports. Finally, in Chapter 15, "Working with Subscriptions," you learn how to create and manage report subscriptions as an alternative method for viewing reports.

Chapter 13
Accessing Reports Online

After completing this chapter, you will be able to:

- Search for a report in Report Manager.

- Use the HTML Viewer or the SharePoint Report Viewer to change the display of a report or to print a report.

- Store reports in a personalized folder on a native-mode report server.

- Create a dashboard on a SharePoint integrated-mode server.

- Export reports to alternative formats for online viewing, analysis, data-driven document creation, analysis, printing, and data exchange.

This chapter introduces you to Reporting Services from the perspective of a user who uses either Report Manager or a SharePoint Web application to find and view reports online. You learn how to use the available online functions to change pages in a report, to change the page size, to change visibility of a report's document map or parameters, or to print a report. If you're running a native-mode report server, you continue by learning how to save your favorite reports to a personalized folder. If you're running an integrated-mode report server, you learn how to create a dashboard to display multiple reports on a single page. For both server modes, native and integrated, you learn about the different export formats that enable you to use report data in other applications.

 Important The procedures in this chapter assume that you have deployed and organized reports by completing the procedures in Chapter 10, "Deploying Reports to a Server."

Using Report Manager

In Chapter 10, you learned how to use Report Manager to organize and view reports deployed to the native-mode report server. But you should learn a few more features in Report Manager to understand the functionality available to users who access reports online. Instead of navigating through the folder hierarchies to locate a report, you can search for a report. After you open a report, you can use the HTML Viewer to manage the report display. The HTML Viewer also includes a print control that you can use to print one or more pages of the report for offline reference.

> **Note** You learn how to access reports on a SharePoint integrated-mode report server in the section entitled "Accessing Reports in SharePoint," later in this chapter.

Searching for a Report

When you aren't sure where to find a report, you can search for it by name or by description. The Search For feature in Report Manager also includes folders, shared data sources, report models, and other items stored on the report server in the search results. Regardless of the current folder you are viewing in Report Manager, the search begins at the Home folder and searches through all nested folders to which you are assigned at least the Browser role. The search results do not include any item or folder that you don't have permission to see (as described in Chapter 11, "Securing Report Server Content").

In this procedure, you search for report server content that includes *sales* in the report name.

Search report server content

1. In Windows Internet Explorer, in the address bar, type **http://<*servername*>/Reports**, where <*servername*> is the name of your server, to open the Home page of Report Manager.

2. Click the Sales folder link.

   Although the name of a report folder might indicate the type of reports that it con-tains, similar reports might also be found elsewhere. For example, the Sales folder currently contains two sales reports, Pacific Reseller Sales Margin Analysis and Reseller Sales Margin Analysis By Sales Territory. You can search the report server to locate other reports that include *sales* in the report name or the report description. All content on the report server is searched.

3. In the Search For text box, type **sales**, as shown here.

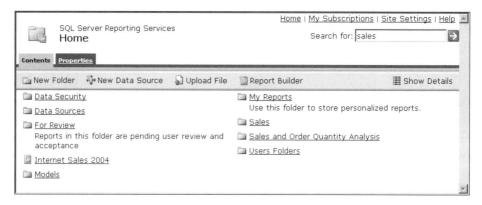

4. Click the button to the right of the Search For text box to perform the search and view the results, as shown here.

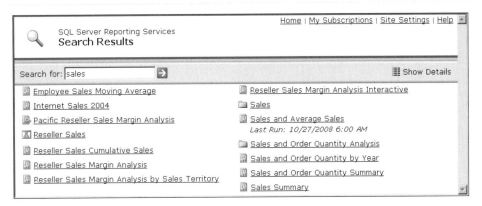

Notice that the search retrieves reports, folders, and report models containing the word *sales*. If you have not completed all procedures in this book, the list on your computer might be different from the list shown in the illustration.

5. Click Show Details to view the folder containing the items meeting the search criteria and the last execution date for report snapshots.

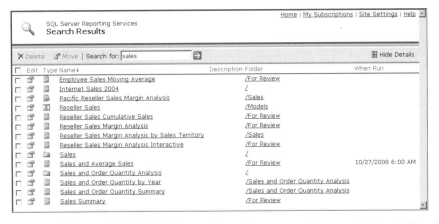

You can click on a link in the Name column to open an item or click the link in the Folder column to open Contents tab of the selected folder.

6. Click the Reseller Sales Cumulative Sales link to display the report. Leave the window open for the next procedure.

Using the HTML Viewer

When you open a report in Report Manager, a special toolbar called the HTML Viewer displays above the report. You can use the HTML Viewer to control the elements visible on screen, to change the zoom factor of the report, to navigate between pages, and to search for text within a report. You also use the HTML Viewer to change the parameter selections for the report if parameters are enabled and visible on the report.

The HTML Viewer, shown in Figure 13-1, includes the following functions for managing the report view:

- **Show/Hide Document Map**   This button allows you to toggle the display of the document map. This function is not visible if a document map does not exist for the report.

- **First Page**   This button allows you to jump to the beginning of the report. This function is disabled when viewing the first page.

- **Previous Page**   This button allows you to scroll to the previous page of the report. This function is disabled when viewing the first page.

- **Current Page**   Type a page number in this text box and press Enter to jump to the specified page.

- **Next Page**   This button allows you to scroll to the next page of the report. This function is disabled when viewing the last page.

- **Last Page**   This button allows you to jump to the last page of the report. This function is disabled when viewing the last page.

- **Zoom**   This drop-down list allows you to reduce or enlarge the size of the report.

- **Find Text**   Type a search string and click the Find link to find the first instance of the string following the current position in the report. Click the Next link to find each subsequent instance of the string. The links are disabled when the Find Text text box is empty.

- **Export Formats**   Select an alternate file type for viewing or saving the report, and then click the Export link.

- **Refresh**   This button allows you to reload the report definition and re-execute the dataset queries.

- **Print**   This button allows you to print one or more pages of the report to a selected printer.

- **Show/Hide Parameters**   This button allows you to toggle the display of the parameters section of the HTML Viewer. This function is not available if the report contains no parameters.

- **Parameters**   Use the drop-down list(s) to select a new value or type a new value in a text box, as applicable, and then click View Report to change a parameter selection. Parameters do not display if they are hidden in the report definition or the report properties.

Current Page

First Page   Last Page   Parameters   Refresh

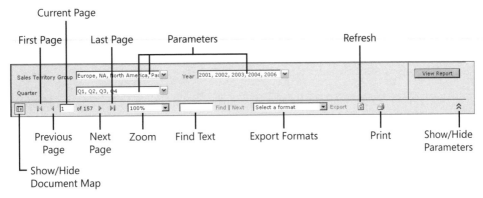

Previous   Next   Zoom   Find Text   Export Formats   Print   Show/Hide
Page   Page   Parameters

Show/Hide
Document Map

FIGURE 13-1 HTML Viewer

In this procedure, you explore the features of the HTML Viewer while viewing the Reseller Sales Cumulative Sales.

Use the HTML Viewer

1. In the Reseller Sales Cumulative Sales report (opened in the previous procedure), click the Show/Hide Document Map button in the HTML Viewer to close the document map.

   You can click the button again to open the document map when you want to locate a different section of the report.

   To allocate more screen space to your report, you can hide other elements on the screen, such as the parameters or the portion of the screen above the HTML Viewer.

2. In the lower-right corner of the HTML Viewer, click Show/Hide Parameters.

   Notice that the direction of the arrows on the Show/Hide Parameters button has reversed. You can click the button to show the parameters again later when you want to change a parameter selection.

3. In the upper-right corner of the HTML Viewer, click Full Screen.

   The Full Screen button becomes the Restore Down button when the report displays in Full Screen mode. You can click the button again later when you want to navigate to a different location on the report server.

   When the report is in Full Screen mode, the maximum space is available for viewing the report. You can display more of the report on your screen by adjusting the zoom factor to a smaller size.

4. In the Zoom drop-down list (to the right of the Last Page button), select 75%.

After resizing the report, you can view a different page of the report by using HTML Viewer buttons to page forward or backward, to jump to the first page or last page of the report, or to jump to a specific page.

5. In the Current Page text box, type **5** and press Enter.

   You can also search for text in the report. The search begins from the page you are currently viewing.

6. In the Find Text text box, type **brakes**, and click the Find link.

   Notice that the page number has changed in the Current Page text box and that the first instance of the search text is highlighted on the screen. You can continue to search for additional instances in the report.

7. Click the Next link to find the next instance of *brakes*, and then keep the report open for the next procedure.

   In this example, you started the search on page 5 of the report. If you were to continue clicking the Next link to find each additional instance (of which there are many), the search would continue through the last page of the report, and then start again at the first page of the report until all pages have been searched. If you click the Next link after the last instance has been displayed, a message box displays the message, "The entire report has been searched." You must click OK to close this message box.

Printing a Report

The print feature of the browser includes Web elements of the Report Manager application, so you should use the Print button on the HTML Viewer when you want a printed copy of the report that you are currently viewing online. This button opens an ActiveX control that you can use to preview the layout, change the orientation, define new margins, and select a range of pages to print if you don't want to print the entire report.

In this procedure, you use the Print button to preview the print layout of the Reseller Sales Cumulative Sales report.

Preview the print layout of a report

1. In the Reseller Sales Cumulative Sales report (which you used in the previous procedure), in the HTML Viewer, click Print.

2. If this is the first time that you have tried to use this feature, in the Internet Explorer – Security Warning message box, click Install to install the print control, shown here.

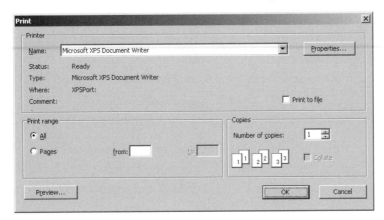

In the Print dialog box, you can use the Name drop-down list to select a printer. Use the Properties button to open a dialog box that allows you to choose between portrait or landscape orientation. You can also choose to print all pages of the report, specify a range of pages, and select the number of copies to print. The Preview button allows you to check the layout of the report before printing.

3. In the Print dialog box, click Preview.

Notice the Margins button, which you can use to increase or decrease margins as necessary. You can use the Next and Previous buttons to preview different pages of the report or use the Page spinner control to jump to a specific page. When you're ready, you can click the Print button to print the report.

4. Click Close, and then, in the Print dialog box, click Cancel.

Using the My Reports Folder

The My Reports folder is a user-specific folder available in Report Manager where you can publish and manage reports separately from reports available to other Reporting Services users. Only you and report server administrators have access to your My Reports folder. The My Reports feature is disabled on the server by default and must be enabled by a report administrator before you can start using it. The My Report folder is visible on the Home page of the Report Manager if the feature is enabled and if you have been assigned to the My Reports role.

You can add content to the My Reports folder by creating a linked report and storing it in the My Reports folder. You can also upload a file directly from the file system within Report Manager. If you have Business Intelligence Development Studio (BI Dev Studio), you can develop your own reports and deploy them to the My Reports folder.

> **Tip** To publish a report from BI Dev Studio, type the following value in the TargetReportFolder text box: **Users Folders/<*servername*> <*username*>/My Reports**, replacing <*servername*> with the domain name on your network or the name of the report server if no domain exists and replacing <*username*> with the user's Microsoft Windows account.

> **Important** The following procedure assumes that you have added EuropeMgr as a Windows account by completing the "Add Windows group and user accounts" procedure in Chapter 11 and that you have enabled My Reports as described in the "Update and review server properties procedure" in Chapter 12, "Performing Administrative Tasks."

In this procedure, you create a personal linked report for the EuropeMgr account based on the Sales and Order Quantity by Year report.

Create a personal linked report for the My Reports folder

1. Open Internet Explorer as EuropeMgr. If your computer runs Windows Vista or Windows Server 2008, you must log off and then log in using EuropeMgr as both the user name and password, and then open Internet Explorer. If your computer runs Windows XP, Windows Server 2000, or Windows Server 2003, click Start, select All Programs, right-click Internet Explorer, and select Run As. Select The Following User, and then type **EuropeMgr** in the User and Password text boxes.

2. In Internet Explorer, open Report Manager at *http://<servername>/reports*, replacing <*servername*> with the name of your server.

   When the user opens Report Manager for the first time after the My Reports feature has been enabled, the My Reports folder is added, and the role assignment specified in server properties (described in Chapter 12) is added to the folder's security. Now that the My Reports folder is added, the user with the My Reports role assignment can up-load report definition files directly to this folder (or a folder that the user creates within that folder) if a report author has provided the files to the user via e-mail or a network file share. If users are able to develop reports with Report Builder or BI Dev Studio, they can publish those reports to the My Reports folder.

3. Click the My Reports folder link, and click Upload File.

4. On the Upload File page, click Browse, navigate to the Microsoft Press\Rs2008sbs \Chap13 folder, and double-click Sales And Order Quantity By Year.

   By saving reports to the My Reports folder, a user can keep all favorite reports in a common location rather than having to remember where to find these reports in the Reporting Services folder hierarchy.

5. In the Name text box, type **My Sales And Order Quantity By Year**, and click OK to upload the report, as shown here.

The report displays in the user's My Reports folder. If the report contained parameters (which this report does not), the user could access the Parameters page of the report to set the preferred default value for each parameter in the linked report (as described in Chapter 10).

6. Close Internet Explorer, and switch to the Internet Explorer window running under your own credentials.

7. Click the Home link, click the Users Folders folder link, click the *<servername>* EuropeMgr folder link (where *<servername>* is the name of your server), and click the My Reports folder link to confirm that you can view the My Sales And Order Quantity By Year report in the user's My Report folder.

As a report server administrator, you can view the contents of the My Reports folder for each user below the User's Folders folder. If a user has developed a report that you both agree should be available to additional users, you can move the report from this folder to a different folder on the report server. You can also delete reports from this folder if necessary.

Accessing Reports in SharePoint

In Chapter 10, you learned how to open a report in the reports library, a special type of document library in a SharePoint Web application. If the Office SharePoint Server Search service has been configured on the SharePoint server, you can search for reports if you don't know which reports library contains the report that you want to access. A toolbar in the SharePoint Report Viewer allows you to manage the report display much like the HTML Viewer in Report Manager. You can view a report in isolation by clicking the report link in the reports library, or you can combine multiple reports for display on a single page by creating a dashboard.

Configuring Search in SharePoint

Because the search feature in SharePoint is not enabled by default and is independent of Reporting Services integration, there are several steps that you must complete before users can search for reports. For in-depth information about this feature, refer to the topic "Configure the Office SharePoint Server Search service (Office SharePoint Server)" at *http://technet.microsoft.com/en-us/library/cc262700.aspx*.

> **Important** You must be an administrator on your server to complete these steps to configure the search function in SharePoint. You can skip this procedure if you don't want to implement the search service.

In this procedure, you perform the minimum configuration steps for the Office SharePoint Server Search service.

Configure the search function in SharePoint

1. Click Start, right-click My Computer (or, if using Windows Vista, right-click Computer), and select Manage.

2. Expand Local Users And Groups, right-click the Users folder, and select New User.

    To implement the Search service in SharePoint, you must create a service account that the Web application uses as an application pool identity. You cannot use a built-in account, such as NT AUTHORITY\NETWORK SERVICE, for the Web application.

3. Type a name for a service account to run the Search service in the User Name, Password, and Confirm Password text boxes, clear the User Must Change Password At Next Login check box, click Create, and then click Close.

    You must give this account Read permission to the Report Center site so that the published reports can be indexed.

4. In Internet Explorer, navigate to the Report Center site at *http://<servername>/sites /ssrs* (replacing *<servername>* with the name of your server), click Site Actions, select Site Settings, and select People And Groups.

5. In the navigation bar, click the Reporting Services Step By Step Owners link, and click New.

    In this procedure, the Search service account is assigned to the Owners group to ensure that all reports will be included in the crawl. In Chapter 11, the security for several reports and folders were changed to restrict access to specific users, although the Owners group continues to have access to these folders. When a user who is not a member of the Owners group performs a search, the security for that user still applies and the user sees only permitted reports in the search results list.

6. On the Add Users: Reporting Services Step By Step page, in the Users/Groups text box, type the service account name, click the Check Names icon below the text box to validate the name, and click OK to save the assignment.

    Now that you have created the service account and granted it the Read permission to the Report Center site, you are ready to configure the Search service.

7. Click Start, select All Programs, select Administrative Tools, and then select SharePoint 3.0 Central Administration.

8. In the navigation bar on the left side of the window, click Shared Services Administration.

9. If a Shared Services Provider (SSP) already exists and is associated with a Web application that uses a service account instead of a built-in account for the application pool identity, skip to step 17. Otherwise, click New SSP.

10. On the New Shared Services Provider page, click the Create A New Web Application link.

11. In the Application Pool section, in the User Name text box, type the name of the service account that you created in step 3 in the form ***<domain>\<serviceaccount>,*** where *<domain>* is the name of the Windows domain to which your server belongs (or the name of the server if it does not belong to a domain).

12. In the Password text box, type the password for the service account, keep all other defaults on the page, and click OK.

13. On the New Shared Services Provider page, in the Username text box, type the name of the service account that you created in step 3 in the form ***<domain>\<serviceaccount>,*** where *<domain>* is the name of the Windows domain to which your server belongs (or the name of the server if it does not belong to a domain).

> **Important** In a production environment, you should use a different service account for the SSP service credentials than you established for the Web application's application pool identity.

14. In the Password text box, type the password for the service account, keep all other defaults on the page as is, and click OK.

15. On the Warning page, click OK.

> **Tip** The warning on this page recommends that you use a separate Web application for My Sites, but you can safely ignore that for the purposes of completing the procedures in this chapter. In a production environment, you should follow this recommendation and create a new Web application for My Sites, which you can do from the New Shared Services Provider page just as you did to create a Web application for the SSP.

16. When the creation of the SSP is complete, on the Success page, click OK.

17. In the navigation bar, click the name of the SSP. For example, if you just created the first SSP on the SharePoint server and kept the default SSP name, click SharedServices1.

18. On the Shared Services Administration page, in the Search section, click the Search Settings link.

19. Click the Default Content Access Account link. In the Account text box, type the name of the service account that you created in step 3 in the form ***<domain> \<serviceaccount>,*** where *<domain>* is the name of the Windows domain to which your server belongs (or the name of the server if it does not belong to a domain). In the Password and Confirm Password text boxes, type the password for the service account, and click OK.

20. Click the Content Sources And Crawl Schedules link, and click the Local Office SharePoint Server Sites.

    On this page, you define the start addresses for crawling, which by default include the local sites on your servers. You also define the crawl schedules on this page. For the purposes of completing the next procedure in this chapter, you start only a full crawl of the content source rather than establish schedules for the full crawl and incremental crawl. If reports are deployed to the report server between crawl schedules, the new reports do not appear in a search results list.

> **More Info** A full explanation of content crawling is beyond the scope of this book. For more information, refer to the topic "Crawl Content (Office SharePoint Server 2007)" at *http://technet.microsoft.com/en-us/library/cc262794.aspx.*

21. Select the Start Full Crawl Of This Content Source check box, and click OK. A crawl of the current content begins, and the status displays in the Status column.

> **Tip** If you later deploy more content to the report server but have not yet implemented crawl schedules, you can start a full crawl from this page by pointing to Local Office SharePoint Server Sites, clicking the arrow that appears to the right of the content source name, and selecting Start Full Crawl.

22. Periodically click Refresh on the Manage Content Sources page to update the status. When the status is Idle, you can continue to the next procedure.

Searching for a Report

After you configure the SharePoint Search service and this service browses the site containing the reports library, you can search for reports by using keywords used in the report name or its properties. The Search service also finds data sources, report models, and other items stored on the SharePoint site that meet the search criteria so long as you have permission to view these items. (Item-level security is described in Chapter 11.)

In this procedure, you search for items on the SharePoint site that include *sales* in the item name.

Search a SharePoint site

1. If you need to open the Report Center site, in Internet Explorer, in the address bar, type **http://<servername>/sites/ssrs**, where *<servername>* is the name of your server.

2. In the navigation bar, click the Reports link.

   This folder currently contains two sales reports, Pacific Reseller Sales Margin Analysis and Reseller Sales Margin Analysis By Sales Territory. When you want to locate other reports that include *sales* in the report name or the report description, you can use the search function to search all content in the selected scope.

3. In the upper-right corner of the window, in the Enter Search Words text box, type **sales**, as shown here.

   The search scope is specified in the drop-down list to the left of the Enter Search Words text box. You can limit the search to the current Reports Library or you can change the scope to the entire site.

4. Click the magnifying glass icon to the right of the Enter Search Words text box to perform the search and view the results, as shown here.

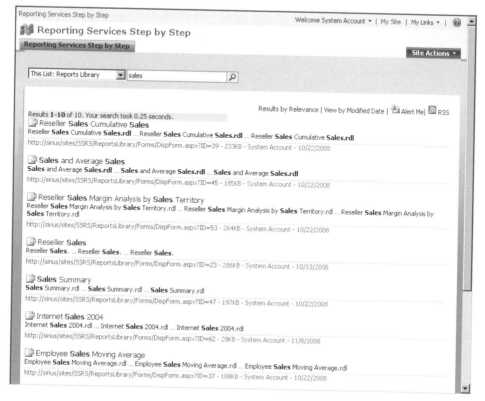

The search retrieves reports, folders, and report models containing the word *sales*. If you have not completed all procedures in this book, the list on your computer might be different from the list shown in the illustration.

5. Click the Reseller Sales Cumulative Sales link to open the report's properties page, and then click the Reseller Sales Cumulative Sales link on the properties page to open the report. Leave it open for the next procedure.

> **Note** If the report displays an invalid data source reference error, the link between the report and the data source must be re-established. Click the Reporting Services Step By Step link at the top of the page, click the Reports link in the navigation bar, click the For Review folder, point to Reseller Sales Cumulative Sales, click the Edit button that appears to the right of the report title, and select Manage Data Sources. On the Manage Data Sources: Reseller Sales Cumulative Sales page, click the AdventureWorksDW2008 link. On the AdventureWorksDW2008: Reseller Sales Cumulative Sales page, to the right of the Data Source Link text box, click the ellipsis button. Click Up twice, click Data Connections, double-click AdventureWorksDW2008, and click OK. Click Close, and then click the Reseller Sales Cumulative Sales report to view the report.

Using the SharePoint Report Viewer

The SharePoint Report Viewer includes all the same functionality for controlling the display of the report as the HTML Viewer that you use in Report Manager, although the toggle to show or hide the document map and parameters is not included on the toolbar. The SharePoint Report Viewer shown in Figure 13-2 includes the following functions for managing the report view:

- **Expand/Collapse Document Map**   This button toggles the display of the document map, if one exists for the report.

- **Actions Menu**   This menu accesses the following commands: Open With Report Builder, Subscribe, Print, and Export.

- **Refresh**   This button reloads the report definition and re-executes the dataset queries.

- **First Page**   This button allows you to jump to the beginning of the report. This function is disabled when viewing the first page.

- **Previous Page**   This button scrolls to the previous page of the report. This function is disabled when viewing the first page.

- **Current Page**   Type a page number in this text box and press Enter to jump to the specified page.

- **Next Page**   This button allows you to scroll to the next page of the report. This function is disabled when viewing the last page.

- **Last Page**   This button allows you to jump to the last page of the report. This function is disabled when viewing the last page.

- **Find Text**   Type a search string and click the Find link to find the first instance of the string following the current position in the report. Click the Next link to find each subsequent instance of the string. The links are disabled when the Find Text text box is empty.

- **Zoom**   This button reduces or enlarges the size of the report.

- **Parameters**   As applicable, use the drop-down list to select a new value or type a new value in a text box, and then click View Report to change a parameter selection. Parameters do not display if hidden in the report definition or the report properties.

- **Expand/Collapse Parameters**   This function toggles the display of the parameters, if they exist for the report.

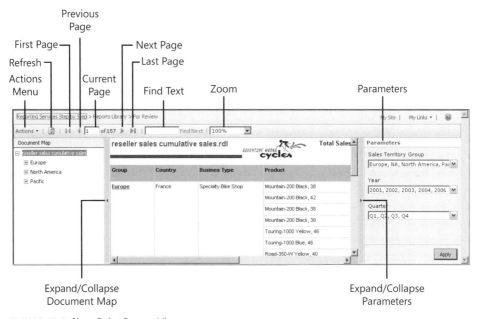

FIGURE 13-2 SharePoint Report Viewer

In this procedure, you explore features of the SharePoint Report Viewer while viewing the Reseller Sales Cumulative Sales.

Use the SharePoint Report Viewer

1. In the Reseller Sales Cumulative Sales report (opened in the previous procedure), click the Collapse button on the left side of the window to close the document map.

When the document map collapses, the button name changes to Expand. You can click this button to open the document map when you want to locate a different section of the report.

You can also hide the parameters to allocate more screen space to the report.

2. Click the Collapse button on the right side of the window to close the parameters.

The Expand button appears when the parameters pane is collapsed.

3. In the Zoom drop-down list (to the right of the Next link), select 75%.

After resizing the report, you can use the toolbar buttons to page forward or backward, to jump to the first page or last page of the report, or to jump to a specific page of the report.

4. In the Current Page text box, type **5** and press Enter.

You can also search for text in the report. The search begins from the page you are currently viewing.

5. In the Find Text text box, type **brakes**, and click the Find link.

Notice the new page number in the Current Page text box. The first instance of the search text is now highlighted on the screen. You can now continue to search for additional instances in the report.

6. Click the Next link to find the next instance of *brakes*, and then keep the report open for the next procedure.

Remember that you started the search on page 5 of the report. By clicking the Next link to find each additional instance, you could continue through the last page of the report and then start again at the first page of the report until all pages have been searched. If you click the Next link after the last instance has been displayed, a message box displays the message, "The entire report has been searched." You must click OK to close this message box.

7. Click Actions, and select Print.

8. If this is the first time that you have tried to use this feature, in the Internet Explorer – Security Warning message box, click Install to install the print control.

The print control is the same control available in the Report Manager. In the Print dialog box, you can use the Name drop-down list to select a printer, to select all pages of the report or a specific range, and to select the number of copies to print. Click Properties to switch between portrait or landscape orientation. The Preview button allows you to check the layout of the report before printing.

9. In the Print dialog box, click Preview.

You can use the Margins button to change the size of the margins as necessary. You can scroll through the pages of the report by using the Next and Previous buttons or jump to a specific page by using the Page spinner control. When you're ready, you can click the Print button to print the report.

10. Click Close, and then, in the Print dialog box, click Cancel.

Creating a Dashboard

You can combine multiple reports on a single page by creating a dashboard. A *dashboard* in SharePoint is a special type of report that includes several Web Parts that you can configure to display a Reporting Services report, a Microsoft Office Excel spreadsheet, or other items.

> **More Info** There are many features that you can use in a SharePoint dashboard in SharePoint Server 2007, but these features are beyond the scope of this book. You can learn more about creating SharePoint dashboards by reading "Understanding the Report Center and Dashboards in SharePoint Server 2007" at *http://msdn.microsoft.com/en-us/library/bb966994.aspx*.

In this procedure, you create a simple dashboard using the Sales And Order Quantity Analysis and Sales And Order Quantity Summary reports.

Create a dashboard

1. Start BI Dev Studio. On the File menu, select Open, and then select Project/Solution. Navigate to the Microsoft Press\Rs2008sbs\Chap13 folder in your Documents folder, and double-click the Sales And Order Quantity Analysis.sln file.

Although you can use any report in a Web Part on a dashboard page, it is typically best to use reports that display limited information or charts, such as the reports in this project.

2. In Solution Explorer, right-click Sales And Order Quantity Analysis, and select Properties.

3. In the TargetDataSourceFolder, TargetReportFolder, and TargetServerURL text boxes, replace localhost in each URL with the name of your server, and click OK.

4. Switch to Internet Explorer, and open the SharePoint Report Center at *http://\<servername>/sites/ssrs* (replacing *\<servername>* with the name of your server).

5. In the navigation bar, click Dashboards.

The Dashboards link opens the Reports Library, which is the same document library in which your reports are stored. Notice the View drop-down list in the upper-right side of the page now says "Dashboards." Dashboards are simply a different content type than reports and are displayed separately in the Dashboards view. You can select All Reports And Dashboards in the Views drop-down list to see all content in the Reports Library.

6. Click the arrow next to New on the Reports Library toolbar, and select Dashboard Page.

   If you simply click New, you create a new report instead of a new dashboard. You must open the New menu to select the correct content type.

7. On the New Dashboard page, in the File Name text box, type **SalesAnalysis**, and then, in the Page Title text box, type **Sales Analysis**.

   For this dashboard, you keep all the default values except that you exclude the key performance indicator (KPI) list. That is, you keep the dashboard in the upper-level folder of the Reports Library document library, add a link to the navigation bar for the new dashboard under the Dashboards heading, and use the two-column vertical layout for the dashboard.

8. In the Key Performance Indicators section, select Do Not Add A KPI List To This Dashboard, and click OK.

   The dashboard page opens in the browser window, and includes two Excel Web Access Web Parts, which you delete and replace with Web Parts for the reports that you just deployed.

9. On the toolbar above the dashboard page, click Edit Page.

   When the dashboard is in edit mode, you can see six separate zones on the page, such as Top Left Zone, Middle Left Zone, and so on. Each zone can contain one or more Web Parts. Empty zones do not display in the published dashboard page.

10. In the Middle Left Zone, click the Add A Web Part link.

    In the Add Web Parts – Webpage Dialog dialog box, a list of available Web Parts displays, but the Web Part that you need in order to display a Reporting Services report is not visible.

11. Scroll to the bottom of the list, expand All Web Parts, scroll to locate the Miscellaneous group, select the SQL Server Reporting Services Report Viewer check box, and click Add.

    The Report Viewer Web Part displays in the dashboard page, as shown here.

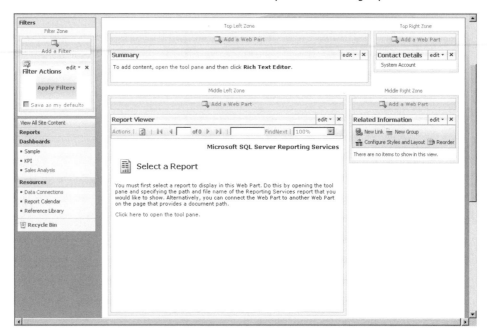

Now you need to configure the Web Part to display a specific report.

12. In the Report Viewer Web Part, click the Click Here To Open The Tool Pane link to open the Report Viewer tool pane at the right side of the browser, as shown here.

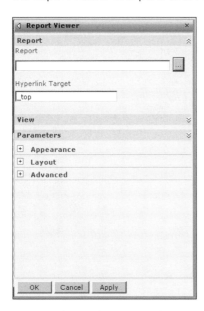

You use the tool pane to select a report, to configure parameter default values if ap-plicable, and to configure the appearance and layout properties of the Web Part. For example, you can change the height and width of the Web Part from its default size of 400 x 400 pixels. The View and Parameters sections of the tool pane can be expanded by clicking the arrows to the right of the section name, and the Appearance, Layout and Advanced sections of the tool pane can be expanded by clicking the plus sign to the left of the section name.

13. To the right of the Report text box, click the ellipsis button.

A list of reports in the current document library displays. You can navigate to a different document library if necessary.

14. In the Select An Item – Webpage Dialog dialog box, double-click Sales And Order Quantity By Year, and then, in the Report Viewer tool pane, click OK to apply the selection and close the tool pane.

The report executes and displays in the Web Part.

15. In the Related Information Web Part in the Middle Right zone, click Edit, and then select Delete to remove the Web Part from the zone. Click OK to confirm.

16. Repeat steps 10 to 14 to add a Report Viewer Web Part for the Sales And Order Quantity Summary report to the Middle Right Zone.

You could continue to add Web Parts to the dashboard page and remove unwanted Web Parts, but for now your next step is to publish the page.

17. On the toolbar above the dashboard page, click Publish to make the dashboard page available to all users, as shown here.

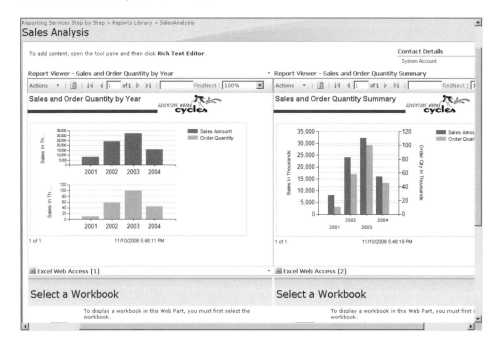

You could instead check in the dashboard as a draft to share with limited users before finalizing the layout. You could also set up a workflow for reviewers and approvers of the dashboard layout. These actions are SharePoint features that you can learn more about by reading "Understanding the Report Center and Dashboards in SharePoint Server 2007" at *http://msdn.microsoft.com/en-us/library/bb966994.aspx*.

Exporting Reports

Online report access is a common way to provide information to a wide variety of users, but sometimes users need to view information when they are disconnected from the network or they want to use the information in different ways. They might need to share information from a report in an e-mail, or they might want to analyze report data by using a spreadsheet. Users might want to use a report as a mechanism for retrieving corporate data that they then can import into a document for rich formatting. They might want to share report information in a print-ready paginated file or they might simply need access to raw data to import into another application. Reporting Services includes seven different rendering formats as alternatives to the online Hypertext Markup Language (HTML) format used to display reports. In this section, you compare the differences between these formats and learn how some report design features are more compatible with certain formats than with others.

> **More Info** For complete information about support for specific report design and behavior and rendering limitations, refer to the topic "Exporting Reports" in SQL Server Books Online.

> **Note** Many of the steps to follow in the procedures in this section depend on whether your target report server is native mode or SharePoint integrated mode. Each step includes instructions for both architectures.

Exporting a Report for Online Viewing

When you access a report online using Report Manager or the SharePoint Report Viewer, the report is rendered as HTML by default and all interactive features in the report definition are supported. An HTML report might have multiple pages if explicit page breaks have been defined or if the HTML rendering extensions inserts soft page breaks to improve the viewing of large reports. When you want to save a multipage report as a one-page HTML file or embed it as a single page into an e-mail message, you can export the report as a Web archive file which saves the report as a MIME Encapsulation of Aggregate HTML Documents (MHTML) file.

In this procedure, you export the Reseller Sales Margin Analysis by Sales Territory report to a Web archive file.

Export a report using the Web archive format

1. Open the Reseller Sales Margin Analysis by Sales Territory report.

    ❏ *Native mode:* Click the Home link at the top of the browser window, click the Sales folder link, and then click the Reseller Sales Margin Analysis by Sales Territory link.

    ❏ *Integrated mode:* Click the Reports Library link at the top of the SharePoint Report Viewer if currently viewing a report. Otherwise, navigate to *http://<servername> /sites/ssrs/ReportsLibrary* (replacing *<servername>* with the name of your server). Click the Reseller Sales Margin Analysis by Sales Territory link.

    Notice on the toolbar that the report contains two pages.

2. Export the report to the Web archive format.

    ❏ *Native mode:* In the Export Formats drop-down list, select MHTML (Web Archive), and then click the Export link.

    ❏ *Integrated mode:* Click Actions, select Export, and then select MHTML (Web Archive).

    When you export a report to a file, you have the option to open the file immediately in the new format or save the file to disk.

3. In the File Download message box, click Open.

4. Scroll to the bottom of the window to confirm that the second page of the report displays in the window, as shown here.

Country Total	$53,607,801					
Group Total	$67,985,727					
Pacific						
1 of 2		Filters: Europe,North America,Pacific - 2001,2002,2003,2004,2006 - Q1,Q2,Q3,Q4			·		
Australia						
Specialty Bike Shop	$327,172				◆	
Value Added Reseller	$799,552				◆	
Warehouse	$467,612				◆	
Country Total	$1,594,335					
Group Total	$1,594,335					
2 of 2		Filters: Europe,North America,Pacific - 2001,2002,2003,2004,2006 - Q1,Q2,Q3,Q4				

The exported file does not include the interactive features to expand or collapse the rows as possible in Report Manager or the SharePoint Report Viewer. If you want to display the hidden rows in the exported file, you must toggle the desired items manually to display them in the report before exporting the report.

5. Close the browser window.

Exporting a Report for Analysis

Many users like to export data into Excel to perform analysis with added formulas or to combine the data with information from other sources. Formatting in the report is preserved in the worksheet wherever possible. Explicit page breaks in the report definition produce one worksheet per page. If your report includes a document map, the first worksheet in the file includes the document map links, which you can then use to jump to the target location in the worksheet containing the report data. Other interactive features such as the hyperlink and bookmark actions are also supported in the Excel version of the report.

> **Important** Because Reporting Services creates a file compatible with Excel 97, there are limitations to the amount of data that can be exported to Excel. Your report must have no more than 65,536 rows and no more than 256 columns, even if you are opening the exported file in a later version of Excel that supports a larger amount of data.

In this procedure, you export the Reseller Sales Margin Analysis by Sales Territory report to an Excel file.

Export a report using the Excel format

1. Open the Reseller Sales Margin Analysis by Sales Territory report, if not already open.

   ❑ *Native mode:* Click the Home link at the top of the browser window, click the Sales folder link, and then click the Reseller Sales Margin Analysis by Sales Territory link.

   ❑ *Integrated mode:* Click the Reports Library link at the top of the SharePoint Report Viewer if currently viewing a report. Otherwise, navigate to *http://<servername> /sites/ssrs/ReportsLibrary* (replacing *<servername>* with the name of your server). Click the Reseller Sales Margin Analysis by Sales Territory link.

2. Export the report to the Excel format.

   ❑ *Native mode:* In the Export Formats drop-down list, select Excel, and then click the Export link.

   ❑ *Integrated mode:* Click Actions, select Export, and then select Excel.

3. If you have Excel installed on your computer, in the File Download message box, click Open. Otherwise, click Save and save the file to a location from which you can access it from a computer on which Excel is installed.

   Because this report contains only soft page breaks, all data is rendered to a single worksheet in the Excel file. The rendering process converts the hidden rows in the report into Excel outlines that you can expand or collapse.

4. In Excel, click the Row Level 2 button, shown here, to display the detail rows.

Row Level 2

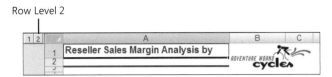

The detail rows are now visible in the report, as shown here.

	Product	Sales Amount	Profit Margin	Profit Margin Pct	Pct Contribution
6	Europe				
7	France				
8	Specialty Bike Shop	$418,644			
9	Mountain-200 Black, 38	$42,343	$4,096.78	9.675%	10.114%
10	Mountain-200 Black, 42	$27,294	$2,610.26	9.564%	6.52%
11	Mountain-200 Black, 38	$17,901	$1,625.17	9.079%	4.276%
12	Mountain-200 Black, 38	$17,212	$1,731.08	10.057%	4.111%
13	Touring-1000 Yellow, 46	$15,735	($566.45)	-3.60%	3.759%
14	Touring-1000 Blue, 46	$15,735	($566.45)	-3.60%	3.759%
15	Road-350-W Yellow, 40	$15,309	($928.74)	-6.067%	3.657%
16	Touring-1000 Yellow, 60	$14,686	($6,061.26)	-41.273%	3.508%
17	Touring-1000 Yellow, 60	$14,304	($514.96)	-3.60%	3.417%
18	Mountain-200 Silver, 42	$13,671	$1,374.95	10.057%	3.266%
19	Mountain-200 Black, 42	$12,295	$1,236.49	10.057%	2.937%
20	Touring-1000 Blue, 46	$11,444	($411.97)	-3.60%	2.733%
21	Touring-2000 Blue, 54	$8,018	($288.65)	-3.60%	1.915%
22	Mountain-200 Silver, 38	$7,457	$749.98	10.057%	1.781%
23	Touring-1000 Blue, 60	$7,152	($257.48)	-3.60%	1.708%
24	Road-650 Red, 62	$7,047	($253.69)	-3.60%	1.683%
25	Mountain-200 Silver, 46	$6,214	$624.98	10.057%	1.484%
26	Road-350-W Yellow, 48	$6,124	($371.50)	-6.067%	1.463%

Reseller Sales Margin Analysis

All data that you see in the worksheet has been converted from expressions to a constant value. Notice on your screen that the conditional formatting in the Pct Contribution columns displays the first value in the detail row in green font. The conditional formatting expression in the report sets the font color here, but it does not become a conditional formatting rule in the worksheet.

Also, notice the key performance indicator images in the final column did not render in the Excel file, although the logo image was rendered. Background images in the report are not supported in Excel and are consequently eliminated.

5. Close Excel without saving the file.

Creating a Data-Driven Document

You can easily create a Microsoft Office Word document that presents data from your organization's databases by exporting a report to Word. The exported file is compatible with Word 2000 and later. You can then enhance the exported report with additional information or modify the formatting. Interactive features such as hyperlinks and actions are preserved after export, but the ability to toggle the visibility of items is not. The page header and page footer in the report are converted to a header and footer in the document, but the *Height* property for each of these items is not converted. The Word document includes most images found in the report definition, such as a logo, but excludes the background images.

In this procedure, you export the Pacific Reseller Sales Margin Analysis report to a Word file.

Export a report using the Word format

1. Open the Pacific Reseller Sales Margin Analysis report.

   ❏ *Native mode:* Click the Home link at the top of the browser window, click the Sales folder link, and then click the Pacific Reseller Sales Margin Analysis link.

   ❏ *Integrated mode:* Click the Reports Library link at the top of the SharePoint Report Viewer if currently viewing a report. Otherwise, navigate to *http://<servername> /sites/ssrs/ReportsLibrary* (replacing *<servername>* with the name of your server). Click the Pacific Reseller Sales Margin Analysis link.

2. Expand Specialty Bike Shop to display the detail rows.

3. Export the report to the Word format.

   ❏ *Native mode:* In the Export Formats drop-down list, select Word, and then click the Export link.

   ❏ *Integrated mode:* Click Actions, select Export, and then select Word.

4. If you have Word installed on your computer, in the File Download message box, click Open to view the exported file, as shown here. Otherwise, click Save and save the file to a location from which you can access it from a computer on which Word is installed.

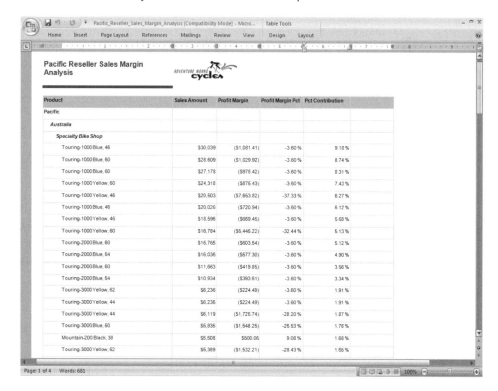

If you scroll through the document, you find that, unlike the Excel file, the detail rows in the report are visible only if you expanded a group in the online report before exporting to Word. The logo image exports successfully, but background images like the key performance indicator in the last column do not.

5. Close Word without saving the file.

Exporting a Report for Printing

For offline viewing in a print-ready format, you can save a report as a Tagged Image File Format (TIFF) or Portable Document Format (PDF) file. The PDF format of a report supports the document map feature, which is useful for large reports, but other interactive features are not supported. When designing reports that will be primarily accessed by users in one of these printable formats, you should be sure to set correctly the report size properties *Width* and *Height* and the margin properties *Left*, *Right*, *Top*, and *Bottom*.

In this procedure, you export the Reseller Sales Cumulative Sales report to a PDF file.

Export a report using the PDF format

1. Open the Reseller Sales Cumulative Sales report.

   ❏ *Native mode:* Click the Home link at the top of the browser window, click the For Review folder link, and then click the Reseller Sales Cumulative Sales link.

   ❏ *Integrated mode:* Click the Reports Library link at the top of the SharePoint Report Viewer if currently viewing a report. Otherwise, navigate to *http://<servername> /sites/ssrs/ReportsLibrary* (replacing *<servername>* with the name of your server). Click the For Review folder link, and then click Reseller Sales Cumulative Sales link.

   This report has a document map that renders as bookmarks in the PDF file.

2. Export the report to the PDF format.

   ❏ *Native mode:* In the Export Formats drop-down list, select Acrobat (PDF) File, and then click the Export link.

   ❏ *Integrated mode:* Click Actions, select Export, and then select Acrobat (PDF) File.

3. If you have Adobe Acrobat Reader installed on your computer, in the File Download message box, click Open. Otherwise, click Save and save the file to a location from which you can access it from a computer on which Acrobat Reader is installed.

4. In Acrobat Reader, click the Bookmarks icon to open the Bookmarks panel.

   The document map in your report renders as a set of bookmarks in the PDF file that you can use to click to access any sales territory group, sales territory country, or business type in the report.

5. In the Bookmarks panel, select Canada. The report appears as shown here.

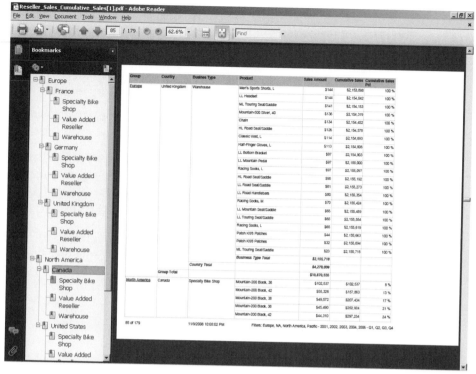

The report is difficult to read at this resolution, but you can use the magnification button or change the zoom percentage to increase the resolution for a more legible report.

6. Close the PDF file.

Exporting a Report for Data Exchange

Some users simply want the raw data in a Comma Separated Values (CSV) format to import into a spreadsheet or other analytical application. Or your organization might want to provide information in Extensible Markup Language (XML) format, such as a purchase order or sales invoice, for integration into a partner's business processes. For these formats, the export file contains only data and excludes all the formatting that makes a report more readable for users.

When you export a report to a CSV file, the Reporting Services rendering extension converts the report data to the lowest level of detail with a comma delimiter between each field and a carriage return and line feed at the end of each record. A header for in the file provides the names of each column.

A report exported to XML format tags the hierarchical structure of the data. The names of report items in the report definition become XML elements in the exported file, so you should take care to rename report items rather than keep the default names (such as Textbox1).

In this procedure, you export the Reseller Sales Margin Analysis by Sales Territory report to both a CSV file and an XML file.

Export a report using CSV format and XML format

1. Open the Reseller Sales Margin Analysis by Sales Territory report.

   ❏ *Native mode:* Click the Home link at the top of the browser window, click the Sales folder link, and then click the Reseller Sales Margin Analysis by Sales Territory link.

   ❏ *Integrated mode:* Click the Reports Library link at the top of the SharePoint Report Viewer if currently viewing a report. Otherwise, navigate to *http://<servername> /sites/ssrs/ReportsLibrary* (replacing *<servername>* with the name of your server). Click the Reseller Sales Margin Analysis by Sales Territory link.

   Although the detail rows in this report are hidden when the document opens, an export to the CSV or XML formats includes all detail rows whether visible or not.

2. Export the report to the CSV format.

   ❏ *Native mode:* In the Export Formats drop-down list, select CSV (Comma Delimited), and then click the Export link.

   ❏ *Integrated mode:* Click Actions, select Export, and then select CSV (Comma Delimited).

3. In the File Download message box, click Save, and save the file to a location on your computer.

   In this step, you save the file rather than open it because the file opens by default in Excel if you have that program installed on your computer. To view the export file in Notepad or other text viewer, you must first save the file to disk and then open the file with the desired application.

4. Open Windows Explorer, navigate to the location to which you saved the CSV file, right-click the Reseller_Sales_Margin_Analysis_By_Sales_Territory.csv file, select Open With, and then select Notepad to view the raw data, which looks similar to this when word wrap is turned off:

```
Textbox4
Reseller Sales Margin Analysis by Sales Territory

SalesTerritoryGroup,SalesTerritoryCountry,BusinessType,BusinessTypeTotal2,EnglishProductName,SalesAmount,ProfitMargin,Text
Europe,France,Specialty Bike Shop,"$418,644","Mountain-200 Black, 38","$42,343","$4,096.78",9.68 %,10.11 %,"$418,644","$4,
Europe,France,Specialty Bike Shop,"$418,644","Mountain-200 Black, 42","$27,294","$2,610.26",9.56 %,6.52 %,"$418,644","$4,6
Europe,France,Specialty Bike Shop,"$418,644","Mountain-200 Black, 38","$17,901","$1,625.17",9.08 %,4.28 %,"$418,644","$4,6
Europe,France,Specialty Bike Shop,"$418,644","Mountain-200 Black, 38","$17,212","$1,731.08",10.06 %,4.11 %,"$418,644","$4,
Europe,France,Specialty Bike Shop,"$418,644","Touring-1000 Yellow, 46","$15,735",($566.45),-3.60 %,3.76 %,"$418,644","$4,6
Europe,France,Specialty Bike Shop,"$418,644","Touring-1000 Blue, 46","$15,735",($566.45),-3.60 %,3.76 %,"$418,644","$4,607
Europe,France,Specialty Bike Shop,"$418,644","Road-350-W Yellow, 40","$15,309",($928.74),-6.07 %,3.66 %,"$418,644","$4,607
Europe,France,Specialty Bike Shop,"$418,644","Touring-1000 Yellow, 60","$14,686",($6,061.26),-41.27 %,3.51 %,"$418,644",
Europe,France,Specialty Bike Shop,"$418,644","Touring-1000 Yellow, 60","$14,304",($514.96),-3.60 %,3.42 %,"$418,644","$4,6
Europe,France,Specialty Bike Shop,"$418,644","Mountain-200 Silver, 42","$13,671","$1,374.95",10.06 %,3.27 %,"$418,644","$4
Europe,France,Specialty Bike Shop,"$418,644","Mountain-200 Black, 42","$12,295","$1,236.49",10.06 %,2.94 %,"$418,644","$4,
Europe,France,Specialty Bike Shop,"$418,644","Touring-1000 Blue, 46","$11,444",($411.97),-3.60 %,2.73 %,"$418,644","$4,6
Europe,France,Specialty Bike Shop,"$418,644","Touring-2000 Blue, 54","$8,018",($288.65),-3.60 %,1.92 %,"$418,644","$4,607,
Europe,France,Specialty Bike Shop,"$418,644","Mountain-200 Silver, 38","$7,457","$749.98",10.06 %,1.78 %,"$418,644","$4,607
Europe,France,Specialty Bike Shop,"$418,644","Touring-1000 Blue, 60","$7,152",($257.48),-3.60 %,1.71 %,"$418,644","$4,607,
Europe,France,Specialty Bike Shop,"$418,644","Road-650 Red, 62","$7,047",($253.69),-3.60 %,1.68 %,"$418,644","$4,607,538"
Europe,France,Specialty Bike Shop,"$418,644","Mountain-200 Silver, 46","$6,214","$624.98",10.06 %,1.48 %,"$418,644","$4,607
Europe,France,Specialty Bike Shop,"$418,644","Road-350-W Yellow, 48","$6,124",($371.50),-6.07 %,1.46 %,"$418,644","$4,607,
Europe,France,Specialty Bike Shop,"$418,644","Road-650 Black, 52","$6,107",($219.86),-3.60 %,1.46 %,"$418,644","$4,607,538
```

Notice the report title and the name of the text box containing the report title, Textbox4, display at the top of the file because all data is exported even if the data is not found within a data region. The fourth row of the file is the header row for the data region containing the report data. The CSV export ignores dynamic visibility defined in the report. All remaining rows are the details found in the report that are hidden in the HTML format of the report. Notice also the quotation marks used as a text qualifier when a field contains an embedded comma.

5. Close Notepad, and switch to the browser window displaying the report.

6. Export the report to the XML format.

   ❑ *Native mode:* In the Export Formats drop-down list, select XML File With Report Data, and then click the Export link.

   ❑ *Integrated mode:* Click Actions, select Export, and then select XML File With Report Data.

7. In the File Download message box, click Open, and the following display appears:

```
<?xml version="1.0" encoding="utf-8" ?>
- <Report
    xsi:schemaLocation="Reseller_x0020_Sales_x0020_Margin_x0020_Analysis_x0020_by_x0020_Sales_x0020_Territory
    http://localhost/ReportServer?%2fSales%2fReseller+Sales+Margin+Analysis+by+Sales+Territory&rs%
    3aCommand=Render&rs%3aFormat=XML&rs%3aSessionID=ep5ddrqgab441055jkk52ayi&rc%3aSchema=True"
    Name="Reseller Sales Margin Analysis by Sales Territory" Textbox4="Reseller Sales Margin Analysis by Sales
    Territory" xmlns:xsi="http://www.w3.org/2001/XMLSchema-instance"
    xmlns="Reseller_x0020_Sales_x0020_Margin_x0020_Analysis_x0020_by_x0020_Sales_x0020_Territory">
  - <Tablix1>
    - <SalesTerritoryGroup_Collection>
      - <SalesTerritoryGroup SalesTerritoryGroup="Europe" Textbox21="10870534.7989">
        - <SalesTerritoryCountry_Collection>
          - <SalesTerritoryCountry SalesTerritoryCountry="France" Textbox17="4607537.9350">
            - <BusinessType_Collection>
              - <BusinessType BusinessType="Specialty Bike Shop" BusinessTypeTotal2="418643.6974"
                BusinessTypeTotal="418643.6974">
                - <Details_Collection>
                    <Details EnglishProductName="Mountain-200 Black, 38" SalesAmount="42342.5649"
                     ProfitMargin="4096.7793" Textbox13="0.0967532153443071182492301027"
                     PctContribution="0.101142248558786018403820834" />
                    <Details EnglishProductName="Mountain-200 Black, 42" SalesAmount="27293.9879"
                     ProfitMargin="2610.2649" Textbox13="0.0956351600053284994678260263"
                     PctContribution="0.0651962231117061598930928991" />
```

Just like the CSV file, the XML file also includes data that uses dynamic visibility and it preserves the grouping structure defined in the report. In this example, the *SalesTerritoryGroup_Collection* represents the outermost element and contains elements for each *SalesTerritoryGroup* which in turn contain a *SalesTerritoryCountry _Collection* and so on to represent each grouping in the report. Attributes for each element correspond to field names from the applicable group in the report.

8. Close the XML file.

In addition to accessing reports online, as you learned how to do in this chapter, you might want to create new reports based on a report model using the Report Builder 1.0 application. In Chapter 14, "Creating Ad Hoc Reports," you learn how to start this application from Report Manager or your SharePoint site and how to share the reports that you build with other users.

Chapter 13 Quick Reference

To	Do This
Search report server content	*Native mode:* In Report Manager, in the Search For text box, type a search string, and click the green button. *Integrated mode:* If search in SharePoint is configured for the Report Center site, open the reports library, type a search string in the Enter Search Words text box, and click the magnifying glass icon.
Print a report	*Native mode:* Open a report, and click Print in the HTML Viewer. *Integrated mode:* Open a report, click Actions, and select Print.
Create a personal linked report for the My Reports folder	When My Reports is enabled in Server Properties in SQL Server Management Studio, open the General Properties page of a report, and click Create Linked Report. Type a name for the report, and click Change Location. In the folder tree, select My Reports. Set parameter default values on the linked report's Parameter Properties page, if desired.
Configure the search feature on SharePoint	In SharePoint 3.0 Central Administration, create a new SSP and assign it to a Web application with a Windows account as the application pool identity. Open the SSP's Shared Services Administration page, click the Search Settings link, click the Default Content Access Account link, assign a Windows account with read permissions to the site to search, and click OK. Click the Content Sources And Crawl Schedules link, and click the Local Office SharePoint Server Sites. Specify schedules for full crawl and incremental crawl, and click Start Full Crawl Of This Content Source check box.
Create a dashboard with a Report Viewer Web Part on an integrated-mode report server	In Internet Explorer, open the Reports Library, select Dashboard Page on the New menu, type a name and page title for the dashboard, click OK, and click Edit Page. In a dashboard zone, click the Add A Web Part link, expand All Web Parts in the Add Web Parts – Webpage Dialog dialog box, select the SQL Server Reporting Services Report Viewer check box, and click Add. In the Report Viewer Web Part, click the Click Here To Open The Tool Pane, click the ellipsis button to the right of the Report text box, and select a report. Close the tool pane, and click Publish.
Export a report to a new format	*Native mode:* Open a report in Report Manager, select a format in the Export Formats drop-down list, and then click the Export link. Open the file or save the file to your computer. *Integrated mode:* Open a report in the Reports Library, click Actions, select Export, and select a format. Open the file or save the file to your computer.

Chapter 14
Creating Ad Hoc Reports

After completing this chapter, you will be able to:

- Use Report Builder to create a table, matrix, or chart report.

- Enhance the appearance of a Report Builder report with formatting.

- Create a new field for the report by using an expression.

- Apply a filter to the report data.

- Change the sort order of report data.

- Set report properties to control the use of interactive features.

- Save a report to the report server.

- Work with default and custom clickthrough reports.

In Chapter 9, "Developing Report Models," you created a report model to support ad hoc reporting. The report model presents a list of available fields from the data source that the user can include in a report. The report server translates the user's selection into a query that it uses to retrieve data from the data source. In this way, users can produce reports when they need access to information and thereby relieve some of the pressure on the IT department to create managed reports. Professional report developers can use the report model as a data source when developing with Report Builder 2.0 or the Report Designer in Business Intelligence Development Studio (BI Dev Studio), but nontechnical users develop ad hoc reports based on the report model by using Report Builder 1.0. Report Builder 1.0 is a completely different application from Report Builder 2.0, and it is the focus of this chapter.

> **Important** To complete the procedures in this chapter, you must have completed Chapter 9 successfully so that you have a report model available on the report server.

Developing Reports with Report Builder

Report Builder is a tool you can use to create a simple report quickly and easily. You start by selecting a report model and deciding how you want to arrange the data in the report. Then you explore the report model and select the fields that you want to include in the report. You can preview the report at any time during the development process. When you're finished, you can save the report to the report server or you can save it to a local file.

Introducing Report Builder

Because Report Builder is intended for use by nontechnical businesspeople, the interface is kept simple and the range of functionality is limited. Ad hoc reports typically are used to answer a specific question at a point in time, so consequently people don't spend a lot of time arranging and formatting the data in a precise way. Other report development tools are available in Reporting Services to support more sophisticated reporting requirements.

> **Note** Many of the steps in the procedures in this chapter depend on whether your target report server is native mode or SharePoint integrated mode. Each step includes instructions for both architectures where applicable.

In this procedure, you explore the Report Builder interface.

Explore Report Builder

1. In Windows Internet Explorer, open the Web application for your report server type.

   ❑ *Native mode:* Navigate to *http://*<servername>*/reports*, replacing *<servername>* with the name of your server.

   ❑ *Integrated mode:* Navigate to *http://*<servername>*/sites/ssrs*, replacing *<servername>* with the name of your server. In the navigation bar, click the Reports link, and then click the Ad Hoc Reports folder link. (You created the Ad Hoc Reports folder in Chapter 11, "Securing Report Server Content.")

2. Start Report Builder.

   ❑ *Native mode:* In Report Manager, on the toolbar, click Report Builder.

   ❑ *Integrated mode:* Click the arrow to the right of the New button on the document library toolbar, and select Report Builder Report.

3. If this is the first time that you have run Report Builder, in the Application Run – Security Warning dialog box, click Run to download the client application to your computer from the report server.

   After the application installs on your computer, the Microsoft Report Builder window opens and displays only the Getting Started pane on the right side of the window, as shown here for a native-mode report server.

At the top of the Getting Started pane is a link to the current report server. If report models are stored on multiple native-mode report servers or in multiple document libraries on a SharePoint integrated-mode report server, you can click this link to open the Select Site Or Server dialog box and navigate to a new location.

When you select a location, the available models at that location appear in the Select A Source Of Data For Your Report list. If you select the Show Path check box, you see the folder hierarchy containing the report model displayed as a prefix to the report model name in the list. If you plan to create a new report, you must select a report model to use as a source for the report query.

If reports created by using Report Builder have been published to the report server, you can open any of those reports for which you have the necessary permissions and then view or edit the report. You can choose to open a report on the report server or one that has been saved to your local file system.

4. If you're running a SharePoint integrated-mode report server, click the *http: //<servername>/sites/ssrs/ReportsLibrary/Ad Hoc Reports* link at the top of the Getting Started pane, and then, in the Select Site Or Server dialog box, double-click *http: //<servername>/sites/ssrs/ReportsLibrary* to open the library that contains the report model.

5. In the report model list, expand the Reseller Sales model.

In Chapter 9, you created the Basic Reseller Sales perspective to organize a subset of entities, attributes, and roles. You can use this perspective to build a report instead of using its parent report model. For this procedure, you use the parent report model as you learn how to work with Report Builder.

Below the report model list, the three layout options display: Table (Columnar), Matrix (Cross-tab), and Chart. You can choose only one layout type for your report. If you need to create a report that displays more than one data region, such as a matrix and a chart, then you must use either Report Designer or Report Builder 2.0. For now, you keep the default selection, Table (Columnar).

6. In the report model list, select Reseller Sales, and click OK to view the new report in Design mode, as shown here.

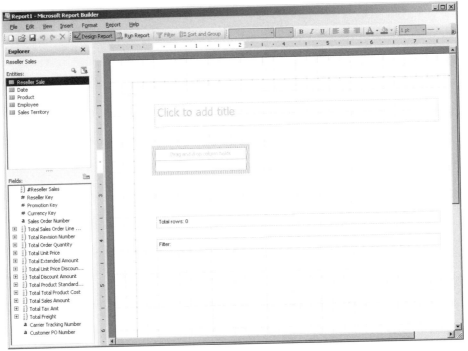

In the Explorer pane on the left side of the window, the Entities list shows all the report model entities and the Fields list shows the list of fields (called *attributes* in the report model) related to the selected entity. The main section of the window is the report design surface, which contains text boxes for the title, a row count, and a filter description. In the center of the design surface is a table that contains a single column and a single row. You can add columns to the table by selecting fields from the report model.

7. In the Entities list, select Reseller Sale.

In the Fields list, the icon that displays to the left of the field name identifies the field's data type. For example, the three yellow blocks next to #Reseller Sales tells you the field is an aggregate numeric value, just like Total Order Quantity. The pound (#) symbol indicates that the field is a scalar numeric value. The letter *a* next to Sales Order Number identifies the field as a string.

8. On the Help menu, select Report Builder Help.

   The Help file for Report Builder includes basic information about Report Builder and provides instructions for creating and editing a report in this application.

Building a Table

A table is a simple structure with one or more columns based on fields from the report model. The selection of fields that you add to the table determines whether your report displays detail rows or grouped rows. You can add only columns to the table layout; you cannot add rows.

In this procedure, you create a simple table to display total sales and average sales by sales territory.

Build a table

1. In the Entities list, select Sales Territory.

2. Drag Sales Territory Group from the Fields list onto the Drag And Drop Column Fields area of the table data region.

3. Drag Sales Territory Country from the Fields list to the table, and, when you see an I-bar to the right of Sales Territory Group, as shown here, drop Sales Territory Country at the insertion point.

   The table now looks like this:

4. In the Fields list, double-click Sales Territory Region.

   Rather than use dragging, you can double-click a field to add it as the last column in the data region. After a field is in the data region, you can rearrange the order of the columns by dragging columns to new locations in the table.

Now that the table has all the fields needed from the Sales Territory entity, you need to switch to the Reseller Sales entity to select the numeric values to include in the table. As shown here, notice that the Entities list shows the current entity selection, Sales Territory, and only two other entities appear below it, Reseller Sales and Employees. After you add the first field to a report, the Entities list displays only the current entity selection and the entities that share a role with it. (Roles are explained in more detail in Chapter 9.)

5. In the Entities list, select Reseller Sales.

6. In the Fields list, expand Total Sales Amount to view its related fields, as shown here.

You use the Total Sales Amount field when you want to group detail data by the non-numeric fields in the report, but use the Sales Amount field when you want to see each detail row listed in the report.

7. Drag Total Sales Amount from the Fields list to the right of Sales Territory Region on the report design surface.

Notice that subtotal rows are added automatically when you add an aggregate field like Total Sales Amount. You can disable this behavior by right-clicking the column header or the column's detail row and clearing the Show Subtotal selection.

8. Drag Avg Sales Amount from the Fields list, and drop it to the right of Total Sales Amount.

9. Double-click the text box above the table (containing Click To Add Title), and type **Reseller Sales**.

10. Click Run Report on the toolbar to preview the report, as shown here.

Reseller Sales

Sales Territory Group	Sales Territory Country	Sales Territory Region	Total Sales Amount	Avg Sales Amount
Europe	France	France	$4,607,537.94	$1,305.25
		Total	$4,607,537.94	$1,305.25
	Germany	Germany	$1,983,988.04	$1,078.84
		Total	$1,983,988.04	$1,078.84
	United Kingdom	United Kingdom	$4,279,008.83	$1,215.63
		Total	$4,279,008.83	$1,215.63
	Total		$10,870,534.80	$1,222.92
NA	NA	NA		
		Total		
	Total			
North America	Canada	Canada	$14,377,925.60	$1,256.37
		Total	$14,377,925.60	$1,256.37
	United States	Central	$7,906,008.18	$1,360.29
		Northeast	$6,932,842.01	$1,193.47
		Northwest	$12,435,076.00	$1,579.66
		Southeast	$7,867,416.23	$1,325.15
		Southwest	$18,466,458.79	$1,380.26
		Total	$53,607,801.21	$1,381.32

11. Scroll down to review the subtotals for each country and the grand total.

If the report is satisfactory, you can save the report to the report server or to your local computer by clicking the Save button on the Standard toolbar. You can also use the Export button (which looks like a diskette and is located next to the Zoom drop-down list) to save the report to a different file type, such as Portable Document Format (PDF) or Microsoft Office Excel.

12. On the toolbar, click Save.

13. Save the report to the report server.

❑ *Native mode:* In the Save As Report dialog box, in the Look In drop-down list, select *http://<servername>/ReportServer* (where *<servername>* is your server name), and then, in the Name text box, type **Reseller Sales**. Click Save.

❑ *Integrated mode:* In the Save As Report dialog box, double-click the Ad Hoc Reports folder, and then, in the Name text box, type **Reseller Sales**. Click Save.

You can save a report to the report server only if you have been assigned to the Content Manager role on a native-mode report server or if you are an Owner or Member of the report server content site on a SharePoint integrated-mode report server. If My Reports is enabled on a native-mode report server, you can also save reports to your personal folder.

14. Close Report Builder, and then, in Internet Explorer, press F5 to refresh the page.

15. Click the Reseller Sales report link to open the report.

    You can use the Web application to view a report created by using Report Builder just as you can view a report created by using BI Dev Studio or Report Builder 2.0.

    Notice that each column header in the Report Builder report displays the interactive sort icon. Interactive sort is included automatically in the report design. When the user chooses to sort data by column values, the group definitions applicable to the rows are preserved. That is, rows sort within the group to which they belong.

16. Click the arrows to the right of Total Sales Amount to apply an ascending sort.

    Notice that the only change to row order occurs in the United States group because this group is the only one with multiple rows in the Total Sales Amount column.

17. Click the arrows to the right of Sales Territory Country to apply a descending sort.

    This time, the rows in the Europe and North America groups sort in descending order alphabetically by country name. Notice that the rows in the United States group continue to sort in ascending order of sales amount. You can continue applying new sorting to the table without losing the existing sorting.

Building a Matrix

You can create a matrix layout with groups on both rows and columns just as you can in the other Reporting Services development tools. In Report Builder, multiple groups are collapsed to produce a drilldown report by default.

In this procedure, you create a simple matrix to display total sales by sales territory and by calendar year.

Build a matrix

1. Start Report Builder.

    ❏ *Native mode:* In Report Manager, click the Home link, and then click Report Builder.

    ❏ *Integrated mode:* At the top of the page, click the Reports Library link, click the arrow to the right of the New button, and select Report Builder Report.

2. In the Report Layout section of the Getting Started pane, keep the default selection of Reseller Sales for the Data Source, select Matrix (Cross-tab) for the Report Layout, and then click OK.

3. Double-click the title text box, and type **Reseller Sales Matrix**.

4. In the Entities list, double-click Sales Territory.

When you double-click an entity, the default attributes defined in the report model (and described in Chapter 9) are added to the report layout as a group. Because the field names in the column header are too long for the default text box size, you must adjust the report layout. One adjustment you might make is to widen the text box.

5. Point to the line between the first and second column, and when the pointer becomes a double-headed arrow, drag the line to the right until you can see the entire field name.

If you decide not to use some of the columns that were added automatically to the report layout, you can remove them easily, as you learn in the next step.

6. Right-click the column header in the second column, and select Delete to delete any columns that you want to remove.

> **Tip** The order of the fields from left to right is not the correct arrangement. It is deter-
> mined by the order of the attributes in the entity's *DefaultDetailAttributes* property in
> the report model. To ensure the arrangement on the report layout is always correct, you
> should adjust the report model and redeploy the updated model to the report server.

The correct sequence of fields is Sales Territory Group, Sales Territory Country, and Sales Territory Region to display data in the correct hierarchical order.

7. Drag the third column containing Sales Territory Group in front of the first column (containing Sales Territory Region), and then drag the new third column, Sales Territory Country, between the first and second columns to produce the desired sequence of fields.

Rather than widen the columns to display the full field name in the column header, you can replace the field name with alternate text.

> **Note** The goal of step 7 is to rearrange the columns and to create three separate groups.
> Each group in a matrix has its own Total row. If you see only two Total rows in the matrix
> after rearranging the columns, you need to click Undo and repeat the process of drag-
> ging the columns. If you release the mouse button too early when dragging Sales Territory
> Country between the first and second columns, your matrix contains only two groups.
> When you release the mouse button when the pointer is on the line between the two col-
> umns, you should see three groups with three Total rows in the matrix.

8. Click twice in the first column, type **Group**, click twice in the second column, type **Country**, click twice in the third column, and type **Region**.

Your matrix now looks like this:

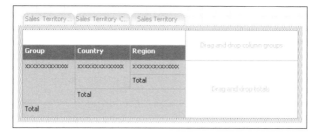

9. On the toolbar, click the Run Report button.

   An error message displays to alert you that the matrix must have at least one row group, column group, and a total before you can run the report.

10. Click OK to close the message box. In the Entities list, select Reseller Sales, and then, in the Fields list, drag Total Sales Amount to the Drag And Drop Totals area in the matrix.

11. Select Order Date in the Entities list.

12. Expand the Total Calendar Year field in the Fields list, and then drag Calendar Year to the Drag And Drop Column Groups area.

> **Tip** You might be wondering why the Fields list contains Total Calendar Year, Avg Calendar Year, Min Calendar Year, and Max Calendar Year. When you used the Report Model Wizard to generate the report model in Chapter 9, the wizard recognized Calendar Year as a numeric value and created aggregate fields for the report model so that users can build a report to perform *SUM, AVERAGE, MIN*, and *MAX* functions without the need to build an expression. Because you selected Calendar Year as the column group in step 12, the query generator retrieves the distinct Calendar Year values from the source table rather than perform an aggregate function. Although you can use this report model as it is to build a report successfully, the report model requires further refinement to be as simple and easy to understand as possible for nontechnical users. The typical process of report model development includes several cycles in which the report model is developed, deployed to the report server, and then tested with Report Builder. By interacting with the model from the user perspective, you more easily find anomalies in the report model (such as you see here with Calendar Year and other date fields) and can make adjustments in the report model as needed.

Notice that the text that displays in the column group header is not clearly visible. When you run the report, the width of the text box increases and you can then read the text. You can type alternate text for the column group header if you want.

13. Click the Run Report button again.

   Notice that some of the sales amount values are too large for the current text box width. You must resize the value columns to accommodate the largest values.

14. Click Design Report, point to the line between the two columns in the Calendar Year group until the double-headed arrow appears, and drag the line to the right until the text box is approximately 1 inch wide.

15. Click Run Report to view the updated report, as shown here.

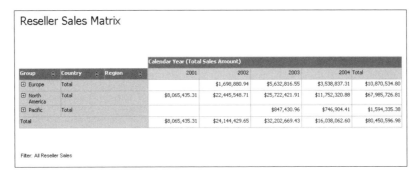

When you add multiple fields to the rows or columns of a matrix, Report Builder automatically collapses the innermost fields. This behavior is similar to using the *Hidden* and *ToggleItem* properties as explained in Chapter 6, "Adding Interactivity."

16. Expand North America, and then expand United States to view the lowest level of detail in the report.

17. On the File menu, select Save To File. Navigate to the Microsoft Press\Rs2008sbs \Workspace folder in your Documents folder. In the File Name text box, type **Reseller Sales Matrix**, and click Save.

As an alternative to publishing reports to the report server, you can save a Report Builder report to a local hard drive or a network share.

Building a Chart

You can present data visually by building a chart report. Report Builder uses a different set of chart controls than Report Builder 2.0 and Report Designer and supports only the following chart types: column, bar, area, line, pie, and doughnut. Formatting options for your chart are also more limited in Report Builder.

In this procedure, you create a simple chart to display total sales by sales territory in a column chart.

Build a chart

1. On the File menu, click New.

2. In the Getting Started pane, in the Report Layout section, select Chart, click OK, and then, in the message box prompting you to save the report that you just created, click No.

> **Note** Although you saved the report to your local drive, Report Builder prompts you to decide whether you want to save the report to the report server before closing the report.

3. Double-click the title text box, and type **Reseller Sales Chart**.

4. Click the chart data region to display the drop zones.

5. In the Entities list, select Sales Territory, and then drag Sales Territory Country to the area labeled Drag And Drop Category Fields.

6. In the Entities list, select Reseller Sales, and then drag the Total Sales Amount field to the area labeled Drag And Drop Data Value Fields

7. Click Run Report to view the report, as shown here.

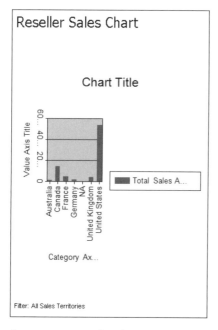

As you can see, the chart settings require adjustment to view the data better. You can start by removing the chart title and then changing the labels for the category and value axes.

8. Right-click the background of the chart, and then select Chart Options.

9. In the Chart Options dialog box, click the Titles tab, clear the text in the Chart Title text box, change the Category Title of Category (X) Axis to **Countries**, and change the Value Title of Value (Y) Axis to **Dollars**.

   Notice that you can also set the font properties for all titles and specify the alignment for axis titles. Next, you can remove the legend because the chart has only one series.

10. Click the Legend tab, and then clear the Show Legend check box.

To add more visual interest to the chart, you can set three-dimensional properties.

11. Click the 3D Effect tab, select the Display Chart With 3-D Visual Effect check box, and then adjust the property values on this tab, as shown in the following table.

Property	Value
Horizontal Rotation (Degrees)	5
Vertical Rotation (Degrees)	0
Perspective (%)	0
Wall Thickness (%)	10

The properties are defined as follows:

❑ The *Horizontal Rotation (Degrees)* property changes your perspective of the column on the horizontal axis. A positive value makes the face of the column appear to turn to your left, whereas a negative value makes it appear to turn to the right. In this step, the perspective change to the left is very slight.

❑ The *Vertical Rotation (Degrees)* property changes your perspective of the column, but along the vertical axis. A positive value makes the chart appear as if you are looking down at the column so you can see the top face of the column. A negative value makes it appear as if you are looking up at the column, allowing you to see the bottom face of the column. In this step, you make no change to the vertical rotation and consequently can see neither the top nor the bottom face of the column.

❑ The *Perspective (%)* property adds depth to the chart by adding a side wall to the chart background to give the appearance of looking past the columns. The *Horizontal Rotation (Degrees)* property also adds depth, but the width of each column is consistent. When you increase the *Perspective (%)* property to more than 0, the width of each column changes such that some columns appear closer to you than others. Although this feature is frequently found in chart tools that offer three-dimensional features, be aware that changing the perspective can distort the appearance of the chart and misrepresent the relative values across categories.

❑ The *Wall Thickness (%)* property changes the thickness of the bottom and side walls of the chart background. Increasing the value of this property can improve the visibility of the edges of the chart background, but you should keep the value at 10 percent or less for the best appearance.

12. Click OK to close the Chart Options dialog box, and then click Run Report to view the modified chart, as shown here.

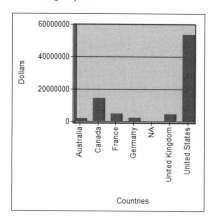

The formatting options for charts in Report Builder are much more limited than those you used in Chapter 8, "Visualizing Data."

13. On the File menu, select Save To File. Navigate to the Microsoft Press\Rs2008sbs \Workspace folder in your Documents folder. In the File Name text box, type **Reseller Sales Chart**, and click Save.

Testing Security

In Chapter 11, you configured the report model to secure individual model items. Specifically, you secured the *Employee* entity so that only members of the Managers group can use it.

In this procedure, you review the Reseller Sales report model when impersonating the Analyst user and the VP user.

Review model item security by impersonating users

1. Open Internet Explorer as Analyst. If your computer runs Windows Vista or Windows Server 2008, you must log off and then log in using Analyst as both the user and password, and then open Internet Explorer. If your computer runs Windows XP, Windows Server 2000, or Windows Server 2003, click Start, select All Programs, right-click Internet Explorer, and select Run As. Select The Following User, type **Analyst** in the User and Password text boxes, and then click OK.

2. In Internet Explorer, navigate to the upper-level folder for report server content.

   ❏ *Native mode:* Open Report Manager at *http://localhost/reports*.

   ❏ *Integrated mode:* Open the Reports library at *http://localhost/sites/ssrs /ReportsLibrary*.

3. Start Report Builder.

   ❑ *Native mode:* In Report Manager, on the toolbar, click Report Builder.

   ❑ *Integrated mode:* Click the arrow to the right of the New button on the document library toolbar, and select Report Builder Report.

4. If this is the first time that you have run Report Builder for this user, in the Application Run – Security Warning dialog box, click Run to download the client application to your computer from the report server.

5. If you're running a SharePoint integrated-mode report server, click the *http://<servername>/sites/ssrs/ReportsLibrary/Ad Hoc Reports* link at the top of the Getting Started pane, and then, in the Select Site Or Server dialog box, double-click *http://<servername>/sites/ssrs/ReportsLibrary* to open the library that contains the report model.

6. In the report model list, select Reseller Sales, keep the default selection of Table (Columnar), and click OK.

   In the Entities list, notice that only four entities display: *Reseller Sale, Date, Product,* and *Sales Territory.* The *Employee* entity is missing because you restricted this model item in Chapter 9.

7. Close Report Builder, close Internet Explorer, and, if necessary, log off your computer. Repeat steps 1 through 6, running Internet Explorer with the user as VP and the password as VP (if necessary, log on to your computer as VP).

   This time, you should see all five entities display in the Entities list: *Reseller Sale, Date, Product, Employee,* and *Sales Territory.*

8. Close Report Builder, close Internet Explorer (or log off your computer, if necessary), and then log on again using your administrator credentials.

Enhancing Reports

Although you might not take the time to format an ad hoc report that you intend to discard after viewing once or twice, you might decide to format a report that you want to share to make it easier to read for others or implement other features that make it easier to use. Report Builder formatting options are basic compared to Report Designer but are typically sufficient for ad hoc reports. You can also enhance your reports by adding a calculation to your report, by adding filters to limit the data in your report, or by providing a default sort order for the data. Finally, if you want, you can disable the interactive sort feature that you saw in the Reseller Sales report or the expand/collapse capability in the Reseller Sales Matrix report.

Formatting a Report

Report Builder aims to provide users with a quick and easy way to access and display information with minimum effort and little emphasis on formatting. Nonetheless, when you create a table or matrix layout, you have much more control over formatting than you do with a chart. You can use the Formatting toolbar to set properties such as font size, font color, and text alignment.

In this procedure, you modify the formatting of the subtotal rows in the Reseller Sales report.

Apply formatting

1. In Report Builder, with Internet Explorer running under your own credentials, open the Reseller Sales report.

   ❏ *Native mode:* Click the Open button on the toolbar, click No to decline saving the chart report, select *http://<servername>/ReportServer* in the Look In drop-down list, select Reseller Sales, and then click Open.

   ❏ *Integrated mode:* Click the Open button on the toolbar, click No to decline saving the chart report, double-click the Ad Hoc Reports folder, and double-click Reseller Sales.

2. Click the Sales Territory Group column header, then, while pressing Shift, click Avg Sales Amount to select all five column headers.

   You can apply formatting to multiple selections in a single step by using the Formatting toolbar.

3. On the Formatting toolbar, click the Centered button, and then, in the Font Size drop-down list, select 10.

   Although the text in the first three column headers is not completely visible, the text boxes expand vertically when the report renders. You can also change the text in these text boxes if you want, as you learned in the procedure, "Build a Matrix," earlier in this chapter.

   The total rows for each group in the matrix display with a light blue fill color by default. You can change the fill color or font properties for an individual text box or for the entire row.

4. Click the Total cell in the Sales Territory Region column, and then, while pressing Shift, click the last cell in the same row to select a total of three cells. Right-click one of the selected cells, select Format, click the Fill tab, and then select White.

5. Click the Font tab, select Bold in the Font Style list, and click OK.

6. Click the Total cell in the Sales Territory Country column, and then, while pressing Shift, click the last cell in the same row to select a total of three cells. Right-click one of the

selected cells and select Format. Click the Font tab, select Bold Italic in the Font Style list, and click OK.

You can change the label for the subtotal row by typing a new value.

7. Click twice in the first text box in the bottom row of the table to edit the label, click to position the cursor in front of the existing text, and then type **Grand** and press the spacebar to insert text rather than replace the existing text.

Rather than open the Format dialog box to change the properties for the total row, you can use the Formatting toolbar as you did for the column headers.

8. Click anywhere outside the table, click the Grand Total cell in the Sales Territory Group column, and then, while pressing Shift, click the last cell in the same row to select a total of three cells, and click the Bold button on the Formatting toolbar.

9. Point to the line between Total Sales Amount and Avg Sales Amount until the double-headed arrow appears, and drag the line to the right until the text box is approximately 1 inch wide.

10. Point to the right edge of the Avg Sales Amount text box until the double-headed arrow appears, and drag the line to the right until the text box is approximately 1 inch wide.

11. Click Run Report to preview the report, as shown here.

Reseller Sales

Sales Territory Group	Sales Territory Country	Sales Territory Region	Total Sales Amount	Avg Sales Amount
Europe	France	France	$4,607,537.94	$1,305.25
		Total	**$4,607,537.94**	**$1,305.25**
	Germany	Germany	$1,983,988.04	$1,078.84
		Total	**$1,983,988.04**	**$1,078.84**
	United Kingdom	United Kingdom	$4,279,008.83	$1,215.63
		Total	**$4,279,008.83**	**$1,215.63**
	Total		*$10,870,534.80*	*$1,222.92*
NA	NA	NA		
		Total		
	Total			
North America	Canada	Canada	$14,377,925.60	$1,256.37
		Total	**$14,377,925.60**	**$1,256.37**
	United States	Central	$7,906,008.18	$1,360.29
		Northeast	$6,932,842.01	$1,193.47
		Northwest	$12,435,076.00	$1,579.66
		Southeast	$7,867,416.23	$1,325.15
		Southwest	$18,466,458.79	$1,380.26
		Total	**$53,607,801.21**	**$1,381.32**

12. Scroll to the bottom of the page to review the formatting of the Grand Total row.

13. Click the Print Layout button on the toolbar to see the print preview of the report.

 Tip Before you print a report, you should view the print preview to ensure that the report fits the page correctly. You can click the Page Setup button on the toolbar to change the paper size, orientation, and the size of the margins.

14. Click the Print Layout button again to return to the online view of your report.

Adding Formula Fields

Sometimes you need to include a calculation in a report that is not already provided in the report model. You can easily create a field that uses a formula definition to perform the needed calculation. The new field persists only in the report and is not added to the report model. If other users need to use the same field in their reports, you should update the report model to include the formula definition field so that it is available to all users.

In this procedure, you create a field to calculate profit margin and add it to your report.

Create a new field using a formula

1. Click Design Report.

2. In the Entities list, select Reseller Sales, and then click the New Field button, shown here, which appears above the Fields list.

3. In the Define Formula dialog box, in the Field Name text box, type **Profit Margin**.

4. Click the Functions tab, and in the Function list, expand the Aggregate folder.

5. Double-click SUM to add it to the Formula text box.

 Tip You can type the field name as the argument for the *SUM* function, but you can avoid typographical errors by selecting it from the Fields list.

6. Click the Fields tab, and in the Fields list, double-click Sales Amount to add it to the formula box.

7. Click the – button, and then double-click Total Product Cost in the Fields list.

8. Position the cursor at the end of the expression, and click the / button.

9. Click the Functions tab, double-click SUM, click the Fields tab, and double-click Sales Amount to complete the expression, as shown here.

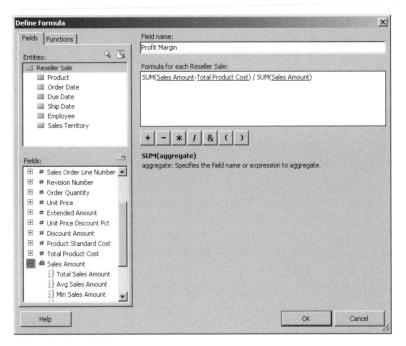

10. Click OK to close the Define Formula dialog box.

Profit Margin appears as a new field at the top of the Fields list. You can now use this field like any other field from the report model.

> **Tip** Adding a field to perform a calculation is a simple task for report developers accustomed to building expressions, but casual users might find it intimidating. You should ask users to tell you about commonly used expressions that you can add to the report model to simplify the report development process for them.

11. Drag Total Total Product Cost to the right of Avg Sales Amount in the table, and then drag Profit Margin to the right of Total Total Product Cost.

12. Click the Total Total Product Cost detail cell (the cell below the column header), and then, while pressing Shift, click the last cell in the column to select all four data cells in the column. Right-click one of the selected cells, and then select Format.

13. In the Format dialog box, in the Format list, select $1,234.56, and click OK.

14. Click the Profit Margin detail cell (the cell below the column header), and then, while pressing Shift, click the last cell in the column to select all four data cells in the column. Right-click one of the selected cells, and then select Format.

15. In the Format dialog box, in the Format list, select 1,234.56%.

16. Click the Alignment tab, select Right in the Horizontal drop-down list, and then click OK.

17. Click Run Report to preview the report, as shown here.

Reseller Sales

Sales Territory Group	Sales Territory Country	Sales Territory Region	Total Sales Amount	Avg Sales Amount	Total Total Product Cost	Profit Margin
Europe	France	France	$4,607,537.94	$1,305.25	$4,644,847.54	-0.81 %
		Total	**$4,607,537.94**	**$1,305.25**	**$4,644,847.54**	-0.81 %
	Germany	Germany	$1,983,988.04	$1,078.84	$2,095,241.74	-5.61 %
		Total	**$1,983,988.04**	**$1,078.84**	**$2,095,241.74**	-5.61 %
	United Kingdom	United Kingdom	$4,279,008.83	$1,215.63	$4,272,626.92	0.15 %
		Total	**$4,279,008.83**	**$1,215.63**	**$4,272,626.92**	0.15 %
	Total		*$10,870,534.80*	*$1,222.92*	*$11,012,716.19*	*-1.31 %*
NA	NA	NA				NaN
		Total				NaN
	Total					*NaN*
North America	Canada	Canada	$14,377,925.60	$1,256.37	$14,199,698.51	1.24 %
		Total	**$14,377,925.60**	**$1,256.37**	**$14,199,698.51**	1.24 %
	United States	Central	$7,906,008.18	$1,360.29	$7,765,449.57	1.78 %
		Northeast	$6,932,842.01	$1,193.47	$6,855,591.62	1.11 %
		Northwest	$12,435,076.00	$1,579.66	$12,214,179.23	1.78 %
		Southeast	$7,867,416.23	$1,325.15	$7,747,344.30	1.53 %
		Southwest	$18,466,458.79	$1,380.26	$18,482,078.69	-0.08 %
		Total	**$53,607,801.21**	**$1,381.32**	**$53,064,643.42**	1.01 %
	Total		*$67,985,726.81*	*$1,352.87*	*$67,264,341.93*	*1.06 %*

 Tip The NaN value in the Profit Margin column indicates an error caused by an attempt to divide by zero. To prevent this error from appearing on the report, you could modify the expression to include the *IF* function to test the value of SUM(SalesAmount) and perform the division only if SUM(SalesAmount) is not equal to zero. To edit the expression, right-click the field in the Fields list, select Edit to open the Define Formula dialog box, and change the expression as needed.

18. On the File menu, select Save.

Filtering a Report

When viewing a report by using Report Builder, you can apply a filter to constrain the result set returned by the report query generated by Report Builder. If you plan to publish the report to a report server, you can create a dynamic filter that allows any user to change the filter condition on demand without opening Report Builder.

In this procedure, you add filters to your report to exclude the NA sales territory and to prompt the user to select one or more product categories.

Apply a filter

1. On the toolbar, click Filter.

2. In the Filter Data dialog box, in the Entities list, select Reseller Sales, and then select Product.

3. In the Fields list, double-click Category.

   By default, the filter condition uses the Equals operator to limit the filter criteria to a single value. You can change the operator to In A List to support multiple selections as filter criteria. To create a condition that compares a field value to the filter criteria, you can also use the Greater Than, Greater Than Or Equals, Less Than, or Less Than Or Equals comparative operators. You can also use the range operator From...To to filter for a range of values. Additional options for string fields include Is Blank Or Empty, Is Blank, Is Empty, and Contains.

4. To the right of Category, click the Equals link (which does not appear as a link until you point to it), and then select In A List to change the operator.

5. Click the (No Values Selected) link, select the Bikes check box in the drop-down list, and then click anywhere in the dialog box to close the drop-down list.

   If you click OK at this point, the report displays the filtered data, but the only way to change the filter criteria is to open the Filter dialog box, which you can do only when viewing the report with Report Builder. To enable users accessing the report on the report server to change the filter criteria, you should add a prompt.

6. Click the Category link in the filter expression, and select Prompt.

   Notice that the shortcut menu that displays when you click the Category link also includes the Edit As Formula command to allow you to replace the selected field with a complex expression. The shortcut menu also includes a Remove Prompt command to delete the filter when it's no longer needed.

   When you select Prompt on the shortcut menu, a question mark icon appears to the left of the filter expression as a visual cue that the prompt feature has been enabled.

7. In the Entities list, select Sales Territory, and then, in the Fields list, double-click Sales Territory Group.

   Rather than use a filter to choose which values to include in the report, you can also use it to exclude a specific value.

8. Click the Equals link, and then select Not.

9. In the (Unspecified) drop-down list, select NA.

The Filter Data dialog box now looks like this:

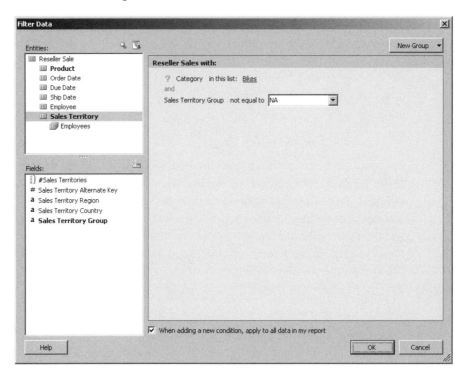

When you use multiple conditions in the filter, you can specify the relationship between the conditions for evaluating the filter criteria. The two conditions in the Filter Data dialog box are currently connected with the And operator, which requires both conditions to be true. You can click the And link to change to the Or operator when you want to define a filter for which either condition could be true.

You can also create condition groups that you can consider to be the logical equivalent of placing parentheses around a set of conditions to control the order of processing. To create a condition group, click the New Group button in the upper-right corner of the Filter Data dialog box. The type of group that you select after clicking this button determines which operator is used between conditions in the group. For example, if you select the All Of group type, the And operator is used to link the group's conditions, but if you select the Any Of group type, the Or operator is used instead. You can nest condition groups by dragging one condition group into a second group or create adjacent condition groups by dragging a condition group out of its parent group.

10. Click OK to close the Filter Data dialog box.

Notice that a Category prompt displays above the report, but there is no prompt for Sales Territory Group.

11. Scroll to the bottom of the page to view the description of filters applied to the report, as shown here.

Filter: Reseller Sales with: All of (Category in (prompted), Sales Territory Group ≠ "NA")

Although there is no prompt for Sales Territory Group prompt, the filter to exclude NA is specified in the filter description on the report.

12. In the Category drop-down list, clear the Bikes check box, select the Accessories check box, and then click View Report.

Sorting Data

Report Builder includes the Sort and Group button on the toolbar so that you can specify the default sort order of the data by group. You can also indicate whether to add page breaks between groups. The user can still use the interactive sort feature to apply a custom sort.

In this procedure, you define a sort order to list rows in descending order of profit margin and then alphabetically by sales territory group.

Apply a default sort order to each group

1. In the toolbar, click Sort And Group.

2. In the Sort dialog box, in the Select Group list, select Sales Territory Group.

3. In the Sort By drop-down list, select Profit Margin, and select Descending.

4. In the first Then By drop-down list, select Sales Territory Group, as shown here.

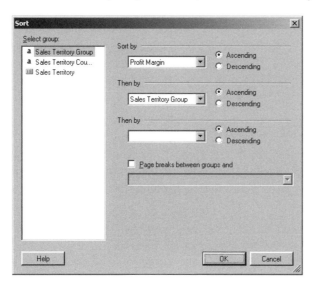

With this sort definition, the Sales Territory Group field values display the most profit-able sales territory group first and then each subsequent sales territory group displays in descending order of profitability. When a profit margin tie exists, alphabetical order prevails.

5. In the Select Group list, select Sales Territory Country, select Profit Margin in the Sort By drop-down list, select Descending, and then, in the first Then By drop-down list, select Sales Territory Country, and keep the default sort order as Ascending.

6. In the Select Group list, select Sales Territory, select Profit Margin in the Sort By drop-down list, select Descending, and then, in the first Then By drop-down list, select Sales Territory Region, and click OK.

The sorted report looks like this:

Sales Territory Group	Sales Territory Country	Sales Territory Region	Total Sales Amount	Avg Sales Amount	Total Total Product Cost	Profit Margin
		Northwest	$10,400,537.66	$3,163.18	$10,402,404.30	-0.02 %
		Southeast	$6,698,867.28	$2,623.92	$6,705,876.62	-0.10 %
		Northeast	$5,669,526.09	$2,321.67	$5,718,845.38	-0.87 %
		Southwest	$15,305,362.16	$2,728.71	$15,657,361.03	-2.30 %
		Total	**$44,832,751.73**	**$2,723.90**	$45,229,001.68	-0.88 %
	Canada	Canada	$11,636,380.59	$2,619.63	$11,748,166.57	-0.96 %
		Total	**$11,636,380.59**	**$2,619.63**	$11,748,166.57	-0.96 %
	Total		*$56,469,132.32*	*$2,701.74*	$56,977,168.24	-0.90 %
Europe	United Kingdom	United Kingdom	$3,405,747.21	$2,566.50	$3,484,974.94	-2.33 %
		Total	**$3,405,747.21**	**$2,566.50**	$3,484,974.94	-2.33 %
	France	France	$3,560,665.65	$3,032.93	$3,696,178.99	-3.81 %
		Total	**$3,560,665.65**	**$3,032.93**	$3,696,178.99	-3.81 %
	Germany	Germany	$1,543,015.65	$2,453.13	$1,678,793.37	-8.80 %
		Total	**$1,543,015.65**	**$2,453.13**	$1,678,793.37	-8.80 %
	Total		*$8,509,428.50*	*$2,718.57*	$8,859,947.30	-4.12 %
Pacific	Australia	Australia	$1,323,820.73	$1,721.48	$1,455,965.91	-9.98 %
		Total	**$1,323,820.73**	**$1,721.48**	$1,455,965.91	-9.98 %
	Total		*$1,323,820.73*	*$1,721.48*	$1,455,965.91	-9.98 %
Grand Total			**$66,302,381.56**	**$2,673.48**	$67,293,081.45	-1.49 %

Disabling Interactive Features

A Report Builder report automatically includes certain interactive features. As you have already seen in your reports, interactive sort is enabled for all columns in a table and for all row group columns in a matrix. If your report has a specific sort order defined, you might not want to allow the user to use the interactive sort feature. Similarly, in a matrix report, you can expand and collapse groups that you might want to disable. You can change the report's properties to turn off these features when necessary.

In this procedure, you disable the interactive sort in the Reseller Sales report and disable the group expansion feature in the Reseller Sales Matrix report.

Disable interactive sort and group expansion

1. On the Report menu, select Report Properties.

2. In the Report Properties dialog box, clear the Allow Users To Sort The Report Data When They View It check box, as shown here.

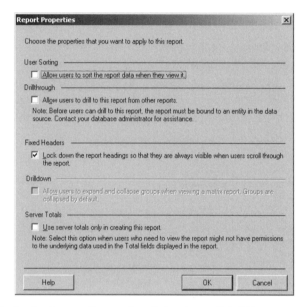

3. In the Report Properties dialog box, click OK.

   Notice that the interactive sort icons have been removed from the report.

4. In the toolbar, click Save.

5. On the File menu, select Open From File.

6. In the Open dialog box, navigate to the Microsoft Press\Rs2008sbs\Workspace folder in your Documents folder, and double-click Reseller Sales Matrix.

7. Click Run Report.

   The report currently permits the user to expand Group to view Country, and to expand Country to view Region. Open the report properties to disable this capability.

8. In the Report Properties dialog box, clear the Allow Users To Expand And Collapse Groups When Viewing A Matrix Report check box, and click OK.

   The report now expands all groups so that you can see Group, Country, and Region, but you cannot collapse the groups to return to the original view of the report.

9. On the File menu, select Save To File, and then, in the File Name box, type **Reseller Sales Matrix Expanded**, and click Save.

Working with Clickthrough

If you are using Microsoft SQL Server Enterprise or SQL Server Developer, Report Builder includes a special feature called clickthrough. If the report model is designed to support clickthrough (which is called drillthrough in the report model and described in Chapter 9), then a user can explore data interactively by clicking a text box to view the underlying details comprising the selected value (such as a sales amount) or associated with a selected record (such as a product name).

Opening a Clickthrough Report

A user can detect that a clickthrough report is available by pointing to a text box on the report. If the pointer changes to a hand symbol, then the user can click the text box and a new report is created based on the selected text box. If the text box displays summary data, then the new report will contain all the records that are included in that summary. On the other hand, if the text box represents a single item, then the report will show additional information about that item.

In this procedure, you explore reseller sales information by opening clickthrough reports.

Open clickthrough reports

1. In the Reseller Sales Matrix report, click the text box in the details row at the intersection of France and 2002 to view the sales transactions that comprise this sales amount in a clickthrough report, as shown here.

Reseller Sales

Sales Order Number	Sales Order Line Number	Product Product	Order Date Date	Sales Amount	Order Quantity
SO46623	1	Mountain-300 Black, 38	7/1/2002	$647.99	1
SO46623	2	ML Mountain Rear Wheel	7/1/2002	$141.62	1
SO46623	3	HL Mountain Frame - Silver, 42	7/1/2002	$1,488.55	2
SO46626	1	Half-Finger Gloves, M	7/1/2002	$42.39	3
SO46626	2	Women's Tights, L	7/1/2002	$179.98	4
SO46626	3	Long-Sleeve Logo Jersey, M	7/1/2002	$57.68	2
SO46626	4	LL Mountain Rear Wheel	7/1/2002	$52.65	1
SO46626	5	Mountain-200 Black, 46	7/1/2002	$3,688.38	3
SO46626	6	Men's Bib-Shorts, M	7/1/2002	$215.98	4
SO46626	7	Mountain-300 Black, 40	7/1/2002	$1,295.99	2
SO46626	8	Mountain-300 Black, 44	7/1/2002	$647.99	1
SO46626	9	Sport-100 Helmet, Blue	7/1/2002	$45.42	3
SO46626	10	HL Mountain Frame - Silver, 38	7/1/2002	$744.27	1
SO46626	11	ML Mountain Frame - Black, 48	7/1/2002	$837.02	4
SO46626	12	HL Mountain Rear Wheel	7/1/2002	$392.66	2
SO46626	13	Mountain-300 Black, 48	7/1/2002	$2,591.98	4
SO46626	14	Sport-100 Helmet, Red	7/1/2002	$30.28	2
SO46626	15	Men's Bib-Shorts, S	7/1/2002	$269.97	5
SO46626	16	Mountain-200 Black, 38	7/1/2002	$9,835.67	8

You can determine whether a clickthrough report is available when the pointer changes to a hand symbol. By default, the clickthrough report is generated on demand by the report server when you click a field for which the *EnableDrillthrough* property value is *True*, as defined by the report model developer. The columns in the clickthrough report's table are defined by the *DefaultDetailAttributes* property for the parent entity of the field in the selected text box and are used in the SELECT clause for the click-through report query. The query also depends on the context of the text box that you clicked. That is, the field values on the row and column of that text box, in addition to the filter specifications on the report, become conditions in a WHERE clause for the clickthrough report query.

If the query generated for the clickthrough report returns multiple instances, the results display in a table with a row for the column headers and with details in rows below the column headers. In the next step, you see the clickthrough report for a single instance.

2. Click the first Sales Order Number, SO46623, to view the transaction detail for the sale of the Mountain-300 Black, 38 bike, as shown here.

Reseller Sale

Sales Order Number	SO46623
Sales Order Line Number	1
Product Product	Mountain-300 Black, 38
Order Date Date	7/1/2002
Sales Amount	$647.99
Order Quantity	1
#Reseller Sales	1
Reseller Key	337
Promotion Key	1
Currency Key	100
Revision Number	1
Unit Price	647.99
Extended Amount	647.99
Unit Price Discount Pct	0.0
Discount Amount	0.0
Product Standard Cost	598.44
Total Product Cost	598.44
Tax Amt	51.84
Freight	16.20
Carrier Tracking Number	7E34-4681-95
Customer PO Number	PO13514159069

When the clickthrough report query returns a single instance, the result is displayed as a simple table, with field headings in the first column and the field values in the second column. The single-instance clickthrough report first lists the fields that are configured in the *DefaultDetailAttributes* property in the report model, and then lists all other fields associated with the entity.

You can continue generating a new clickthrough report so long as the report you are currently viewing displays a field that supports clickthrough.

3. Click Mountain-300 Black, 38 to view the details for this product.

At any time, you can return to the previous report.

4. Click the Back To Parent Report button on the toolbar, shown here, three times to return to the original report.

Back to Parent Report

Configuring a Custom Clickthrough Report

Instead of defining the structure of the clickthrough report in the report model, you can use Report Builder to develop a custom clickthrough report. After you construct the report, you must change the report server properties to make it accessible for clickthrough.

In this procedure, you configure report properties for clickthrough and modify the report in Report Designer.

Configure a report for clickthrough

1. On the File menu, click New.

2. In the Getting Started pane, select Table (Columnar), click OK, and click No when prompted whether to save changes.

3. In the Entities list, double-click Product to add the default attributes to the report.

> **Note** In a production environment, you would spend more time designing the report. In this procedure, your focus is on the configuration of the report rather than its design. Later in this procedure, you learn about enhancing the format of a custom clickthrough report.

4. On the Report menu, select Report Properties, select the Allow Users To Drill to This Report From Other Reports check box, and then click OK.

   Setting this property adds a special drillthrough parameter to the report. When you deploy the report to the report server, you cannot open the report directly. You can view the report only when it opens in response to a clickthrough request and only when you associate the report with an entity in the report model, which you will do in the next procedure. Before you associate the report with the report model, you must deploy the report to the report server, and then you can edit it in BI Dev Studio.

5. Save the report to the report server.

   ❑ *Native mode:* On the File menu, select Save As, select *http://<servername> /ReportServer* in the Look In drop-down list, type **ProductDetail** in the Name text box, and click Save.

   ❑ *Integrated mode:* On the File menu, select Save As, double-click Ad Hoc Reports, type **ProductDetail** in the Name text box, and click Save.

6. In Internet Explorer, in the Web application, download the report definition file from the properties page of the report.

   ❑ *Native mode:* Navigate to *http://<servername>/reports* (replacing *<servername>* with the name of your server), click the Refresh button on the toolbar, click the ProductDetail link, click the Properties tab, click the Edit link, click Save in the File

Download message box, navigate to the Microsoft Press\Rs2008sbs\Workspace folder in your Documents folder, and click Save twice.

❏ *Integrated mode:* Navigate to *http://<servername>/sites/ssrs*, replacing *<servername>* with the name of your server. In the navigation bar, click the Reports link, click the Ad Hoc Reports folder link, point to the ProductDetail report, click the Edit button that appears to the right of the report title, select Send To, and select Download A Copy. In the File Download message box, click Save, navigate to the Microsoft Press\Rs2008sbs\Workspace folder in your Documents folder, and click Save twice.

7. Start BI Dev Studio. On the File menu, select New, and select Project.

8. In the New Project dialog box, in the Name text box, type **Clickthrough**.

9. Click Browse, navigate to the Microsoft Press\Rs2008sbs\Workspace folder in your Documents folder, and then click OK twice.

10. In Solution Explorer, right-click the Reports folder, select Add, select Existing Item, navigate to the Microsoft Press\Rs2008sbs\Workspace folder in your Documents folder, and double-click ProductDetail.rdl.

11. In Solution Explorer, double-click ProductDetail.rdl.

12. Click the text box containing <Expr> at the bottom of the page to select it, and then press Delete. Repeat this step to delete the other two text boxes for the report title and footer on the page.

You can modify the formatting of this report in any way you like. You can add rows, delete columns, and rearrange or reformat fields in the data region. You can even add additional data regions to which you can add fields from the dataset. However, you cannot add new datasets or parameters to the report.

13. In the Report Data window, right-click the Images folder, select Add Image, navigate to Microsoft Press\Rs2008sbs\Chap04, select BMP Files in the Files Of Type drop-down list, and double-click Logo.bmp.

14. Drag the logo image from the Report Data pane to the upper-left corner of the report, click OK to close the Image Properties dialog box, and then, if necessary, drag the image up so that it does not overlap the data region.

15. In Solution Explorer, right-click Clickthrough, and select Properties.

16. Update the project properties to specify the target destination for the report.

❏ *Native mode:* In the TargetServerURL text box, type **http://<servername>/reportserver** (replacing *<servername>* with the name of your server), and click OK.

❏ *Integrated mode:* Change the TargetDataSourceFolder to **http://<servername>/sites/ssrs/Data Connections**, change the TargetReportFolder to **http://<servername>/sites/ssrs/ReportsLibrary/Ad Hoc Reports**, and change the

TargetServerURL to **http://<*servername*>/sites/ssrs**. Replace <*servername*> with your computer name in all these instances. Click OK.

> **Tip** In a production environment, you might consider deploying the reports to a folder dedicated to clickthrough reports.

17. In Solution Explorer, right-click ProductDetail.rdl, and select Deploy.

> **Note** An error message tells you that the shared data source cannot be found. You can safely ignore this message. The report model is configured correctly in the report definition.

Now that you have configured the report successfully for clickthrough and enhanced the report by adding an image, your next task is to link the report to the report model, which you learn to do in the next procedure.

Assigning a Custom Clickthrough Report to a Report Model

You can replace the default generic clickthrough report generated by the report server with a custom report. You must create the report in Report Builder, but you can enhance the report in Report Designer. You can then associate the custom report with a specific entity in the report model. When you configure the association between the custom report and the report model, you must indicate whether the report should be used when the clickthrough action returns a single instance or when it returns multiple instances.

In this procedure, you assign a custom clickthrough report as a single-instance report for the Product entity in the Reseller Sales report model.

Assign a custom clickthrough report to a report model

1. In Internet Explorer, open the top-level folder for report server content.

   ❑ *Native mode:* Navigate to *http://<servername>/reports*, replacing <*servername*> with the name of your server.

   ❑ *Integrated mode:* Navigate to the Report Center site at *http://localhost/sites/ssrs*, and then, in the navigation bar, click the Reports link.

2. Open the clickthrough management page for the report model.

   ❑ *Native mode:* Click the Models folder, click the Reseller Sales link, and then click the Clickthrough link.

   ❑ *Integrated mode:* Point to the Reseller Sales link, click the Edit button that appears to the right of the model title, and select Manage Clickthrough Reports.

3. Assign the Product Detail report as the single-instance report for the Product entity.

❏ *Native mode:* In the model tree, select Product, click the Browse button to the right of the Single Instance Report box, expand the Clickthrough folder, select ProductDetail, and click OK to assign the single-instance report, as shown here.

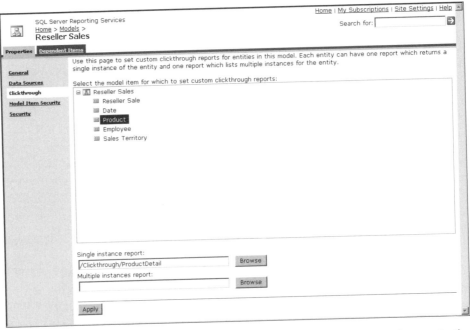

❏ *Integrated mode:* In the model tree, select Product, click the ellipsis button to the right of the Single Instance box, click the Ad Hoc Reports folder link, and double-click ProductDetail to assign the single-instance report, as shown here.

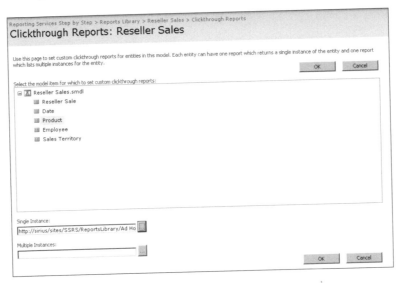

4. Save your changes.

❑ *Native mode:* Click Apply.

❑ *Integrated mode:* Click OK.

Now you're ready to test the clickthrough report.

5. Open the Reseller Sales report and clickthrough to the Product Details report, as shown here.

❑ *Native mode:* Click the Home link, click the Reseller Sales link, click the text box at the intersection of Central and Total Sales Amount, and then click the text box on the top detail row in the Product column.

❑ *Integrated mode:* Click the Ad Hoc Reports folder link, click the Reseller Sales link, click the text box at the intersection of Central and Total Sales Amount, and then click the text box in the Product column containing Mountain-100 Silver, 44.

To ensure a positive user experience in Report Builder, it's very important that you take care when building the report model to include only the fields required for ad hoc reporting and to set properties used for aggregations, sorting, and clickthrough correctly. You should invest the time to test your report model by building ad hoc reports that explore each field and clickthrough path.

Chapter 14 Quick Reference

To	Do This
Start Report Builder	*Native mode:* In Report Manager, click Report Builder.
	Integrated mode: In a SharePoint document library that is configured to use the Report Builder Report content type, click the arrow to the right of the New button on the document library toolbar, and select Report Builder Report.
Create a report	In Report Builder, in the Getting Started pane, select a report model, select a report layout option, and click OK.

To	Do This
Apply formatting	Select one or more text boxes, click a button on the Formatting toolbar or right-click one of the selected text boxes, select Format, and set options in the Format dialog box.
Add a formula field	In the Entities list, select an entity to associate with the field, and then click New Field. In the Define Formula dialog box, type a name, and then select items from the Fields list and from the Function list to construct a formula.
Add a filter	On the toolbar, click Filter, select an entity, and then double-click a field, click the operator link to change it if necessary, and specify a value for the filter criteria. If you want, click the first link in the expression and select Prompt to create a parameter for the report.
Apply a default sort order	In the toolbar, click the Sort And Group button. In the Sort dialog box, select a group, select a field in the Sort By drop-down list, and select a sort direction. You can add second- and third-level sorts by using the two Then By drop-down lists in the Sort dialog box.
Disable interactive features	On the Report menu, select Report Properties, and clear the Allow Users To Sort The Report Data When They View It check box or clear the Allow Users To Expand And Collapse Groups When Viewing A Matrix Report check box.
Open a clickthrough report	Click a text box that changes the pointer to a hand symbol.
Return to a parent report	Click the Back To Parent button on the toolbar.
Configure a clickhrough report	On the Report menu, select Report Properties, and select the Allow Users To Drill to This Report From Other Reports check box. Deploy the report to a report server.
Download a report definition file from a report server	*Native mode:* In Report Manager, click the report link, click the Properties tab, click the Edit link, click Save in the File Download message box, navigate to the target folder, click Save, and click Close. *Integrated mode:* In a SharePoint document library, point to the report, click the Edit button that appears to the right of the report title, select Send To, and select Download A Copy. In the File Download message box, click Save, navigate to the target folder, click Save, and click Close.
Assign a custom clickthrough report to a report model	*Native mode:* In Report Manager, click the model link, click the Clickthrough link, select an entity, click Browse to the right of the report type to assign, and select a report from the report server. *Integrated mode:* In a SharePoint document library, point to the model, click the Edit button that appears to the right of the model title, select Manage Clickthrough Reports, select an entity, click the ellipsis button to the right of the report type to assign, and select a report from the report server.

Chapter 15
Working with Subscriptions

After completing this chapter, you will be able to:

- Create a standard subscription to send a file to an e-mail recipient or a file share.

- Create a data-driven subscription to send a report to multiple destinations in multiple formats with different parameter values.

- Create a shared schedule.

- Review the status of a subscription.

- Delete a subscription.

Rather than require users to connect to the report server to view reports, you can use Reporting Services to send reports to users via e-mail or to a network folder. If you're running a report server in SharePoint integrated mode, you can also send reports to a Microsoft SharePoint document library. Regardless of which delivery method you use, you can send a report in any rendering format so that users can get reports when they want in the file type they want. In this chapter, you learn how to create and manage subscriptions to provide flexible report delivery.

 Important To complete the procedures in this chapter, you must have successfully completed Chapter 10, "Deploying Reports to a Server," so that you have the reports that are used in these procedures available on the report server and so that the data source is configured to use stored credentials, which is required to create a subscription.

Creating Standard Subscriptions

A *standard subscription* is a subscription that delivers a specific report to one or more e-mail accounts or to a designated network file share on a scheduled basis. By default, the Browser role (described in Chapter 11, "Securing Report Server Content") gives users permission to manage individual subscriptions. That is, users can create, view, modify, and delete the subscriptions that they own. The Content Manager role can manage subscriptions created by anyone. Not only must the user be assigned to the proper security role to create a new subscription, but the data source for the report must use stored credentials, as you learned in Chapter 10.

Creating an E-Mail Subscription

Recipients of a report created by an e-mail subscription receive an identical copy of the report. When you define the subscription, you provide a list of recipients and specify the contents of the e-mail. For example, you can specify whether the e-mail includes the report as an attachment for offline viewing in addition to or instead of a link to the report on the report server. At a minimum, you can send just a notification that the report is ready for viewing on the report server. You then establish a schedule for the subscription using either a schedule specific to the report or a global schedule established on the report server. If you want, you can override the report's default parameter values.

Before you can create an e-mail subscription, Reporting Services requires you to specify a Simple Mail Transport Protocol (SMTP) server in the report server configuration settings. Using the Reporting Services Configuration Manager (described in Chapter 2, "Installing Reporting Services"), you configure the SMTP server address and an e-mail address to use as the From: address. If you skip the configuration, the e-mail delivery option is not available when you try to create a subscription.

> **Important** The SQL Server Agent service must be running before you start creating a subscription. If the service is not running, an error message displays when you attempt to save the subscription settings.

In this procedure, you create an e-mail subscription for the Reseller Sales Margin Analysis By Sales Territory report to send the report to yourself on a report-specific schedule as an embedded MIME Encapsulation of Aggregate HTML Documents (MHTML) message.

Create an e-mail subscription

1. In Windows Internet Explorer, open the Web application for your report server type and navigate to the folder containing the Reseller Sales Margin Analysis By Sales Territory report.

   ❑ *Native mode:* Navigate to *http://<servername>/reports*, replacing *<servername>* with the name of your server, and then click the Sales folder link.

   ❑ *Integrated mode:* Navigate to *http://<servername>/sites/ssrs*, replacing *<servername>* with the name of your server. In the navigation bar, click the Reports link.

2. Open the subscriptions page of the Reseller Sales Margin Analysis By Sales Territory report.

   ❑ *Native mode:* Click the Reseller Sales Margin Analysis By Sales Territory link. Notice the New Subscription button above the HTML Viewer. Click the

Subscriptions tab, and notice the New Subscription button on this page. Each button opens the same subscription definition page.

❑ *Integrated mode:* Point to the Reseller Sales Margin Analysis By Sales Territory report, click the Edit button that appears to the right of the report title, and select Manage Subscriptions.

3. Create a new subscription.

❑ *Native mode:* Click New Subscription.

❑ *Integrated mode:* Click Add Subscription.

4. Review the delivery extension options.

If you have configured the report server's e-mail settings properly, the default delivery extension is E-mail. Otherwise, your only option is to use Windows File Share (which you use in the next procedure). You can develop or purchase third-party delivery extensions to provide additional delivery methods to users.

❑ *Native mode:* Open the Delivered By drop-down list to review the options, but keep the default value of E-mail.

❑ *Integrated mode:* Open the Delivery Extension drop-down list to review the options, but keep the default value of E-mail.

5. In the To text box, type your e-mail address.

> **Tip** If you are using Windows Server 2003, you can use an alias instead of an e-mail address. This operating system resolves the correct e-mail address automatically. However, you must use an e-mail address if you are using Windows Vista or Windows Server 2008 because neither of these operating systems performs the same type of alias resolution as Windows Server 2003.

If you are a member of the Browser role, you can create a subscription only for yourself and cannot add other recipients to the subscription. Your Microsoft Windows account displays in the To: text box and cannot be changed. If you are a member of the Content Manager role, you can create a subscription for multiple recipients by adding e-mail addresses to the To:, Cc:, and Bcc: text boxes.

When configuring the e-mail subscription, you can specify a Reply-To address that is different from the e-mail's sender address. You can also establish a priority and add a comment, if you want.

If you want to send the report as an attachment only, you select the Include Report check box and clear the Include Link check box. Conversely, if you want to send only a link to the report, you select the Include Link check box and clear the Include Report check box. You also can select these two check boxes to include both the report and the link, which is the default configuration for the e-mail subscription. If you intend to send the report in the attachment, you must specify a render format. All the render formats available for export when viewing a report are also available for the e-mail subscription. However, the MHTML (Web Archive) format is not sent as an attachment, but is embedded into the body of the e-mail message.

6. Clear the option to include a link to the report in the body of the e-mail.

   ❏ *Native mode:* Clear the Include Link check box.

   ❏ *Integrated mode:* Clear the Include A Link To The Report check box.

7. Set the render format for the subscription to MTHML (Web Archive) to embed the message as MHTML in the body of the e-mail.

   ❏ *Native mode:* Open the Render Format drop-down list to review the options, but keep the default value of MHTML (Web Archive).

   ❏ *Integrated mode:* Open the Format drop-down list to review the options, but keep the default value of MHTML (Web Archive).

8. Specify a report-specific schedule for the report to execute once at a specific time.

   A report-specific schedule applies only to the subscription that you are creating. If you have several reports, each with its own report-specific schedule, any change that you might want to make to the schedules later requires you to open each report and modify the schedule settings. On the other hand, if you create a shared schedule that you use with multiple subscriptions (as described in the section entitled "Creating a Shared Schedule" later in this chapter), you need only change the settings of the shared schedule. For now, you create a report-specific schedule so you can see how it works.

   ❏ *Native mode:* Click Select Schedule, select Once to specify the frequency of the report, enter a start time that is 3 minutes ahead of the current time, select the correct A.M. or P.M. option, as shown here, and click OK.

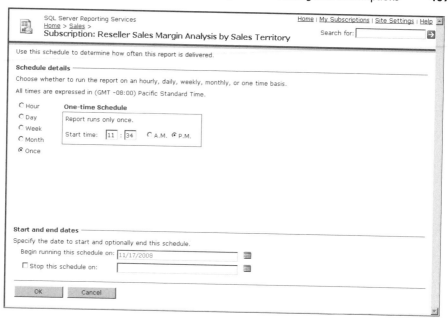

- ❏ *Integrated mode:* Click Configure, and select Once in the Frequency section. In the Start Time text box, type a time that is 3 minutes ahead of the current time, select the correct A.M. or P.M. option, and click OK.

If you are running a SharePoint integrated-mode report server, in addition to the report-specific or shared schedule options, you also have the option to send a report using an e-mail subscription when a report snapshot is created.

9. Replace the Sales Territory Group parameter value with Pacific.

- ❏ *Native mode:* In the Report Parameter Values section, in the SalesTerritoryGroup drop-down list, clear the Europe and North America check boxes (leaving only the Pacific check box selected), as shown here, and click OK.

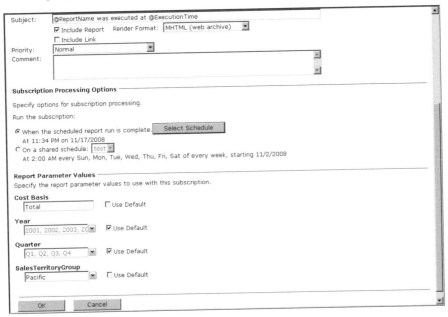

- □ *Integrated mode:* In the Parameter section, under SalesTerritoryGroup, select Override Report Default, select Pacific in the drop-down list, and select OK.

10. After three minutes, click the Refresh button on the Internet Explorer toolbar to view the status of the subscription.

When the subscription runs successfully, the Last Run column displays the date and time of the subscription execution, and the Status column shows the action taken, such as Mail Sent, and the target of the delivery, such as the e-mail recipient.

Tip If the Status displays The E-Mail Address Of One Or More Recipients Is Not Valid, and you know that you have specified a valid e-mail address, you should check the SMTP server properties. If you have implemented an SMTP server by using Internet Information Services (IIS), in the Administrative Tools program group on the SMTP server, open Internet Information Services (IIS) Manager. Right-click Default SMTP Virtual Server and select Properties. In the Default SMTP Virtual Server Properties dialog box, click the Access tab, and then click Relay. In the Relay Restrictions dialog box, if Only The List Below is selected but the list is empty, you can change the selection to All Except The List Below and click OK until all dialog boxes are closed. By making this change, the SMTP server should accept the e-mail addresses defined in the subscription. If the relay restrictions list is not empty, then you should work with your network administrator and refer to the topic "Troubleshooting Subscription and Delivery Problems" in SQL Server Books Online to resolve the problem.

Creating a Windows File Share Subscription

Another commonly used method for sharing reports is to make them accessible on a Windows file share that you identify by using the Universal Naming Convention (UNC) for the folder. For example, you might store a PDF version of files on a Web server for access by external users that do not have access to your internal network. A single copy of the report created by a Windows file share subscription is placed in the target location. You must configure the subscription to use a Windows account that has permissions to write to the target location. If you create a recurring subscription, you can specify whether an existing file on the file share is overwritten by the new file or if you want to append a number to the file name that automatically increments as each new file is added to the file share. Just as you do with e-mail subscriptions, you define a schedule for Windows file share subscription using a report-specific schedule or a shared schedule. You can also override the report's default parameter values, if you want.

In this procedure, you create a Windows file share and then create a subscription for the Pacific Reseller Sales Margin Analysis report to store a copy of the report in the shared folder on a report-specific schedule.

Create a Windows file share subscription

1. Share the Workspace folder, which is located in the Microsoft Press\Rs2008sbs folder in your Documents folder, with a specific Windows account.

    > **Important** This step explicitly grants the Change permission to your Windows account on the Workspace folder, which is a permission level your account already implicitly has. In a production environment, the folder to share would not be in your Documents folder and you must therefore configure permissions to the shared folder for the Windows account that you associate with the subscription later in this procedure.

    ❑ *Windows Server 2003 or Windows XP with simple file sharing disabled:* Open Windows Explorer, navigate to the Microsoft Press\Rs2008sbs folder in your Documents folder, right-click the Workspace folder, and then select Sharing And Security. On the Sharing tab of the Workspace Properties dialog box, select Share This Folder, and then click Permissions. In the Permissions For Workspace dialog box, click Add. In the Select Users Or Groups dialog box, click Advanced, then click Find Now. In the Search Results list, double-click your Windows account, and click OK. In the Permissions For Workspace dialog box, select Change in the Allow column, and then click OK twice to close all dialog boxes.

❑ *Windows Vista or Windows Server 2008*: Open Windows Explorer, navigate to the Microsoft Press\Rs2008sbs folder in your Documents folder, right-click the Workspace folder, and then select Share. Notice that your account already has Owner permissions, therefore no further action is required. If you were to specify a different account in a production environment, you would select the appropriate user account from the drop-down list that appears to the left of the Add button. If the user account is not visible, then select Find from the drop-down list. In the Select Users Or Groups dialog box, click Advanced, then click Find Now. In the Search Results list, double-click the name of the account, and click OK. In the Permission Level column for the newly added account, click the arrow next to Reader, select Contributor, click Share, and click Done.

2. In Internet Explorer, navigate to the folder containing the Pacific Reseller Sales Margin Analysis report.

❑ *Native mode:* Navigate to *http://<servername>/reports*, replacing *<servername>* with the name of your server, and then click the Sales folder link.

❑ *Integrated mode:* Navigate to *http://<servername>/sites/ssrs*, replacing *<servername>* with the name of your server. In the navigation bar, click the Reports link.

3. Open the subscriptions page of the Pacific Reseller Sales Margin Analysis report.

❑ *Native mode:* Click the Pacific Reseller Sales Margin Analysis report, and then click the Subscriptions tab.

❑ *Integrated mode:* Point to the Pacific Reseller Sales Margin Analysis report, click the Edit button that appears to the right of the report title, and select Manage Subscriptions.

4. Create a new subscription.

❑ *Native mode:* Click New Subscription.

❑ *Integrated mode:* Click Add Subscription.

5. Select the Windows File Share delivery method.

❑ *Native mode:* In the Delivered By drop-down list, select Windows File Share.

❑ *Integrated mode:* In the Delivery Extension drop-down list, select Windows File Share.

When you specify the Windows File Share delivery extension, the screen changes to prompt you for the settings specific to the selected extension.

6. Specify the Workspace folder as the destination for the subscription.

> ❏ *Native mode:* In the Path text box, type **\\\<*servername*>\Workspace**, replacing
> <*servername*> with the name of your server. The file name defaults to the report
> name, but you can change this value if you want.

> ❏ *Integrated mode:* In the File Name text box, type **Pacific Reseller Sales Margin
> Analysis**, and then, in the Path text box, type **\\\<*servername*>\Workspace**,
> replacing <*servername*> with the name of your server.

7. Configure the subscription to add a file extension to the file name.

> ❏ *Native mode:* Keep the Add A File Extension When The File Is Created check box
> selected.

> ❏ *Integrated mode:* In the File Extension drop-down list, select True.

8. In the Render Format drop-down list, select Acrobat (PDF) File.

The same render formats are available for the Windows file share subscription as were
available for the e-mail subscription. Notice that there is an additional render format
called RPL Renderer, which is a special format that combines the report layout and
the data in an intermediate format that can be used by the ReportViewer Web server
control.

9. In the User Name text box, type your account in the format *domain\user name* (or
servername\user name if your computer is not part of a domain), but leave the password blank for now.

Because the password will be removed when you configure the schedule later in this
procedure, you do not need to provide the password in this step.

10. Select the option to increment file names.

> ❏ *Native mode:* In the Overwrite Options section, select Increment File Names As
> Newer Versions Are Added.

> ❏ *Integrated mode:* In the Write mode drop-down list, select Autoincrement.

11. Specify a report-specific schedule for the report to execute once at a specific time.

> ❏ *Native mode:* Click Select Schedule, select Once to specify the frequency of the
> report, enter a start time that is 3 minutes ahead of the current time, select the
> correct A.M. or P.M. option, as shown here, and click OK.

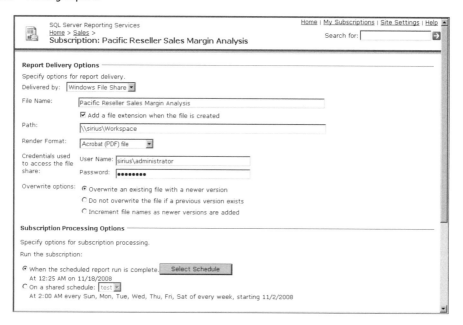

Note In this example, the Sirius server name in the Path string and in the User Name string is fictitious, included for illustration purposes only.

- ❏ *Integrated mode:* Click Configure, and select Once in the Frequency section. In the Start Time text box, type a time that is 3 minutes ahead of the current time, select the correct A.M. or P.M. option, and click OK.

12. In the Password text box, type your password, and click OK.

    For this procedure, you keep the default values for the parameters, although notice that you can override the default values for the subscription.

13. After waiting three minutes, click the Refresh button on the Internet Explorer toolbar to view the status of the subscription.

    If you're running a SharePoint integrated-mode report server, the status looks like this:

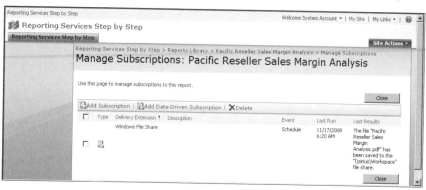

> **Note** In this example, and later in this chapter, the Sirius server name in the file share path that appears in the Last Results column is fictitious, included for illustration purposes only.

14. In Windows Explorer, open the Microsoft Press\Rs2008sbs\Workspace folder.

15. Double-click the Reseller Sales Margin Analysis by Sales Territory.pdf file to open the file in Acrobat Reader.

Understanding the Other Delivery Extensions

There are two additional delivery extension types that might be useful for your reporting environment: Null Delivery Provider and SharePoint Document Library.

Null Delivery Provider

The Null Delivery Provider is available on a report server running in native mode or SharePoint integrated mode. This delivery extension doesn't actually deliver a report; instead, it executes the report so that the report can be cached and ready for viewing on demand. By using this delivery extension, all your users can experience the benefits of a cached report, not just the users that view the report after someone else viewed it.

SharePoint Document Library

The SharePoint Document Library delivery extension is available only on a report server running in SharePoint integrated mode. It delivers a copy of the report to the specified document library, which must be on the same SharePoint site as the report on which the subscription is based. Because the report is a copy, the user experience might not be as fully interactive as the source report. If you have enabled versioning in the document library, the subscription always creates a major version of the report copy, unless you specifically choose no versioning. If you limit the retention of versions, the oldest report version is removed with the newest subscription delivery.

Creating Data-Driven Subscriptions

A *data-driven subscription* is a subscription that delivers the same report to many destinations, each of which might receive a different render format of the report and a different set of parameter values on a recurring basis. The recurrence of a subscription can be defined by a schedule or by the creation of a report snapshot. As you learned in Chapter 10, a report snapshot can be created manually or on a schedule.

You must be assigned to the Content Manager role to configure a data-driven subscription. You must also have a relational table that stores the mapping between destinations (an e-mail address or a file share), report settings, and parameter values. When you configure the data-driven subscription, you provide the query to this table and then assign the values in the query results to specific settings in the subscription configuration.

> **Important**   To create a data-driven subscription, you must be running Microsoft SQL Server 2008 Enterprise or SQL Server 2008 Developer.

Creating a Subscription Delivery Table

Because Reporting Services does not include a table for you to use for storing subscription delivery information, you must create and maintain a table yourself to use the data-driven subscription feature. You can create a table that contains a single column of e-mail addresses for the simplest data-driven subscription, or you can define columns for every subscription setting that can be changed by a value from this table. This flexibility allows you to manage customized subscriptions for individual users easily.

In this procedure, you use SQL Server Management Studio to run a script that creates the SubscriptionDelivery table in the AdventureWorksDW2008 database, and then you review the contents of the new table.

Create a table to support a data-driven subscription

1. Click Start, select All Programs, select Microsoft SQL Server 2008, and select SQL Server Management Studio.

2. In the Connect To Server dialog box, in the Server Type drop-down list, select Database Engine.

3. In the Server Name text box, if necessary, type **localhost** (or the name of your report server), and then, in the Authentication drop-down list, select Windows Authentication. Click Connect.

4. On the File menu, select Open, and then select File.

5. Navigate to the Microsoft Press\Rs2008sbs\Chap15 folder in your Documents folder, and double-click SubscriptionSetup.sql.

This script adds the EuropeMgr and PacificMgr e-mail accounts to the Subscription-Delivery table in the AdventureWorksDW2008 database in addition to the corresponding subscription settings that set the render format type and default parameter values.

6. On the SQL Editor toolbar, click Execute.

7. In Object Explorer, expand the Databases folder, expand the AdventureWorksDW2008 folder, expand the Tables folder, right-click dbo.SubscriptionDelivery, and select Select Top 1000 Rows to view the new table and its contents, as shown here:

	To	IncludeReport	RenderFormat	IncludeLink	ReportParameter
1	EuropeMgr@adventure-works.com	1	Excel	1	Europe
2	PacificMgr@adventure-works.com	1	PDF	0	Pacific

Notice that the render format and the default report parameter for each manager are different. Also, the IncludeLink value determines whether the user can click a link in the e-mail message to open the report on the Web server. When you create a data-driven subscription in the next procedure, you map all data in this table to specific subscription settings.

Creating a Data-Driven Subscription

When you created the standard subscriptions earlier in this chapter, you set the subscription settings manually. In a data-driven subscription, these settings are set dynamically and might change for each row retrieved from the subscription delivery table.

In this procedure, you create a data-driven subscription for the Reseller Sales Margin Analysis by Sales Territory report based on the SubscriptionDelivery table and using a report-specific schedule.

Create a data-driven subscription

1. In Internet Explorer, navigate to the folder containing the Reseller Sales Margin Analysis By Sales Territory report.

- ❏ *Native mode:* Navigate to *http://<servername>/reports*, replacing *<servername>* with the name of your server, and then click the Sales folder link.

- ❏ *Integrated mode:* Navigate to *http://<servername>/sites/ssrs*, replacing *<servername>* with the name of your server. In the navigation bar, click the Reports link.

2. Open the subscriptions page of the Reseller Sales Margin Analysis By Sales Territory report.

    ❏   *Native mode:* Click the Reseller Sales Margin Analysis By Sales Territory report, and then click the Subscriptions tab. There is no option to create the new subscription on the View page of the report. You must access the Subscriptions page.

    ❏   *Integrated mode:* Point to the Reseller Sales Margin Analysis By Sales Territory report, click the Edit button that appears to the right of the report title, and select Manage Subscriptions.

3. Create a new subscription.

    ❏   *Native mode:* Click New Data-Driven Subscription.

    ❏   *Integrated mode:* Click Add Data-Driven Subscription.

4. In the Description text box, type **Reseller Sales Margin Subscription**.

    The description appears in the list of subscriptions on the Subscriptions page for a report. When you need to change or delete a subscription, you can use the description to help you identify it.

5. Specify the shared data source AdventureWorksDW2008 as the source for the subscription delivery table.

    ❏   *Native mode:* In the Specify How Recipients Are Notified drop-down list, select E-mail, select Specify A Shared Data Source, and click Next. In the list of folders, expand Data Sources, select AdventureWorksDW2008, and click Next.

    ❏   *Integrated mode:* Click the ellipsis button to the right of the Data Source Link text box. In the Select An Item - Webpage Dialog dialog box, click Up, click the Data Connections folder link, and double-click AdventureWorksDW2008.

6. Configure the subscription query.

    ❏   *Native mode:* In the text box, type **select * from SubscriptionDelivery**.

    ❏   *Integrated mode:* In the Query text box, type **select * from SubscriptionDelivery**.

7. Click Validate, and then click Next.

8. Configure the subscription's delivery settings (if running in native mode) or configure the subscription's parameter values (if running in integrated mode).

    ❏   *Native mode:* Configure the delivery extension settings according to the following table:

Delivery Setting	Option	Value
To	Get The Value From The Database	To
Reply-To	Specify A Static Value	reports@adventure-works.com
Include Report	Get The Value From The Database	IncludeReport
Render Format	Get The Value From The Database	RenderFormat
Include Link	Get The Value From The Database	IncludeLink

❑   *Integrated mode:* For the SalesTerritoryGroup parameter, select Override Report Default With Value From Database, and then select ReportParameter in the drop-down list.

9. Click Next.

10. Configure the subscription's parameter values if running in native mode or configure the subscription's delivery settings if running in integrated mode.

❑   *Native mode:* For the SalesTerritoryGroup parameter, select Get The Value From The Database, then select ReportParameter in the drop-down list.

❑   *Integrated mode:* In the Delivery Type drop-down list, keep the default, E-Mail. Configure the delivery extension settings according to the following table:

Delivery Setting	Option	Value
To	Select A Value From The Database	To
Reply-To	Specify A Static Value	reports@adventure-works.com
Include Report	Select A Value From The Database	IncludeReport
Render Format	Select A Value From The Database	RenderFormat
Subject	Specify A Static Value	Reseller Sales Margin Analysis
Include Link	Select A Value From The Database	IncludeLink

11. Click Next.

12. Specify a report-specific schedule for the report.

❑   *Native mode:* Select On A Schedule Created For This Subscription, click Next, click Once to specify the frequency of the report, enter a start time that is 3 minutes ahead of the current time, select the correct A.M. or P.M. option, and click Finish.

❑   *Integrated mode:* Select Once in the Frequency section. In the Start Time text box, type a time that is 3 minutes ahead of the current time, select the correct A.M. or P.M. option, and click Finish.

13. After waiting three minutes, refresh the browser window to check the status of the subscription.

Managing Subscriptions

You can manage subscriptions effectively by creating shared schedules, viewing active subscriptions, and deleting subscriptions. A shared schedule makes it easier for users to assign a subscription to a schedule. To view active subscriptions, you must open a report's subscriptions page. There, you can see when the subscription was last run and the status of the last subscription execution. If you are running a native-mode report server, you can also open the My Subscriptions page to view all subscriptions on the server in a single location. You can edit the schedule for a subscription at any time, and when a subscription is no longer needed, you can delete it.

Creating a Shared Schedule

You should create a shared schedule to better manage when reports are executing in the background. You can then pause all subscriptions associated with a schedule at one time whenever you need to perform server maintenance. Your use of a shared schedule is not limited to subscriptions. You can also use shared schedules to generate a report snapshot or to expire the report cache.

In this procedure, you create a shared schedule to run on the first day of every month.

Create a shared schedule

1. In Internet Explorer, open the Web application for your report server.

   ❑ *Native mode:* Click the Site Settings link, and click the Schedules link.

   ❑ *Integrated mode:* Click Site Actions, select Site Settings, and then select Modify All Site Settings. In the Reporting Services section, click the Manage Shared Schedules link.

2. Add a monthly schedule.

   ❑ *Native mode:* Click New Schedule. In the Schedule Name box, type **First Day Of Month**. In the Schedule Details section, select Month. Select On Calendar Day(s), and then in the On Calendar Day(s) text box, replace the default text by typing **1**. Keep the default start date. If you want, you can select the Stop Running This Schedule On check box, and then use the calendar control to select a date. Click OK.

   ❑ *Integrated mode:* Click Add Shared Schedule. In the Schedule Name box, type **First Day Of Month**. In the Frequency section, select Month. In the On Calendar Day(s) text box, replace the default text by typing **1**. Keep the default start date. If you want, you can select the Stop Running This Schedule On check box, and then type a date or use the calendar control to select a date, as shown here. Click OK.

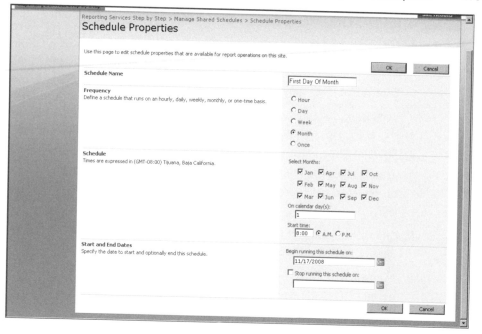

Using the My Subscriptions Page

If you create many subscriptions, you might find it challenging to locate each report on the report server to check the status of each subscription. If you are running a native-mode report server, you can use the My Subscriptions page to see all your own subscriptions. (There is no equivalent available in SharePoint integrated mode.) The link to this page appears at the top of every page in Report Manager. If you are a Content Manager, you cannot use the My Subscriptions page to manage subscriptions for other users. Instead, you must open each report individually and open the report's subscription page to manage subscriptions created by other users.

In this procedure, you create a subscription for the EuropeMgr account and check the results of subscription execution by using the My Subscriptions page.

Review the status of a subscription by using the My Subscriptions page

1. In Report Manager, click the My Subscriptions link in the upper-right corner of the browser window to view all your subscriptions.

2. Click the Last Run link to change the sort order of the subscriptions.

    When you have many subscriptions, you might find it useful to sort the subscriptions in ascending or descending order. Each time you click the Last Run link, the sort order reverses.

3. Click the Edit link to the left of the file share delivery subscription.

4. Click Select Schedule.

5. Change the start time to 5 minutes ahead of the current time, and then click OK.

6. Enter **VP** as both the user name and password, and then click OK.

    Because this account does not have permissions to write a file to the Workspace file share, an error occurs and the status on the My Subscriptions page changes to reflect the error.

7. After waiting five minutes, click the Click the Pacific Reseller Sales Margin Analysis link for the file share subscription, click the Properties tab, and then click the Data Sources link.

8. Change the Connect Using option to The Credentials Supplies By The User Running The Report, then click Apply.

9. After waiting five minutes, refresh the browser window to view the error, as shown here.

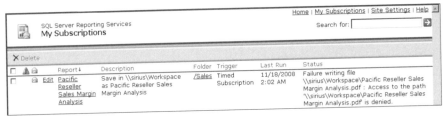

When you see a subscription status with a message stating that access to the file share is denied, you should probably check the permissions for that folder. After fixing the permissions issue, you can open the subscription, edit the schedule, and then save the subscription. The error message does not clear until the subscription executes successfully.

Deleting a Subscription

When you no longer need a subscription, you can delete it from the report's subscription page or the My Subscriptions page. You can delete subscriptions by selecting all the subscriptions you want to delete and then clicking the Delete button. The Delete button is not active until you select at least one subscription.

In this procedure, you delete the Windows file share subscription for the Pacific Reseller Sales Margin Analysis report.

Delete a subscription

1. In Internet Explorer, navigate to the folder containing the Pacific Reseller Sales Margin Analysis report.

   ❑ *Native mode:* Navigate to *http://<servername>/reports*, replacing *<servername>* with the name of your server, and then click the Sales folder link.

   ❑ *Integrated mode:* Navigate to *http://<servername>/sites/ssrs*, replacing *<servername>* with the name of your server. In the navigation bar, click the Reports link.

2. Open the subscriptions page of the report.

   ❑ *Native mode:* Click the Pacific Reseller Sales Margin Analysis report, and then click the Subscriptions tab.

   ❑ *Integrated mode:* Point to the Pacific Reseller Sales Margin Analysis report, click the Edit button that appears to the right of the report title, and select Manage Subscriptions.

3. Delete the subscription.

   ❑ *Native mode:* Select the check box to the left of the Windows File Share subscription, click Delete, and click OK to confirm.

   ❑ *Integrated mode:* Select the check box to the left of the Windows File Share subscription, click the Delete link, and click OK to confirm.

Congratulations! Now that you have completed all the procedures up to this point in the book, you have also completed the reporting life cycle. You should now understand how to use each Reporting Services feature to develop, administer, and access reports. Although Reporting Services satisfies most requirements of a reporting platform, there might be additional functionality that you require that is not included. Because Reporting Services is as much a development platform as it is an application, you can easily extend the capabilities of Reporting Services with custom development for each stage in the reporting life cycle, which you learn about in Chapter 16, "Programming Reporting Services."

Chapter 15 Quick Reference

To	Do This
Create an e-mail subscription	*Native mode:* In Report Manager, open the report, click the Subscriptions tab, and click New Subscription. Type the recipient e-mail addresses, select whether to include a link to the report, and select a rendering method. Choose whether to send the description when a snapshot is created or to use a custom or shared schedule. If applicable, select the parameter values if you don't want to use the default values.
	Integrated mode: In SharePoint, point to the report, click the Edit button that appears to the right of the report title, select Manage Subscriptions, click Add Subscription, type the recipient e-mail addresses, select whether to include a link to the report, and select a rendering method. Choose whether to send the description when a snapshot is created or to use a custom or shared schedule. If applicable, select the parameter values if you don't want to use the default values.
Create a Windows File Share subscription	*Native mode:* In Report Manager, open the report, click the Subscriptions tab, and click New Subscription. In the Delivered By drop-down list, select Windows File Share. Type the UNC path for the destination folder. Select whether to add a file extension to the file name, and select a rendering method. Type a user name and password with access to the shared folder, and then select an overwrite option. Choose whether to send the description when a snapshot is created or to use a custom or shared schedule. If applicable, select the parameter values if you don't want to use the default values.
	Integrated mode: In SharePoint, point to the report, click the Edit button that appears to the right of the report title, select Manage Subscriptions, and click Add Subscription. In the Delivery Extension drop-down list, select Windows File Share. Type the file name to assign the subscription output and type the UNC path for the destination folder. Select whether to add a file extension to the file name, and select a rendering method. Type a user name and password with access to the shared folder, and then select an overwrite option in the Write drop-down list. Choose whether to send the description when a snapshot is created or to use a custom or shared schedule. If applicable, select the parameter values if you don't want to use the default values.

To	Do This
Create a data-driven subscription	Create and populate a table containing recipient e-mail addresses or target folder destinations and the subscription options for each recipient or destination. Open the Subscriptions page of a report, and click New Data-Driven Subscription. Choose a delivery method, specify the connection string for the subscription query, provide the credentials to use to execute the query, and type the query to retrieve information from the subscription table. Configure the settings for the delivery extension and the parameter values, using static values or values from the subscription query. Specify a schedule for the subscription.
Create a shared schedule	*Native mode:* In Report Manager, click the Site Settings link, click the Schedules link, click New Schedule, type a name for the schedule, select a frequency, and configure the frequency options. You can set a start and stop date for the schedule.
	Integrated mode: In SharePoint, click Site Actions, click the Manage Shared Schedules link, click Add Shared Schedule, type a name for the schedule, select a frequency, and configure the frequency options. You can set a start and stop date for the schedule.
Review the status of a subscription	Open the report subscription page and check the values in the Last Run and Last Results columns. If you are running a native-mode report server, you can also click the My Subscriptions page from any page in Report Manager to view the status of all of your subscriptions.
Delete a subscription	Open the report subscription page, select the subscription's check box, click Delete, and click OK to confirm.

Part V
Using Reporting Services as a Development Platform

As you have learned by completing the procedures throughout this book, Reporting Services includes all the tools that you need to complete the entire reporting life cycle. In the final chapter of this book, you discover how you can also use Reporting Services as a development platform to develop, manage, and access reports. With a better appreciation of the full range of capabilities that Reporting Services supports, you can decide the best way to use Reporting Services in your organization.

Chapter 16
Programming Reporting Services

After completing this chapter, you will be able to:

- Use custom code in expressions.

- Use the Rs utility to manage content on a native-mode report server.

- Create an application that uses Windows Management Instrumentation (WMI) classes to list and update report server settings.

- Use a URL to access report server content.

- Embed reports into a Microsoft Windows application using the *ReportViewer* control.

In this chapter, you explore the range of programmability available in the Reporting Services reporting life cycle. You start by learning how to incorporate custom code into the report development process. Then you learn how to use the Reporting Services application programming interface (API) to create additional tools that you can use to manage the report server. You complete the chapter by exploring alternative techniques for accessing reports that you can incorporate into applications.

Programming Report Design Components

As part of the report development phase of the reporting life cycle, you learned in Chapter 5, "Developing Expressions," how to use expressions to calculate a value that displays in your report or to change a property value that affects the behavior or appearance of a report item. When you need to use the same complex expression many times in the same report, you might find it easier to write one custom function that you can use as many times as you need throughout the report. Then you have only one place in the report to update the expression if the report requirements change later. Another advantage of using custom functions is the ability to use more advanced logic in your expressions, such as loops that use FOR or WHILE statements or conditions that use IF...THEN or CASE statements. In Reporting Services, you can use custom functions either by embedding code into a single report or by creating a custom assembly that you can then reference in any of your reports.

Embedding Code in a Report

Embedded code gives you the flexibility of reusing a custom function that you create anywhere in your report, but you should consider its limitations before taking this approach. First, you cannot share the code that you embed in one report with other reports. You must physically add the code to any report in which you want to use the custom function. Furthermore, you must write your custom function using Microsoft Visual Basic .NET. If you want to use your custom function in multiple reports or want to use a different language, you should create a custom assembly, as explained in the section entitled "Using Assemblies to Share Custom Code," later in this chapter.

For simple requirements, you might decide that using embedded code is easier to implement even if you must copy the code to multiple reports. The process is very easy, although you need to know how to use the Visual Basic .NET programming language. You start by adding a custom function to the report properties, and then you call your function using the global *Code* member in an expression.

Creating a Custom Function

You use the *Code* property of a report to store the custom functions that you create. You can use arguments to pass a constant, field, parameter, variable, or expression value to your custom function. Although you create only one custom function in the next procedure, you can add as many custom functions as you need to your report.

In this procedure, you add a custom function to a report to return a color or an image name for conditional formatting.

Add a custom function to a report

1. In Business Intelligence Development Studio (BI Dev Studio), on the File menu, select Open Project, navigate to Microsoft Press\Rs2008sbs\Chap16, and double-click Programmability.sln.

2. In Solution Explorer, double-click EmbeddedCode.rdl.

3. In the Properties window, in the drop-down list at the top of the window, select PctContribution Text Box, and point to the expression in the Color text box to view the expression in a tooltip window.

    This expression compares the value of PctContribution Text Box to threshold values that determine whether to use a red, black, or green font color to display the text box value.

4. In the Properties window, in the drop-down list at the top of the window, select Textbox25, expand the BackgroundImage property, and point to the expression in the Value text box to review the expression in a tooltip window.

    Here you see a similar expression that determines which key performance indicator (KPI) image to display. You can find this same expression in the Textbox41 text box's *Value* property in the BackgroundImage section. If the business rules change later, you must edit the applicable property expression for each text box. Although making a change to properties in three text boxes might not seem very tedious in this report, you might have a report that uses the same expression in many more places in the report. Fortunately, you can use embedded code to store the business rule logic in one location, and then change the property expressions to refer to that embedded code. Then, each time that the business rules change, you can update the logic in one place.

5. On the Reports menu, select Report Properties.

6. In the Report Properties dialog box, click Code.

7. In the Custom Code text box, type the following code (or copy and paste this code from the EmbeddedCode.txt file in the Microsoft Press\Rs2008sbs\Chap16 folder in your Documents folder):

```
Function GetStatus(ByVal StatusType As String, ByVal StatusCondition As Decimal, ByVal
StatusThreshold As Decimal) As String
Dim ReturnValue As String = Nothing
      Select Case StatusType
           Case "Color"
                Select Case StatusCondition
                     Case Is < .02
                          ReturnValue = "Red"
                     Case Is > StatusThreshold
                          ReturnValue = "Green"
                     Case Else
                          ReturnValue = "Black"
                End Select
          Case "KPI"
                Select Case StatusCondition
                     Case Is < .02
                          ReturnValue = "redkpi"
                     Case Is > StatusThreshold
                          ReturnValue = "greenkpi"
                     Case Else
                          ReturnValue = Nothing
                End Select
     End Select
     Return ReturnValue
End Function
```

This function takes three arguments. You use the first argument, *StatusType*, to indicate whether you are using this function to get a value to set font color or to define a KPI when you use the string *Color* or *KPI*, respectively. You then use the second argument, *StatusCondition*, to provide the current value of the report item for comparison to a constant value, *.02*, or to a variable, *StatusThreshold*. You pass the value of *StatusThreshold* as the third argument of this function. Based on the result of the comparison, the function returns a color or an image name to the report item.

Important When you type code into the Custom Code text box, you should check your typing carefully. No IntelliSense alerts you to an error in the code, and you have no mechanism for debugging your function.

8. Click OK, then save and preview the report.

Although you haven't yet called the custom function in your report, you can validate the syntax of your custom function by previewing the report. An error displays if a problem is found. Otherwise, the report renders normally.

Using a Custom Function in an Expression

You can use a custom function in any property that accepts an expression. To call your custom function, you create an expression that references the *Code* member, the function name, and any arguments that are required for your function.

In this procedure, you replace the conditional formatting expressions in your report with a reference to the *GetStatus* custom function.

Call a custom function in an expression

1. In the Properties window, in the drop-down list at the top of the window, select PctContribution Text Box, and then, in the Color drop-down list, select Expression.

First, you replace the expression for the color conditional formatting with your custom function.

2. In the Set Expression For: Color text box, replace the current expression by typing the following expression:

```
=Code.GetStatus("Color", ReportItems!PctContribution.Value, Variables!GroupThreshold.
Value)
```

Notice that you can use a constant or an expression as function arguments. Notice also that the IntelliSense feature indicates that the *GetStatus* function is invalid in this expression, but you can safely ignore this warning.

 Note In this expression, you are using a group variable, *GroupThreshold*, to provide a value for the *StatusThreshold* argument in the *GetStatus* function. In the Group Properties dialog box for the SalesTerritoryGroup group, on the Variables page, you can view the expression that assigns a value to this variable based on the current instance of the group. You learned how to work with group variables in Chapter 5.

3. Click OK.

4. In the Properties window, in the drop-down list at the top of the window, select Textbox25 Text Box, expand BackgroundImage, and then, in the Value drop-down list, select Expression.

Here, you use the custom function to replace the expression for the KPI conditional formatting.

5. In the Set Expression For: Value text box, replace the current expression by typing the following expression:

```
=Code.GetStatus("KPI", ReportItems!PctContribution.Value, Variables!GroupThreshold.
Value)
```

6. Click OK.

7. In the Properties window, in the drop-down list at the top of the window, select Textbox41 Text Box, expand BackgroundImage, and then, in the Value drop-down list, select Expression.

Again, you replace the KPI conditional formatting expression with your custom function.

8. In the Set Expression For: Value text box, replace the current expression by typing the following expression:

```
=Code.GetStatus("KPI", ReportItems!PctContribution.Value, Variables!GroupThreshold.
Value)
```

9. Click OK, and then save and preview the report.

10. Click Next Page, and expand the Specialty Bike Shop group under Australia.

This set of detail records includes rows that illustrate both possible results of the custom function. The first row displays the Pct Contribution using a green font and displays the green KPI image. All the rows with a Pct Contribution value below 2 percent display the value using a red font and display the red KPI image. All other rows in this set display the value using a black font and have no KPI image to display.

Keep the project open in preparation for the next procedure.

Using Assemblies to Share Custom Code

For maximum flexibility and reusability, you can create an assembly for your custom functions using any language supported by the Microsoft .NET Framework. You start by creating a class library and then building the assembly. You must then install the assembly on the report server and on your report development workstation so that you can test functions in the Report Designer before deploying reports to the report server. After installing the assembly, you can then call your custom function by adding a reference to your report and creating an expression that references the namespace and class for your function and includes any required arguments.

Creating a Custom Assembly

Using Microsoft Visual Studio 2008, you can create a class library as a container for all the custom functions that you want to use in your reports. After you add functions to the class library, you use the Build command to produce the assembly file as a .dll file that you can then copy to the Bin folders for Report Designer and for the report server.

> **Note** To complete the following procedure, you must install Visual Studio 2008 Standard or Professional Edition with either the Visual Basic .NET or Microsoft Visual C# .NET library. You must also install Visual Studio 2008 Service Pack 1 if you develop the custom assembly on a workstation on which BI Dev Studio, Integration Services, or Management Tools (Basic or Complete) are installed.
>
> The steps and the code samples in the following procedure assume that you are using Visual Basic .NET. If you prefer to use Visual C# .NET, you can find the corresponding code samples in the Microsoft Press\Rs2008sbs\Chap16\CS folder. The completed project is in the Microsoft Press\Rs2008sbs\Answers\Chap16\CS folder.

In this procedure, you create and deploy a class library to store a custom function for conditional formatting.

Create and deploy a class library for a custom function

1. In BI Dev Studio, on the File menu, select Add, and then select New Project.

2. In the Add New Project dialog box, in the Project Types list, select Visual Basic, and then, in the Templates list, select Class Library.

3. In the Name text box, change the project name to Rs2008sbs.VB.Extensions and, in the Location text box, change the location to the Microsoft Press\Rs2008sbs\Workspace folder in your Documents folder, as shown here. Click OK.

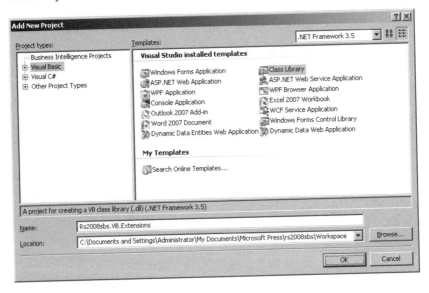

4. In Solution Explorer, right-click Class1.vb, select Rename, and type **ReportFunctions.vb**.

5. Type the following code to the class definition between the *Public Class ReportFunctions* and *End Class* statements (or copy and paste this code from the ReportFunctions_VB.txt file in the Microsoft Press\Rs2008sbs\Chap16\VB folder in your Documents folder):

```
Public Shared Function GetStatus(ByVal StatusType As String, ByVal StatusCondition As
Decimal, ByVal StatusThreshold As Decimal, ByVal AlertThreshold As Decimal) As String
        Dim ReturnValue As String = Nothing
        Select Case StatusType
            Case "Color"
                Select Case StatusCondition
                    Case Is < AlertThreshold
                        ReturnValue = "Red"
                    Case Is > StatusThreshold
                        ReturnValue = "Green"
                    Case Else
                        ReturnValue = "Black"
                End Select
            Case "KPI"
                Select Case StatusCondition
                    Case Is < AlertThreshold
                        ReturnValue = "redkpi"
                    Case Is > StatusThreshold
                        ReturnValue = "greenkpi"
                    Case Else
                        ReturnValue = Nothing
                End Select
        End Select
        Return ReturnValue
End Function
```

The code for this function is almost identical to the code that you added as embedded code in the previous procedure. Notice that the code includes a new argument, *AlertThreshold*, to replace the constant *0.02* value in the embedded code and is consequently more flexible. You can then customize the alert threshold value in each report.

6. On the File menu, select Save ReportFunctions.vb.

The document window looks like this:

```
(General)                                                          (Declarations)
Public Class ReportFunctions
    Public Shared Function GetStatus(ByVal StatusType As String, ByVal StatusCondition As Decimal, ByVal StatusThre
        Dim ReturnValue As String = Nothing
        Select Case StatusType
            Case "Color"
                Select Case StatusCondition
                    Case Is < AlertThreshold
                        ReturnValue = "Red"
                    Case Is > StatusThreshold
                        ReturnValue = "Green"
                    Case Else
                        ReturnValue = "Black"
                End Select
            Case "KPI"
                Select Case StatusCondition
                    Case Is < AlertThreshold
                        ReturnValue = "redkpi"
                    Case Is > StatusThreshold
                        ReturnValue = "greenkpi"
                    Case Else
                        ReturnValue = Nothing
                End Select
        End Select
        Return ReturnValue
    End Function
End Class
```

7. In Solution Explorer, right-click Rs2008sbs.VB.Extensions, and select Build.

When you build a project, you create the assembly file that you can deploy to the report development workstation and to the report server.

8. Open Windows Explorer and navigate to the Microsoft Press\Rs2008sbs\Workspace \Rs2008sbs.VB.Extensions\Bin\Debug folder.

The Rs2008sbs.VB.Extensions.dll is the assembly file that you must deploy to the report development workstation by copying to the folder used by Report Designer. If you want other report developers to use your custom function, they must also deploy this file to the same location on their workstations.

9. Right-click the Rs2008sbs.VB.Extensions.dll file, select copy, navigate to C:\Program Files\Microsoft Visual Studio 9.0\Common7\IDE\PrivateAssemblies, and press CTRL+V to paste the file into the folder.

Next, you deploy the same file to the report server.

10. Navigate to C:\Program Files\Microsoft SQL Server\MSRS10.<*Instance*>\Reporting Services\ReportServer\Bin, where <*Instance*> is the instance identifier for your report server, such as MSSQLSERVER as described in Chapter 2, "Installing Reporting Services." Press CTRL+V to paste the file into the folder.

Now you are ready to develop reports that reference the new assembly and deploy those reports to the report server.

Calling a Custom Assembly in an Expression

When you want to use functions from a custom assembly in an expression, you must add a reference to that custom assembly as a report property. Then, in the expression, you include the namespace and the name of the class in which the function is defined. You also include any arguments required by the function.

In this procedure, you replace the conditional formatting expressions in your report with a reference to the *GetStatus* custom function in the Rs2008sbs.VB.Extensions assembly.

Call a function from a custom assembly in an expression

1. In Solution Explorer, double-click CustomAssembly.rdl.

2. On the Report menu, select Report Properties.

    First, set the value for the alert threshold for this report to *0.01*.

3. In the Report Properties dialog box, click Variables, and click Add. In the Name text box, type **AlertThreshold**, and then, in the Value text box, type **0.01**.

    Next, add a reference to the assembly as a report property.

4. In the Report Properties dialog box, click References. Below Add Or Remove Assemblies, click Add, and then click the ellipsis button that appears.

5. In the Add Reference dialog box, click the Browse tab, navigate to C:\Program Files \Microsoft Visual Studio 9.0\Common7\IDE\PrivateAssemblies, and double-click Rs2008sbs.VB.Extensions.dll to add the assembly reference to the Report Properties dialog box, as shown here.

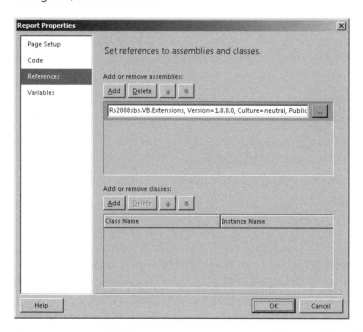

Now you can modify the property expressions used for conditional formatting in this report.

6. Click OK.

7. In the Properties window, in the drop-down list at the top of the window, select PctContribution Text Box, and then, in the Color drop-down list, select Expression.

8. In the Set Expression For: Color text box, replace the current expression by typing the following expression:

```
=Rs2008sbs.VB.Extensions.ReportFunctions.GetStatus("Color", ReportItems!
PctContribution.Value, Variables!GroupThreshold.Value, Variables!AlertThreshold.Value)
```

Your expression must include the namespace, the class name, and the function name in addition to the arguments required by the function. Just like the embedded code expression, you can use constant values or expressions as arguments. Again, the IntelliSense feature indicates that the *GetStatus* function is invalid in this expression because it is unaware of external functions, but you can ignore this warning here.

9. Click OK.

10. In the Properties window, in the drop-down list at the top of the window, select Textbox25 Text Box, expand BackgroundImage, and then, in the Value drop-down list, select Expression.

11. In the Set Expression For: Value text box, replace the current expression by typing the following expression:

```
=Rs2008sbs.VB.Extensions.ReportFunctions.GetStatus("KPI", ReportItems!PctContribution.
Value, Variables!GroupThreshold.Value, Variables!AlertThreshold.Value)
```

12. Click OK.

13. In the Properties window, in the drop-down list at the top of the window, select Textbox41 Text Box, expand BackgroundImage, and then, in the Value drop-down list, select Expression.

14. In the Set Expression For: Value text box, replace the current expression by typing the following expression:

```
=Rs2008sbs.VB.Extensions.ReportFunctions.GetStatus("KPI", ReportItems!PctContribution.
Value, Variables!GroupThreshold.Value, Variables!AlertThreshold.Value)
```

15. Click OK, then save and preview the report.

16. Click Next Page, and expand the Specialty Bike Shop group under Australia.

Just as you saw in the EmbeddedCode report, the detail records here include rows with both possible results of the custom function. The first row displays the Pct Contribution using a green font and displays the green KPI image, while all the rows with a Pct Contribution value below 1 percent (as defined by the report variable *AlertThreshold*) display the value using a red font and display the red KPI image. All other rows in this set display the value using a black font and have no KPI image to display.

Programming Report Server Management

Any task that you can perform in Report Manager can also be done programmatically by using the Reporting Services API to communicate with the report server through a Web service. For example, you might prefer to script repetitive tasks if you're managing a native-mode report server. You can deploy reports, set properties, define security, and create schedules or subscriptions. Or you might use a custom application to check report server configuration settings. Regardless of which method you use to communicate with the Web service, you must implement a proxy class in your code to use the methods and properties available in the Web service library. In this section, you learn how to build tools to accomplish some of the objectives that are common in the management phase of the reporting life cycle.

Scripting Administrative Tasks

If you're running a native-mode report server, you can streamline repetitive administrative tasks by creating a script file (written in Visual Basic .NET) that you can execute by using the Rs utility. A script file is a much simpler approach to performing administrative tasks than developing a Microsoft Windows or Web application to interact with the Reporting Services Web service. In Chapter 10, "Deploying Reports to a Server," you first used the Rs utility to deploy reports to the server, but you can accomplish much more with scripts. You might take a modular approach by creating multiple script files that perform a specific task each and then creating a batch file to execute the scripts as a batch process.

The Rs utility uses the following syntax:

```
Rs -i input_file -s ReportServerURL -u username -p password -l timeout -b -v variable_
key=variable_value -t
```

You must be a local administrator on the report server to use the Rs utility. At minimum, you provide the name of the script file as the *input_file* argument and the Web service URL for a local or remote report server. All the following arguments are optional:

- **-u username -p password**   You provide the *username* and *password* arguments when you need to replace your current Windows credentials with alternate credentials.

- **-l timeout**   To override the default time-out value of 8 seconds, you can include the *timeout* argument. You can use a value of 0 to prevent timing out altogether.

- **-b**   You use this argument if you want to handle the commands in your script as a batch and roll back the transaction if a command fails that is not otherwise handled as an exception in the script.

- **-v variable_key=variable_value**   You can pass a variable and its value to the script as an argument. You can repeat this argument when you have multiple variables to pass to the script.

- **-t**   To record the script output in the trace log, use this argument.

When the Rs utility executes, the utility finds the Web Services Definition Language (WSDL) document that describes the public members available in the Web service and creates a proxy class called *rs* that you use in your script to interact with the Web service. You can also use members from the following .NET Framework namespaces: *System, System.IO, System.Xml,* and *System.Web.Services.*

> **Note** This chapter shows you how to use only a few of the available Reporting Services methods and properties. Refer to the topic "Reporting Services Class Library" in SQL Server Books Online for more information. In some cases, SQL Server Books Online includes code samples that show you how to use the Reporting Services API.

Deploying Reports

As you learned in Chapter 10, the Rs utility is useful for deploying a set of reports to the server. You can use the Web service's *CreateFolder* method to create a folder to store the reports, if necessary, and then use the *CreateReport* method to copy the report definition to the report server. If your report uses any shared data sources, you must use the *SetItemDataSources* method to establish the link between the report and the shared data sources.

> **Important** The Rs utility is not supported for use with an integrated-mode report server.

In this procedure, you create a script that deploys the reports in the Programmability solution.

Create a script to deploy reports to a native-mode report server

1. In BI Dev Studio, on the File menu, select Open, Open File, navigate to Microsoft Press \Rs2008sbs\Chap16 within your Documents folder, and double-click DeployReports.rss.

   The script file currently contains placeholders for code that you add as you complete the steps in this procedure.

2. In the document window, below 'INSERT CODE #1: 1_Variables.txt, add the following code (or copy and paste this code from the 1_Variables.txt file in the Microsoft Press \Rs2008sbs\Chap16\Deploy folder in your Documents folder):

```
Dim definition As [Byte]() = Nothing
Dim warnings As Warning() = Nothing
Dim parentFolder As String = "Programmability"
Dim parentPath As String = "/" + parentFolder
Dim filePath As String = "Programmability\"
Dim fileName As String = "*.rdl"
```

At the beginning of the script, you declare global variables that can be used by any function in the script. The *definition* variable is a byte array that you use later in the script to store data read from a report definition file. The *warnings* variable is an array that you use to store any warnings that might result from executing a Web service method. The remaining four variables—*parentFolder, parentPath, filePath*, and *filename*— are used to provide constant values to the script for the location and name of the files to be deployed. Notice that you can use a wildcard value, such as *.rdl*, rather than a specific report name when you want to deploy multiple reports. Although you declare and assign values to these variables in this script, you could pass these values to the script as arguments, which you learn how to do in the next procedure.

> **Important** RSS scripts are case-sensitive. When developing code for RSS scripts, be careful that you maintain the proper case when referring to objects in the code.

3. In the document window, below 'INSERT CODE #2: 2_Main.txt, add the following code (or copy and paste this code from the 2_Main.txt file in the Microsoft Press\Rs2008sbs \Chap16 folder in your Documents folder):

```
Public Sub Main()
    rs.Credentials = System.Net.CredentialCache.DefaultCredentials
    'Create the parent folder
    Try
        rs.CreateFolder(parentFolder, "/", Nothing)
        Console.WriteLine("Parent folder {0} created successfully", parentFolder)
    Catch e As Exception
        Console.WriteLine(e.Message)
    End Try

    'Publish the sample reports
    Dim hostFolder As System.IO.Directory
    Dim reports As String() = hostFolder.GetFiles(filePath, fileName)
    Dim report As String
    For Each report In reports
        PublishReport(report)
    Next
End Sub
```

The first line in the *Main* procedure assigns the current user credentials to the proxy class to establish the security context for the subsequent commands in the script. In this way, the security model is enforced even when using script to perform administrative tasks instead of using Report Manager. The Web service compares the credentials to the role assignments to determine what items you can access and what tasks you can perform when using the Web service methods.

The *Try-Catch* block calls the *CreateFolder* method of the Web service and passes the *parentFolder* as the folder name to create on the report server. The second argument is the parent folder for the new folder, which in this case is a constant value for the root folder, *Home*. You use the third argument to pass an array of properties for the folder, but in this script, there are no properties to set for the new folder. If the creation of the new folder succeeds, a message displays in the command prompt window to indicate the status. Otherwise, a message displays that describes the error that was encountered.

> **Tip** There is no way to use Visual Studio to debug your script. In addition to recording the status of executing a method, you can include more *Console.WriteLine()* statements in your code as a debugging technique. For example, you can display the current value of a variable at a particular point in the execution of the code.

The next three lines in the code declare variables that are local to the *Main* procedure—*hostfolder*, *reports*, and *report*. You use *hostfolder* to store the current directory name in which the Rs utility is executing. Then the code uses this directory with the *GetFiles* method to retrieve from one or more files as defined by *filename* in the *filePath* directory. In this procedure, the file path for all files with the .rdl extension in the Programmability folder below the Microsoft Press\Rs2008sbs\Chap16 directory (which is the directory in which you execute the Rs utility) is retrieved and stored in a string array called *reports*. Then the For-Next loop iterates through each file path in the array and assigns the current file path as a string in the *report* variable, which is then passed as an argument to the local *PublishReport* function.

4. In the document window, below 'INSERT CODE #3: 3_PublishReport.txt, add the following code (or copy and paste this code from the 3_PublishReport.txt file in the Microsoft Press\Rs2008sbs\Chap16 folder in your Documents folder):

```
Public Sub PublishReport(ByVal reportPath As String)
  Try
    Dim stream As FileStream = File.OpenRead(reportPath)
    definition = New [Byte](stream.Length - 1) {}
    stream.Read(definition, 0, CInt(stream.Length))
    stream.Close()
  Catch e As IOException
    Console.WriteLine(e.Message)
  End Try
  Try
    Dim reportPieces As String() = Microsoft.VisualBasic.Strings.Split(reportPath, "\")
    Dim reportName As String = reportPieces.GetValue(reportPieces.Length - 1)
    reportName = reportName.Substring(0, reportName.Length - 4)
    warnings = rs.CreateReport(reportName, parentPath, False, definition, Nothing)
    If Not (warnings Is Nothing) Then
      Dim warning As Warning
      For Each warning In warnings
        Console.WriteLine("Report: {0} published with the following warning: " +
warning.Message, reportName)
      Next warning
    Else
```

```
        Console.WriteLine("Report: {0} published successfully with no warnings",
    reportName)
        End If
    'Set single shared data source value
        Dim ds(0) as DataSource
        Dim s as New DataSource
        Dim dsr as New DataSourceReference
        dsr.Reference = "/Data Sources/AdventureWorksDW2008"
        s.Item = dsr
        s.Name = "AdventureWorksDW2008"
        ds(0) = s
        Dim myItem as String = parentPath + "/" + reportName
        rs.SetItemDataSources(myItem, ds)
        Console.WriteLine("The shared data source reference for {0} has been updated",
    reportName)
      Catch e As Exception
        Console.WriteLine(e.Message)
      End Try
    End Sub
```

The first *Try-Catch* block in this section of code starts by reading the Report Definition Language (RDL) that's passed (as the variable *reportPath*) into the *PublishReport* function and storing the RDL as a filestream object in the *stream* variable. Then the code initializes a byte array, *definition*, into which *stream* contents are then transferred.

In the second *Try-Catch* block, the first three lines parse the value of *reportPath* to separate the file extension from the report name and assign the result to the local variable *reportName*, which is passed, along with the global variable *parentPath* to the Web service's *CreateReport* method as the first and second arguments. The third argument, *False,* ensures that you don't overwrite an existing file of the same name in the same location. The fourth argument, *definition*, is the RDL in the byte array. Finally, the fifth argument specifies the properties to modify when the report is added to the Report Server. The result of executing the *CreateReport* method is stored in the *warnings* array. If any warnings are found, the warning displays in the command prompt window. If not, then a success message displays.

After the report is added to the report server, the remaining lines of code in this section assign the shared data source AdventureWorksDW2008 to the report. Otherwise, the link to the data source is broken and the report cannot execute.

5. Save the file, and then open a command prompt window.

6. Type the command to navigate to the folder containing the script file. For example, if you're running Windows XP or Windows Server 2003, type **cd C:\Documents and Settings\<*username*>\My Documents\Microsoft Press\Rs2008sbs \Chap16**. If you're running Windows Vista or Windows Server 2008, type **cd C:\Users\<*username*>\Documents\Rs2008sbs\Chap16**.

7. To run the Rs utility, type **rs -i DeployReports.rss -s http://<*servername*> /ReportServer** (replacing <*servername*> with the name of your server or localhost),

and press Enter to view the results of executing the utility in the command prompt window, as shown here.

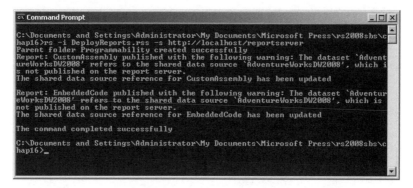

8. To confirm the successful deployment of the reports, switch to Windows Internet Explorer, navigate to *http://<servername>/Reports* (replacing *<servername>* with the name of your server), and click the Programmability link in Report Manager and view the list of reports. Open the reports to confirm that they each are properly associated with the shared data source and can therefore execute and render properly.

Creating a Linked Report

Another task that you might find useful to automate is the creation of a linked report. You use the *CreateLinkedReport* method to define the base report, the name of the linked report, its location, and the properties to set for the linked report. If you want to provide new default values for the linked report, you build an array of *ReportParameter* objects and use the *SetReportParameters* method to assign the *ReportParameter* array to the linked report.

In this procedure, you create a script that creates a linked report using information passed as variables to the script at run time.

Create a script to create a linked report on a native-mode report server

1. In BI Dev Studio, on the File menu, select Open File, navigate to Microsoft Press \Rs2008sbs\Chap16, and double-click CreateLinkedReport.rss.

   In this script file, you can see placeholders for code that you add as you complete the steps in this procedure.

2. In the document window, below 'INSERT CODE #1: 1_Main.txt, add the following code (or copy and paste this code from the 1_Main.txt file in the Microsoft Press\Rs2008sbs \Chap16\Link folder in your Documents folder):

```
CreateLinkedReport(sourceReport, linkedReport, newFolder)
```

   This line of code passes three variables as arguments to the local function, *CreateLinkedReport*. Although the name of the location function matches the name of the Web service method, the omission of the *rs* class lets you know that in this case, the call to a function is local. Notice that the script file does not declare any of these variables. For maximum flexibility, you can use global variables to define arguments at run time.

3. In the document window, below 'INSERT CODE #2: 2_Parameters.txt, add the following code (or copy and paste this code from the 2_Parameters.txt file in the Microsoft Press \Rs2008sbs\Chap16\Link folder in your Documents folder):

```
Dim params(3) as  ReportParameter

Dim paramCostBasis as New ReportParameter
paramCostBasis.Name = "CostBasis"
Dim paramCostBasisDefaults(0) as String
paramCostBasisDefaults(0) = "Total"
paramCostBasis.DefaultValues = paramCostBasisDefaults
paramCostBasis.PromptUser = False
params(0) = paramCostBasis

Dim paramYear as New ReportParameter
paramYear.Name = "Year"
Dim paramYearDefaults(0) as String
paramYearDefaults(0) = "2004"
paramYear.DefaultValues = paramYearDefaults

paramYear.PromptUser = False
params(1) = paramYear

Dim paramQtr as New ReportParameter
paramQtr.Name = "Quarter"
Dim paramQtrDefaults(3) as String
Dim i as Integer
For i = 0 to 3
  paramQtrDefaults(i) = Cstr(i + 1)
Next i
paramQtr.DefaultValues = paramQtrDefaults
paramQtr.PromptUser = True
paramQtr.PromptUserSpecified = True
params(2) = paramQtr

Dim paramTerritory as New ReportParameter
paramTerritory.Name = "SalesTerritoryGroup"
Dim paramTerritoryDefaults(0) as String
paramTerritoryDefaults(0) = "Pacific"
paramTerritory.DefaultValues = paramTerritoryDefaults
paramTerritory.PromptUser = False
params(3) = paramTerritory
```

This code creates an array of *ReportParameter* objects called *params*. Each of the four report parameters—*CostBasis, Year, Quarter,* and *SalesTerritoryGroup*—in the report is set to specific default values in the linked report, and the prompt to the user is disabled for all report parameters except *Quarter.* In this script, the parameter names and default values are defined as constant values for simplicity, but you could add more flexibility to this report by using global variables to set the values at run time.

4. In the document window, below 'INSERT CODE #3: 3_CreateLinkedReport.txt, add the following code (or copy and paste this code from the 3_CreateLinkedReport.txt file in the Microsoft Press\Rs2008sbs\Chap16\Link folder in your Documents folder):

```
Try
  Dim linkedReportPath as String = "/" + newFolder
  CreateNewFolder(newFolder)
  Console.WriteLine("Parent folder created: {0}", newFolder)
  rs.CreateLinkedReport(linkedReport, linkedReportPath, baseReport, Nothing)
  Console.WriteLine("Linked report created: {0}", linkedReport)
  rs.SetReportParameters(linkedReportPath + "/" + linkedReport, params)

Catch e As Exception
  Console.WriteLine(e.Message)
End Try
```

In this *Try-Catch* block, a new folder is created in preparation for creating the linked report by calling the script's *CreateNewFolder* method. Then, to create the linked report, the Web Service's *CreateLinkedReport* method is called with four parameters. You use the first parameter, *linkedReport*, to provide a name for the linked report. For the second parameter, *linkedReportPath*, you pass a string that combines the root path ("/") with the *newFolder* string to define the folder path just created with the *CreateNewFolder* method. You then use the third parameter, *baseReport*, to identify the full path to the base report from which the linked report is created. In this script, you pass *Nothing* as the fourth parameter to specify that no report properties are to be updated in the linked report.

5. Save the file.

6. If necessary, open a command prompt window and type the command to navigate to the folder containing the script file. For example, if you're running Windows XP or Windows Server 2003, type **cd C:\Documents and Settings\<*username*>\My Documents\Microsoft Press\Rs2008sbs\Chap16**. If you're running Windows Vista or Windows Server 2008, type **cd C:\Users\<*username*>\Documents\Microsoft Press\Rs2008sbs\Chap16**.

7. To run the Rs utility, type **rs -i CreateLinkedReport.rss -s http://localhost /ReportServer -v sourceReport="/Programmability/EmbeddedCode" -v linkedReport="Pacific Margin Analysis 2004" -v newFolder="Pacific Sales**, and press Enter. The results of executing the utility display in the command prompt window.

Important It is important to exclude spaces between the input variable file name, the equal sign, and the value, as shown in the previous command.

8. To confirm the successful deployment of the report, switch to Internet Explorer, navigate to *http://*<servername>*/Reports* (replacing *<servername>* with the name of your server), and click the Pacific Sales link in Report Manager.

9. Click the Pacific Margin Analysis 2004 link to open the linked report, and then, in the Quarter drop-down list, select the (Select All) check box. Click View Report to view the report, as shown here.

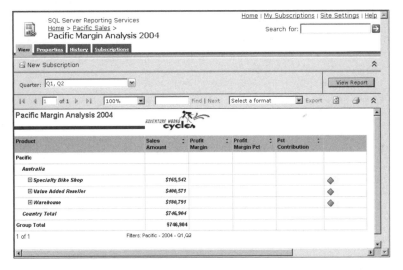

Notice the icon in the upper-left corner, which indicates that this report is a linked report. Also notice that *Quarter* is the only visible report parameter with default values specified to include only the two quarters available for 2004 in the data source. Any changes that you make to the base report also update the linked report, with the exception of changes to report parameters or report parameter default values.

Using the WMI Provider

To review and change the report server configuration settings programmatically, you can use WMI classes. Reporting Services includes the following two classes:

- **MSReportServer_Instance**   This class provides basic information about the report server, such as the edition, version, instance name, and SharePoint integration status. All these configuration settings are read-only.

- **MSReportServer_ConfigurationSetting**   This class provides access to the configuration settings in the configuration file. Some settings are read-only, but several methods are available to make changes to configuration settings, such as *DeleteEncryptionKey* or *ReserveURL*.

The Reporting Services Configuration Manager uses the WMI provider to view and change the configuration settings. However, if you want to have access to this functionality without installing Reporting Services, you can use a custom application instead. You might create a console application as an easy tool that allows you to check the current settings of all Report Server instances on a target server. Or you might create a management application that allows you to update settings in the report server configuration file. To use either of these techniques, you must be a member of the local administrator group on the target report server.

> **Note**   To complete the following procedure, you must install Visual Studio 2008 with either the Visual Basic .NET or Visual C# .NET library.
>
> The steps and the code samples in the following procedure assume that you are using Visual Basic .NET. If you prefer to use Visual C# .NET, you can find the corresponding code samples in the Microsoft Press\Rs2008sbs\Chap16\CS folder. The completed project is in the Microsoft Press\Rs2008sbs\Answers\Chap16\CS folder.

In this procedure, you create a console application to display report server settings by using the WMI provider.

Create an application to list report server settings

1. In BI Dev Studio, on the File menu, select New Project.

2. In the New Project dialog box, in the Project Types list, select Visual Basic, and then, in the Templates list, select Console Application.

3. In the Name text box, change the project name to WMIQueryVB and, in the Location text box, if necessary, change the location to the Microsoft Press\Rs2008sbs\Workspace folder in your Documents folder. Click OK.

4. In the document window, above the *Module* statement, type the following code:

```
Imports System
Imports System.Management
Imports System.IO
```

To work with the WMI provider, you must add the *System, System.Management,* and *System.IO* namespaces to your project.

5. In Solution Explorer, right-click the WMIQueryVB project, and then select Add Reference.

6. In the Add Reference dialog box, in the Component Name list, select System .Management, and click OK.

   Your code does not build properly unless you add a reference to System.Management in your project. When you add the reference, it might be hidden.

> **Tip** If you want to see the project references that are currently hidden, you can display them by clicking the Show All Files button on the toolbar in Solution Explorer.

7. In the document window, below the *Sub Main()* statement, add the following code (or copy and paste this code from the WMIQuery_VB.txt file in the Microsoft Press \Rs2008sbs\Chap16\VB folder in your Documents folder):

```
Const WmiNamespace As String = _
"\\localhost\root\Microsoft\SqlServer\ReportServer\RS_MSSQLSERVER\v10\Admin"
Const WmiRSClass As String = _
"\\localhost\root\Microsoft\SqlServer\ReportServer\RS_MSSQLSERVER\v10\admin:
MSReportServer_ConfigurationSetting"
Dim serverClass As ManagementClass
Dim scope As ManagementScope
scope = New ManagementScope(WmiNamespace)
'Connect to the Reporting Services namespace.
scope.Connect()
'Create the server class.
serverClass = New ManagementClass(WmiRSClass)
'Connect to the management object.
serverClass.Get()
If serverClass Is Nothing Then Throw New Exception("No class found")
'Loop through the instances of the server class.
Dim instances As ManagementObjectCollection = _
serverClass.GetInstances()
Dim instance As ManagementObject
For Each instance In instances
Console.Out.WriteLine("Instance Detected")
Dim instProps As PropertyDataCollection = _
instance.Properties
Dim prop As PropertyData
Console.WriteLine("Property Name".PadRight(35) + "Value")
For Each prop In instProps
Dim name As String = prop.Name
Dim val As Object = prop.Value
Console.Out.Write(prop.Name.PadRight(35))
If val Is Nothing Then
Console.Out.WriteLine("<null>")
    Else
```

```
Console.Out.WriteLine(val.ToString())
    End If
Next
Next
Console.WriteLine("Press any key to continue")
Console.ReadKey()
```

This code starts by assigning the Reporting Services WMI namespace and class to strings and assumes that you are creating the application to run on a local report server. You can replace *localhost* with the name of a remote report server, if necessary. Notice also the reference to RS_MSSQLSERVER in the string. This instance name is specific to Reporting Services 2008. If, for some reason, the instance name has been changed on your server, you must update the reference in this code to the applicable value.

> **Tip** To find the correct instance name, open the Reportingservices.mof file in the C:\Program Files\Microsoft SQL Server\MSRS10.*<Instance>*\Reporting Services \ReportServer\Bin folder of the report server, where *<Instance>* is the instance identifier for your report server, such as MSSQLSERVER if you followed the instructions in Chapter 2. In the Reportingservices.mof file, look for a line containing Root\Microsoft\SqlServer \ReportServer and note the instance name on the same line.

The code then connects the WMI namespace and creates a server class so that it can connect to the management object. Using this object, the code can then iterate through the instances that it contains. Within each instance, the code iterates through the property collection and writes the name of the property and its value to the command prompt window.

8. Save the file.

9. Press F5 to test the application and view the results, as shown here.

```
C:\WINDOWS\system32\cmd.exe                                          _ □ ×
Instance Detected
Property Name                           Value
ConnectionPoolSize                      100
DatabaseLogonAccount
DatabaseLogonTimeout                    -1
DatabaseLogonType                       2
DatabaseName                            reportserver
DatabaseQueryTimeout                    120
DatabaseServerName                      localhost
InstallationID                          {bc63afb0-08a4-4608-9139-fe2a81c53a73}
InstanceName                            MSSQLSERVER
IsInitialized                           True
IsReportManagerEnabled                  True
IsSharePointIntegrated                  False
IsWebServiceEnabled                     True
IsWindowsServiceEnabled                 True
MachineAccountIdentity
PathName                                C:\Program Files\Microsoft SQL Server\MSRS10.
MSSQLSERVER\Reporting Services\ReportServer\RSReportServer.config
SecureConnectionLevel                   0
SenderEmailAddress                      administrator@sirius.com
SendUsingSMTPServer                     True
ServiceName                             ReportServer
SMTPServer                              localhost
UnattendedExecutionAccount
Version                                 10.0.1600.22
VirtualDirectoryReportManager           Reports
VirtualDirectoryReportServer            ReportServer
WindowsServiceIdentityActual            NT AUTHORITY\NETWORK SERVICE
WindowsServiceIdentityConfigured        NT AUTHORITY\NETWORK SERVICE
Press any key to continue
```

This application allows you to view the report server configuration without opening the configuration file. To use the application, copy the WMIQueryVB.exe file from the Microsoft Press\rs2008sbs\Workspace\WMIQueryVB\WMIQueryVB\Bin\Debug folder and place it in a location that is easier to access. You can then start the application on demand by running the executable file.

10. Press any key to close the console application.

Programming Reporting Access

To complete the final phase of the reporting life cycle, you can provide access to reports programmatically. As one example, you can create Web pages that include links to reports managed on your report server and thereby bypass Report Manager or SharePoint to display reports. As another example, you can easily develop a Windows or Web application that uses the *ReportViewer* control that ships with Visual Studio 2008 to embed your Reporting Services reports into custom applications.

Linking to Reports with URL Access

Although using Report Manager or SharePoint as the central access point for reports is often satisfactory for most reporting needs in an organization, you might find it useful to provide direct links to your reports on a corporate portal page by using a different URL than you see in the Address bar when you use Report Manager or SharePoint. Not only can you provide a link to open a report for online viewing, you can include commands in a report link to set parameter value selections or to specify an alternate rendering format.

Viewing a Report

You can quickly find the correct URL for a report by navigating to the report server's virtual directory and locating the report. You can then append values in that URL to override parameter default values, to hide all or part of the HTML Viewer, or to render the report to a different format. Although you are not using Report Manager to access a report, the same security permissions continue to apply and you can access only those items that your role assignment includes.

 Note Many of the steps in the following procedure depend on whether your target report server is native mode or SharePoint integrated mode. Each step includes instructions for both architectures.

In this procedure, you open the Pacific Margin Analysis 2004 report by using a URL access command.

Open a report by using a URL access command

1. If you are running a native-mode report server, skip to step 9. If you are running a SharePoint integrated-mode report server, on the File menu, select Open Project, navigate to Microsoft Press\Rs2008sbs\Chap16, and double-click Programmability.sln.

> **Important** You must have completed at least the "Add a custom function to a report" and "Call a custom function in an expression" procedures earlier in this chapter, before continuing with this procedure. This procedure requires deployment of the Programmability solution.

2. In Solution Explorer, right-click Programmability, and then select Properties. In the Programmability Property Pages dialog box, in the TargetDataSourceFolder text box, type **http://<*servername*>/sites/ssrs/Data Connections**, replacing <*servername*> with the name of your server. In the TargetReportFolder text box, type **http://<*servername*>/sites/ssrs/ReportsLibrary**. In the TargetServerURL text box, type **http://<*servername*>/sites/ssrs**, replacing <*servername*> with the name of your server, and click OK.

3. In Solution Explorer, right-click Programmability, and select Deploy.

4. In Internet Explorer, navigate to *http://*<servername>*/sites/ssrs/ReportsLibrary* (replacing <*servername*> with the name of your server), point to the EmbeddedCode report, click the Edit button located to the right of the report title, point to Send To, and select Other Location. On the Copy: EmbeddedCode.rdl page, in the Destination Document Library Or Folder box, append **/ReportsLibrary** to the existing URL. In the File Name For The Copy box, replace the default text by typing **Pacific Margin Analysis 2004**, and click OK.

5. In the Copy Progress message box, click OK, and then, when the copy operation completes, click Done.

6. In Internet Explorer, point to the Pacific Margin Analysis 2004 report in the list, click the Edit button located to the right of the report title, and select Manage Parameters. Configure the parameters by following these steps:

    a. Click the CostBasis link, select the Hidden option, and click OK

    b. Click the Year link, select Use This Value, and then, in the corresponding drop-down list, type **2004**. Select the Hidden option, and click OK.

    c. Click the SalesTerritoryGroup link, select Use This Value, and then, in the corresponding drop-down list, type **Pacific**. Select the Hidden option, and click OK.

7. On the Manage Parameters: Pacific Margin Analysis 2004 page, click Close.

8. In the Reports Library list, point to the Pacific Margin Analysis 2004 report, click the Edit button located to the right of the report title, and select Manage Data Sources. Click the AdventureWorksDW2008 link, and then click the ellipsis button to the right of the Data Source Link box. In the Select An Item dialog box, click Up, click the Data Connections link, select AdventureWorksDW2008, click OK twice, and click Close.

The shared data source is now associated correctly with the new report.

9. View the report server contents in the virtual directory root.

> ❏ *Native mode:* Open Internet Explorer and navigate to *http://*<servername> */reportserver* (replacing *<servername>* with the name of your server) to view the report server contents in the virtual directory root.

Your screen should look similar to this:

```
sirius/ReportServer - /
_____

     Friday, November 14, 2008 10:00 AM      <dir> Clickthrough
Wednesday, October 29, 2008 9:11 PM          <dir> Data Security
    Monday, October 13, 2008 1:44 PM         <dir> Data Sources
    Monday, October 20, 2008 8:27 AM         <dir> For Review
    Sunday, August 17, 2008 3:24 PM          28594 Internet Sales 2004
    Monday, October 13, 2008 1:44 PM         <dir> Models
  Sunday, November 30, 2008 10:10 AM         <dir> Pacific Sales
   Friday, November 14, 2008 11:18 AM        25696 ProductDetail
   Sunday, November 30, 2008 8:20 AM         <dir> Programmability
 Thursday, November 13, 2008 5:52 AM         92741 Reseller Sales
   Sunday, October 19, 2008 9:09 PM          <dir> Sales
   Sunday, November 30, 2008 5:39 AM         <dir> Sales and Order Quantity Analysis
   Sunday, November 02, 2008 10:01 AM        <dir> Users Folders
                                             <dir> My Reports
_____

Microsoft SQL Server Reporting Services Version 10.0.1600.22
```

By using the Web Service URL, *http://*<servername>*/reportserver* (where *<servername>* is the name of your server), you can bypass the Report Manager or SharePoint interface to navigate through the folders and access report server content. The security permissions that are defined for the reports also apply when you use the Web Service URL, so you will see only those reports that you are allowed to see.

> ❏ *Integrated mode:* Open Internet Explorer and navigate to *http://*<servername> */reportserver* (replacing *<servername>* with the name of your server) to view the directory listing in the virtual directory root. Click the *http://*<servername>*/sites* */ssrs* link, and then click the ReportsLibrary link to view the report server contents in the document library, as shown here.

sirius/ReportServer - http://sirius/sites/SSRS/ReportsLibrary

```
[To Parent Directory]
    Thursday, October 30, 2008 1:19 PM      <dir> Ad Hoc Reports
  Wednesday, October 22, 2008 2:20 AM       <dir> For Review
    Thursday, October 30, 2008 2:43 PM      <dir> DataSecurity
      Sunday, November 09, 2008 3:28 PM     <dir> Miscellaneous Sales Reports
      Monday, November 10, 2008 3:32 PM    189850 Sales and Order Quantity Summary.rdl
      Monday, November 10, 2008 3:32 PM    195272 Sales and Order Quantity by Year.rdl
      Monday, December 01, 2008 12:38 PM   271109 Pacific Margin Analysis 2004.rdl
      Friday, August 08, 2008 7:07 PM       32644 SampleWorkbook.xlsx
  Wednesday, October 22, 2008 4:00 AM      270571 Pacific Reseller Sales Margin Analysis.rdl
      Friday, August 08, 2008 7:07 PM       11757 Sample Dashboard.aspx
      Monday, November 10, 2008 3:53 PM     11234 SalesAnalysis.aspx
      Monday, November 10, 2008 3:46 PM     14454 Report.xlsx
      Monday, December 01, 2008 12:16 PM   270915 CustomAssembly.rdl
      Monday, December 01, 2008 12:16 PM   271109 EmbeddedCode.rdl
  Wednesday, October 22, 2008 3:58 AM      270572 Reseller Sales Margin Analysis by Sales Territory.rdl
    Saturday, November 08, 2008 9:53 PM     28594 Internet Sales 2004.rdl
      Monday, October 13, 2008 3:16 AM     298276 Reseller Sales.smdl
```

Microsoft SQL Server Reporting Services Version 10.0.1600.22

10. Open a report.

❑ *Native mode:* Click the Pacific Sales link, click the Pacific Margin Analysis 2004 link, select the (Select All) check box in the Quarter drop-down list, and click View Report to view the report, as shown here.

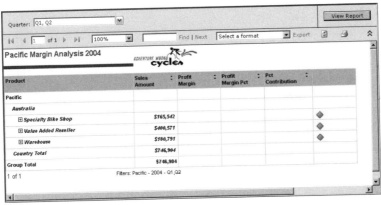

❑ *Integrated mode:* Click the Pacific Margin Analysis 2004.rdl link to view the report, as shown here.

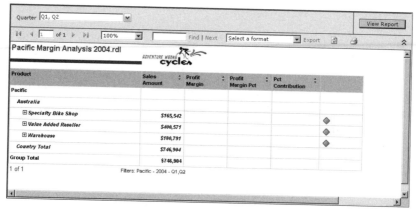

Because the report renders by default as Hypertext Markup Language (HTML), the HTML Viewer also displays with the report, even on a SharePoint integrated-mode report server. In the next procedure, you learn how to hide the HTML Viewer.

Look at the Address bar to see the URL for the link that you selected in the previous step: *http://<servername>/ReportServer/Pages/ReportViewer.aspx?%2fPacific+Margin+Analysis+2004+&rs%3aCommand=Render* (where *<servername>* is the name of your server) on a native-mode report server. If you're running a SharePoint integrated-mode report server, the URL is *http://<servername>/ReportServer/Pages/ReportViewer.aspx? http%3a%2f%2f<servername>%2fsites%2fssrs%2fReportsLibrary%2f Pacific+Margin+Analysis+2004.rdl+&rs:Command=Render*.

If you want to create a link to this report in a Web page, you don't need to know this URL. Just navigate to the report by starting with the Web Service URL and navigating through the folders to locate and open the report. Then you can copy the URL and paste it into the HTML code for the Web page.

> **Tip** The URL that you see in the Address text box is fully encoded, but you can use an abbreviated version of the URL by eliminating the /Pages/ReportViewer.aspx and &rs%3aCommand=Render sections. You can also replace the *%2f* with a forward slash (/) and the plus sign (+) with a space. However, you must include the path to the report. By making these changes, your URL for a native-mode report server looks like this: *http://<servername>/ReportServer?/Pacific Sales/Pacific Margin Analysis 2004*. The corresponding URL on a SharePoint integrated-mode report server looks like this: *http://<servername>/ReportServer?http://<servername>/sites/ssrs/ReportsLibrary /Pacific Margin Analysis 2004.rdl&rs:Command=Render*.

Using URL Access Parameters

You can append URL access parameters that provide additional options in viewing report server content by enabling control of report parameter values, toolbar settings, and rendering formats. For example, for each parameter that you want to override in the report, you include a name/value pair as a string that you append to the report's URL using the following syntax: &rc:ParameterName=ParameterValue. Because these parameter values are sent as plain text, you should implement Secure Sockets Layer (SSL) in your Reporting Services environment if parameters include confidential data.

Another option for using URL access parameters is to control the appearance of the HTML Viewer. If you add parameter values in the URL, you might decide not to display the Parameters section of the HTML Viewer so that more of the computer screen is available for the report display. To remove the Parameters section and otherwise leave the HTML Viewer intact, you add the following URL access parameter to the report's URL: &rc:Parameters=false. To remove the HTML Viewer entirely, you use the following syntax: &rc:Toolbar=false.

You can also use URL access parameters to specify the format used to display the report. To render the report as a Microsoft Office Excel workbook, for example, use the following syntax: &rc:Format=Excel. Possible rendering format values include HTML3.2, HTML4.0, MHTML, IMAGE, Excel, Word, CSV, PDF, XML, and NULL.

Not only can you use URL access parameters to view reports, but you can also send commands to the report server. You can append the command &rs:Command=ListChildren to the URL for a folder on the report server to view its contents. Or you can append the command &rs:Command=GetResourceContents to the URL of a file (other than a report) on the report server to render the resource as an HTML page.

> **Tip** For more information about other options for using URL access, refer to the topic "URL Access" in SQL Server Books Online.

In this procedure, you view the Pacific Margin Analysis 2004 report by using various URL access commands.

Use URL access commands to view a report

1. In Internet Explorer, in the Address text box, use the URL to view the report for Q1 only.

   ❑ *Native mode:* Type **http://<*servername*>/ReportServer?/Pacific Sales/Pacific Margin Analysis 2004&Quarter=1** (replacing <*servername*> with the name of your server).

❏ *Integrated mode:* Type **http://<*servername*>/ReportServer?http: //<*servername*>/sites/ssrs/ReportsLibrary/Pacific Margin Analysis 2004 .rdl&Quarter=1** (replacing <*servername*> with the name of your server).

You must know a valid value for the parameter because you cannot pass the parameter label, such as Q1, in the URL string.

2. In the Address text box, change the URL to view the report with both available values for the *Quarter* parameter.

❏ *Native mode:* Type **http://<*servername*>/ReportServer?/Pacific Sales/Pacific Margin Analysis 2004&Quarter=1&Quarter=2** (replacing <*servername*> with the name of your server).

❏ *Integrated mode:* Type **http://<*servername*>/ReportServer?http: //<*servername*>/sites/ssrs/ReportsLibrary/Pacific Margin Analysis 2004 .rdl&Quarter=1&Quarter=2** (replacing <*servername*> with the name of your server).

When a parameter accepts multiple values, you include each value separately with the parameter name.

3. In the Address text box, change the URL to view the report with both available values for the *Quarter* parameter, but without the Parameters section of the HTML Viewer, as shown here.

❏ *Native mode:* Type **http://<*servername*>/ReportServer?/Pacific Sales /Pacific Margin Analysis 2004&Quarter=1&Quarter=2&rc: Parameters=false** (replacing <*servername*> with the name of your server).

❏ *Integrated mode:* Type **http://<*servername*>/ReportServer?http: //<*servername*>/sites/ssrs/ReportsLibrary/Pacific Margin Analysis 2004 .rdl&Quarter=1&Quarter=2&rc:Parameters=false** (replacing <*servername*> with the name of your server).

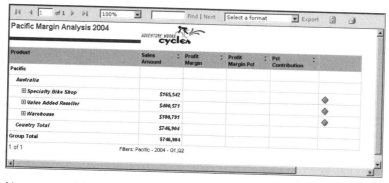

Now more of the screen is available to display the report. In the report footer, you can see the current selections for the *Quarter* parameter are Q1 and Q2. When you hide the

Parameters section of the HTML Viewer, you can change the parameter selection only by changing the URL.

> **Important** Do not use URL access to address a report directly from a Web page as a security measure to filter report content because a user can see the parameter values in the Address bar. The user can freely remove the parameter values from the URL or change the parameter values to change the report content.
>
> If you want to use URL access and secure the parameters, you can render a report programmatically, as explained in the topic "Using URL Access in a Windows Application," or use a POST request in a form submission, as explained in the topic "Using URL Access in a Web Application," both in SQL Server Books Online.

4. In the Address text box, change the URL to view the report with both available values for the *Quarter* parameter, but without the HTML Viewer, as shown here.

   ❑ *Native mode:* Type **http://<*servername*>/ReportServer?/Pacific Sales /Pacific Margin Analysis 2004&Quarter=1&Quarter=2&rc:Toolbar=false** (replacing <*servername*> with the name of your server).

   ❑ *Integrated mode:* Type **http://<*servername*>/ReportServer?http: //<*servername*>/sites/ssrs/ReportsLibrary/Pacific Margin Analysis 2004 .rdl&Quarter=1&Quarter=2&rc:Toolbar=false** (replacing <*servername*> with the name of your server).

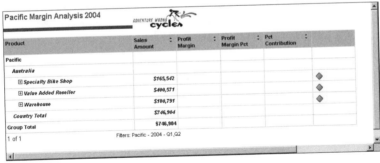

You can omit the *&rc:Parameters=false* command in the URL when you hide the HTML Viewer by using the *&rc:Toolbar=false* command.

5. In the Address text box, change the URL to render the report as an Excel workbook.

   ❑ *Native mode:* Type **http://<*servername*>/ReportServer?/Pacific Sales /Pacific Margin Analysis 2004&Quarter=1&Quarter=2&rs:Format=Excel** (replacing <*servername*> with the name of your server), and, in the File Download message box, click Open to view the report as an Excel document if you have Excel installed on your computer.

❑ *Integrated mode:* Type **http://<*servername*>/ReportServer?http:
//<*servername*>/sites/ssrs/ReportsLibrary/Pacific Margin Analysis 2004
.rdl&Quarter=1&Quarter=2&rs:Format=Excel** (replacing <*servername*> with
the name of your server), and, in the File Download message box, click Open to
view the report as an Excel document if you have Excel installed on your computer.

You can render the report in any format other than HTML by adding the *&rs:Format*
command and providing the format type.

6. In the Address text box, change the URL to display the contents of a folder.

❑ *Native mode:* Type **http://<*servername*>/ReportServer?/Pacific Sales
/&rs:Command=ListChildren** (replacing <*servername*> with the name of your server).

❑ *Integrated mode:* Type **http://<*servername*>/ReportServer?http:
//<*servername*>/sites/ssrs/ReportsLibrary/&rs:Command=ListChildren**
(replacing <*servername*> with the name of your server).

Using the *ReportViewer* Control

Visual Studio 2008 includes the *ReportViewer* control to support application development
that requires embedded reports. Because this control works independently of Microsoft SQL
Server 2008, you don't need a SQL Server license to create reports. However, when you have
a Reporting Services infrastructure in place, you can use the *ReportViewer* control to access
reports from your report server.

> **Note** To complete the following procedure, you must install Visual Studio 2008 with either the
> Visual Basic .NET or Visual C# .NET library.
>
> The steps and the code samples in the following procedure assume that you are using Visual
> Basic .NET. If you prefer to use Visual C# .NET, you can review the completed project in the
> Microsoft Press\Rs2008sbs\Answers\Chap16\CS folder.

In this procedure, you create a Windows application with a *ReportViewer* control to display
the Pacific Margin Analysis 2004 report.

Create a Windows application with a *ReportViewer* control

1. In BI Dev Studio, on the File menu, select New Project.

2. In the New Project dialog box, in the Project Types list, expand Visual Basic, select
   Reporting, and then, in the Templates list, select Reports Application.

3. In the Name text box, change the project name to ReportAppVB and, in the Location
   text box, change the location to the Microsoft Press\Rs2008sbs\Workspace folder in
   your Documents folder, as shown here. Click OK.

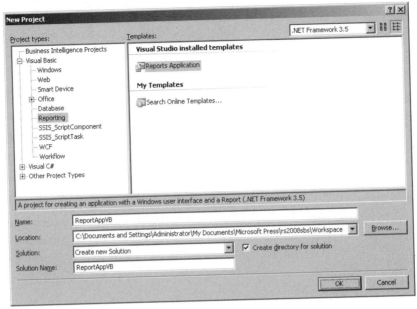

4. In the Report Wizard, click Cancel.

You can use the Report Wizard to step through development of a report independent of Reporting Services. In this procedure, however, you instead access a report from the report server for your application.

After you click Cancel, the application form displays with a *ReportViewer* control already added to the form, as shown here.

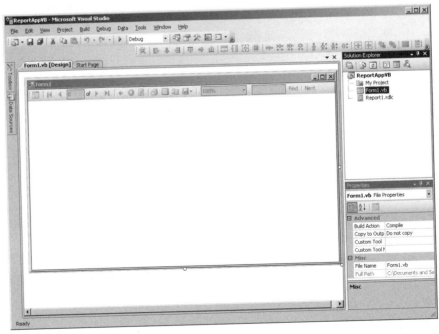

Tip If you create a form manually, you can add a *ReportViewer* control by opening the Toolbox window, expanding the Reporting section, and dragging the *MicrosoftReportViewer* control to the form.

In the Solution Explorer window, notice the Report1.rdlc item. If you want to create a report without accessing the report server, you can open this item and use Report Designer. However, Report Designer includes only the features available for designing SQL Server 2005 Reporting Services reports. Because you are developing this application to use a report from the report server, you can delete this file from the project safely.

5. In Solution Explorer, right-click Report1.rdlc, select Delete, and click OK to confirm deletion.

You can set properties for the *ReportViewer* control to suit your purposes. For example, you might want to resize the control.

6. In the design window, click the title bar of the form to set the focus of the Properties window to Form1.

7. Locate the Size text box and type **600,500**.

Resizing the form automatically resizes the *ReportViewer* control that it contains.

8. In the design window, click anywhere in the center of the *ReportViewer* control to set the focus of the Properties window to ReportViewer1.

9. In the Properties window, scroll to locate the ServerReport section and expand Server Report to view the properties, as shown here.

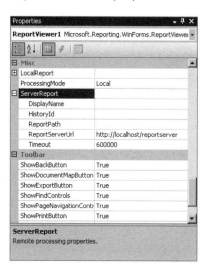

At a minimum, you must configure the *ReportViewer* control's *ProcessingMode*, *ReportPath,* and *ReportServerURL* properties. To use reports managed by Reporting Services, you must change the *ProcessingMode* property to Remote. When you define *ReportPath*, you provide only the folder and report name. You cannot include URL access commands. For *ReportServerURL*, you use the Web Service URL, which is the same URL that you use when deploying reports from BI Dev Studio.

Notice the properties in the Toolbar section of the Properties window. You can remove buttons from the HTML Viewer by setting the corresponding property to *False*.

10. In the ProcessingMode drop-down list, select Remote.

11. In the ReportPath text box, provide the path to the report.

   ❏ *Native mode:* Type **/Pacific Sales/Pacific Margin Analysis 2004**.

   ❏ *Integrated mode:* Type **http://<*servername*>/sites/ssrs/ReportsLibrary /Pacific Margin Analysis 2004.rdl** (replacing *<servername>* with the name of your server). Notice that you must provide the full path to the report.

12. In the ReportServerURL, provide the URL for the report server.

   ❏ *Native mode:* Type **http://<*servername*>/ReportServer**, replacing *<servername>* with the name of your server.

   ❏ *Integrated mode:* Type **http://<*servername*>/sites/ssrs/_Vti_bin/ReportServer** (replacing *<servername>* with the name of your server). Notice that you must provide the full URL to the SharePoint equivalent of the report server.

13. In Solution Explorer, right-click ReportAppVB, and click Build.

When you build the application, Visual Studio creates the ReportAppVB.exe in the bin\Debug folder for your application. You can then distribute this executable file to anyone who has access to your report server and has permissions to the report. Using a custom application to access the report does not override the security defined on the report server.

14. Press F5 to test the application, and click View Report to display the report, as shown here.

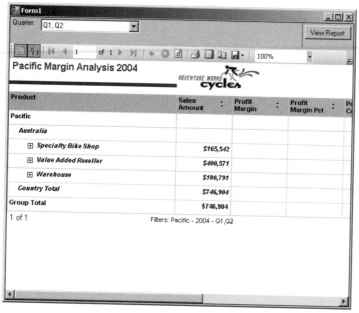

15. Close the form to return to Visual Studio.

    At this point, the application is very basic. You could extend the application by adding a menu that lists available reports (using the *ListChildren* method, for example) and then changing the report path when the menu selection changes. By using the *ReportViewer* control in your applications, you can focus your development efforts on application logic and save the time required to build the same reporting capabilities that Reporting Services already includes.

Congratulations! You have successfully completed the reporting life cycle programmatically in this chapter. If you have completed all the procedures in the earlier chapters of this book, you also know how to use Reporting Services features to develop, manage, and access reports. Now you're ready to test your skills by creating and deploying projects that meet the reporting requirements of your organization.

Chapter 16 Quick Reference

To	Do This
Add embedded custom code to a report	In BI Dev Studio, select Report Properties on the Report menu, click Code, and then enter a Visual Basic .NET code block in the Custom Code text box. Call the function in an expression using the following syntax: `Code.method(arguments)`. For example: `=Code.GetStatus("Color", ReportItems!PctCon tribution.Value, Variables!GroupThreshold. Value)`
Use a custom assembly in a report	Create a class library using a .NET language in Visual Studio and deploy the assembly to the Report Designer and report server Bin folders. In BI Dev Studio, open a report. On the Report menu, select Report Properties, and click References. Click Browse in the Add Reference dialog box, navigate to the Report Designer's Bin folder, and select the .dll file for the assembly. Call a function from the custom assembly using the following syntax: `Namespace.Class.Method(arguments).` For example: `=Rs2008sbs.VB.Extensions.ReportFunctions. GetStatus("Color", ReportItems!PctContribution.Value, Variables!GroupThreshold.Value, Variables!AlertThreshold. Value)`
Create a folder on the report server	Use the *CreateFolder* method. For example, to create a folder that is accessible from the Home folder, use the following code: `Rs.CreateFolder(newFolder, "/", Nothing)`
Read a report definition file into memory	Read the file into a filestream object, initialize a byte array to a size that is one character smaller than the filestream object, and then read the filestream into the byte array like this: `Dim stream As FileStream = File. OpenRead(reportPath) definition = New [Byte](stream.Length - 1) {} stream.Read(definition, 0, CInt(stream.Length)) stream.Close()`

To	Do This
Deploy a report to the report server	Use the *CreateReport* method. For example: ``` CreateReport(reportName, parentPath, False, definition, Nothing) ```
Assign a shared data source to a report	Use the *SetItemDataSources* method. For example: ``` Dim ds(0) as DataSource Dim s as New DataSource Dim dsr as New DataSourceReference dsr.Reference = "/Data Sources/ AdventureWorksDW2008" s.Item = dsr s.Name = "AdventureWorksDW2008" ds(0) = s Dim myItem as String = parentPath + "/" + reportName rs.SetItemDataSources(myItem, ds) ```
Create a linked report	Use the *CreateLinkedReport* method. For example: ``` rs.CreateLinkedReport(linkedReport, linkedReportPath, baseReport, Nothing) ```
Set report parameters	Create an array of *ReportParameter* objects and set the *Name, DefaultValues,* and *PromptUser* properties as applicable. Then assign the *ReportParameter* array to the report. For example: ``` rs.SetReportParameters(linkedReportPath + "/" + linkedReport, params) ```
Execute a script by using the Rs utility	Open a command prompt window and execute the Rs utility by using the following syntax: ``` Rs -i input_file -s ReportServerURL - u username -p password -l timeout -b -v variable_key=variable_value -t ```

To	Do This
| Review report server management properties | Create a console application that includes the following namespaces: *System, System.Management*, and *System .IO*. Create a *ManagementScope* object using the WMI namespace definition at \\<*servername*>\Root\Microsoft \SqlServer\ReportServer\RS_MSSQLSERVER\v10\Admin. Create a *ManagementClass* object using the WMI class definition at \\<*servername*>\Root\Microsoft \SqlServer\ReportServer\RS_MSSQLSERVER\v10 \Admin:MSReportServer_ConfigurationSetting. Create a Report Server instance as a *ManagementObject* object, and iterate through this object's *PropertyData* collection. For example: <br><br>```
For Each prop In instProps
Dim name As String = prop.Name
Dim val As Object = prop.Value
Console.Out.WriteLine("Name:"+ prop.Name)
If val Is Nothing Then
    Console.Out.WriteLine("Value: <null>")
Else
    Console.Out.WriteLine("Value: "+val.
ToString())
End If
Next
``` |
| Display a report by using URLs | *Native mode:* Navigate the folder hierarchy starting from *http://*<servername>*/ReportServer* to locate the report.
or
Type the URL of the report in your browser. For example: **http://<*servername*>/ReportServer?/Pacific Sales /Pacific Margin Analysis 2004**.

Integrated mode: Navigate the folder hierarchy starting from *http://*<servername>*/ReportServer?http://*<servername> */sites/ssrs* (or the site name you created) to locate the report.
or
Type the URL of the report in your browser. For example: **http://<*servername*>/ReportServer?http://<*servername*> /sites/ssrs/ReportsLibrary/Pacific Margin Analysis 2004.rdl.** |
| Specify report parameter values in a URL | Create a string using the following syntax &rc:
ParameterName=Parameter-
Value and append the string to the URL.
For example:
Native mode: http://<servername>*/ReportServer?/Pacific Sales/Pacific Margin Analysis 2004&Quarter=1&Quarter=2*
Integrated mode: http://<servername>*/ReportServer? http://*<servername>*/sites/ssrs/ReportsLibrary/Pacific Margin Analysis 2004.rdl&Quarter=1&Quarter=2* |
```

To	Do This
Control the features of the HTML Viewer	Create a string using the following syntax: &rc:URLAccessParameterName=URLAccessParameterValue and append the string to the URL. For example, to hide the HTML Viewer toolbar, use the following URL: *Native mode: http://<servername>/ReportServer?/Pacific Sales/Pacific Margin Analysis 2004&Quarter=1&Quarter= 2&rc:Toolbar=false* *Integrated mode: http://<servername>/ReportServer? http://<servername>/sites/ssrs/ReportsLibrary/Pacific Margin Analysis 2004.rdl&Quarter=1&Quarter=2&rc:Toolbar=false*
Render a report to an alternate format	Create a string using the following syntax: &rs:Format=Excel and append the string to the URL. For example: *Native mode: http://<servername>/ReportServer?/Pacific Sales/Pacific Margin Analysis 2004&Quarter=1&Quarter= 2&rs:Format=Excel* *Integrated mode: http://<servername>/ReportServer? http://<servername>/sites/ssrs/ReportsLibrary/Pacific Margin Analysis 2004.rdl&Quarter=1&Quarter=2&rs:Format=Excel*
Configure a *ReportViewer* control to use Reporting Services reports	In Visual Studio, create an application using the Reports Application template in the Reporting section and cancel the Report Wizard. Select the form and change its *Size* property values. Select the *ReportViewer* control and set the *ProcessingMode* property to Remote, set the *ReportPath* property to the report's path (such as /Pacific Sales/Pacific Margin Analysis 2004 in native mode or *http://<servername>/sites/ssrs/ReportsLibrary/Pacific Margin Analysis 2004.rdl* in integrated mode), and set the *ReportServerURL* to *http://<servername>/ReportServer* in native mode or *http://<servername>/sites/ssrs/_vti_bin /ReportServer* in integrated mode (replacing *<servername>* with the name of your server).

Glossary

Ad hoc report A report that can be developed by a user with limited technical skills and saved privately or shared with others by publishing to the Reporting Services centralized store.

Attribute A report model object that represents a column in a table.

Authentication The process of confirming the user's identity through the use of a login name and password.

Authorization The process of granting permissions to access content on the report server and to perform specific actions.

Cascading parameters Two report parameters for which the available values list for one report parameter is based on the user's selection of a value for the other report parameter.

Clickthrough The feature in Reporting Services that automatically generates a drillthrough report in Report Builder.

Column handle The top edge of a tablix data region represented as a gray border when the data region is selected.

Complex expression An expression that references multiple fields, parameters, or built-in fields, includes operators to combine several expressions into a compound expression, and specifies calls to functions.

Conditional formatting The use of an expression to set a report item's appearance and behavior properties (such as *Color* or *Hidden*) dynamically at run time.

Dashboard A special type of SharePoint report that includes several Web Parts that you can configure to display one or more Reporting Services reports, Microsoft Office Excel spreadsheets, or other items.

Data-driven subscription A subscription that delivers the same report to many destinations, each of which might receive a different render format of the report and a different set of parameter values.

Data region A special type of report item that you add to the report layout that is bound to a data set.

Data set A container for the information used by the Report Processor to execute a query and return the following results: a pointer to the data source, the query string to execute, and a field list describing the data types of the query results.

Drilldown report A report in which only the summary data displays when the user opens the report and the detail data displays when the user clicks a text box that has been configured to toggle the visibility of detail data.

Embedded data source A data source that is associated only with a single report and requires editing of the report to change the connection string of the data source.

Embedded report A report integrated into an organization's portals or custom applications.

Entity A report model object that corresponds to a table in the data source view.

Group A collection of detail rows that share a common field value.

Job A report that is currently being executed by the report server.

Key Performance Indicator Abbreviated as KPI, this is a special type of calculation stored in the Analysis Services cube to compare actual values to target values.

Managed report Information gathered from one or more data sources in report form and formally managed in a central report repository.

Named query A logical object in the report model that is analogous to a view in a relational database.

Nonadditive value A value that cannot be summed because it is derived from a multiplication or division of other values that must be summed before the multiplication or division is performed, such as a ratio or percentage value.

Online Analytical Processing (OLAP) A method of interaction with data that uses a multidimensional data structure known as a *cube* to provide fast responses to queries and to centralize and simplify business logic for calculations by using spreadsheet-style formulas.

Permission level A set of tasks that a user is allowed to perform on a SharePoint integrated-mode report server.

Rendering The conversion of the report layout and report data into a specific file format, such as Microsoft Office Excel or Portable Document Format (PDF).

Report A structured arrangement of information, such as business data.

Report model A logical description of the tables and columns in a database in a user-friendly format.

Reporting platform An integrated set of applications that supports all activities related to a report, including report development, server management, and access to reports.

Report server project A folder created to store a set of reports and shared data sources.

Role (1) A report model object that defines the relationship between two entities. (2) A named definition of a set of tasks, such as System Administrator or Content Manager, that includes the necessary permissions to perform those tasks. By assigning a user to a role, you enable that user to perform the role's tasks on a native-mode report server.

Row handle The left edge of a tablix data region represented as a gray border when the data region is selected.

Server extension A processor with a very specific function, such as authentication, data processing, rendering, or delivery.

Simple expression A reference to a single dataset field, parameter, or built-in field.

Shared data source A set of data source connection properties that is stored independently of reports. These properties contain the necessary information for connecting to a database. Storing this information independently of reports enables you to define the data source only once and then use this definition for multiple reports.

Standard subscription A subscription that delivers a specific report to one or more e-mail accounts or to a designated network file share on a recurring basis.

Subreport A report item used to display another report inside the current report.

Tablix A hybrid data region that provides a flexible grid layout that can use fixed columns and dynamic rows like a table, or dynamic columns and dynamic rows like a matrix.

URL access parameter A string value appended to a URL that provides additional options in viewing report server content by enabling control of report parameter values, toolbar settings, and rendering formats.

URL reservation A description of one or more URLs used to access a Web service or Web application.

Index

C

Resources for SQL Server 2008

Microsoft® SQL Server® 2008
Administrator's
Pocket Consultant
William R. Stanek
ISBN 9780735625891

Programming Microsoft
SQL Server 2008
Leonard Lobel, Andrew J. Brust,
Stephen Forte
ISBN 9780735625990

Microsoft SQL Server 2008
Step by Step
Mike Hotek
ISBN 9780735626041

Microsoft SQL Server 2008
T-SQL Fundamentals
Itzik Ben-Gan
ISBN 9780735626010

MCTS Self-Paced
Training Kit (Exam 70-432)
Microsoft SQL Server 2008
Implementation and
Maintenance
Mike Hotek
ISBN 9780735626058

Smart Business Intelligence
Solutions with Microsoft
SQL Server 2008
Lynn Langit, Kevin S. Goff,
Davide Mauri, Sahil Malik,
and John Welch
ISBN 9780735625808

COMING SOON

Microsoft SQL Server 2008 Internals
Kalen Delaney et al.
ISBN 9780735626249

Inside Microsoft SQL Server 2008: T-SQL Querying
Itzik Ben-Gan, Lubor Kollar, Dejan Sarka
ISBN 9780735626034

Microsoft SQL Server 2008 Best Practices
Saleem Hakani and Ward Pond
with the Microsoft SQL Server Team
ISBN 9780735626225

Microsoft SQL Server 2008 MDX
Step by Step
Bryan C. Smith, C. Ryan Clay, Hitachi Consulting
ISBN 9780735626188

Microsoft SQL Server 2008 Reporting Services
Step by Step
Stacia Misner
ISBN 9780735626478

Microsoft SQL Server 2008 Analysis Services
Step by Step
Scott Cameron, Hitachi Consulting
ISBN 9780735626201

Microsoft®
Press

For Web Developers

Microsoft® ASP.NET 3.5 Step by Step

George Shepherd
ISBN 9780735624269

Teach yourself ASP.NET 3.5—one step at a time. Ideal for developers with fundamental programming skills but new to ASP.NET, this practical tutorial delivers hands-on guidance for developing Web applications in the Microsoft Visual Studio® 2008 environment.

Microsoft Visual Web Developer 2008 Express Edition Step by Step

Eric Griffin
ISBN 9780735626065

Your hands guide to learning fundamental Web-development skills. This tutorial steps you through an end-to-end example, helping build essential skills logically and sequentially. By the end of the book, you'll have a working Web site, plus the fundamental skills needed for the next level—ASP.NET.

Introducing Microsoft Silverlight™ 2, Second Edition

Laurence Moroney
ISBN 9780735625280

Get a head start with Silverlight 2—the cross-platform, cross-browser plug-in for rich interactive applications and the next-generation user experience. Featuring advance insights from inside the Silverlight team, this book delivers the practical, approachable guidance and code to inspire your next solutions.

Programming Microsoft ASP.NET 3.5

Dino Esposito
ISBN 9780735625273

The definitive guide to ASP.NET 3.5. Led by well-known ASP.NET expert Dino Esposito, you'll delve into the core topics for creating innovative Web applications, including Dynamic Data; LINQ; state, application, and session management; Web forms and requests; security strategies; AJAX; Silverlight; and more.

JavaScript Step by Step

Steve Suehring
ISBN 9780735624498

Build on your fundamental programming skills, and get hands-on guidance for creating Web applications with JavaScript. Learn to work with the six JavaScript data types, the Document Object Model, Web forms, CSS styles, AJAX, and other essentials—one step at a time.

Programming Microsoft LINQ

Paolo Pialorsi and Marco Russo
ISBN 9780735624009

With LINQ, you can query data—no matter what the source—directly from Microsoft Visual Basic® or C#. Guided by two data-access experts who've worked with LINQ in depth, you'll learn how Microsoft .NET Framework 3.5 implements LINQ, and how to exploit it. Study and adapt the book's examples for faster, leaner code.

ALSO SEE

Developing Service-Oriented AJAX Applications on the Microsoft Platform
ISBN 9780735625914

Microsoft ASP.NET 2.0 Step by Step
ISBN 9780735622012

Programming Microsoft ASP.NET 2.0
ISBN 9780735625273

Programming Microsoft ASP.NET 2.0 Applications: Advanced Topics
ISBN 9780735621770

Microsoft®
Press

microsoft.com/mspress

About the Author

Stacia Misner is the founder of Data Inspirations, which delivers global business intelligence (BI) consulting and education services. She is a consultant, educator, mentor, and author specializing in business intelligence and performance management solutions using Microsoft technologies. Stacia has more than 20 years of experience in information technology and has focused exclusively on Microsoft BI technologies since 2000. She is the author of *Microsoft SQL Server 2000 Reporting Services Step by Step, Microsoft SQL Server 2005 Reporting Services Step by Step,* and *Microsoft SQL Server 2005 Express Edition: Start Now!* and the coauthor of *Business Intelligence: Making Better Decisions Faster, Microsoft SQL Server 2005 Analysis Services Step by Step,* and *Microsoft SQL Server 2005 Administrator's Companion.* She is also a Microsoft Certified IT Professional-BI and a Microsoft Certified Technology Specialist-BI. Stacia lives in Las Vegas, Nevada, with her husband, Gerry.

Contributing Author

Erika Bakse is a consultant at Data Inspirations, where she specializes in developing custom solutions using Microsoft business intelligence technologies. Erika has a B.S. in Mathematics from the Massachusetts Institute of Technology and is a Microsoft Certified Technology Specialist. She currently lives in Las Vegas, Nevada.

What do you think of this book?

We want to hear from you!

Your feedback will help us continually improve our books and learning resources for you. To participate in a brief online survey, please visit:

microsoft.com/learning/booksurvey

...and enter this book's ISBN-10 or ISBN-13 number (appears above barcode on back cover). As a thank-you to survey participants in the U.S. and Canada, each month we'll randomly select five respondents to win one of five $100 gift certificates from a leading online merchant. At the conclusion of the survey, you can enter the drawing by providing your e-mail address, which will be used for prize notification only.*

Thank you in advance for your input!

Where to find the ISBN on back cover

ISBN-13: 000-0-0000-0000-0
ISBN-10: 0-0000-0000-0

9 0 0 0 0

0 000000 000000

Example only. Each book has unique ISBN.

Microsoft
Press

* No purchase necessary. Void where prohibited. Open only to residents of the 50 United States (includes District of Columbia) and Canada (void in Quebec). For official rules and entry dates see: **microsoft.com/learning/booksurvey**

Stay in touch!

To subscribe to the *Microsoft Press* *Book Connection Newsletter*—for news on upcoming books, events, and special offers—please visit:

microsoft.com/learning/books/newsletter